T0286989

Named in remembrance of

the onetime *Antioch Review* editor

and longtime Bay Area resident,

the Lawrence Grauman, Jr. Fund

supports books that address

a wide range of human rights,

free speech, and social justice issues.

The publisher and the University of California Press
Foundation gratefully acknowledge the generous support
of the Lawrence Grauman, Jr. Fund.

Love's Next Meeting

Love's Next Meeting

*The Forgotten History of Homosexuality
and the Left in American Culture*

Aaron S. Lecklider

UNIVERSITY OF CALIFORNIA PRESS

University of California Press
Oakland, California

© 2021 by Aaron S. Lecklider

First Paperback Printing 2023

Library of Congress Cataloging-in-Publication Data

Names: Lecklider, Aaron, author.
Title: Love's next meeting : the forgotten history of
  homosexuality and the left in American culture /
  Aaron S. Lecklider.
Description: Oakland, California : University of
  California Press, [2021] | Includes bibliographical
  references and index.
Identifiers: LCCN 2020045477 | ISBN 9780520381421
  (cloth) | 9780520395589 (pbk) 9780520381438
(ebook)
Subjects: LCSH: Homosexuality—Political aspects—
  United States—History—20th century. | Right and left
  (Political science)—United States—History—20th
  century.
Classification: LCC HQ76.3.U5 L59 2021 |
  DDC 306.76/60973—dc23
LC record available at https://lccn.loc.gov/2020045477

Manufactured in the United States of America

30 29 28 27 26 25 24 23
10 9 8 7 6 5 4 3 2 1

For Avram Finkelstein, who taught me much and inspires me to do more

Contents

Illustrations

Acknowledgments

The best thing about finishing a book that you've been working on for, um, several years is that you finally have a chance to thank all the many people who made it all possible. Ultimately its mistakes and flaws are my own, but the good parts of this book belong to everyone who gave so much of themselves to help me along the way.

I was fortunate to have an opportunity to visit many archives during the course of my research. Nothing reveals the collective labor of historical research more than working with archivists, librarians, and staff at these institutions—from those who catalogue materials and suggest research leads to those who move banker boxes and remind us to wear gloves when handling documents. Endless thanks go to the amazing folks working at the Smithsonian Archives of American Art, Newberry Library, University of Delaware Special Collections, University of Illinois at Chicago Special Collections and University Archives, ONE National Gay and Lesbian Archives, Beinecke Library at Yale University, Houghton Library at Harvard University, Longfellow House–Washington's Headquarters National Historic Site Archives, Princeton University Library Department of Special Collections, Harry Ransom Center at the University of Texas Austin, Harvard Law School Special Collections, New York Public Library Archives and Manuscripts, Schomburg Center for Research in Black Culture, Tamiment Library and Robert F. Wagner Labor Archives at New York University, San Francisco Gay, Lesbian, Bisexual, and Transgender Historical Society, San Francisco Library

Special Collections, Smith College Special Collections, University of Oregon Special Collections and University Archives, Howard Gotlieb Archival Research Center at Boston University, Northern Illinois University Rare Books and Special Collections, University of Chicago Library's Special Collections Research Center, UCLA Special Collections, Southern California Library, University of Michigan Special Collections, and the Norman McLaren Archive, University of Stirling. For assistance with permissions, I would like to thank Joey Cain, Jarrett Earnest, Raymond Foye, Bonnie Kirschstein, and Diana Lachantanere.

In addition to the archives I visited for research, I also would like to thank the workers at libraries I relied upon for fulfilling interlibrary loan requests, tracking down elusive books and periodicals, and providing space to write. In particular, Joanne Riley and the workers at the Healey Library at the University of Massachusetts Boston, the workers at Boston Public Library, and Tom Ruane and the workers at the Provincetown Public Library were especially resourceful. I finished writing this book at the Provincetown Commons, and I am grateful to the folks who funded and staff this little community space.

Research costs money, and I don't have a lot of it. I am therefore grateful for funding from a Joseph P. Healey Research Grant at UMass Boston, a Dean's Research Fund grant at UMass Boston, and the American Studies Department at UMass Boston. I would also like to thank the retired UMass Boston faculty for assisting my research through an Endowed Faculty Career Development Award.

Several talented students at UMass Boston assisted me with research for this book. Thanks to Jordan Pouliot Latham, Adam Koltun, and Sarah Duncan for their invaluable labor and research skill. I would also like to thank Andrew Lester for his inspiring scholarship and friendship both during his time as a graduate student at UMass Boston and, more recently, as a colleague in the field of American Studies.

Many scholars helped me think through the tricky parts of this project, read drafts of chapters, and offered useful feedback. I am particularly grateful to John D'Emilio, Michael Denning, Molly Geidel, Dayo Gore, Christina Hanhardt, Cheryl Higashida, Patricia Hills, Emily Hobson, Gary Edward Holcomb, Kwame Holmes, Regina Kunzel, Greta LaFleur, Jen Manion, William Maxwell, Joanne Meyerowitz, Julia Mickenberg, Ryan Murphy, Paula Rabinowitz, Rachel Lee Rubin, Jim Smethurst, Judith Smith, Chris Vials, Stephen Vider, Alan Wald, and Mary Helen Washington. Others provided materials such as FBI files, which, if I had had to wait on the benevolence of government employees administering FOIA requests, would likely have arrived several years following my already-delayed book's publication: thank you to William Maxwell, Barry Reay, and Hugh Ryan. Still others offered me the gift of solidarity and engaged with critical questions about this project at important stages of my research and writing. Particular thanks to Sam Alexander, Bettina Aptheker, Benjamin Balthaser, Ross Barrett, Brooke Blower, Darius Bost, Matt Brim, David Brody, Margot Canaday, Christopher Capozzola, George Chauncey, Floyd Cheung, David Churchill, Danielle Coriale, Lisa Duggan, Roderick Ferguson, Jonathan Flatley, Glenda Gilmore, Scott Herring, Hua Hsu, Daniel Hurewitz, David Johnson, Jonathan Ned Katz, Will Kuby, Helen Langa, Marisol LeBrón, Steven Lee, Ian Lekus, Amanda Littauer, Heather Love, Alex Lubin, Anita Mannur, Curtis Marez, Patrick McKelvey, Jeffrey Melnick, LaShonda Mims, David Mislin, Devon Muchmore, Ani Mukherji, John Munro, Jecca Namakkal, Nadia Nurhussein, John Ott, Anthony Petro, Sarah Phillips, Joey Plaster, Elliott Powell, Patrick Pritchett, Kim Reilly, Tom Roach, David Román, Don Romesburg, Gabe Rosenberg, Hugh Ryan, Christopher Schmidt, Rebecca Schreiber, Bruce Schulman, Sarah Schulman, Cathy Schlund-Vials, Nayan Shah, Nina Silber, Salomé Aguilera Skvirsky, Marc Stein, Shelley Streeby, Timothy Stewart-Winter, Patricia Stuelke, Nick Syrett, and Phil Tiemeyer.

At the University of Massachusetts Boston, I wish to thank my many wonderful colleagues, especially Ping-Ann Addo, Lillian-Yvonne Bertram, Chris Bobel, Matt Brown, Neil Bruss, Andrés Fabián Henao Castro, Philip Chassler, Elora Chowhury, Reyes Coll-Telechea, Doreen Drury, Shoshanna Ehrlich, Amani El Jack, Jennifer Gregg, Renee Hudson, Rafael Jaen, Keith Jones, Denise Khor, Stephen Levine, Scott Maisano, Carney Maley, Bonnie Miller, Marisol Negrón, Lorenzo Nencioli, Mickaela Perina, Pratima Prasad, Joanne Riley, Emilio Sauri, Rajini Srikanth, Steve Striffler, Karen Suyemoto, Shirley Tang, Len Van Morzé, Cedric Wood, Kevin Wozniak, and Chris Zurn, each of whom has generously offered me a ton of solidarity and guidance over the years. As Dean of the College of Liberal Arts, David Terkla supported this project from its inception, and it breaks my heart that he passed away before I was able to hand deliver a copy of this book to him. His legacy lives on.

Lynnell Thomas has read so many documents and fielded so many frantic emails and phone calls that she should probably be listed as this book's coauthor. Heike Schotten has done the same. Come to think of it, so have Sari Edelstein and Holly Jackson. And, of course, Susan Tomlinson and Erin O'Brian. Jeez. The fact that each of these colleagues and friends continues to share meals and movies and conversation and gifs with me in spite of my seemingly endless litany of demands—in addition to producing brilliant and inspiring scholarship of their own—says everything about their generosity and brainpower. I'm lucky to work with each of you, and I'm even more grateful for having you in my life after I punch the clock. Next dinner's on me, as long as you're good with pizza and chocolate milk.

I love all my colleagues in academia, but I would lose my mind if I didn't have a bunch of friends and comrades outside the ivory tower. Phoebe Sung, Peter Buer, Gillian Mason, Jon Dyen, Jason Dionne, Christopher Vyce, Stephanie Vyce, Avram Finkelstein, Cindy Staton, Allison Lentino, Melissa Mack, Bob Burns, Derek McCormack (both of them), Stephen McCauley, Sebastian Stuart, Kristin James, Adam Singer, Dan Samson, Tony Paine, Shauna Peck Slome, David Stankiewiez, Jeffrey Perkins, Chris Muther, Keith O'Brien, Matt Gavin, Josh Hecht, Tim Famulare, Hedi El Kholti, Bhavin Patel, Mike Sullivan, Michael Cox, Damian Barr, Utah Nickel, Greg Kornbluh, Tim Barry, Lili Taylor, Tradd Sanderson, John Koran, Steve Yablonski, and Chloe Teston: thank you for being my friends, traveling down the road, et cetera. Billy Hough: thanks for providing the soundtrack.

Julio Capó Jr. and Kevin Murphy arrived in my life at the perfect moment, and your friendship has anchored me when life was at its most turbulent. I'm amazed by you. I love you even when I say I have no sisters, and let the record show that I did *not* steal that raffle ticket. Mark Adams: thanks for texting me back and for rebuilding the world with the good stuff. Christopher Castellani and Michael Borum: thank you for the film screenings and book reports, and for providing Rosie's alternate seating. Jason Ruiz: thank you for dog pics and for your Lifetime channel password. Matthew Limpede: thank you for being my lifeline; for *LDWD,* MK, and SPKs.

Douglas Mitchell championed this project when it was still just a research idea and continued supporting me throughout. His passing remains a tremendous loss to the field of queer studies, and I'm grateful for the many conversations, meals, and mocktails we were able to share over the years. The amazing dedication of the folks at University of California Press has been truly extraordinary. Niels Hooper has been an exemplary editor and an astute reader, and I'm endlessly grateful for all he has done to improve this book and bring it into the world. His commitment to both queer and radical history has made publishing with UC Press a joyous enterprise. Thank you as well to Robin Manley, Madison

Wetzell, Jessica Moll, Julie Van Pelt, Katryce Lassle, and Teresa Iafolla for all your work making my manuscript into a book people can actually read. Thanks also to Carl Walesa for his careful and attentive copyediting, and to Jim O'Brien for providing the index.

Thank you, finally, to Brian Halley for everything else. When this pandemic ends, let's dance at the A-House with everyone we know. Then Spiritus.

Introduction

Deviant Politics

Between July 1954 and June 1955, the New York City Police Department swept through Times Square in a series of carefully orchestrated raids designed to rid the area of its undesirables. As the action unfolded, Edward Melcarth, a radical artist who had exhibited paintings at New York's left-leaning ACA Gallery, drafted an essay voicing his objection to the police's effort to crack down on drug users, gamblers, sex workers, homosexuals, and other dissidents.[1] Titled "Guerilla Warfare," Melcarth's essay attacked the "latest 'Search and Kill-joy' operation in the Times Square zone," which, he complained, had recently "netted fifty bodies." This "War on Undesirables" was conducted by "special forces of policemen and police-women acting as entrapment agents" who "dropped [in] at bars[,] counters of cafeterias, and even into men's lavatories." This elite brigade had been "trained in purse-swinging, solicitation, shooting crap, etc." They made up a "highly dedicated group" who "disguise themselves by day as businessmen, professors, actors, hostesses and Seventh avenue models," while "after dark they don black leather, bright shirts, low-cut blouses, boots and other para-sexual uniforms to set up ambushes along some of the main highways of Mid-town and Greenwich Village." While "undesirables" made up a large portion of the New York populace, "under no circumstances, will a 'habitual user' be returned to the City Council by Greenwich Village nor Times Square be represented in Congress by a bearded female impersonator."[2] Sexual dissidents and other undesirables, in Melcarth's analysis, constituted a disenfranchised group that was targeted by the police while remaining excluded from American political institutions. Their deviance cast them as enemies of the state, and their undesirability placed them outside political channels conceived as legitimate.

As a former Communist Party member, long-time fellow traveler, and full-time homosexual who had himself been targeted by the FBI (an informant advised the bureau that Melcarth "was a Communist and makes no effort to conceal his feelings"), Edward Melcarth had little tolerance for—and well-tuned sensitivity to—the state suppression of undesirables.[3] Having grown up in privilege, Melcarth was radicalized by a number of scenes witnessed during his childhood travels—a trajectory that, in his recounting, "started with the bread-riots I saw as a kid in Vienna, with the General strike in 1926 in England and of course with the depression when I returned to the United States. In other words the only politics that I could see led me to sympathise with the aims of the Left." While Melcarth acknowledged that if he "were asked what I was in the thirties and early forties, I should have begun by saying a 'liberal' and perhaps by 1939 'a socialist,'" several events "turned me further and further towards the Communists." Among these were his visits to New York during college, which, he noted, "were not entirely devoted to learning to 'Lindy' and looking for sex and at pictures." He had also visited the Soviet Union with a male companion, and during that trip, Melcarth "had not been unfavorably impressed." More significantly, the "Spanish Civil War was the first real pressure" that impelled him to "contribute quite a bit of time and what little money I might to encourage the 'loyalists.'" He determined that "[o]nly the Communists seemed sincerely antifascist and serious about a socialist economy." Shortly thereafter, Melcarth joined the Merchant Marine, at which time he became

> very impressed by the way The N.M.U. [National Maritime Union] was run . . . it was then Communist dominated. It was the first time that I had seen party members on a day to day basis and their devotion and idealism was particularly noteworthy at a time in which the great American slogans were 'liberate' meaning steal and 'kick the shit out of' meaning more often than not little kids begging in Naples or the Coolies desperately trying to augment their fifteen cents a day wages.[4]

Melcarth joined the Communist Party in 1944 and remained an active member until 1948, when he departed due to a minor disagreement with the official line on Yugoslavia, where Melcarth had visited in 1938.

After leaving the Party, Melcarth remained a dedicated fellow traveler, committing himself to working "with Communist Fronts" on issues such as supporting the Trenton Six, an important civil rights case in 1948 concerning six Black men accused of murder that was taken up by the Communist-affiliated Civil Rights Congress. He wrote to *Life* magazine complaining of anti-Communism in their coverage of Willie McGee, a Black man convicted of assault on a white woman. "If *LIFE* hoped by this article to suggest that Negroes condemned to death should abjure Communist support," Melcarth wrote, "*LIFE* has merely succeeded in suggesting that only the Communists make a serious and concerted effort to abolish or abrogate our infamous Southern Law code."[5] He also remained committed to an anticolonial program in the United States. "[L]op off our arms race, our colonies official or otherwise," he wrote, "and capitalist prosperity will collapse."[6]

As an artist, Melcarth explored themes connected to labor, class, and sexuality. While he included many classical themes in his paintings, he was also, like many artists on the Left, interested in the art of social concern. In 1946, for example, he sketched a National Maritime Union strike in New York City. One of these drawings featured two men, one tenderly touching the sandwich-board sign of the other (figure 1). Another sketch from this time, labeled "Picket Line," depicted a jumble of indistinguishable bodies in a writhing mass, while a third featured two prone men being beaten. Violence among workers fascinated Melcarth, as further evidenced in a 1945 painting, titled *Fight in Central Park,* depicting sailors and men in working-class clothes midbrawl. An avid photographer, Melcarth took many pictures of striking workers. Later, his repertoire expanded to include hustlers and drug users, suggesting that his interest in undesirables was not reducible to his homosexuality.[7] He continued producing images of labor unrest, as in a 1948 painting of a demonstration on a city street—an image that included a prone man in its foreground. Melcarth was fascinated by urban landscapes, including among his sketches one of an "old woman pissing" and another of two men in various stages of undress in a beach changing room, and his photographs included images of a red-light-district peep show.[8] Two 1951 paintings, *Sit Down Strike* and *Construction,* show that his interest in labor themes continued past the 1940s.[9]

Though he was committed to the Left, Melcarth was also open about his homosexuality. He had affairs with various men, which he wrote about in poems that he kept in his personal papers:

FIGURE 1. Edward Melcarth, untitled, 1946, Edward Melcarth Papers, Archives of American Art, Smithsonian Institution.

No hustler
 With a sullen face,
Sellin love
 In the market-place
can ever e-rase
 the memory of you

No pocket
 With a bulgin' hand
No promise
 Of a one night stand
can ever disband
  the memory of you

Those bad things . . . were good things
 when I did them with you[10]

The distance between good things and bad things was a significant pre-occupation for Melcarth, who conceived wage theft, racism, crack-downs on homosexuality, and policing as bad, and leftist resistance to them good. He enjoyed spending time with hustlers, drug users, and queers more than respectable company anyway.

Under McCarthyism, Melcarth remained unapologetic about his history with the Communist Party. "[A]s long as the Smith Act remains on the books," he wrote in a letter criticizing the 1940 legislation that criminalized membership in the Party, "we Americans cannot castigate the Communists. The difference is only one of degree." Though he was no longer a Communist Party member when the red scare reached its peak, he remained committed to the good things for which he continued to fight. "I will be damned if I will 'clear' myself under the present stipulations," he continued;

> I may not be as fanatical as you suppose about turning America into a carbon copy of Soviet Russia past or present . . . but I *am* fanatical about seeing to it that America does not become a nation of Stool-pigeons. Fortunately I am not marrying Marilyn Monroe . . . I merely stand to lose a three thousand a year teaching job . . . no Hollywood contracts . . . no civil service seniority . . . no kids of mine are forced to starve . . . I can afford the rarest American privilege today . . . I can say what I think . . . unfortunately I may be almost unique.[11]

In accounting for his impassioned refusal to remain silent as the United States descended into anti-Communist hysteria, Melcarth pointed to both his artistic career and his nonprocreation as reasons for his radical resistance. He did so with good humor, contrasting his bachelor life with that of Arthur Miller, the latter of whom was caught up in a very public affair with Marilyn Monroe. Melcarth's deviance impelled his commitment to social justice.

Though he might not have realized it, Melcarth was not as unique as he believed. His history as a gay Communist who cast his lot with undesirables connects his personal and political history to a motley assortment of sexual dissidents on the Left before 1960. By developing sensitivity to class inequality, moving into clarity about the ways this was exacerbated by the Great Depression, participating in radical labor campaigns, sympathizing with the Soviet Union, contributing to the Republicans in the Spanish Civil War, opposing police and state harassment, resisting racial discrimination, and aligning himself with the dispossessed, Melcarth trod a well-worn path. Like him, a broad cross-section of sexual dissidents, especially culture workers who eschewed normative family structures, took advantage of their space on the margins of American society to throw themselves into leftist campaigns. His evident willingness to "not conceal his feelings," rather than presenting himself as an upstanding American citizen, further links him with his fellow travelers. Whether they were themselves straight, gay, or otherwise queer, many leftists, like Melcarth, brought sexual dissidence and the Left into conversation.

That conversation is the subject for this book. *Love's Next Meeting: The Forgotten History of Homosexuality and the Left in American Culture* reconsiders the relationship between radical anticapitalism and homosexuality in the United States. Throughout, I revisit a relationship often characterized as a series of misgivings, betrayals, dismal disappointments, and interpretive dead ends. Much of the prevailing scholarship on queer history discounts the Old Left due to its perceived homophobia, suggesting that emerging gay subcultures were more historically significant than movements that did not centralize LGBT identities.[12] Though my book does not ignore the failures of the Left to build a cultural movement centralizing sexual dissidence as a political concern, *Love's Next Meeting* explores a counterhistory where possibility, visibility, and resistance converged at the intersection of homosexuality and the Left.

I also consider the impact of both sexual conservatism and anti-Communism on overly simplified narratives about homosexuality and the Left, suggesting that at least some of their narrative friction has been generated and maintained through a capricious application of McCarthyism and historical amnesia about sexual politics before 1969. The powerful effect of a century's worth of red scares, state-sponsored repression, cultural opprobrium, moral condemnation, police harassment, and FBI surveillance would be hard to overstate. These forces have further restricted the availability of sources documenting this history, providing a significant stumbling block to historians attempting to write about it. "There is no evidence current that you loved me," wrote the Black gay leftist poet Owen Dodson in a 1946 poem, "Or witnesses: there was fire for the letters, / And those I told are promised, sealed." "Chrisesakes, man," wrote Harry Hay in a letter to Jonathan Ned Katz in 1974, "who among us Reds was stoopid enough to keep records through TWO Witch-hunts."[13]

Who indeed? One would certainly be hard-pressed to find a central repository dedicated to collecting material relating to sexual dissidence and the Left before 1960. Yet if imagining the history of an intimate relationship between homosexuality and the Left has been challenging, it is not entirely for want of evidence. As Regina Kunzel writes in a different context, "[W]hile deviant sexuality—forced out of hiding, interrogated, surveyed, and policed—leaves a paper trail, the normal covers its tracks."[14] Cultural works such as novels, poems, autobiographies, and short fiction reveal unique aspects of the Left that were central to participants but not necessarily found in the official records of the Communist Party—the political hub of the Left especially after the onset of the Great Depression. It is within cultural spaces that homosexuality was most visible. At speakeasies, nightclubs, and cabarets; within bohemian spaces such as Chicago's Dil Pickle Club and private parties; on the outskirts of, and sometimes deep inside, public parks; within working-class and transient communities; and in incipient political parties and organizations, leftists engaged, sometimes willingly and sometimes unwittingly, with sexual dissidents in their midst, blurring the line between these categories. In the process they laid the foundation for building a radical movement through which homosexual lives and experiences were given shape and new political identities were constructed.

Though its primary concern is with homosexuality, *Love's Next Meaning* explores the cultural logic that linked sexual dissidents with radical working-class politics in ways that challenge the homo/hetero binary. In discussing male prostitution, for example, leftists often foregrounded work rather than pleasure, and the practice of buying and selling sex frustrated efforts at connecting sexual behavior with identity. Same-sex object choice among male hustlers did not necessarily speak to desire as much as economics. Yet this linking of sex and economics further suggests how entwined sexuality was with the political economy—a topic

Kevin Mumford points to in his discussion of "interzones," those urban spaces where "cultural, sexual, and social interchange" occurred.[15] Radical writers such as Willard Motley, a best-selling novelist in the 1940s, refused to treat sex workers as abject or tragic figures who sublimated erotic pleasure as they made their money. Instead, in concert with other leftists, Motley explored the affective relationship between sex, class, race, and work.

Though the Left consisted of a variety of anticapitalist organizations and movements, members of the Communist Party were especially adept at balancing homosexual desire and leftist commitment, in part because they were already cast as sexual and political outsiders within American society. As one leftist member of the National Marine Cooks and Stewards, a radical labor union, described the situation, many were "drawn to the Party, to Marxism, simply because it was a rebellious group working for recognition and acceptance. And that, fundamentally, was the same thing that a homosexual—as we used that term in those days—as a gay person was working for."[16] The act of joining a revolutionary party seeking to overthrow the government of the United States pushed against the boundaries of respectability, morality, and decency that governed American life. It also threatened the dominance of bourgeois values. Homosexuality was associated with a similar refusal to submit to American norms, creating discursive overlap between sexual dissidents and leftists that blurred the line separating one group from the other. "Doctor, I'm a gay fellow, so what do I care about social position?" wrote a homosexual to the sexologist David O. Cauldwell in 1949. "I don't want to go to any tea parties."[17]

The impossibility of assimilating into mainstream America society primed many gay women and men to reject mainstream politics in favor of radical liberation. Their experiences as outsiders further informed gay leftists' capacity for tolerating situations where antipathy toward homosexuality appeared within the Communist Party, just as their skillful navigation of public and private sexualities made it possible for them to commit themselves to a political movement where they maintained some circumspection about their personal relationships. Arthur Laurents, a self-identified "Jew and a homosexual," found himself drawn into the orbit of the Depression-era Communist Party because leftists were "friends to the outsider."[18] Similarly, in a 1938 letter to sexologist William J. Fielding, a self-described homosexual noted that "peculiarities that go with this are an intense love of life (I have never taken the life-blood of anything)," as well as "pacifism" and "socialism."[19] Leftist belonging attracted those inclined toward transgression. As literary scholar Glyn Salton-Cox succinctly puts it, "Communists are queer creatures."[20]

In an influential essay dissecting the post-1960s New Left, cultural critic Stuart Hall describes how "the crisp distinction between socially and politically deviant behavior is increasingly difficult to sustain."[21] Political deviants privilege activities that "tend to fall outside the consensual norms which regulate political conflict, and they are willing to employ means commonly defined as 'illegitimate' to further or secure their ends. In life-style, attitude, and relationships they are socially unorthodox, permissive, even subversive."[22] Hall's analysis of deviance offers tremendous explanatory power for understanding iterations of the Left appearing in earlier decades of the twentieth century. Sexual values never emerged wholly from sexual identities. The lived experiences of sexual dissidents on the Left illuminate how the state-sponsored act of defining deviance shaped American sexual and political values in uneven ways.

The distance between sexual dissidents and leftists was further diminished through the shared institutions, tight spaces, and intersecting communities that brought them into close contact with one another. Just as the policing of homosexual behavior produced spaces for homosexual contact in working-class neighborhoods, prisons, and other places that were already considered outside the bounds of respectable middle-class life, the Left emerged from within industrial workplaces, working-class communities, and public spaces similarly located on the peripheries of polite society. Many who aligned with the Left or were targeted by Communist organizers had already been exposed to sexual diversity through population density, urban zoning, and sex districting, as well as the porous borders of public and private spaces. The YMCA, for example, was a significant site of homosexual-Left intersection. A 1928 exposé by George Jarrboe in the leftist magazine *New Masses* reported that among "lady-like boys" using the facilities, "obscene pictures were freely shown. 'Queer' men summoned those interested in trysts, with delicate whistles one to the other." Meanwhile, "now and then came a whiff of politics," and, Jarrboe notes, "to my amazement I discovered advocates of communism, Reds!"[23] Cafeterias, urban parks, boxcars, prisons, working-class bars, skid rows, and slums all represented spaces where both Communists and homosexuals could be found. Though working-class communities were subjected to police harassment and surveillance, sexual dissidence was more visible in areas catering to economically disadvantaged populations. The organization of modern urban spaces segregated by class produced vice districts in poor and working-class neighborhoods that fell between the cracks of the law and attracted radicals seeking to organize—and sometimes rub against—the lawless.

Until 1924, the Communist Party was organized into underground cells where members remained invisible even to one another—a structure that precluded public identification with the Party and prevented members from defending themselves against slanderous attacks. Draconian laws policing sexuality ensured that sexual dissidents were similarly relegated to subterranean corners at this time. In spite of such obstacles, many leftist sexual dissidents exploited these coalescing forces to resist the machinery of oppression: urban marginalization led to the building of counterpublics; criminalization produced solidarity among outlaws; enforced silence introduced subcultural codes that built alliances. As Michel Foucault famously writes, "[T]here is not one but many silences, and they are an integral part of the strategies that underlie and permeate discourses."[24] Neither homosexual nor Communist silence was ever absolute, and sexually dissident leftists were especially versatile in negotiating the restrictions on forbidden features of their American lives by stitching together shreds of political discourse that incited them to speech.

In a US context, the intellectual scaffolding that connected sexual dissidence with leftist politics derived most clearly from efforts to combat racism. Particularly beginning in the 1920s, leftists worked to theorize race, challenge racism, build momentum around antilynching laws, and advocate for Black Americans. These campaigns emerged out of a longer history of Black Marxism that critiqued racial capitalism from an internationalist perspective, connecting racism to a global history of colonization, enslavement, and diaspora.[25] The commitment to radical antiracism adopted by many American leftists suggests how attention to the meanings of racial identities for collecting power, resisting capitalism, confronting inequality, and organizing working women and men sometimes opened the door to reflexivity around sexual dissidence as a political category. There was, to be sure, much conflict and debate as leftists struggled to work out antiracist politics within a movement that too often replicated racist structures and practices. Yet the sensitivity of leftist writers to marginalized identities; the shared geographies for leftists, homosexuals, and African Americans in urban spaces; and an emphasis upon representing the brutality of the American way of life for people of color opened avenues of discourse that aligned antiracist and sexually dissident perspectives within leftist culture. Though the theorization of race in the Communist Party was far more robust than the attention given sexuality, writers on the Left frequently explored sexual dissidence and race in ways that defied official Party prohibitions on homosexuality.

The Left in the United States was also commonly associated with immigrant populations, many of them clustered in ethnic neighborhoods in the nation's cities. German immigrants had been foundational to the formation of the Socialist Labor Party in 1877. But these associations became especially pronounced after new patterns of migration emerged beginning in the late nineteenth century. Large numbers of Italian Americans participated in turn-of-the century anarchist and syndicalist movements. A sizable population of Jewish immigrants to the United States, many of them eastern European migrants, embraced radical politics and founded leftist organizations, magazines, and newspapers that connected ethnic identities with radical politics. Publications such as the *New Yorker Volkszeitung, Morgen Freiheit,* and *Novy Mir* offered leftist perspectives on issues of particular concern to readers with deep connections to immigrant communities in the United States.

In addition to their attraction to the Left, immigrants from nations outside western Europe were frequently accused of adhering to nonnormative sexual values. During periods of heightened nativism, immigrants, especially those conceived as nonwhite, were dogged by pernicious myths about their presumed criminality and, often, sexual deviance. Immigrant neighborhoods were accused of incubating depraved sexual behavior. Charges of "moral degeneracy" that rendered immigrants unassimilable were added to the nation's xenophobic playbook. The 1875 Page Law had restricted Chinese women from entering the United States for "lewd and immoral" purposes. Beginning in 1917, the United States banned "persons with abnormal sexual instincts" from immigrating, and the Johnson-Reed Act of 1924 further restricted immigration by targeting groups that, not incidentally, were broadly condemned as comprising both political and sexual dissidents.[26] Much of the surveillance of the Left, then, emerged out of deep suspicion of racial and ethnic minorities in the United States who were perceived as both politically and sexually different. Discrediting the Left was never reducible to ideological disagreement, and radicals carried with them the burden of their ethnic and racial identities being connected to sexual deviance. Yet even as American legal and cultural apparatuses were instrumentalized to squelch the voices of sexually dissident immigrants and people of color, many of those targeted responded not by dampening their voices but rather by increasing the volume in their outcries against injustice.

The clearest articulations of homosexuality on the Left appeared within expressive works rather than in official transcripts of Communist organizations and meetings. Representations of homosexuality in leftist literature and visual culture reveal a sometimes crude but nonetheless vital engagement with class, race, sex, and gender that was evidently important enough to become commonplace in leftist culture while rarely taken up by the Party leadership. Though their work was to some extent shaped by the Communist Party line and bound up in internecine debates about the proper application of Marxist ideology to artistic expression, leftist writers and artists were shaped through their collective grappling with often-contradictory ideas about aesthetic politics cultivated within organizations such as the John Reed Clubs and the League of American Writers.

Writing for working-class audiences or readers sharing political sympathies, and often published by presses accustomed to pushing against censorship, writers on the Left created spaces for representing diverse perspectives on homosexuality that were more dynamic and sophisticated than what was generally considered publishable outside their radical milieu.[27] Though the literary scholar Walter Rideout claimed in 1956 that "for the proletarian novelist homosexuality came to stand arbitrarily as a convenient, all-inclusive symptom of capitalist decay," the novels themselves suggest otherwise.[28] It was particularly within proletarian fiction that homosexuality was confronted directly, honestly, and without the tenor of moral opprobrium that so often dominated both mainstream and pulpy accounts of tragic third-sex disappointment. "Attack the filthy, the blood-stained luxuries of the rich all you want to," the Communist writer Michael Gold advised Upton Sinclair, "but don't moralize against the poor little jug of wine and hopeful song of the worker."[29] Leftist writers may have gotten a little preachy from time to time, but they mostly avoided moralizing against the vices of the lower class.

Love's Next Meeting unfolds in eight chapters. In chapter 1, I examine the lived experiences of sexual dissidents on the Left. Queer leftists negotiated their sexual and radical politics in ways that defy simple narratives that treat these concerns as entirely discrete. Rather than imagining their sexual dissidence as separate from their leftist sympathies, the subjects of this chapter brought those concerns into alignment. Chapter 2 expands this discussion to think about how leftists conceived sexual politics more generally. Within radical publications, discussions of interracialism and prostitution, challenges to censorship and obscenity law, interest in birth control, and engagement with free love framed sexual dissidence within a movement that has been mischaracterized as singularly focused on reductive class analysis. Chapter 3 focuses more narrowly on leftist analysis and interpretation of homosexuality within radical newspapers, magazines, and books in the 1920s and 1930s. I suggest how the Left allowed for an expansive narrative about homosexuality that connected leftist politics to sexual dissidence.

In the three following chapters, I emphasize key constituencies in leftist organizing: workers, women, and the urban poor. In chapter 4, I consider industrial labor unions, workplaces, and sex work to think about how leftists imagined labor as a site for exploring homosexuality. Chapter 5 analyzes leftist approaches to "the woman question" to centralize sexual dissidence in discussions of radical gender politics. Chapter 6 focuses on formal dimensions of proletarian fiction—in particular, novels by writers of color—as vehicles for addressing poverty in US cities. In *Knock on Any Door,* which was ruthlessly edited for publication, Willard Motley positioned homosexuality as a key feature of the proletarian urban landscape. H. T. Tsiang's *The Hanging on Union Square* depicted performances of sexual dissidence in New York as a tool for dismantling capitalism.

Love's Next Meeting's final two chapters consider homosexuality in relation to two seismic historical shifts that affected both sexual dissidents and leftists: the rise of fascism and the onset of the Cold War. Chapter 7 focuses on the emergence of antifascism in the Popular Front—a period marked by a dramatic about-face in Communist politics and culture. Leftist discourse moved closer to the center of American politics as the Communist Party responded to a global crisis by positioning Communism as 100 percent Americanism. This move set the stage for sexual dissidents to envision themselves as essential figures in the ongoing project of democratizing the United States. Chapter 8 considers how the lingering effects of the Popular Front played out during the Cold War, when sexual dissidence and Communism were collapsed in the public imagination and the homophile movement attempted to position homosexuals as American citizens deserving of equal rights.

It is my hope that careful consideration of the sexual and political deviance of the Left in American culture will demystify the attraction of the Left for many sexual dissidents, suggest the complexity in the relationship between homosexuality and the Left before sexual liberation, and reframe the politics of sexuality in moments when repression too often has been made into the whole story. In his memoir of his life in the Communist Party, Junius Scales recalls how he "felt that because homosexuals were a segment of the population subjected to prejudice and persecution, the Party should accept them freely."[30] *Love's Next Meeting* explores spaces where prejudice and persecution were transformed into political action. Even in the face of tremendous pressure, many leftist sexual dissidents, like Edward Melcarth, refused to conceal their feelings. This is their story.

CHAPTER I

"Flaunting the Transatlantic Breeze"

Sexual Dissidents on the Left

Two months before his thirtieth birthday, the radical poet, editor, and literary critic John Malcolm Brinnin set sail for the Soviet Union on the MS *Sidier,* a ship "loaded to the water level with intellectuals and other bores who are Doing Books." Brinnin, a former John Reed Club writer and Young Communist League member, embarked on his travels in July 1936, at the height of America's red decade, leaving behind his comrade Jack Thompson, whom he had met while working at a used bookstore, and with whom Brinnin had founded the leftist literary magazine *Signatures: Work in Progress.*[1] This latter venture, which aimed to publish emerging work from established leftist writers—and which Lillian Hellman described as "a damn good job"—was about to bring its first issue into print in a spring volume.[2] Brinnin also left behind in Michigan Kimon Friar, a fellow poet, critic, and Young Communist League member, as well as Brinnin's same-sex lover. Writing to Friar from a ship that "brightly flies the hammer and sickle," and which was propelling him to a nation cited by fellow Communists around the world as the model for a global anticapitalist revolution, en route to Leningrad, Brinnin waxed poetic to the lover he had fleetingly left behind. "Russia looms great before me now," Brinnin typed on a piece of stationery emblazoned with a red banner also brightly bearing the hammer and sickle, "and I am ready to meet it fullhearted. Hold with your communist lover, Kimon, you are more to him than manifestoes, banners, or a thousand nations."[3]

For Brinnin, identifying as a Communist and a sexual dissident held no contradiction. The depth of his love for Friar was made particularly evident through his holding him above those trappings of the committed leftist orientation—banners, manifestos, and internationalism—that had impelled Brinnin's Russian pilgrimage, a journey that left him "stunned, bewildered, exhilarated, depressed, infinitely thoughtful and lonely for you."[4] Brinnin's fullhearted affection for both the revolution and his romantic partner made frequent appearance in his correspondence with Friar over the next decade, and his relationship with his Communist lover was intimately connected with their shared investment in leftist politics, radical community, and the Soviet dream.

Brinnin's story might represent a particularly well-documented case study for unpacking the lives of gay leftists in the 1930s, but in his joining of Communism and homosexuality, he was hardly alone. Many women and men pursuing same-sex affairs, intimacy, and relationships were drawn to the Depression-era Left, and their biographies reveal the complexity of balancing homosexuality and Communism in the twentieth-century United States. Yet the marginalization of radicals and sexual dissidents from the mainstream currents of American life might also have drawn these strange bedfellows even closer. Straddling theoretically incompatible political and sexual identities, gay leftists eschew neat historical narratives about sexual politics and culture in American history.

This chapter explores the interrelations between the sexual, political, and artistic lives of sexually dissident leftists between 1920 and 1950. Though in many instances leftists openly puzzled through the relationship between their homosexuality and radical cultural politics as part of a shared project opposing both capitalism and bourgeois morals, the women and men detailed in this chapter also struggled to maintain same-sex contacts and relationships while building a leftist movement. Like John Malcolm Brinnin, many vacillated between attempting to connect sexual and class politics and treating personal relationships as beyond the scope of revolutionary struggle.

About both his sexual and political attachments, Brinnin was unashamed. His biography, along with those of many fellow queer leftists, demonstrates how the deviant politics of the Communist Party, a group pushed to the margins of political discourse and cast by liberals and conservatives as outside cultural norms, obviated the need for Communists to disavow their homosexuality while also suggesting an incipient interest in repurposing political revolution to articulate sexual politics. Sexual dissidents on the Left exploited a fundamental ambiguity between desire for revolution and for one another, refusing to yield primacy to one or the other and mapping a romantic yearning for sexual and political objects that charted a confluence of queer-Left passion. Though this perplexing admixture might be interpreted as denoting a failure on the Left to attend to the needs of its homosexual members or to centralize sexual politics, the radicals in this chapter unreservedly embraced the Left even while maintaining active sexual lives and pursuing same-sex relationships.

CRUISING THE LEFT

Hobos and itinerant workers occupied cruisy, intersectional spaces where sexual dissidents and leftists found one another.[5] In a 1937 "autobiography," Box-Car Bertha Thompson, a fictional vagrant invented by the renowned anarchist, sex doctor, syphilis expert, founder of Hobo College, and regular rider of the rails Ben Reitman, described a motley cast of radical queer characters found among transients in the early decades of the twentieth century. Among this crew, Bertha included a memorable portrait of Lizzie Davis, a Communist organizer who "knew the dirt about everybody. She knew if a man was 'queer.' . . . The lesbians and the fairies and the 'queens' could keep nothing from her."[6] Bertha also encountered Yvonne the Tzigane, a bisexual woman who "had several lesbian relationships which lasted varying lengths of time" and who both dished on the queer underworld to Bertha—"she said that there were a number of lesbians on the road and that usually they traveled in small groups"—and introduced her to a "Mickey Mouse's party" where lesbian women gathered.[7] Though not a wholly sympathetic portrait of homosexuality and hobohemia, Box-Car Bertha's emphatically proletarian narrative acknowledged the central role of lesbians, queers, and butch women with finely tuned gaydar in both shaping radical working-class communities and challenging "straight" culture. Even after Bertha's seeming transformation into a reformed mother, she included in her newly extended vagrant family "Ed Hammon, a fellow who was organizer for the painters' union; and a thin fairy called Hazel," who offered that Bertha "can claim the bunch of us as father for your child."[8]

The itinerant life represented a significant site of overlap between homosexuality and radicalism. In an unpublished manuscript from the 1930s titled "The Joys and Hazards of Sex," Reitman reflected further on the "homosexuals" who were "accepted in full fellowship" within the "Bohemian and Hobohemian circles" where he traveled. "No one insults them by calling them queer or kids them for being sissies," Reitman remarked. "In Bohemia, the 'homos' can speak their own language." Though he did not provide a glossary to assist his readers in parsing out this vocabulary, the language Reitman referenced was both familiar to and shared among homosexuals and leftists. "Two male 'homos' will meet a Radical," Reitman wrote, "and say, 'You know, this is my wife, Ella,' or 'I brought Kitty along; she is looking for trade.'"[9] This spirited moment of campy approval points to a serendipitous intersection of homosexuality and radicalism that was common within the Depression-era United States, when homos and radicals both found themselves riding the rails.[10] Reitman's "male homo" named his "wife" Ella, drawing immediate associations with prominent Communist Ella Reeve "Mother" Bloor and suggesting an irreverent relationship between homosexuality and radicalism that was instantiated through common use of the spaces where both communities traveled and within the shared language they used as they passed through life. So long as capitalism produced an unequal class structure and homosexuality was treated as deviant, homosexual and leftist communities' fates remained intertwined.

Areas such as Union Square in New York, Pershing Square in Los Angeles, and Washington Park in Chicago—the latter a well-known site for gay cruising and a venue for Marie Houston's Marxist lectures to large crowds of African Americans—were central meeting places for sexual dissidents that were also seen by leftists as fertile ground for organizing the working class.[11] Radicals working in these locations often capitalized on the proximity of leftists and sexual dissidents to build bohemian spaces where homosexuality was made political. Washington Square Park, popularly known as Bughouse Square, attracted soapbox radicals and cruising homosexuals. Jack Jones's infamous Dil Pickle Club, in its location in nearby Tooker Alley, brought both into a Bohemian, leftist, and decidedly queer space.[12] Jones, the Dil Pickle's proprietor and MC—the *Chicago Daily News* reported that "Jack Jones is the father, the mother and the ringmaster of the Dill Pickle"— routinely invited speakers to talk about sex to audiences of intellectuals, artists, and radicals.[13] Jones, who was married for a spell to the Communist organizer Elizabeth Gurley Flynn, herself a free-love supporter who had a long-term affair with Marie Equi while living in Oregon, was a teetotaler whose nightclub became a scene known for fostering unbridled behavior. To gain entrance to the Dil Pickle Club, visitors were required to squeeze through a tight alley to a tiny illuminated door emblazoned with instructions to "stoop low, step high, leave your dignity outside."[14] Once inside, visitors found themselves amid an energetic, often rowdy crowd prone to screaming fights and howls of disagreement, and especially attracted to topics pushing the boundaries of sexuality. At the Dil Pickle, dissidents of all stripes could finally, as a flier for one evening's event advertised, "Liberate the Libido!"[15]

Balancing lectures, performance, and generally bad behavior from the audience, the Pickle included lectures on homosexuality. Ben Reitman recalled "the guy called Theda Bara"—presumably named, in a typical instance of film-inspired camp, after the famous silent-film actress known popularly as "the Vamp"—who "talk[ed] about his life as a homosexual."[16] The German sexologist Magnus Hirschfeld, founder of the Institute for Sex Research, delivered a packed lecture on homosexuality that promised "beautiful revealing pictures."[17] Other topics included "Do Perverts Menace Society?," with two speakers answering yes and two answering no; "Are We Sex Crazy?"; and "Shall Society Accept Intermediates?"[18] H. H. Lewis, a Missourian Communist poet, contributed a poem to the Pickle's program, dedicated to Jack Jones, that was far more racy than his typical proletarian screeds:

> With fond regrets I oft remember
> The happy days of sport and fun
> When all my bones were young and limber
> Did I say all? Well, all but one.
>
> Now I'm becoming old and feeble
> The happy days of youth are gone
> Now all my bones are getting stiffer
> Did I say all? Well, all but one.[19]

Ben Reitman recalled that "most of the labor leaders who numbered among the early Dill Picklers followed the workers' movement through the syndicalism and the Workers' Party to the Communist Party. Several old members of the Dill went to Russia to become active as Bolshevists."[20] Down the street, radical revelers could also go to leftist Ed Clasby's similarly radical and Bohemian Seven Arts Club, which outlasted the Dil Pickle, though it never achieved quite the same level of popularity. Clasby was gay and decidedly open about it: "A sodomist," he declared, "is one who enlarges his circle of friends."[21] Clasby enlarged his own circle by inviting all kinds to the discussions at the Seven Arts. One homosexual habitué noted in a 1931 letter that Clasby was "still dragging widows and old maids to Seven Arts Club discussions." In spite of his interest in salons delving into the profane, Clasby was apparently naive enough that he "doesn't know anything about such things" as "rough trade." Nonetheless, the letter writer noted that "many of these gatherings have been really amusing. They were to me."[22]

The working-class spaces claimed by homosexuals and leftists in urban settings represented a significant point of intersection for constructing a homosexual-Left axis. In the 1940s, Communist Party member Jim Kepner, who later became one of the earliest members of the Mattachine Society and a founder of ONE, Inc., recalled having met "a tall, fairly handsome young radical in Pershing Square" who "seemed to be very knowledgeable about Marxism and radical history."[23] Kepner was "inspired by his virile good looks and superior knowledge" and "invited him to [his] party meeting."[24] Kepner's relationship to the Communist Party was informed and inflected by relationships with and attraction to other men in the park, which functioned as a site for both seduction and revolution. Pershing Square, where Kepner met his virile radical (who turned out to be a Trotskyist), was a common space where leftists delivered soapbox oratory and men met one another for sex.[25] This was a spot Kepner frequented to satisfy both his leftist and his homosexual desires. "Pershing Square," he recalled, "was one of the chief centers in the country for public open-air debate, officially designated as a 'free speech area,' ostensibly free from police harassment of persons whose views they might find offensive, and also popular for gay cruising."[26] Kepner's acknowledgment of the shared uses of this park suggests the particular value of working-class public spaces for connecting leftists and sexual dissidents. It was here where relative freedom from police harassment facilitated both radical organizing and gay sex.

Pershing Square's physical geography made it easy to brush up on radicals and same-sex partners, presenting opportunities for the line between homosexuality and the Left to blur. "Queens and gay hustlers generally occupied the park's East side, on the path along Hill Street," Kepner notes. "In the 40's, radicals and freethinkers were heaviest on the wide diagonal path from the Southwest corner to the large fountain plaza in the center."[27] Kepner cruised both paths. The easy relationship between homosexuality and radicalism in the public commons eventually crystallized into Kepner's radical homophile organizing. In conversations with his leftist comrades in the 1940s, Kepner tentatively started conversations about the responsibility for Communists to support homosexual rights. "I suggested that since the C.P. was rightly proud of its record of aggressively defending the rights of minorities," Kepner recalled, "it should be expected to defend gays also."[28]

Kepner also gestured toward sites of homosexual-leftist cross-polli-nation outside Los Angeles. While he was working for the Communist Party in New York, Kepner "had a few other homosexual encounters, some with guys I met in Union Square or Columbus Circle." These same spaces were critical to his work as a Communist organizer: "I became a regular in the Union Square and Columbus Circle debates, finding that I could often win people over to specific Marxist ideas (as long as I didn't call them that) while most cliché-spouting Marxists turned them off."[29] Kepner's language betrays the slippage between the cruising and Party recruitment that consumed his time in New York. His concern in both contexts was to make sure that when he encoun-tered potential sexual or political partners, he did not, above all, "turn them off." In Central Park, Kepner also met

> an incredibly beautiful, slender young Greek, with a bevy of handsome younger disciples, [who] was also a sharp progressive advocate, with an aggressive and witty style, not quite in the CP line but not far from it, as was a tall, elegant Black composer whom I also met several times in my wander-ings through Central Park, and with whom I later discreetly discussed gay concerns. I had several more contacts with Trotskyists. They seemed so often physically attractive. The SWP [Socialist Workers Party] and the WP [Work-ers Party], aka, the Canonites and Schachmanites, were early-on Trotskyite splinters, both still active. In practice if not in theory, the SWP seemed more tolerant of male gays, especially in New York, Minneapolis and Seattle.[30]

Alan M. Wald confirms Kepner's claim about the openness of the Social-ist Workers Party to male same-sex intimacy, but the Left seemed to attract homosexual denizens regardless of party affiliation.[31] Kepner's recounting of the sexual cruising that accompanied his radicalization illustrates his careful attention to both sexual attractions and political factions. His offhanded comment about the SWP's tolerance of "male gays" suggests that Kepner was perceptive about the ways leftist organ-izations treated homosexual members even at a time when he was not officially organizing homosexuals in his own work on the Left. His memories drift between detailed physical descriptions of his sexual partners and a deliberate parsing out of his partners' party affiliations.

Within homosexual-leftist memoirs, where sex and politics both were made symptomatic of particular forms of desire, discussions about the intricacies of party politics often took on the character of dishy gossip. As with exhaustive diaries of homosexuals such as Donald Vining, whose extensive journals were published in multiple volumes to accommodate accounts of his myriad sexual liaisons, homosexual-Left autobiographies tend to be extremely long and exhaustingly digressive.[32] Kepner's never-completed autobiography exceeded a thousand pages and was rewritten repeatedly without his ever finding a publisher. Samuel Steward, the working-class homosexual and tattoo artist who wrote gay pulp as Phil Andros and inked a sizable sample of working-class Chicago, exhaustively catalogued his sexual liaisons in a "stud file" that was used by Alfred Kinsey as he prepared his influential *Sexual Behavior in the Human Male*.[33] Just as each sexual experience was individually meaningful for constructing a gay autobiographical narrative, so the relationship between leftists and their chosen party was subjected to fetishistic, often emotionally charged detail, and the nuances and minutiae of every strike and direct action revealed something integral and essential about the meanings of the Left. Kepner's discussion of Central Park suggests how public parks could become spaces accommodating, constructing, and uniting sexual practices and political communities.

Whether in parks or nightclubs or wandering city streets, leftists found one another in spaces where they interacted with, and sometimes sought out, sexual dissidents. These interactions produced urban geographies where the culture of the Left and the sexual underground overlapped, producing political and erotic interzones that blurred the boundaries of deviant politics. While some of these relationships were fleeting, meetings between homosexual leftists sometimes developed into radical partnerships in which sexual, emotional, and political desires were fully enmeshed.

ANXIOUS ARCHITECTS: JOHN MALCOLM BRINNIN AND KIMON FRIAR

John Malcolm Brinnin and Kimon Friar were animated by both their commitment to the Left and their deep love for one another. After sending his letter to Friar from the MS *Sidier*, Brinnin wrote him another lonely, beseeching letter, this time from Kiev, where Brinnin had been exploring the Soviet Union and experiencing a confusing complex of mixed emotions. "To begin to tell you what I have seen here would be impossible because the very thought of it all chokes me," he wrote. "It will be months before I have assimilated for my personal self and for my abstract intellect just what importance it all has." As had the anticipation of his sojourn, actually being in Russia without his beloved Kimon left Brinnin feeling bittersweet. "If thoughts were actualities," he pined, "you would have identity in Red Square, the palace of the Tsars, the

teeming streets of Moscow, the lonely steppes—every spot I have been."
Again, the experience of visiting the Soviet Republic—a land that symbolized all their shared political aspirations—while Friar languished at
home put Brinnin in a desperately romantic mood. "We have so much
to build together," he wrote, "that it is a whole life itself,—and I am
such an anxious architect."[34] Whether they would be building a romantic union or Communist utopia this architect would not say. The fundamental ambiguity introduced through the world to be built seeped into
each of the missives Brinnin dispatched from his journey, as it did in his
ongoing relationship with Friar. It was, in fact, this precise melding of
sexual longing, romantic desire, and radical vision that best characterized Brinnin's relationship to homosexuality and the Left. If he failed to
produce a political narrative that brought these pursuits into alignment,
his capacity for highlighting their potential for cross-pollination suggests a common theme among those radicals who also balanced homosexuality and leftist politics between 1920 and 1950.

Friar responded to Brinnin's queer revolutionary overtures in kind.
In reply to Brinnin's Kiev letter in 1936, Friar sent a poem titled "Revolutionary Love: An Intimate Mosaic," which included the following
stanzas:

Poet whose soul resembles mine,
O heart whose heart is like my own,
The young only outface despair
To fashion out of dream and rime
Radiant firm new voices flown
In luminous signatures of air.

We shall exalt with love like ours,
Flaunting the transatlantic breeze,
Poets whose resolute songs foment
Hammer and sickle thru risen shores
Planting a joyous, blossoming peace
Where we may lie together in the end.[35]

In this poem, Friar blurred the distinction between his same-sex relationship and his revolutionary commitment to the point of irrelevance.
His Communist utopia, where the hammer and sickle rose as proud
symbols of peace, represented a future where he and Brinnin, together,
might eventually find their rest.

In the face of contradictory positions assumed by Moscow on sexual
matters, sexual dissidents continued to join the Communist Party in the
United State and, in some cases, discovered opportunities to express

resistance to both capitalism and sexual conservatism by looking to the Bolshevik Revolution for inspiration. The Soviet Union offered both a model for envisioning a postrevolutionary society and a location many Communists actually visited. There are many documented instances of American travel to the Soviet Union that allowed for sexual awakenings in contradistinction to US homosexual oppression. Claude McKay's suggestively labeled photographs of members of the Red Army ("fine type of Soviet soldier"), collected during the trip to the USSR that yielded his book, *Negry v Amerike,* in 1923, point to a libidinal investment in the Soviet Union that exceeded his revolutionary politics.[36] Boston Communist Henry Wadsworth Longfellow Dana collected among his many photographs of naked men a number of pictures of himself posed heroically in Cossack attire.[37] In the American imagination, the Soviet Union was sometimes even imagined as a livelier and more sexually open version of the United States. "Drinking, jazzing, petting, free love—these make for the social chaos of Soviet Russia," complained a reverend to *New Masses* in 1926.[38] The magazine's editors looked upon social chaos with more optimism. "I haven't been to Russia yet," Hugo Gellert, a leftist artist and *New Masses* contributor confessed in September 1927, "but I believe that they'll let you wear your hair as long as you like."[39] For Friar, flaunting the transatlantic breeze was inseparable from lying "together in the end."

John Brinnin first experienced same-sex desire as an adolescent. The earliest manifestations of his homosexuality spoke to a cultural element beyond mere sexual attraction. "Twelve years old," Brinnin recalled in an unpublished memoir, "and I'm reading Proust and Krafft-Ebing."[40] That he exposed himself to queer modernist literature and cutting-edge sexology—Krafft-Ebing's *Psychopathia Sexualis,* which appeared in its first English translation in 1903, was both highly scientific and extraordinarily sensationalistic, delving into subjects ranging from homosexuality to sadomasochism—before he became sexually active suggests the cerebral orientation of Brinnin's sex life.[41] He had his first homosexual experience several years later, and he tended to focus on cultivating sentimental and romantic relationships with other men rather than pursuing promiscuity.

Kimon Friar had been in a deeply affecting love affair with a boy in his high school. "My intense *love* for a boy has, without a doubt, been the chief influence in my high school development," Friar wrote in his diary in 1929, the year he graduated. "I am told my intense liking for him is unusual."[42] Friar was not inclined to care too much about what was considered unusual, though he was acutely aware of the pain he experienced as a result of the inability for his desire to find expression in a society that saw his attractions as unnatural. In 1929 he published a poem, titled "Camouflage," in his high school newspaper. The poem was only four lines long, simplified to a flat recitation of the most benign pleasantries:

> I meet you in the hall.
> You say, 'How are you?'
> And I answer,
> 'Fine; how are you?'[43]

In this simple and abbreviated verse, Friar captured both the anxiety of performing heterosexuality and the thrill of queer sexual frisson. Friar was acutely attuned to the contours of heteronormativity and seemed eager to push against such social restrictions, anticipating the political refusal that impelled his turn to the Left. In a diary entry detailing his same-sex crush during his high school years, Friar both justified his homosexual feelings and envisioned a future world that would affirm his queer desire:

> Though I feel so wretched in this wanting him, I'd rather feel thus than not to have that feeling at all. I know that when I have a son I will do all in my power to help him in case he should feel this way about another boy. I hope to God that he *will* feel so for I think it is the most wonderful experience in the world. I know that I have gotten a better, cleaner outlook of life, have wanted to do more things, know more of the world and life, and lead a clean, upright moral life since I met Ed.[44]

Friar dismissed criticism of same-sex desire, rather than homosexuality itself, as immoral and unclean. In 1930, after he began attending the University of Wisconsin, a longtime friend of Friar's attempted to alleviate his mother's fear that he was "allowing his moral character to go to ruin. . . . He not only has not gone out with bad women," she cheekily reassured her in a letter, "he has not gone with girls at all."[45] Indeed, Friar was avidly pursuing a number of men with whom he sought physical contact, especially a fellow cafeteria worker about whom he wrote longingly to his friend "Ed the Communist":

> He walked close to me, tantalizing close, and once in a while, his warm brown arm, pendulum-swinging, would brush against mine and tinge my blood with a delicious warmth. Somehow, the conversation developed on our lodgings, and I, though I did not want to and though I listened to myself as though to a person acting against his will, invited him up to my room, being immediately aware with what enthusiasm he accepted the invitation.[46]

Brinnin and Friar were both fairly forthcoming about their sexual partnership. "No, I do not closet anything," Friar wrote Brinnin in 1938, "I am much too afraid of skeletons."[47] Brinnin confessed the full dynamic of his and Friar's relationship to his heterosexual comrade Jack Thompson in 1940 without any apparent impact on their friendship. "I am glad that you know," Friar wrote to Thompson after that conversation. "He [Brinnin] has kept it pent up within himself too long, and he needs someone who might be sensitive to his feelings, that he might not feel so alone."[48] Both Friar and Brinnin maintained an intimate, though nonsexual, relationship with Phillips Garman, a union activist and labor radical. The three men's relationship balanced intimacy with aesthetics and politics. In a 1934 letter to Friar, Garman recounted visiting the leftist painter Diego Rivera's famous *Detroit Industry* murals at the Detroit Institute of Arts. "I can't express their simple, vivid strength in words, but he certainly captures some of the essences of our civilization and with glowing power preserves them for everyone to experience," Garman effused. "I wish we could look at the murals together," Garman added, "for powerful as they are to me alone I know that you can see much more deeply into them than can I."[49]

Despite the intensity of his and Friar's friendship, Garman did not desire Kimon sexually. "I'm sure Kimon that I'll never love a man that way," he wrote in 1934, "because I believe I am fundamentally incapable of it." Yet Garman attracted much attention from men seeking his affection, as when, in the case of one man, Garman "sensed after awhile that he was a person who felt and lived as Calamus, and in a sense admired him for his sincerity."[50] Friar diligently instructed Garman to hold steady against these advances, but he urged him to also recognize his own role in attracting Calami. "When you next buy a suit of clothes," Friar wrote, "please—and I am sure you do not realize the excessive importance of this—buy trousers of greater width than you are wearing both around the thighs and the groin, even though you have to have them tailor made."[51]

Friar maintained close friendships with many Communists from whom he sought to learn more about Marx and the Party line. Chief among these was Shigeto Tsuru, a Japanese economist with whom Friar maintained a long-term friendship that began at Wisconsin. Long after they graduated, Friar continued seeking clarity from Tsuru on Communist principles.[52] Friar joined the Communist Party after immersing himself in activities that were part of the broader cultural front. In 1935, he was assigned to the American Guide group in the Works Progress

Administration, a New Deal agency that was particularly amenable to left-wing politics. At the same time, he became involved in a group he referred to as "the New Theatre Movement Against War and Fascism."[53] Though he was not inclined to expound on Marxist theory, Friar did not shy away from expressing anticapitalist viewpoints in his correspondence. "Not only do these wily capitalists store up treasures on earth," he complained in one such letter, "but they take great care to leave an opening for compound interest in heaven."[54]

Brinnin became aware of the labor movement around the time of his adolescent sexual awakening. "On the way across Cadillac Square one afternoon I ran smack into a crowd reaching to the steps of City Hall. Workers from the auto plants," Brinnin recalled. "They'd lost their jobs and were sore about it. Some walking two or three abreast carried banners and in different spots around the Square speakers stood on boxes and yelled out what they had to say." Witnessing the power of a mobilized working class animated Brinnin to join the Young Communist League. He became particularly interested in the cultural side of the Left after taking a job working in a bookstore, where he discovered "a stridently smudgy issue of something called New Masses." It was here that Brinnin also first stumbled upon "the blue paper-bound Ulysses from Shakespeare & Company recently devalued because of a Supreme Court decision overturning the ban imposed by United State Customs," as well as "the actual fever chart affixed to the foot of Walt Whitman's hospital bed."[55] In the space of a bookstore, Brinnin was able to explore radical politics, obscenity, modernism, and sexual dissidence.[56] Brinnin's orientation toward aesthetics perhaps also allowed for a more individualized relationship to the Left. "I believe they are much more flexible in the things they ask from people talented in artistic ways than they used to be," Phillips Garman wrote to Brinnin of the Communist Party in 1936. "And that's as it should be, for you can certainly do far more through your writing to help other people to want to live better than in any other way—and incidentally live better and more fully yourself."[57]

Brinnin was especially drawn to modernist writers—an attraction that defined his emerging career as a poet and biographer. Though Max Eastman had attempted to discredit the "artist in uniform,"[58] Brinnin acknowledged that one need not choose between modernist and political writing—a viewpoint presented especially persuasively in his unpublished essay "The Poet as Political Man." Here Brinnin perceptively noted how "readers have a tendency to call that poem didactic whose premises they disagree with; the same readers will protest that charge brought against a poem that echoes their belief or comforts it."[59] He submitted his writings to *New Masses* under the name Isaac Gerneth.[60] Even after he moved away from the Party in 1945, he continued to advance, as literary scholar Alan Filreis argues, a "sense of 'deliberate innocence' as a radical form of honesty."[61]

Brinnin followed the Party line in the late 1930s and early 1940s, excising from his circle—and even his bookshelves—writers whose politics strayed from approved positions, as when Kay Boyle, an active participant in New York's artistic circles, was believed to have betrayed the cause in 1936. "Kay Boyle has gone unforgivably fascist," Brinnin moaned, "and I am wretched about it; her books stand in mute betrayal on my shelves, their art become suddenly beautifully vicious."[62] Yet his own published literary output rarely adhered to the formal demands of proletarian literature of the period. Brinnin favored surrealist and romantic strains that captured waves of emotion in modernist housing but hardly announced a partisan perspective. "You, being a fastidious worker of images and rhythms, are not easy to grasp," Norman Rosten, the poetry editor for *New Masses,* wrote him after he submitted work for publication. "A compliment, really, but the revolution must go on— even with lousy poetry."[63]

Brinnin's sexual dissidence and leftist politics cross-pollinated. On his nightstand table, Brinnin kept a photograph of Kimon "along side of Henri Barbusse," the noted French Communist writer whose fidelity to the Soviet Union was well established. "You know, dearest," Brinnin wrote Kimon, "I was never really sentimental about anybody before."[64] In spite of such protestations, Brinnin's sentimentality often spilled over into overwhelming feelings of affection for the promise of working-class revolution and same-sex love. Recounting a trip to Detroit, Brinnin reported how

> this has been very wonderful for many reasons: first, oh so terribly first, I have discovered how unbelievably much I love you; second, I have sung with raised fist the Internationale among nine thousand people in Detroit; I have joined that creative, directive channel of comradeship in my first actual party contact: I have met Waldo Frank and talked long with him alone and have seen him respond to me until I nearly choked with excitement, have seen him on to his train and have him put his arm around me and assure him I would write to him; I have had a poem accepted by New Masses.[65]

The tone of Brinnin's letter remained consistent as he declared his abiding affection for his romantic partner and his solidarity with the working class of Detroit. Brinnin celebrated his deepening involvement in the

Communist Party along with his "unbelievable" love for Kimon. Where one might expect a bifurcation of Brinnin's political and sexual identities, instead Brinnin reveals a deeply affective resonance that unites along axes of longing and belonging. Both love and politics affirmed him as an individual within a radical community. Political gestures often doubled for Brinnin as romantic ones. "Several days ago I ordered two copies of SPAIN," Brinnin wrote to Friar of Auden's famous work, "one for you and one for me!! Was ever there a more loving identity in the practical world or in the sentimental?"[66] Probably not, and Brinnin was quite the master of uniting the practical and the sentimental.

At times Brinnin admitted the work involved in bringing homosexuality into alignment with Communism. In 1939, Brinnin described to Friar two male comrades who "*are* lovers, and are consciously trying to mold the course of their relationship in channels that will fit their new sense of responsibility since they've become Marxists."[67] Brinnin frankly acknowledged these men's explicit desire to maintain both their sexual relationship and their leftist politics. A resolution to the presumptive conflict between homosexuality and Marxism was within the realm of possibility if only the correct "fit" could be found. Friar also traded gossip with Brinnin about their gay leftist friends and comrades. In a 1937 letter, he dished about a gathering that yielded a wealth of information about the gay leftist circles of the United Kingdom. "They are all abnormal—including [William] Plomer and [Louis] MacNeice," Friar reported. "[Stephen] Spender, it seems, wrote his last book, the advance from liberalism, on an isle in the Aegean sea with his lover Tony. Tony is a charming boy, says Engle."[68]

Brinnin's leftist orientation plugged him into a network of fellow gay writers with whom he shared a sensibility and, occasionally, an arch humor. The problem of the homosexual leftist was sometimes made an object of camp, as when Truman Capote—about whom, decades later, Brinnin wrote an influential biography—sent a trenchant letter to Brinnin about André Gide. Capote knew from gay leftists, having dated the leftist critic Newton Arvin.[69] Gide, meanwhile, was something of a gay Left celebrity in the 1930s. Though his most direct articulation of sexual politics, the *Corydon* dialogues, did not appear in an English translation until 1950, they were published and attributed to Gide in France as early as 1924, and they were eminently accessible to the artistic types for whom knowledge of French was the price of entry into rarified cultural circles.[70] In 1933, *New Masses* published an article celebrating Gide's Communism while acknowledging him as "a troubled though unashamed introvert."[71] In his letter to Brinnin, Capote reported on Gide's move to the United States. "Gide is living here; he sits in the barbershop all afternoon having his face lathered by little boys of ten and twelve," Capote wrote. "There is rather a scandal, not because he likes to take little boys home with him, but because he only pays them two hundred lire."[72] Capote rendered the plight of the Communist struggling to maintain ideological purity within a capitalist society an object of playful camp. For transgression, seeking underage lovers—a charge that was likely exaggerated for comic effect—was trifling when placed next to the exploitation of underpaid service workers.

Within his writing, Brinnin brought his sexual and radical concerns together. The pressures of publishing sometimes forced him to rein in his most outspoken leftist impulses. Brinnin's editor at Macmillan urged him in 1939 to "drop the political poems that have become shopworn in these days when events in Europe move faster than we in the U.S., however quick our eyes reflect their images, can follow."[73] Brinnin pressed forward anyway. His 1944 book of poems, *No Arch, No Triumph,* included "The Insatiables," an anticapitalist poem about the "Café Underground," a most likely fictional interracial gay bar in Paris. "Under the prosperous hospitals and jails," Brinnin writes,

> Under the triumphal arch
> That holds for flags and victories,
> The losers, the perverse, and those who watch
> From the corners of their eyes
> Eternally, put down their ransomed coins
> To bring the mincing entertainers out.
> Like ballet kings and queens
> With blood to spend and nonchalance to flout,
> They watch a shocking symmetry of life
> That owes no debt to grief.[74]

Here, "under the courts and the cagey logic of cash," Brinnin finds at last a counterpublic space that situates losers and perverts in the audience and on the stage.[75] He positions the Café Underground as a seductive alternative to the prosperous brightness and casual cruelty of public spaces where capitalism thrived. Brinnin's deviant queers reject social environments where they are constantly watching out the corner of their eyes in favor a café operating under an alternative political economy. Their labor might have been extracted in exchange for "ransomed coins," but once they entered the Café Underground, sexual dissidents' debt was erased through affective relationships bound by perversion.

The logic of cash was rendered inoperative. No more grief. In a shocking symmetry, by descending deeply underneath the triumphal arch, the losers and perverts at the Café Underground were transformed into Communist lovers.

For both Brinnin and Friar, the relationship between aesthetics, politics, and sexuality was impossible to untangle, and their enthusiastic pursuit of each suggests how leftist artists repurposed their radicalism to affirm sexual dissidence. Though they did not endorse a political revolution that placed their sexuality at the center, neither did Friar and Brinnin conceive their sexuality and radicalism as entirely separate. Through their poetry and politics, they brought sexual dissidence and leftist politics into alignment, anxiously building a world that unsettled comfortable categories of social and political deviance. And as they grappled with the modern, Brinnin and Friar built a movement broadly encompassing both sexual dissidence and working-class revolution.

BISEXUAL COMMUNIST POET: WILLARD MAAS

Brinnin and Friar's relationship to the Depression-era Left, defined by their commitment to one another as well as to the Party, contrasts somewhat with that of Willard Maas, a bisexual leftist poet who gained notoriety decades later for reportedly administering the eponymous act in Warhol's 1964 silent film *Blow Job,* a claim that Warhol disputed. Though he had many same-sex affairs throughout his life, Maas remained married to Marie Menken, a fellow artist and filmmaker whose relationship with Maas was purported to have provided the model for Martha and George, the epically dysfunctional couple in Edward Albee's 1962 play *Who's Afraid of Virginia Woolf?* Maas joined in the signing of the first statement of the League of American Writers, a leftist group that included both Communist Party members and fellow travelers, in 1935. He became increasingly involved with the Party in the later 1930s, and he was a friend and confidant to leftist writers including Ruth Lechlitner and Richard Wright. Wright adopted an unusually campy tone with Maas. "Have you yet laid eyes on Auden," he asked in one letter, "or is he flitting like a ghost around the neighborhood?" Wright also participated in queer world building when he commented to Maas that he "just finished the life of Oscar Wilde by Frank Harris, and did I get the shivers."[76]

Maas contributed poetry to *New Masses* and was committed to leftist literature in the Depression years. He proposed a book anthologizing the poetry of social concern that would have included work by Lechlitner as well as Muriel Rukeyser, the latter a fellow bisexual leftist poet. He edited the July 1935 issue of *Alcestis*, which included a broad assortment of radical poetry. In defining his aesthetic, Maas wrote that "the poet is caught up in the forces of fire and blood of history, and objective force acts upon him."[77]

Though Maas was committed to Communism, he was also something of an iconoclast. In 1938, Raymond Larsson, a fellow poet, attempted to unpack Maas's attraction to the Communist Party. "I think your approach is emotional, and from revolt against other circumstances and states, rather than from a profound conviction of the *rightness* of Communism," Larsson charged. "I think your inclination is toward Communism simply because you've really never thoroughly looked for another solution."[78] Larsson's read of Maas's political deviance suggests how the Left was conceived as appealing to those who rejected the stifling conformity of bourgeois moralism. His accusation that Maas's Communism represented an "emotional" approach acknowledged that one could join the Party to fulfill affective desires.

There is no denying that Maas, like many in the Party, enjoyed the social elements of Communism. In a 1937 letter to Maas from Anna Norma Porter, a poet and journalist, the writer chastised Maas's bad behavior at a gathering with fellow leftists at the home of Tess Slesinger, another leftist writer. "I don't think it was at all funny your getting drunk on Tess Slesinger's whisky under a chair," Porter wrote disapprovingly, "just disgustingly Bohemian."[79] Maas was no stranger to booze-fueled hedonism, but he did not let it interfere with his profound conviction of the rightness of Communism.

Maas carried on with a number of men, including Rupert Barneby and Thomas Doremus, while remaining married to Menken, who was apparently aware of, if not altogether unconcerned about, his same-sex affairs. One of his longest affairs was with Norman McLaren, a Canadian leftist artist who maintained an intense relationship with Maas for several years. McLaren had been a camera operator on *Defence of Madrid,* a film about the Spanish Civil War directed by the Communist filmmaker Ivor Montagu.[80] He was in an open relationship with the actor and theater director Guy Glover and was frustrated by the secrets Maas kept from Marie Menken. "Why did I weep the first time we were alone together," McLaren wrote pleadingly to Mass. "After seeing Marie, I felt like a louse, and knew I was one."[81] McLaren also worried that Maas's sexual affairs would distract from his art. "You are Willard

Maas, the poet," he wrote in another letter, "not Willard Maas, the lover of N. McLaren."[82] McLaren signed off another letter with perhaps history's most extravagantly camp articulation of queer deviance:

WITH LOVE AND LOVE? AND EXTRA LOVE? AND OTHER LOVE AND INVERTED LOVE AND ELONGATED LOVE AND CRUSHED LOVE AND SLICED LOVE AND CUSHIONED LOVE AND VERTICAL LOVE AND SPIRAL LOVE AND LOVE IN CUBES AND LOVE IN OVALS AND LOVE IN SNIPITS AND LOVE IN DOLLOPS AND LOVE IN CURLICUES, AND LOVE THAT'S GUEY, AND LOVE THAT'S CRUNCHY AND LOVE THAT'S BEEN DIGESTED, AND LOVE THAT'S BEEN EXCRETED, AND LOVE THAT'S RETURNED TO THE EARTH AND LOVE THAT'S GROWN INTO LOVE AGAIN AND COMPLETED A CYCLE OF LOVE RETURNING TO ITSELF.[83]

Maas's correspondence reflects the camp sensibility he shared with his friends. In a 1941 letter to Mass, Guy Glover discussed *Let Us Now Praise Famous Men* ("a catalogue documentation of three poor Southern families, with liberal hunks of poetic prose, in the Style Whitman") before recounting the queer pleasure of cruising "the Sodomic Mysteries of Prospect Park" and gossiping about his fellow actor Woody Parker ("a very nice looking youth, [a really quite accomplished actor (I saw him only once, however),] but my! what a bitch!").[84] A letter from Rupert Barneby reported to Maas how he had "found Peggy [Guggenheim] in bed surrounded by little piles of terrier-shit. She *said* she was menstruating."[85] Maas himself wrote a song in rhyming verse titled "Park Avenue Analyst Blues" that offered a ridiculously over-the-top treatment of a psychiatrist's office occupied by a chorus of neurotic queers. "I even love you after you've come as much as I did before," the chorus announces, "but I couldn't love you half as much, loved I not Mother MORE!"[86] Maas evidently appreciated the campy—and sometimes misogynist—vernacular circulating through Depression-era gay culture.

Norman McLaren's letters to Maas frequently incorporated camp style alongside allusions to their shared leftist sympathies. In 1941, he sent Maas a handwritten poem describing how "revolt rises from the deep / cisterns of hunger," impelling "the mind's growth of dialectic / lambent powers."

Atoms of might
    Be ours
new leaves new blood new flowers
in our hands and the hands
of all[87]

Here dialectics coexisted with the heartfelt romance of new beginnings, auguring a time when flowers would belong to everyone. In another letter, McLaren embellished a dull postcard of *Dancing Faun* with stars and mountains penned in blue, staging the statuary in a celestial landscape that rendered its dullness high camp. On the back of his postcard, McLaren entreated Maas to send him "a special kind of underwear" with a "cock-pouch" in "medium," noting that "it looks better when tightly filled."[88] Theirs was not, evidently, a purely romantic friendship. "My love is firm as a rock," McLaren informed Maas, "and rises like a monument."[89]

As a writer, Maas aspired to meet the formal expectations of the literary Left, often emphasizing the erotic undercurrent in homosocial work environments. In an unpublished story Maas set among workers in "the cotton fields of San Joaquin," an unnamed narrator becomes increasingly distressed by Swanson, a "big German over six feet," who arouses great consternation because "he took his drawers only half way when he rubbed himself down. . . . I thought he was some big squarehead for acting like a woman about going naked." The story's denouement occurs when the workers "were all standing stark naked at the edge of the water rubbing soap on our sweaty parts" and "Swanson had his drawers half down as usual. He was going at it like a sixteen year old in front of his old lady." Having finally had enough, the narrator cries out, "Swanson, we all know you got a wang. Off with the pants," and proceeds to "jerk them down." He is knocked unconscious by Swanson, and is told only later that Swanson's penis had been sliced off by a farmer for unnamed sexual indiscretions. Maas's narrative was aimless and far from high art, but it suggests how he repurposed proletarian literature to stage homoerotic scenes.

In another story, a narrator sits in a literal closet with his friend, watching his father have sex with another man's wife. A third describes two merchant marines being cruised by a priest in San Francisco. The priest invites them to his apartment, where he offers them "some very choice wine that was used for sacramental purposes" before initiating sex.[90] As a leftist who was familiar with the kind of fiction one found in venues such as *New Masses*, Maas seemed particularly inclined to repurpose the literature of the Left to indulge queer fantasies. Maas's persistent, if unsuccessful, efforts at writing proletarian fiction demonstrate his desire to put his sexual dissidence in the service of his revolutionary politics.

Though he took some stabs at fiction, Maas was more committed to poetry. In an unpublished poem from the 1940s, he made sport of the stock market's crash, imagining Times Square as a site of investment in sexual cruising:

> "Go, before the crash!" I coward shout, but
> On the arcade of 42nd Street and at
> Downtown stations Wall boys cruise the Johns,
> Dealing in bonds the ticker does not clock.
> Each lily in the market of their arms
> Notes the rising price of preferred cock.[91]

The absurdities of capitalism are repurposed by men cruising for hustlers. The sexual economy functions in Maas's poem as a radically queer alternative to the overinvestment in capitalism on Wall Street. In another poem, Maas describes "the bourgeois gentleman from Chicago" who "discusses supply and demand and the curb price of wheat" while "homosexual young men with a flair for metaphysics / arch their eyebrows and file T.S. Eliot to the archives." Sexual dissidence, Maas seemed to suggest, represented a libidinal investment on which agents of capitalism could not speculate.

Maas published his second full book of poetry, *Concerning the Young*, in 1938.[92] In this volume Maas included a number of poems gesturing toward the seduction of cities and youth, particularly emphasizing parks and the potential they contained for both solidarity and sexual contact. In the poem "Concerning the Young," part of a cycle titled "Journey and Return," Maas describes an apocalyptic urban landscape that teems with sex and revolution:

> Out of the classrooms past the factory wall,
> They stand upon the platform in the square,
> Erecting barricades against the night[93]

Equally suited to a reflection on the Paris Commune or a guidebook to New York's homosexual underworld, Maas's verse features cruisy descriptions that include both working-class signifiers ("the factory wall") and allusive nighttime scenes. In "Journey and Return," another poem in the same cycle, Maas offers a lyrical meditation on urban seduction:

> We were in love with the movie queen
> Kissing the celluloid dark,
> . . . .
> While the pale boys with the luminous eyes
> Passed on the sidewalk arm in arm
> And disappeared in the dangerous park.[94]

Maas describes homosexuals as familiar figures who populate the urban landscape. Yet his idyll is undone in the final line of his poem's concluding stanza, where his fantasy is revealed to be but a dream from which Maas awakens "with machineguns mounted on the window sills."[95] The violence of history intrudes on even the most erotic fantasies.

In 1936, Maas wrote his most important work, "His Image in the Snow." Though it remained unpublished at the time of its composition, Maas included the poem in a 1945 recording of his poetry and later adapted it into an experimental film. "His Image in the Snow" begins with an unnamed man who "brought lilies where they had been forbidden." The associations of lilies with homosexuality appeared regularly in American culture, from Bruce Nugent's 1926 story "Smoke, Lilies, and Jade," published in the inaugural and only issue of *FIRE!!,* to the charged libidinal paintings of Charles Demuth, an artist well known for his phallic watercolors.[96] Maas had himself personified the lily in his earlier poem about sex workers. In "His Image in the Snow," the lily functions for Maas as both a metaphor for and a transubstantiation of the queer body, a "strange and intricate flower / That became more precious though neglected," and that, in the face of contempt, "survived." It marks as deviant those who seek to possess it, but the flower itself also absorbs the scorn and torment of those who target it for elimination. "They named as evil / And destructive that desire," Maas writes, "the hidden / Dream of the subterranean past." His poem articulates a highly coded and deeply symbolic meditation on forbidden and suppressed desire that Maas imbues with the contours of history. The lily also represents "the object of scorn in the merchant's year"—an allusion to the punishing economy of labor and desire under capitalism toward which the Communist Maas demonstrated unusual sensitivity. It "was rejected" and "despised."

Yet the hatred cast upon the lily is precisely what fertilizes the flower. It is "with phlegm and the curse spoken" that the flower "came to be more beautiful / Than all the rare trophies he had won / Through striving." The flower embodies the subtext of deviance emerging out of social rejection. In the conclusion of "His Image in the Snow," lilies are transformed into monuments to the struggle against the brutality of repression. They are "heroes"; their soil beds the "field of battles;" the flowers "dug from the grave / The living statues to endure the constant snows." The meaning of the title is thus made clear at the poem's end: "his image in the snow" is the flower that thrives in those conditions that are supposed to exterminate it. It is the completion of a cycle of love that has been excreted and returned to the earth and grown into love again.

There was, it seems, little that distinguished Maas the Communist from Maas the sexual dissident. Through his deviant politics, Maas aligned himself with the proletariat and the perverse and refused normativity. In contrast to some of the fiery leftist verse of the 1930s, Maas's work tended toward gently romantic and swelling emotion. Though he explored radical themes, his poems rejected tough-guy aesthetics of Depression-era proletarian literature. "We are told," the editors of the influential 1935 collection *Proletarian Literature in the United States* complained, "that intensity over a phase of the class struggle is agitation and therefore not poetry."[97] Maas was a poet who sought agitation. His poetry attempted to offer radical perspective on sexual dissidence, signaling Maas's aesthetic commitment to representing the experiences of both sexual and political deviance, the forces of fire and the blood of history.

LESBIAN LEFTISTS: GRACE HUTCHINS AND ANNA ROCHESTER

Throughout the 1930s and 1940s, women both joined and, in some cases, assumed positions of leadership within the Communist Party. Yet the organization's repeated failure to fully incorporate women's concerns into the Party platform—or to recognize the unique issues confronting women under capitalism as unassimilable into reductive class politics—alienated many women who might otherwise have been sympathetic to revolutionary Marxism.[98] Nevertheless, women on the Left such as Mary Inman and Elizabeth Gurley Flynn, the latter of whom Jim Kepner recalled being "very impressed by[,] half suspecting that she might be a lesbian," expended great energy making their voices heard, and they moved the Communist Party in productive directions that recognized the particular issues women confronted under capitalism.[99] Inman, a California Communist, was particularly invested in fighting against "male chauvinism" within the Party. Her influential book *In Women's Defense* (1940) centralized the devaluation of domestic labor that maintained women's subordination in the Communist Party, and in it she argued that Communists marginalized women at their own peril.[100] Though her book did not attend to sexuality as a significant feature in women's lives, Inman did force Communists to acknowledge that women were not auxiliary to the revolutionary project and deserved to have their particular histories theorized. Other leftist women, such as Rose Pastor Stokes, had established their radical credibility by assuming positions of leadership in feminist movements advocating for suffrage and birth control before they aligned with the Communist Party. Stokes parlayed her long history as a feminist activist into a leading role in the revolutionary working-class struggle. She joined the Communist Party in the 1920s, when it seemed to represent a uniquely open space from within which to advance feminist causes, and within the Party she continued to advocate for women and the need to address women's issues on their own terms. She was also arrested for her leftist work, caught up in the raids of the Chicago Communist Party's offices in 1920.[101]

Still, women's accomplishments in the Party came at something of a cost. Whereas men were often able to ignore those elements of the Left that they found objectionable, women were subjected to tremendous discipline when they stepped out of line, and the pressures of maintaining an oppositional stance from within the Party produced fatigue and frustration among those who took militant stances on gender issues. In addition to confronting exhaustion and occasional disciplinary action, leftist women developed a reputation that further stigmatized them. Though women's sexuality was barely tolerated and rarely even acknowledged on the Left, scholars have noted that "fragments of evidence indicate that [Communist] party members, especially the women, had a loose reputation."[102]

The association of radical women with sexual license had deep roots. In the earlier twentieth century, Socialism had been charged with appealing primarily to "the longhaired men and shorthaired women"; and those short-haired women sometimes transgressed sexual lines as well as gender norms.[103] As prominent Communist Beatrice Lumpkin recalled in her memoir of life in the Party, it was conventional wisdom that "only Communists or prostitutes would be seen in public without a hat."[104] Female sexuality was something of an open secret on the Left, acknowledged by critics as common, yet most often assumed to be transgressive. As chapter 5 details more fully, queer women's struggles against both the sexism and antipathy toward homosexuality in the Communist Party muted their ability to articulate a subjectivity that would place them on the front lines of revolution.

In 1932, Grace Hutchins, identifying herself as a "Bolshevik," announced in an update for the Bryn Mawr alumni newsletter that "Anna Rochester and I . . . have just celebrated the 10th anniversary of our partnership."[105] Though they were typically treated as good friends and comrades, Hutchins and Rochester were Communists in a queer relationship that spanned several decades. The couple was part of the broader Left community, counting among their friends noted radicals including Alexander Trachtenberg, publisher of the Communist press International Publishers, and Norman Thomas. Devoted to the Party since becoming members in 1927, Hutchins and Rochester often framed their romantic partnership, which actually began in 1919, through their shared political commitments, and the pair were treated by their fellow radicals as valued and respected comrades.

Unlike John Malcolm Brinnin's solo excursion, Rochester and Hutchins traveled to Russia together as a couple in 1927, attending political rallies, such as a May Day parade in Red Square; and cultural events, including a performance of *Constantin Teryokhin*—a play about a Comintern youth organization—at the Trade Union Theater. That play aroused for them conflict around to what extent the Communist Party should involve itself in members' personal affairs. Though their opinion on the matter remained unresolved, Rochester and Hutchins' private correspondence following their viewing the play suggests that thinking carefully about how to approach the question of Party control of individual behaviors was more than a trifling issue for the couple.[106] Rochester and Hutchins routinely aligned their personal lives with their political struggle. Following their trip to Russia, which also included stops in China, India, and several other nations, Rochester described in a letter to a friend their sojourn: "[T]ogether we have in a year quite rebuilt our little world," an articulation of shared passion that echoes Brinnin and Friar's anxious architecture.[107] Having experienced "the thrill of the living sense of human solidarity that reached us many times in Russia," the pair declared to a Soviet journalist that they would "devote all of our energy and all our work efforts so that American workers will walk hand in hand with the other proletariat of the world in the class struggle."[108] Their work and lives embodied principles espoused by Alexandra Kollantai, a Soviet writer and theorist who argued that "the ideal of love-comradeship, which is being forged by proletarian ideology to replace the all-embracing and exclusive marital love of bourgeois culture, involves the recognition of the rights and integrity of the other's personality, a steadfast mutual support and sensitive sympathy, and responsiveness to the other's needs."[109]

Rochester and Hutchins had been life partners since they met as young women. Between that meeting and their travels to the Soviet Union, the couple moved from a series of ascetic religious convictions that impelled them to help the poor into labor radicalism that culminated with steadfast commitment to revolutionary Communism by the late 1920s. They ended up purchasing the *Daily Worker* in the 1940s to keep the newspaper afloat. Julia M. Allen writes in her brilliant biography of the pair that they "spent their lives trying to disrupt the systems that held the silence and codes in place, fusing feminism and Marxism-Leninism to create new discourses and then funding the presses that published the writing that ensued."[110] Hutchins and Rochester were devoted to the Party and to one another, and their romantic partnership was often framed through their political commitments. Hutchins signed her letters to Rochester with "I love you," written in Russian—a private intimacy that joined the couple's affective and political bonds.[111] Rochester affectionately referred to Hutchins as "papa."[112]

The community of radical women around Hutchins and Rochester, meanwhile, were implicitly read as queer. Esther Shemitz, who attended classes at the Rand School, worked for the radical International Ladies' Garment Workers Union, and later worked in the advertising department at *New Masses,* eventually marrying Whittaker Chambers. Before this time, the leftist journalist Elinor Ferry describes Shemitz as "an almost deliberate stereotype of the bohemian radical woman. She wore a black beret over her black bobbed hair; a black leather jacket and flat-heeled shoes. She used no makeup, which was scorned as a form of bourgeois decadence. She is remembered also as mannish and harsh in manner, much given to using four-letter words after the emancipated fashion of the time."[113] Shemitz and Grace Lumpkin, the leftist author of proletarian novels including *To Make My Bread* and *The Wedding,* lived together in the East Village, and they "appeared," according to Communist journalist A. B. Magil, "to be lesbians."[114] Hutchins and Rochester, according to Elinor Ferry, "influenced Esther and Grace Lumpkin in their revolutionary zeal. Miss Hutchins and Miss Rochester had money in their own right, and had made loans to the two younger women so that they could pursue their careers as painter and writer."[115] When Shemitz married Whittaker Chambers—after Lumpkin married Mike Intrator, who was rumored to be Chambers's live-in "sweetheart"—Hutchins and Rochester gave the couple a toaster.[116]

After their return from the Soviet Union, Hutchins and Rochester commenced rebuilding their world and society. Hutchins got arrested at a demonstration in Boston, leading her father to call her a "disgrace," and Rochester began writing a series titled "Class War Bulletins" for *New Masses.*[117] Hutchins worked on the book that became *Labor and*

Silk, an account of textile labor published by International Publishers in 1929. Rochester's *Labor and Coal* appeared two years later. *Labor and Silk* foregrounded the experiences of women workers, allowing Hutchins to bring her feminist interests into alignment with her commitment to a workers' revolution. She also contributed pieces to the Communist publications the *Working Woman* and the *Woman Today,* as well as a pamphlet titled *Women Who Work* in 1934.[118] In 1936, she compared her efforts to Susan B. Anthony's "fight to free women."[119]

Though she did not address lesbian themes in her work, Hutchins did attend to the sexual dimensions of capitalism in *Women Who Work,* attacking Madison Avenue for producing advertisements "addressed to women as subordinate to men, simply as vehicles of sex charm, as if their sole end and aim in life should be to attract and please the man."[120] Grace Lumpkin praised Hutchins's book in *New Masses,* commenting that "so much has been written from the point of view of the middle-class feminists who are making a sort of artificial heaven for themselves, with Miss Greta Palmer of the *World-Telegram* as the Gabriel who blows their horn, and Mrs. Roosevelt as the official spokesman, it is time a book written for working women and from their point of view should be published."[121]

Hutchins was also committed to explorations of literary modernism. Even as she dug into works such as Lenin's *Imperialism, the Highest State of Capitalism,* she thrilled to Virginia Woolf's high-modernist novel *Mrs. Dalloway,* a work that delved into lesbian themes and explored women's consciousness.[122] Rochester and Hutchins further developed an intersectional critique of racism during the Communist Party's Third Period. Inaugurated at the Comintern's Sixth World Congress in 1928, the Third Period line set international Communist policy until 1935. Characterized by a belief that the crisis in capitalism would be met with the global rise of Communist internationalism, the Third Period saw an increased militancy within the Communist Party as it abandoned earlier efforts to bring Socialists, trade unionists, and sympathetic liberals into their fold, instead building a separate movement founded upon revolutionary principles. The Third Period line also drew more African Americans into the already diverse organization—70 percent of the Party's membership was foreign-born in 1933—following the adoption of its "Resolution on the Negro Question in the United States," which established the "Black Belt thesis" asserting African Americans' status as colonized people in the American South, where "the main Communist slogan must be: *The Right of Self-Determination of Negroes in the Black Belt.*"[123] It was during the Third Period that the Communist Party became prominently associated with militant antiracism. In a 1930 issue of the *Working Woman,* Grace Hutchins railed against how "of all workers under capitalism, Negro women are the most exploited."[124] The Black internationalist struggle gave the couple a vocabulary to recognize the ways racial, gender, and class identities became entwined in the revolutionary movement.

Within their private correspondence, political intimacies between the two were shared more freely. In 1943 Rochester wrote Hutchins a birthday poem celebrating their joined personal and political struggles and connecting their same-sex intimacy to their revolutionary fervor:

> Warm heart, clear brain
> Straight-back, no pain
> Friend to many, loved by all
> Spring of youth,
> Though nearly sixty, heeds the call
> Of truth
> And struggle
> Dear Grace,
> Beloved Grace[125]

In this light verse, embedded within personal correspondence that was not intended to find a public audience, Rochester encapsulated both the romantic love and the political struggle that marked her relationship with Hutchins. Her partner's strong back, a sign of her firm posture, signaled her unassailable commitment to both her lover and working-class revolution. Far from being conceived as a distraction from or at odds with leftist commitment, same-sex intimacy deepened the couple's investment in the Communist Party. Rochester articulated her affection through reference to the "struggle" and singled out Hutchins's "clear brain," suggesting how their personal relationship was understood to be inextricable from their political work. Yet the structures of deviance that were used to articulate queer leftist commitment were noticeably absent here. The phrase "loved by all" suggests community and solidarity rather than transgression and abjection. In her brief poem, Rochester encapsulated both the romantic love and political struggle that marked their relationship. Far from being a distraction from or at odds with leftist commitment, same-sex intimacy further entwined the couple in radical political movements, particularly through their shared profession as leftist journalists.

Though Hutchins and Rochester mostly maintained a partnership within the Communist Party by maintaining silence about their sexuality, the challenges of commitment occasionally became pronounced in troubling ways, suggesting the precarity of queer-Left lives. Perhaps most significantly, in 1949, Hutchins labeled Whittaker Chambers, a former editor and contributor to *New Masses* and suspected FBI informant, as a "homosexual pervert" in a memo to the Communist Party headquarters, repeating a claim she made to Alger Hiss's lawyers that "Chambers had been a sex pervert when he was employed at the *Daily Worker.*"[126] While it is difficult to know precisely why Hutchins defaulted to outing her former comrade in order to discredit him, it bears noting that her statement indicates that she was attuned to the presence of homosexuals on the Left. Chambers was, we now know, involved in homosexuality for some time prior to Hutchins's 1949 revelation. It is likely, then, that Hutchins had observed signs of his sexual dissidence and filed it away without action before Chambers betrayed Alger Hiss. Her strategic revelation suggests that Hutchins was willing to instrumentalize sexual conservatism, thus confirming that she was aware of the risks associated with public accusations of homosexuality and unresolved in her attitude toward her fellow gay leftists. Hutchins's actions might further lend insight into her own careful reticence around admitting to a relationship deeper than a friendship.

Ultimately, Hutchins's relationship with Rochester suggests how sexual dissidence and radical politics could be imagined as mutually constitutive by parties wholly immersed in both. Though the broader context of American society produced an unwelcoming environment for them to openly address questions about sexuality in relation to the Marxist struggle that consumed them, Hutchins and Rochester did, as did many other homosexual leftists, use their political commitments to strengthen their relationship, just as they used their relationship to further immerse themselves in Party politics and organizing work. Like Brinnin, Friar, and Maas, Hutchins and Rochester privileged the liberation of the working class as the site of historical struggle that defined them, but they also refused to devalue their relationship regardless of the vicissitudes of Communist Party discipline. Their biographies and writings demonstrate the deep desire homosexual leftists had both for the revolution and for one another.

Throughout the 1930s and 1940s, sexual dissidents shared spaces with leftists, aligned with the Left politically, joined the Communist Party, built same-sex relationships shaped by shared political and sexual desire, and produced literary work exploring sexuality and revolution.

Though their biographies matter, gay leftists are most instructive for revealing the limits of the Communist Party's efforts to discipline its members and to discourage Marxist engagement with the politics of sexuality. While much significance has been ascribed to perceptions of leftist homophobia, the general climate of antipathy to sexual dissidents in the 1930s and 1940s meant that perceived animus toward homosexuals within the Communist Party was not necessarily seen by members and fellow travelers as exceptional or even noteworthy. Through shared spaces and leftist sympathies, sexual dissidents carved out space on the Left from which to challenge presumptive heterosexuality and to envision a revolutionary society where multiple facets of desire might be fulfilled.

CHAPTER 2

"After Sex, What?"

Politicizing Sex on the Left

On March 18, 1927, *New Masses,* the foremost cultural magazine of the US Left, hosted an Anti-Obscenity Ball at Webster Hall in New York City's East Village. Responding to critics and government officials who charged the radical magazine with indecency, the editors abandoned their original theme for the spring event ("Pan, the Uncensored") and instead organized a party where attendees were encouraged to "yield to the overwhelming demand for PURITY, even at the expense of art." The tenor of the ball was ironic rather than enraged, the editors adopting a campy tone as they urged readers to put on the humorless affect of moral puritans seeking to usher in the magazine's demise. Attendees were exhorted to arrive in costume, suggested themes for which included "chilled by chastity," "virtue's virtuosi," "passion's Passover," and, of course, "I ain't that kind of a girl." "Clean up the stage!" the editors mockingly advertised. "Get rid of Sex! The human figure as shown in the 'art magazines' is obscene! The fig-leaf is a perversion of nature! Quick! Put the skirts on the piano legs!" (figure 2).[1] Through this gathering, purportedly the "purest, demurest, God-save-our-homest, most RE-spectable costume party ever held in New York," *New Masses* entertained its readers by demonstrating that dangerous working-class sexuality—another costume suggestion was "pity the poor working girl"—was worth preserving. Recreational (and occupational) sex needed not be understood as the property of debauched aristocrats, and perversion was celebrated for providing pleasure and disrupting the status quo.

THE CENSORS HAVE SPOKEN:

Clean up the stage! Get rid of Sex! The human figure as shown in the "art magazines" is obscene! The fig-leaf is a perversion of nature! Quick! Put the skirts on the piano legs!

THE PRUDES HAVE IT!

Yielding to the overwhelming demand for PURITY, even at the expense of Art, the NEW MASSES artists have abandoned their original plan of a SPRING FROLIC—which was to have been a Festival in honor of

PAN, THE UNCENSORED—

and will give instead, the purest, demurest, God-save-our-homest, most RE-spectable COSTUME PARTY ever held in New York. It will be known as the

ANTI— OBSCENITY BALL

Friday Evening, March 18th
Webster Hall

COME AS

THE DRIVEN SNOW, or in a costume appropriate to the occasion. Here are some suggestions:

DON'T RISK THE RISQUE—
LIBERTY NOT LICENSE—
PITY THE PURE WORKING GIRL—
THE RAKE'S REMORSE—
THE SMUT HOUND'S REVENGE—
PRIG'S PROGRESS—
THE CHILDREN'S HOUR—
FARCE OF THE PHARISEES—
CHILLED BY CHASTITY—
VIRTUE'S VIRTUOSI—
PROPS OF PROPRIETY—
I AIN'T THAT KIND OF A GIRL—
PASSION'S PASSOVER—
NUDE'S NEMESIS—

In a word, we shall, with your help, celebrate everything that is clean and wholesome, everything moral, expurgated, unsophist'.ated, virginal and innocently virtuous.

Prize for the DEMUREST COSTUME!
No Booby Prize!
(This means you!)

Official Flower: (You guessed it)
THE LILY!

Are you crestfallen? Down hearted? Have you got

THOSE PURITY BLUES?

Come, then, and listen to our
HARLEM JAZZ BAND.
Irrepressible those fellows!

Come, and

LAFF IT OFF!

Tickets $1.50 in advance.
$3.00 at the door.

By Mail from NEW MASSES
39 Union Square
Telephone 4445 Stuyvesant

Ask about special rates for parties and clubs.

Pierrot: To the pure in heart all things are pure!
Columbine: You said it!

FIGURE 2. Advertisement, *New Masses*, March 1927, p. 32.

The *New Masses* Anti-Obscenity Ball confirms two important dimensions of American leftist history: first, radical culture in the 1920s and 1930s embraced open discussion about sexuality even in the face of threat from censors; and second, leftists adopted a camp style to resist sexual puritanism and offset accusations that they were stentorian ideologues incapable of enjoying the pleasures of the machine age. During a period characterized by a hard-left turn precipitated by the rise of the Communist Party in the 1920s, leftist print culture balanced its reporting on labor struggles and class warfare with efforts at establishing radical positions on sexuality. Those concerns were particularly pronounced within *New Masses,* the splashiest and most infamous leftist periodical of the 1920s and 1930s ("as big and almost as gaudy as its illustrious namesake [*The Masses*]," according to Daniel Aaron).[2] Following in the footsteps of its Bohemian forebears, *New Masses* established its renegade reputation by publishing boldly radical content ranging from the leftist literary criticism of Joseph Freeman to ferocious proletarian screeds by coeditor Michael Gold, alongside racy cartoons by left-wing artists such as William Gropper. The editors and writers in *New Masses* were especially intrepid about publishing work dealing with sexuality in its many and varied forms: monogamous, promiscuous, homosexual, married, free-loving, and paid in cash; pleasurable, private, public, class bound, and interracial. Though these topics were especially welcomed in the Bohemian context of the 1920s, they persisted beyond the Depression era. *New Masses* positioned itself as a youthful, vibrant publication in contrast to the stodgy theoretical journals often associated with the Left. In a 1931 advertisement, the magazine boasted of its "lusty youngsters: full of proletarian vitality."[3]

The price for such editorial libertinism was constant surveillance by the postmaster and scrutiny by vice squads rabidly pursuing obscenity-law violations. Yet rather than caving to powerful forces that threatened to squelch their voices in the wilderness, the editors of *New Masses,* by employing tactics such as the Anti-Obscenity Ball, responded defiantly and deployed camp stylistics to offset persistent challenges concerning their magazine's propriety. Following in the footsteps of the editors and writers in *The Masses,* the magazine's earlier Bohemian iteration that made its mark by eschewing the conservative sexual mores defining middle-class culture at the turn of the century, and its more militant successor, the *Liberator, New Masses'* editors embraced sexual experimentation and routinely featured content pushing the boundaries of respectability. Consuming such radical content implicated readers as themselves seditious comrades, and it established a radical sexual vanguard that incubated the leftist politics of homosexuality.

From their first issue, *New Masses'* editors were ebullient in their rejection of sexual conservatism and bourgeois culture, both of which they mocked mercilessly in editorials, cartoons, and published forums.

MOTHER. WHEN YOU WERE A GIRL WASN'T IT AN AWFUL BORE BEING A VIRGIN?

FIGURE 3. Art Young, untitled, *New Masses*, July 1926, pp. 16–17.

The tendency for mainstream media to imagine sexual liberation as emerging from among the ruling class was satirized in a July 1926 *New Masses* cartoon featuring a languorous flapper reclining legs-up on a chair with a cigarette as she calls out to her scandalized mother, "[W]hen you were a girl wasn't it an awful bore being a virgin?" (figure 3).[4] Significantly, the *New Masses* editors refused to yield their sexual exuberance to the decadent Gatsby-esque roaring-twenties upper crust, instead reminding readers that working-class values offered a far more liberating foundation upon which to build a revolution than the trendy sexual experimentation that emerged out of prosperity's ennui.

When Michael Gold, perhaps the most committed Communist on the magazine's masthead, became *New Masses'* sole editor in 1928, he channeled popular confession magazines as he solicited "letters from hoboes, peddlers, small town atheists, unfrocked clergymen and schoolteachers," as well as "revelations by rebel chambermaids and night club waiters."[5] The people, evidently, yes—and the racier, the better. "The mass of humanity, stupid or intellectual, is fond of any kind of fun, sensuality, relaxation, sport and frivolity," Gold wrote in a letter to Upton Sinclair, "and I am one of them."[6] Gold was not afraid to embrace the obscenity that characterized mass culture as he sought to minimize the distance between sensationalistic pulp confessionals and the leftist

FIGURE 4. William Sanderson, untitled, *New Masses*, January 5, 1937, p. 13.

press. In this regard, Gold had his work cut out for him. Bernarr Macfadden, an astronomically successful publishing entrepreneur who oversaw a variety of popular magazines such as *Photoplay* and *True Story* that perfected the art of balancing sexual titillation with moral condemnation, had already established a winning strategy representing Communists as sexual freaks. Macfadden was notoriously anti-Communist, and his favored strategy was to discredit the whole movement by pointing to leftists' sexual peccadillos. A detail tucked into a 1937 *New Masses* illustration by William Sanderson depicts Macfadden in caveman-esque wrestling garb, dropping papers around him bearing titles such as "Reds in Free Love" and "Sex, Smut, Filth, etc." (figure 4).[7] Radicals were characterized by Macfadden as deviants, but *New Masses* disrupted such claims by representing Macfadden as the real smut peddler, a maniacal beast who was himself lewd and unsophisticated. *New Masses'* editors labored to distinguish themselves, even when publishing sexually renegade content of their own, from the reactionary magazines published by Macfadden and his ilk, tying themselves in knots as they sought to claim a cultural style popular with working-class readers to articulate a radical perspective on sex that admitted sexual pleasure while disavowing reader prurience.[8]

For the *New Masses* crowd, initially a cross section of Bohemians and leftists who turned increasingly to Communism as the years marched on, obscenity was conceived less as a problem than as a mission, and readers were enlisted as comrades on the front lines of sexual revolution. The editors and writers who produced leftist print culture worked relentlessly to associate middle-class values with sexual suppression, thus replacing a narrative of radical prudery with representations of sexual Victorianism as the backbone of the upper class. Their radical vision confirmed a general cultural anxiety (and leftist promise) that sex and revolution went hand in hand. "The revolutionist," declared the radical John Darmstadt (John-Armstead Collier) in 1927, "is going to take down [sex] from the bourgeois altar, strip off its shroud of mystery in which it is embalmed for worship, and tear off the veils of prudery and falsity in which it is bedecked for barter and sale."[9] "It takes two revolutions to make a new world: one in the sphere of economics and one in the sphere of erotics," wrote Samuel D. Schmalhausen that same year in the *Modern Quarterly*, a radical journal he coedited that was especially inclined to take up sexual matters. "A revolution in property-values and a revolution in sex-values. And the economic prepares the sexual revolution."[10] "If one wants to be a revolutionary proletarian," asked Charles Wood in a *New Masses* article, "shall he favor sex or oppose it?" Wood's answer was simple: "[H]e had better favor it, if he wishes to be an efficient revolutionist."[11]

Efficient revolutionists were rarely in short supply. The presence of Communists as organizers, residents, and workers in poor urban neighborhoods, many of them populated with sex workers and establishments catering to vice, further cast leftists under the flickering glow of unseemly red-light districts. Communists disrupted domesticity through their proximity to the sexual economy. Reporting in the *Daily Worker*, H. M. Wicks noted the many sexual options that were available in slums located so far beyond the peripheries of respectable culture that deviance had no margins toward which to be pushed. "Polygamy, polyandry and incest can by no means be regarded as exceptions among a very large strata of the lower proletariat," Wicks wrote. "Their very condition of life deprives them of any other form of relaxation."[12] Sex in red-light districts and poor neighborhoods offered cheap amusements that were incorporated into everyday street life by residents while attracting sex tourists and slumming dilettantes.[13] Leftist proximity to and interest in representing the "lower proletariat" were perceived by the Right as reflecting unseemly sexual values among radicals who, perhaps by osmosis, but more likely as a fundamental factor in their initial attraction to the proletariat, adopted nonnormative sexual proclivities of their own.

The licentious leanings of *New Masses* prompted praise as well as criticism, sometimes simultaneously. "I think even the renowned Mr. Streicher's pornographic library so many people mention these days is hardly over some of your cartoons when it comes to sheer vulgarity," one reader charged in a 1936 *j'accuse*. Making a comparison between *New Masses* and the notorious Nazi pornographer Julius Streicher's infamous images of Germans raping Jews likely elicited strong reactions among radicals during the early years of the antifascist Popular Front. Yet perhaps even more surprising in this letter was its writer's observation that illustrations in New Masses were *more* pornographic than some of the most obscene images in circulation at the time. "I agree with the point, understand me," this scandalized reader concluded, "but *cripes,* the vulgarity!"[14] That vulgarity often *was* the point might have eluded some of the less sexually progressive New Masses readers, but it was a consistent message in the magazine across the decades. Even this letter writer recognized that the shared political goals of readers and editors in New Masses offered something of a carte blanche to push the boundaries of pertinence. Through her blushing, the reader nonetheless acknowledged she did "agree with the point."

As leftists rejected American capitalism, they also repudiated the values that fueled that cruel economic system. "After I have been with good people, formal people, however revolutionary, for more than a month or two," Michael Gold wrote in the 1920s, "I want to bust loose and do something wild."[15] Contrary to conventional wisdom that has produced a mythical Old Left easily characterized as either disinterested in or antagonistic toward sexual dissidence, the Left often represented a loose space and a wild space, as well as a camp space. Sex made up a regular topic of interest in radical circles of the early to mid-twentieth century, and it was within leftist cultural venues that conversations about deviance, obscenity, and sexual experimentation frequently took center stage.

Two primary dimensions of leftist culture intersected with sexual dissidence during the 1920s and 1930s. First, political efforts at combatting censorship aligned radicals with a sexual vanguard. Second, politicizing sex within radical print culture established a set of militant sexual values that were transformed into a touchstone for leftists who adopted radical sexual politics. Envisioning the leftist politics of homosexuality began with imagining a leftist sexual politics more generally—a process that developed in earnest with the ascendance of the Communist-centered Left in the 1920s and 1930s.

RADICALLY OBSCENE: HOW THE LEFT GOT DIRTY

In 1930, a group of prominent radicals including Marxist philosopher Kenneth Burke, radical literary critic Edmund Wilson, Communist writer Isidor Schneider, and leftist artist William Gropper contributed to a satirical book titled *Whither, Whither, or After Sex, What?*[16] Boasting a scandalous cover designed by Gropper that depicted a nude woman chasing after a stork airlifting a baby, this self-described "symposium to end symposiums" poked fun at intellectuals' obsession with sex and obscenity that seemed to be overtaking American culture, imagining an alternative world in which sex was rendered banal and prohibitions on sexuality were treated as deviant. "Little boys who peep through windows," wrote Malcolm Cowley, "can easily learn to peep through microscopes and thus become the bacteriologists of the future."[17] Rather than pushing perverts to the margins of society, Cowley and his comrades envisioned a world where the contributions of the sex obsessed were placed at the forefront of innovation. Social progress depended on peeping toms.

In another of the book's essays, titled "LIBIDO, or the Future of Debauchery," Corey Ford ironically took on "gambling and betting, fighting, stealing, smoking, drinking, birth, love, marriage, sex and other modern perversions"—a list remarkably resonant with many items in Michael Gold's catalogue of preferred vices. Ford, audaciously positing "marriage" and "love" alongside "sex" and "drinking" as forms of modern "perversion," cited a letter he purportedly received from a college student who had read his work on the shocking prevalence of obscenity in the United States. "I have just read an article by you in which you mention that salacious magazines, smutty stories and obscene picture-postcards can be obtained at numerous places in this country," the earnest student wrote. "I wish you would send me the addresses of a few of these places so that I may study these obscene publications and pictures you speak of, and thus acquaint myself with the dangers of this form of literature."[18] Political radicals were well attuned to the overinvestment in obscenity made by the most putatively prudish of readers, and they insisted on exposing the lurid motivations driving the right-wing censoring machine. Radically redefining obscenity, the book's editors echoed the editors of New Masses, who argued in 1936 that "the distortion of a natural impulse into innuendo and veiled reference is obscene."[19]

Radicals were particularly attuned to the intricacies of obscenity law because those laws were frequently instrumentalized to target leftists. Years of harassment by moral scolds had, by the late 1920s, transformed many leftists into vigorous defenders of the right to get nasty. (Historian Leonard Wilcox refers to such radicals as "the libidinal left.")[20] "We see no point in temporizing with the smut-sniffers or attempting to make art safe for Fundamentalists, morons, and Puritan neurotics," New Masses announced in 1926. "We think they ought to mind their own business. What they are really complaining about is not us but the dirt in their own minds."[21] Leftist writer Samuel Ornitz struck a similar tone when he memorably termed the right-wing interest in prurient materials "First Class Dignified Dirt."[22] What was truly obscene was the right-wing obsession with limiting the scope of knowledge and creating a shameful mystique around sexuality. The best way to combat obscenity, leftists seemed to suggest, was by suffusing all subjects with sexuality. They claimed the moral high ground even as they celebrated their own immorality.

Radicals well understood that obscenity laws were most vigorously pursued when both leftist politics and sexual perversion populated the same pages.[23] An editorial in the second issue of *New Masses* slyly observed how investigations of periodicals for publishing explicit sexual content tended to be pursued with particular zeal in cases where "the magazine also commits the cardinal sin of questioning the economic base of our social order."[24] Sexuality was thus intertwined with the Left in the eyes of the law and the public. Anticipating such escalated surveillance, leftist magazine editors steeled themselves against the inevitable legal challenges launched against them by the state officials they mercilessly attacked. In 1921, the left-wing *Liberator* extracted a refund of $14,321.96 from the infamously rigid postmaster general Will Hays after his office, in an effort to hamper the magazine's circulation, improperly refused to classify the *Liberator* as second-class mail.[25] Though Hays's predecessor, Albert S. Burleson, had cited the *Liberator*'s ostensible failure to contribute to the "public good" as a rationale for imposing prohibitively high postal fees on the magazine, the courts subsequently recognized that his underlying motivation was illegal censorship of radical content.[26] The inaugural issue of *New Masses* in May 1926 was similarly suppressed as "lewd and obscene matter" by New York's postmaster, setting an envelope-pushing tone for the magazine—and a tried-and-true legal defense—that persisted well into the 1930s.[27]

Though the appropriate degree of interest in sex among dedicated leftists was routinely debated throughout the 1920s and 1930s, radical writers portrayed squeamishness about sexual matters as inseparable from efforts to advance right-wing political agendas. When two University of Missouri professors were fired in 1929 following their distributing a sex questionnaire among students, the Communist *Daily Worker* ran a front-page article attacking administrative "smut-hounds," suggesting that Missouri's class and racial hierarchies were their actual target. "Missouri is a fundamentalist state with laws against evolution and a ruling class of white, protestant, one hundred percent Americans, fighting hard to keep a subdued working and farming class of Negroes, white packing house workers and small hill farmers," they wrote. "The educational standards are naturally low."[28] The editors pointed to the ways repression of information about sexuality served ruling-class interests at the expense of workers, farmers, and African Americans— otherwise known as the Communist Party's base. The *Daily Worker* followed up its report on the Missouri professors' dismissal with an exuberant article detailing a resolution adopted by three thousand University of Missouri students protesting the professors' firing, drumming up populist support for smut-hounds.[29]

Under the "new Puritan régime" in America, complained critic Harold Stearns in 1921, "healthy sexual impulses have been transformed into a back-of-the-barn sort of affair."[30] Leftist magazines brought those sexual impulses out of the barn and onto the newsstands. In 1925 the *Daily Worker* published an article about a New York censoring board's attack on a play by Eugene O'Neill, splashing a sensational headline across the page: "Vice Body Prefers Bare Legs to Wobblies." Leftists argued that radical labor politics were under attack by the same regulatory killjoys who policed sexual transgression.[31] Those tangled in this puritanical dragnet refused to go down without a fight.

While editors paid little mind to vice squads and censorship boards, their sexual defiance sometimes raised the ire of readers who sought to separate radical politics from sexual impertinence. "I like your magazine. But for the life of me I can't understand why it is necessary to use profanity and smut to bring home your ideas," one *New Masses* reader complained in 1929. "I gather from many of your contributors that all you have to do in order to be a rebel is to use filthy language and make abominable drawings." He might not have approved of it, but this reader correctly grasped how filthy language and abominable drawings were inextricable from radical politics. To justify his distaste for smut and profanity, the reader helpfully clarified, "I am an Upton Sinclairian."[32]

Given the expansiveness of that author's output, the precise definition of an Upton Sinclairian is difficult to pin down. But in this context, the reader invoked Sinclair the sexually modest radical who proudly referred to himself in 1927 as "the prize prude of the radical movement."[33] By all accounts, Sinclair represented an older, less revolutionary radicalism that was waning in the 1920s. He valued hard work and abstention from pleasure over the rougher proletarian culture favored by the Depression-era hard leftists. In a 1927 response to Floyd Dell, a well-established libertine and chronicler of American sexual life—who, in a *New Masses* piece, invited writers to weigh in on the question "What is the proletarian revolutionary attitude towards sex?"—Sinclair wrote a short piece bluntly headlined "Revolution—Not Sex." Sinclair proposed diplomatically, and a little listlessly, that "the test of a sound and proper sex life is that it contributes comradeship and understanding to the cause." Poor Sinclair could hardly have seemed any less modern than when he espoused the virtue of sexual restraint, most markedly when he volunteered that he "rules out any sex life that exposes either party to disease and any that is merely trifling and [a] waste of time, that involves one or both the lovers in a tangle of futile and distracting emotions," blithely comparing sex to "eating and drinking, waking and sleeping, walking and talking."[34] This was hardly the stuff of lusty youth.

Sinclair consistently rejected the Left's sexual vanguard and panned cultural texts that read as even mildly queer. After attending a performance of *The Importance of Being Earnest,* Sinclair reported that he could "not recall that I was ever more bored in a theater," writing that he found Oscar Wilde a "too-clever young esthete." (Wilde fared better than Lord Alfred Douglass, whom Sinclair branded "the most disagreeable little wretch that ever displayed himself in the British world of letters.") Yet Sinclair stopped short of fully condemning Wilde for his "cultured vices," and he acknowledged the genius of Wilde's prison output, especially "De Profundis" and "The Ballad of Reading Gaol," concluding that "decadent poets should be sent to prison and kept there permanently" in order to cultivate their art.[35] Sinclair nearly accomplished that goal with Sergei Eisenstein, the gay Soviet director whose 1930s project for a Mexican film to be titled "¡Que Viva México!" was unable to be completed after Sinclair denounced Eisenstein's sexuality, likely alerting authorities in Moscow to Eisenstein's queer conduct.[36] Sinclair was troubled because Eisenstein "used his leisure in making elaborate drawings of pornography" and because "all his associates were Trotskyites, and all homos. Men of that sort stick together, and we were besieged by them for several years."[37]

Sinclair did occasionally attract some interest from those with progressive positions on sexuality. In 1911, Havelock Ellis responded to an admiring letter from Sinclair by offering that he had "begun" reading *Love's Pilgrimage,* Sinclair's just-published dissection of modern marriage and sex, and welcomed "the frank way in which you face these fundamental problems of life."[38] More often, Sinclair's sexual conservatism was contrasted with sex radicals like V. F. Calverton, a Communist who was later ejected from the Party. On the same page in *New Masses* where Sinclair worried about venereal disease and wasting time, Calverton offered that "the proletarian revolutionary attitude toward sex" was "opposed to monogamy." The pair recycled that debate under the auspices of a *Modern Quarterly* forum, "Is Monogamy Desirable?"[39]

The *Modern Quarterly,* edited by Calverton, had established itself since its founding in 1923 as a prominent vehicle for openly discussing the modern attitude toward sex from an independently radical perspective. Its editors and contributors consistently triangulated between academic Marxism, soapbox grandstanding, and smut peddling.[40] Calverton's maverick tendencies, fortified by an abiding interest in psychology, attracted as many radicals as it repelled. Sidney Hook, a leftist associated with the New York Intellectuals, characterized the *Modern Quarterly* as "an enterprise of a young man in Baltimore trying to storm his way into the literary world under the slogans of revolt—in politics, economics, culture, and especially sex."[41] While Upton Sinclair distanced his revolution from sexual politics, Calverton offered a rousing plea in *New Masses* that the rank and file "oppose the bourgeois family with its marital system of monogamy."[42] With the onset of civilization and its signature innovation of private property, Calverton feistily asserted, "sex was turned from a social reality into a boudoir sport that was enjoyed but not mentioned."[43] Mentioning sex became a marker of a sufficiently radical orientation, but Sinclair generally preferred to maintain at least a pretense of respectable quiet.

It was somewhat ironic, then, that Upton Sinclair found himself just as likely as any other libidinal leftist to be targeted by purity squads, perhaps most famously when Boston's Watch and Ward Society, the morality organization that enshrined "banned in Boston" as a badge of honor for twentieth-century modernists, targeted his 1927 radical novel, *Oil!,* for censorship. *Oil!* was a long, exhaustingly expository book that dissected the engines of corporate capitalism in their extractive (oil) and cultural (movies) forms. The book attracted censors' notice because of Sinclair's depiction of California's sexual debauchery, especially in his critique of so-called petting parties. Echoing the familiar refrain of many leftists facing censorship, Sinclair maintained that it was the "political and social information which is the real cause of the attack upon the book," countering that Boston's superintendent of police "was obscene in his description of obscenity."[44]

It bears noting that petting parties had become all the rage in the 1920s, receiving mention in no less radical a media outlet than the *Daily Worker,* which, in 1924, published an article announcing with some satisfaction that such parties had at last been approved by the chief police inspector of Baltimore. A journalist in the *New Student* reported proudly in 1926 that "petting parties represent the crude, inchoate beginnings made by American youth to break away from this prevalent conception of eroticism as merely a mechanism of propagation, or as a brute, delightful sin."[45] Such affairs, then, were hardly a fringe topic by the time of *Oil!*'s publication, but Sinclair was more scandalized than many of his fellow leftists by young Americans' expanding sexual repertoire, which he described with a curious mix of ethnographic detachment and moralistic censure.

Sinclair equated petting parties with Hollywood's propensity for moral depravity, the latter of which he embodied most trenchantly in the character Eunice Hoyt, a classic vamp and Hollywood actress with an irrepressible sexual appetite who smokes cigarettes and who "scolded Bunny," *Oil!*'s incipient-radical protagonist, because, in her estimation, "he was a horrid little Puritan that wouldn't keep her company." Even as she seduces him, Eunice goads Bunny for his sexual inexperience, baiting him with the taunt "I've always known you were a queer boy." Giving in to sexual temptation, which Bunny does over and over again, not only changes Sinclair's male protagonist; it also unleashes a new emotional richness in Eunice that Sinclair describes with horror as "a dark abyss where pleasure and pain were so mingled you could hardly tell them apart."[46] Eunice's terrifying sexuality, unleashed through these petting parties, becomes a particularly anxious presence in Bunny's life:

> This "petting" was a daily necessity for her, and a girl could not get it unless she was willing to "go the limit." That was the etiquette prevailing in this smart and dashing crowd; the rich high school youths would go out hunting in pairs in their fancy sport-cars, and would pick up girls and drive them, and if the girls did not play the game according to their taste, they would turn them out on the road, anywhere, a score of miles from a town. There was a formula, short and snappy, "Pet or walk!"[47]

Even as he was subjected to censorship and arrest for his sexually explicit passages in *Oil!*, and in spite of having solicited a defense of his work from Havelock Ellis, Sinclair continued to hold to positions on sexuality that distinguished him from those who saw in sex a path to revolution, instead favoring a leftist strategy that characterized nonnormative forms of sexual behavior as decadent and bourgeois.[48]

Though his was not the dominant radical position by the late 1920s, Sinclair had a fair amount of company in holding his puritan line—a fact that suggests how transitional this moment was for building a leftist sexual movement. J. Louis Engdahl, for example, took to the *Daily Worker* to attack "the decadent bourgeoisie" for "seeking stimulation in its pleasure cesspools."[49] John Vincent Healy published a poem in a 1936 issue of *New Masses* that characterized the dreams of a stockbroker who was

> quiet, then disturbed as if by insect stings,
> Sleeping, this time his face toward the door,
> Jerking with orgasms, weeping in dreams,
> Waking and scratching, stepping down on the floor.[50]

The curious, unconscious sexual desires of stockbrokers were the stuff of scandals, even if the "jerks" of orgasm seemed uncomfortably familiar to this particular poet. A 1926 front-page *Daily Worker* story, sensationalistically titled "Investigation of Wild Orgy Is Under Way," reported on a party "at which guests drank wine from a bathtub in which an undraped model was seated."[51] The *Daily Worker* published several follow-ups to this story, reporting that the "girl" in the tub, Joyce Hawley, never received her $1,000 fee.[52]

The competing narratives of sexual deviance in the upper and lower classes had the potential to turn into an impasse: leftists accused the aristocracy of sexual misconduct; in turn, the Left was accused of sexual indiscretion. In 1926, the *Daily Worker* charged that rumors of "illicit practices" were being "industriously circulated by the university authorities against progressive instructors on the [University of] Illinois faculty."[53] Yet the *Daily Worker* staff were themselves not above reproach: "The matter of drunkenness among the staff of the Daily Worker," one-time Communist and staff member Benjamin Gitlow recalled, "who made asses of themselves in public, was the subject of several plenums in the Central Executive Committee."[54]

Sinclair, who protested that "I have never written an indecent book, and resent the charge that I have done so," responded to calls for censorship by trying desperately either to get arrested or to make fools of the Boston police, parading around the city in a sandwich board advertising *Oil*'s "Fig Leaf Edition"; offering for sale a Bible wrapped in his novel's dust jacket to police seeking violations of obscenity law on the Boston Common; and convincing his publisher to print a special edition of his novel with the Hollywood petting scene redacted.[55] "I still remain what is called a Puritan," Sinclair insisted, "but not Puritan enough for Boston."[56] Of course, as Sinclair rightly surmised, he was being attacked for his radicalism. "In the case of 'Oil!' the motive is obviously political," Sinclair wrote to V. F. Calverton, "due to my picture of the control of our government by the petroleum interests."[57] The fact that *Oil!* used sex to signify, among other things, Hollywood's moral decay was, to the purity police, irrelevant: his filth was just another example of leftist deviance.

Though it was undoubtedly Sinclair's politics that made him suspect among the antivice set, the fact that the radical movement's "prize prude" had written a novel that was sexually explicit suggests that it was not mere overreach that led to connections being drawn between sexual permissiveness and the Left. Radical fiction attracted readers owing in part to its illicit content, and literary critics, as well as censoring boards, were well attuned to the transgressive qualities in leftist art. Floyd Dell wrote of Sinclair's fiction that he produced "description so truthful that strong men faint when they try to read it, and upon recovering consciousness demand that the book be burned up and the author put in jail!"[58] Dell was not himself thrown in jail, but he was no stranger to truthful description. In a 1927 *New Masses* article he announced with pleasure that sex outside marriage "is now destroying the old patriarchal concept of the importance of virginity in young women." The free availability of sexual outlets that resulted from casting off outmoded ideas about monogamy and saving oneself for marriage had the added benefit of reducing demand for sex work. "With their giving up of their old-fashioned care for 'purity,'" Dell noted of these young radicals, "commercialized prostitution tends to become obsolescent."[59] Unsurprisingly given their emphasis upon diagnosing economic causes for social problems, prostitution was most often described by leftists as a form of class exploitation. Poverty, one *Daily Worker* article noted in April 1924, was the "mother of prostitution," and a 1927 *Daily Worker* article approvingly reported on a League of Nations committee's determination that "economic conditions, much more than the innate badness of the women or their desire for such a life, is the chief factor in the supply" of sex workers.[60] Significantly, leftists turned backflips to avoid casting women in sex-negative terms or painting prostitutes as themselves inherently bad people, instead ascribing social motivations that essentially gave a free pass to sex workers themselves and avoided blanket moralizing.

Fighting censorship required constant vigilance, but it also presented an occasion for editors and writers on the Left to establish a critical position on the vanguard of shifting sexual mores. In an article recommending Eugene O'Neill's *Desire under the Elms* at Chicago's Princess Theater, a *Daily Worker* reviewer urged readers to rush to see a performance "before the meddlesome creatures who censor plays in Chicago and in general interfere with other people's morals—because they themselves have none to bother about—start their crusade to stop its performance."[61] Another theatrical review, in the Communist *Daily Worker,* complained that a production of the musical revue *Luckee Girl* included a performance of the song "Facts of Life" in which "some of the verses have to be slurred over a little on account of possible censorship."[62] Leftist audiences demanded that every smutty word be annunciated with crystal clarity! Similarly, a *Daily Worker* review of *Sex,* Mae West's controversial play, lamented not its explicit sexuality, but rather West's disappointingly moralistic resolution in the play's conclusion. "For about one act and a half 'Sex' is a vivid and sinewy contribution to the American drama," A. B. Magil wrote, but the play "becomes depressingly moral in the last two acts."[63] *Sex* explored sex within the urban class struggle, precipitating great controversy and generating a flurry of negative reviews in the mainstream media. The *New York Herald Tribune* objected to West's "ruthless, evil-minded, foul-mouthed crooks, harlots, procurers and other degenerate members of that particular zone of society."[64] In the *Daily Worker,* Magil articulated an opposite concern from the pitched moralizing in the *Herald Tribune.* By redeeming her degenerates by the play's end, Mae West became too puritanical for the Communist critic. Despite its reservations about the moralism found in the play's conclusion, the *Daily Worker* reported diligently on efforts by New York officials to prevent its staging, maintaining that radicals' targeting by obscenity laws impelled them to resist censorship and suppression whenever it appeared.[65]

In fact, opposing censorship was one of the few leftist positions that remained unchanged throughout the 1920s and 1930s. In 1925, the *Daily Worker* lamented that Russel M. Arunel's novel *The College Exodus* had been declared obscene by the New York postmaster because of Arunel's "suggestive" descriptions of art and literature departments.[66] In 1929, following the banning of radical writer Theodore Dreiser's novel *An American Tragedy* in Boston, the *Daily Worker* declared that "vicious Massachusetts puritanism and prudery ran true to its past form today."[67] When a local resident in Davenport, Iowa, Hermine Schmed, sought to ban radical writer Floyd Dell's *Janet March,* the *Daily Worker* cheekily observed that "she got her audience of women's civic societies so excited that they have been besieging the library for all forbidden books ever since."[68] *New Masses* regularly included censorship bills among its list of measures to be opposed by zealous readers.

Its editors objected to the 1936 Culkin Bill by noting that the proposed legislation "provides for the establishment of federal censorship over moving pictures to 'protect' morals, opinions, and religious beliefs."[69] Leftists routinely weighed in on censorship cases regardless of whether they targeted sexual content or radical politics, further obscuring the distinction between these categories.

Radicalism and obscenity, then, were connected through both their shared targeting by antivice organizations and because resisting censorship was part and parcel of adopting a radical position. In 1924 the *Daily Worker* editors named the Kansas City censors the "movie censorship board of morons," and that same year, William F. Kruse, an important Communist who studied at the Lenin School in Moscow, decried the politics of censorship by identifying the "chief ideological props of the capitalist system: Law, religion, patriotism and morality."[70] The editors of *New Masses* asserted that "there should be no limitation on free speech in any manner or form, and [the] attempted censorship of the stage, radio, movies, magazines, books, and art by the so-called patriots and moralists is not only illegal under the constitution but decidedly inimical to advancement of knowledge and of human freedom."[71] Such editorial promiscuity introduced space for radical positions on a number of critical sexual matters, and openness about sexuality became a hallmark—and sometimes even a benchmark—of a radical political orientation.

THE LEFT'S UNDIGNIFIED DIRT

"Cupid's Letter Box," an advice column dedicated to matters of love and (more often) sex, appeared in *New Masses* in April 1934, on a page that also updated readers on the latest news from noteworthy leftists Joseph Freeman, John Spivak, and Anna Rochester.[72] Featuring letters from readers such as Hugh S. ("Can a man make two women happy at once?"), Father C. ("I am a priest and not supposed to ——————— or anything like that, but lately I have met several beautiful girls and almost before I knew it the worst happened!"), and—ever so slyly—"Mayor F.L.G." ("I am engaged to a rich girl that would cut me dead if she thought I had ever mixed it up with a working girl. What shall I do?"), the column paired saucy relationship questions with sassy one-liners from "Letter Box" columnist Bill Smith ("Hugh, your troubles are just beginning"; "Nira, I'm afraid you're whole family is hopeless"). "Liberals and Progressives, are you unhappy?" Smith asked readers. "Then tell your troubles to Cupid—*he* will understand." The irreverent tone of the column suggests the louche perspective on sexuality that characterized *New Masses* as a radical venue open to exploring sexual themes and affirming liberated sex as a feature of the classless society, while also recognizing the appeal of pulp magazines to America's working-class readers.[73]

New Masses' playful adoption of pulp's racy sensibility acknowledged the defiantly proletarian appeal of sexual content to mass-culture audiences, as well as the particular sexual progressivism incubated on the Left.[74] The transgressive appeal of proletarian print culture was heralded by leftist magazines and newspapers to attract thrill-seeking readers to their publications. A 1935 *New Masses* advertisement declared that "if you read the *New Masses,* it shows you are sick of the sordidness of the love and movie magazines," yet this same advertisement, after establishing readers' distaste for the sordid, promised content "beside which fake confession and detective stories pale by comparison."[75] "The denial of sex [is] part of the denial of life's wholeness," Jack Lindsay cautioned in a 1936 *New Masses* article, "inevitable in a class-riven society."[76] In opposition to capitalism's sexual rifts, "Cupid's Letter Box" exposed sex as a common stock in American society and poked light fun at both the sensationalistic content that was typically found in mass-produced periodicals of the day and the expectation that readers of *New Masses* would make up a particularly lovelorn and perverse audience.[77] "You're a natural born lout," Cupid advised Father C, "and you know it."[78] *New Masses* readers knew it as well. Pointing out the tendency of those in positions of moral superiority to themselves share more practices with the common lot than they were inclined to admit helped legitimize the liberating possibilities of a working-class sexuality that tilted in the direction of revolution.

"Cupid's Letter Box" also represented a campy commentary on long-standing characterizations of radicals and working-class women and men as sex obsessed. Those crude caricatures were especially pronounced vis-à-vis the Communist Party. In a 1928 review in *The Communist,* Burn Starr had reported—prematurely, it seems—that a recent book had finally put to rest the common belief that "sex perversions and abnormalities markedly increase during revolutionary times"—a "pet capitalist argument" that was "extensively used to create hostility to revolution."[79] Michael Gold complained in 1934 that "in the few Broadway plays recently in which a Communist has been introduced, he is always a sexual superman."[80] Joining the Party represented a repudiation of American society so totalizing that it seemed to demand a wholesale rejection of normative sexuality. In a 1925 study titled *The Sociology of Revolution,* Pitirim Sorokin, an anti-Communist sociologist, argued that the Bolshevik Revolution introduced a "perversion of sexual relations" that loosened divorce laws, reduced marriages, and encouraged sexual license. Even worse, Communists seemed to enjoy this. "Nearly from the first days of the revolution," Sorokin noted with alarm,

> the people started dancing, dancing in a literal sense. Innumerable "hops" were started. "Hops" with concerts, with meetings; "hops" after debates; "hops" in the midst of starvation, typhus, executions. They have not ceased dancing even now. And during all this dancing, primitive, coarse flirtations are being carried on which generally end in amorous embraces.[81]

Former Communist Benjamin Gitlow recalled that "if a young girl who joined the Communist youth organization insisted upon maintaining her chastity, she was frowned upon as bourgeois by the self-styled revolutionists," concluding that "many of the young Communists considered the giving up of one's chastity as a mark of distinction."[82]

In some instances, joining with the Left itself represented a breakdown of normative relationships. The leftist writer Tess Slesinger penned a short story in 1935, winkingly titled "After the Party," that was set during a cocktail party and its aftermath. "After the Party" tells the story of Mrs. Colborne, who recalls the dissolution of her marriage when her husband Henry comes out as a Socialist. The slippage between Socialism and deviance produces the wry humor that animates Slesinger's story as Mrs. Colborne comes to grips with her husband's new identity. "Oh yes, said Mrs. Colborne bravely," Slesinger writes,

> she had always known that Henry was a Socialist, at heart—in principle; he had been inclined that way even when she first met him, when they were both at school. . . . It turned out that the Socialists he picked up were really very presentable and gentlemanly and could be invited anywhere, just fellows like himself who had been to Harvard or, at worst, sons of New England clergymen.[83]

Henry eventually chooses Socialism over his family: "He was very quiet and abstracted for a week or so, and one night said to her quite clearly that they must have a talk. . . . Henry said . . . that he was planning to change the horizon of himself, change his whole way of life."[84] Henry's rejection of marriage as he embraces the Left points to a slippage between radical politics and queer desire: both deviated from heternormative familial structures, and each suggested illicit forms of desire that provoked anxiety and disrupted everyday life.

A 1927 article by Karl Weigand in the conservative *New York American* offered further insight into Communist deviance:

> A provincial control commission of the Communist party, in examining a member as to his conduct and life, something that is often done, asked him about his morals and sex relations. He replied that he was happily married, had a beautiful wife, loved her, and was faithful to her. The commission expelled him from the party on the ground of "holding to small bourgeois principles."[85]

This vignette might read as a joke, complete with a rim-shot-worthy punch line, but it also speaks to a larger cultural belief that Communists were resolutely opposed to family and domesticity.[86] The details of Weigand's story were surely fabricated, but the underlying anxiety he articulated was not wholly incorrect. Opposing marriage remained a significant feature of the Left well into the 1930s. "Marriage," Floyd Dell wrote in the *Liberator* in 1923, "is a monopoly in restraint of reproduction."[87] What good leftist wanted to be associated with any monopoly? "Getting married in bourgeois circles, as everybody knows, is a matter of salesmanship," wrote a *Daily Worker* reporter in 1928. "If you've ever sold anything you know you must have the product in marketable condition."[88] Rejecting marriage capitalism opened the door for American radicals to embrace less bourgeois, or less marketable, arrangements. Unpacking the economics of sex demystified the process by which capitalism sustained normative sexual expression.

Critiquing marriage on the Left did the dual work of promoting sexual modernism and rejecting capitalism. Edward Newhouse, a leftist Hungarian American writer, published his proletarian novel *This Is Your Day* in 1937. The novel opens as Gene, a Communist organizer, and his girlfriend lie in bed discussing getting married. Conversing in casual, detached language, the two blithely consider the practicalities of such an arrangement. They comment on marriage's legal aspects ("license and all"), quotidian details ("we could go down to the Municipal Building before noon"), and practical accoutrements ("I'll wear my brown shoes"). Their incentive for considering marriage ranges from "[M]y folks will love it" to "[I]t would save time and explanations to make it official." Conspicuously absent from this blasé conversation is any discussion of love, religion, or sex, which the pair has apparently just had. Newhouse registers the latter detail through Gene's punctuating the wedding talk with a banal request: "[W]ould you reach out and hand me my underwear?"[89]

For Newhouse, the significance of marriage was reduced to the social sanctioning of a relationship and its bare economic incentive. By making their announcement, Gene hopes to receive a new pair of shoes as a wedding gift. *This Is Your Day* opened, then, with a materialist analysis of weddings that recognized sex as entirely irrelevant to discussion about marriage. Sex between unmarried partners was depicted as unremarkable, lighthearted, and morally neutral. If proletarian literature inaugurated a tendency toward representing communities and behaviors outside the normative structures of middle-class lives, so did the leftist tendency toward pushing against the repressive institutions allow for literary explorations of life beyond marriage and marriage beyond monogamy.

At times, Communists attempted to distance themselves from the sexual avant-garde. In a 1933 article in *The Communist*, Vern Smith discounted the International Workingmen's Association by dismissing its founders as "a collection of freaks, who went off on a crusade for 'free sex relations' and finally had to be expelled."[90] More often, however, perhaps because leftist political belonging so commonly frustrated heteronormative sexual relations, sex among radicals was itself represented as a form of dissidence. Sherwood Anderson's 1932 proletarian novel, *Beyond Desire,* describes a heterosexual relationship between two leftists. One of them, a teacher, "had become first a socialist and then a communist."[91] Her leftist politics extend to her sexual preferences. Rather than waiting until marriage to begin a sexual relationship, she "thought they ought to sleep together, get used to each other"—a proposal the pair wholeheartedly embraces. United in their rejection of marriage, they also push against normative sex practices. They have sex "on the porch of the house or inside, on a couch," and Anderson vividly describes the male of the couple, Neil, narrating his performing cunnilingus. "She sits on the edge of the low porch," Neil describes in a letter to his friend, Red Oliver, "and I kneel on the grass at the edge of the porch. . . . She is like a flower opening."[92] In this scene, the woman's pleasure is foregrounded. Her ideological commitment to rejecting marriage allows her to define their relationship to privilege her own sexual desire. Sex between radicals, freed from the strictures of marital capital, permitted a broadening of sexual relationships and sex acts.

Despite prominent associations with sexual dissidence, the paradoxical smear of sexual asceticism was simultaneously charged against leftists.[93] In a 1927 *Modern Quarterly* article, John Darmstadt attacked the *Daily Worker*'s aversion to sex, complaining that "the subject of sex is never treated seriously outside the reviews of books or plays—and can hardly be spoken of at all without a sneer or smirk."[94] Darmstadt was even more damning when it came to Socialists, who, he claimed, "could, many of them, change places sexually with our old maid aunt, or with the deacon in the church, and nobody would notice the difference. They live straight, vote straight, pay their dues, and 'take part' in party activities."[95] Darmstadt's charge connected the dots of leftist deviance. It was not only sexual practices that made Socialists so boring; their tendency to "vote straight" represented a form of normativity that paralleled their banal sex lives. The most committed radicals were also the least straight.

There was a smattering of truth to Darmstadt's accusation that radicals were insufficiently radical in their sexual politics. Certainly leftists—both Socialist and Communist—were inclined to be critical of sex when it was used to advance consumer culture or to distract audiences from fully embracing anticapitalist critique. Furthermore, the friction between the Modern Quarterly's free-ranging radicalism and the Communist Party's tighter control over the Daily Worker and New Masses set up a conflict between the publications that Collier exploited with his criticism. Yet there was more overlap between sex radicals and labor radicals than even their contemporaries allowed. Writing in the Daily Worker, Samuel D. Schmalhausen celebrated "the new candor in sex" on the Left, noting that "nothing is so wholesome nowadays (thanks to the 'science' of psychoanalysis) as the bright frankness of the intelligentsia regarding the sexual question."[96] In New Masses, V.F. Calverton wrote that "the radical who is enthusiastic about revolution in economic life but timid about revolution in sexual life is narrow-minded and superficial."[97] And when the Daily Worker's editors reported on Hungary's "puritanical" ban on "any man flirting with a female not known to him," as well as prohibitions on "short skirts" and orders to "cover the busts of wax models displayed in the windows 'up to the neck'" under Miklós Horthy's regime, there was hardly a sneer or smirk to be found.[98]

As leftists sought a more radical vision of sexuality, they often turned to practices common outside the United States. The international context helped American leftists envision alternative structures of sexual relationships and buttressed radical criticism of marriage as bourgeois. In 1928, the Daily Worker reported approvingly that in Germany, "the Reichstag will be called upon next week to decide upon a bill introduced by Communists which would permit divorce if one or both of the parties involved simply stated a desire to discontinue marriage relations."[99] The growing influence of sexologists, many of whom were aligned with the Left, further entangled leftists in carving a space for sexual politics. The *Daily Worker* reported approvingly on a gathering of the World Sexology Congress in Berlin in 1926 to "discuss all important sex problems which are intertwined with modern life," demonstrating interest among Communists in shifting sexual mores on an internationalist stage.[100]

In 1925, the *Daily Worker* reported the opening of the Magnus Hirschfeld Foundation, a birth-control clinic in Germany that also treated homosexuals. Though homosexuals were understood to be unhealthy, the *Daily Worker* foregrounded the problem of social stigma against the group, noting that the Hirschfeld clinic "tries to find the remedy rather than merely condemning such unfortunates to social ostracism."[101] This perspective was similar to that expressed by the renowned sexologist Havelock Ellis in the first issue of the magazine *American Spectator,* under the editorial influence of the radical writer (and later Communist) Theodore Dreiser, in November 1932. "Again and again when sexual anomalies are conceived, we find patients complaining that their physician has shown no comprehension of their special difficulties," Ellis wrote, "treating them as vicious, wicked, perhaps disgusting persons."[102] Here again the medical establishment was taken to task for its total disregard of homosexuals as persons. Sexology inaugurated new conversations about sexual politics within leftist magazines, including a suspicion that physicians often served the interests of the upper class. Engaging research unfolding outside the United States freed American publications to espouse more-radical positions.

The career of Wilhelm Reich, an Austrian psychoanalyst who moved from the Social Democratic Party to the Communist Party in 1930, further points to a complicated engagement with sexuality and the Left in a European context. Much of Reich's work balancing Freudian psychoanalysis and Marxist dialectics appeared during the 1930s, including *The Sexual Struggle of Youth* and *The Imposition of Sexual Morality,* both published in 1932. Reich was expelled from the Communist Party in 1933, the same year the Soviet Union recriminalized homosexuality, but he did not abandon the Left. In 1934, he wrote that "the more clearly developed the natural heterosexual inclinations of a juvenile are, the more open he will be to revolutionary ideas; the stronger the homosexual tendency within him and also the more repressed his awareness of sexuality in general, the more easily he will be drawn to the right."[103] Within a decade Reich was mostly associated with his eccentric work building his Orgone Institute, a project that was embraced in limited avant-garde circles.

Leftist attraction to the Soviet Union also had a deviant dimension. "The ecstasy of sex contact" in Russia, V. F. Calverton declared, "the joy of erotic communion, are regarded as private to the participants, and not subject to social intervention and restriction."[104] A series of articles on the topic of "Russia Today" ran in the *Daily Worker* in 1925, and their authors affirmed that in the Soviet Union "sexual morals are greatly matters of personal conduct which must be left to private conscience and can only be dealt with by education and environment, not by legislation."[105] By 1935, *New Masses* showed no hesitance in casually dropping references to Soviet antimarriage sentiments. In an article meditating on contrasting views on love in the United States and the Soviet Union, the bisexual journalist Ella Winter observed that "love, marriage, motherhood, the home and the family, all in a bourgeois society become bourgeois and suffer from the same canker, the same rotting disease as other bourgeois institutions."[106] Winter's list certainly pushed against a broad palette of American institutions. What right-minded leftists would choose to align themselves with marriage—or even love—after they had been disparaged as a bourgeois canker? In contrast, highlighting Soviet sexual freedom served the dual purposes of projecting American hopes for sexual progress onto an existing revolutionary society and correcting representations of bleak Soviet toil that de-emphasized pleasure and denied labor's reward.

In contrast to the constant stream of popular depictions in the United States that insisted upon a dehumanizing Soviet state apparatus that attempted to "make human beings who would be mechanical robots turning out machinery and 'spawning' (to use *Time's* pleasant, if a little undignified, word) children to work those machines," Ella Winter described a sexually open Soviet Union defined by a liberating "freeing of marriage and divorce." Driving this shift in Soviet sexual practices was the apparent equality of women in the revolutionary society. Winter facetiously conjured a nightmarish version of American heterosexual gender roles, ironically invoking bourgeois fantasies of "the arrow-collar husband coming home to his neat little frigidaire wife while Junior plays on the floor in lux-washed woollens . . . and wifey holds up her face to be kissed while shining-eyed she shows him a new dish she has just cooked." Though Winter did not explicitly connect her parodic suburban tableau with its overtones of whiteness, her absurd scene must be read against the backdrop of white migration from American cities to escape ethnic communities that incubated radicalism and embraced sexual dissidence. In contrast, Winter breathlessly reported that it had become simply unimaginable in Soviet society that "a socially desirable though loveless marriage will be forced on a daughter," or that "a marriage will be forbidden by parents because of differences of race, religion, nationality, or economic means."[107] Stripped of the patriarchal energy driving America's marriage complex, the revolutionary society loosened restrictions on marriage and divorce and allowed for shared ownership across gender, race, and religious lines.

For his outspoken leftist analysis of sexuality, V. F. Calverton represents an exceptionally spirited case study, albeit one whose relationship to the Left, especially the Communist Party, ebbed and flowed. Born George Goetz, Calverton developed a distinctly Marxist engagement with the politics of sexuality that culminated with his editorship of the *Modern Quarterly*, a journal he guided from 1923 to 1940. He also wrote popular books such as *Sex in Civilization* (1930) and *The Bankruptcy of Marriage* (1928). Under his editorial guidance, the *Modern Quarterly* published articles on a kaleidoscopic range of sexual subjects from a leftist perspective. "It is dangerous," he announced in 1928, "to touch upon the sex question in a serious manner—in America. The conservatives denounce the practice as revolutionary, and the revolutionaries attack it as decadent."[108] Though that claim was, arguably, overstated, Calverton was indeed roundly criticized by others on the Left for his overinvestment in sexual politics. Joseph Freeman, editor of *New Masses*, satirized Calverton's *Modern Quarterly* debate with Upton Sinclair on the question "Is Monogamy Desirable?" as "Monogamy vs. Lechery."[109] It went without saying which side Calverton was on. Such criticism had little impact on Calverton, other than to loosen his official ties to the Communist Party, with which he fell decidedly out of favor as the 1930s progressed.

Though he did not write specifically about homosexuality, Calverton attempted to enlist psychologist Phyllis Blanchard, a close friend of feminist psychologist Lorine Pruette, to write a book about lesbianism. Blanchard had submitted an article on Sappho to the *Modern Quarterly* that Calverton liked but declined to publish. When she offered for his perusal a partial manuscript of her 1930 book *New Girls for Old*, which included a chapter dedicated to homosexuality, Calverton wrote that "I have just read your two chapters and find the one on 'Homosexuality' most interesting indeed—in point of fact, this chapter reads far better than any of the previous ones I have seen. It is much more humanly written, I should say, and therefore much more gripping."[110] Though Blanchard never wrote that book, Calverton remained interested in producing humane and gripping work on the subject. "You could go ahead with the book yourself," Blanchard urged after confessing she did not have time to write it, "or get someone else to do it, if you still want to bring it out."[111] Calverton did not.

Though he was committed to exploring the role of sex radicalism in leftist politics, V. F. Calverton also acknowledged that sexual dissidence sometimes substituted for deeper radical commitments. For such individuals, "if the erotic protest is solved," Calverton worried, "their economic radicalism becomes nothing more than an empty, spiritless gesture." He worried that homosexuals in particular represented a population who, with their fancy parties and hedonistic pleasure principles, sometimes promoted erotic protest at the expense of the economic. Among those for whom "sex in itself is a revolution" were no small number of radicals who "are drawn willy-nilly into the cabaret-caverns of the aesthetes, and soon learn to acquire the art of painting passion flowers for the *homo-sapiens* of Greenwich Village."[112] It would be generous to characterize Calverton's comments as coded, careful as he was to literally include the word "homo" in his artful dodging. On other sexual matters, however, Calverton was far more progressive, particularly around monogamy and marriage, both of which he recognized as capitalist tools and opposed with tremendous vigor.

As leftists struggled to articulate a position on sexuality, the Communist Party's concern with cultivating interracial solidarity and pushing against American racism further shaped the Left's sexual politics. In particular, leftists mounted vigorous campaigns challenging Jim Crow laws that placed prohibitions on interracial sexuality and fought against spurious charges of black-on-white rape used to justify lynching.[113] State discipline of interracial couples especially raised the ire of leftist journalists, and reports on overreach by authorities into the romantic and sexual lives of differently raced couples advanced the principles of leftist resistance to American racial segregation. "The policemen have been carrying on a reign of terror during the past year by molesting, insulting, assaulting, and arresting Negro and white couples," wrote an incensed *Daily Worker* journalist in 1924. "Fortunately, however, in spite of all the vicious tricks of the capitalist exploiters, Negro and white workers are . . . mixing and mingling together."[114] B. B. Rubinstein, noting that a "bill forbidding marriage between whites and Negroes" had died in committee, pronounced in 1927 that "the Workers Party is the only group which fights for the interest of the Negro workers."[115]

Many Black Americans were skeptical, however, that the Workers Party *was* fighting for their interests. Some denounced the interracial coupling of Black men with white women on the Left as a betrayal of Black solidarity or, more insidiously, as part of a cynical effort designed to draw more Black men into the Left. In spite of these critiques, the Depression-era Communist Party promoted interracial commingling among its members—an enterprise that occasionally resulted in clumsy efforts such as encouraging dancing lessons among white men to make themselves more appealing to Black women.[116] These efforts were, predictably, as ineffective as they were offensive.

Though they did not always approach racism on the Left with the greatest of sensitivity, the Party did take a public stand against racist laws. In contrast to the regulation of interracial relationships advocated by the "white bourgeoisie," the *Daily Worker* reported that "the Communist Party denounces all discriminatory laws against the Negro workers and demands the abolition of laws against intermarriage."[117] The *Daily Worker* also emphasized the specific impact of intermarriage laws on Black women, asserting that "anti-intermarriage laws styled 'race integrity' measures are solely means of safeguarding the lust of white men in having relations sexually with Negro women."[118] This claim was unusually subtle in its recognition that intermarriage laws preserved a system sanctioning white men's sexual objectification of Black women. It also proposed that legal prohibitions on sexual expression had an unconscious motive in actually producing the sexual practices they putatively opposed.

Intersections of race, gender, and sexuality entered more directly into radical conversation via leftist antilynching efforts. The struggle to end lynching in the South was a central concern within the Communist Party in the 1930s. Scottsboro brought its racial, gender, and sexual dynamics into the center of public conversation. The case erupted in 1931, when nine young Black men were accused of raping of two white women on an Alabama freight car. Alabama Communists were especially emboldened by Third Period antiracism, and the Black women and men driving the Left in the region were primed to make the Scottsboro case a centerpiece of their organizing.[119] The struggle over control of the Scottsboro boys' defense revealed fault lines dividing liberal and leftist antiracist organizations, the latter of which tended to connect the case to broader structures of inequality at the nexus of race, class, and gender.

In her sensitive analysis of Scottsboro, Cheryl Higashida notes how southern racism relied upon the "triangulation of race and gender relations that justified lynching by constructing white men as the virile defenders of virtuous white women against black rapists." Yet "the Southern 'lynching triangle'" was "countered by a Communist "homosocial triangle" as "African American and white male workers bonded through negatively libidinizing white women."[120] This homosocial triangle also introduced an additional dimension into the Scottsboro case, as journalists and activists highlighted the gender nonconformity in the widely reported-upon overalls worn by the women making the accusations. Ruby Bates and Victoria Price, the Scottsboro accusers, fit longstanding characterizations of sisters of the road. They had been arrested for vagrancy in the past, and they shared a history as sex workers.[121] Many accounts of the case emphasized how the women were dressed in men's overalls—a detail that confirms how popular narratives about vagrancy were inflected by ideas about gender transgression. "The girls had bobbed hair," Edmund Wilson noted in a *New Republic* article, "and wore overalls."[122] In a 1931 article in *Harper's* titled "The Negro and the Communists," Walter White, a lawyer for the National Association for the Advancement of Colored People (NAACP), stated that

> the officials of the law at Scottsboro intended at first only to charge the nine Negro defendants, who ranged in age from fourteen to twenty years, with the crime of fighting and stealing a ride. But when it was discovered that two of the four white 'men' were women in men's clothing, the girls were vigorously questioned as to whether or not sex offenses had been committed on them by the Negroes.[123]

In White's account, the two women's gender transgression preceded their fabricated accusation of sexual assault. The women's clothing even entered into the second trial of Haywood Patterson, a high-profile defendant who had secured a lawyer in his initial trial through the Communist International Labor Defense. A purported witness to the assault, Ory Dobbins, was questioned by Patterson's attorney, Samuel Liebowitz, who grilled him on how he knew Ruby Price was a woman:

Liebowitz: You know it was a woman don't you?

Dobbins: She had on woman's cloths.

Liebowitz: She had on women's clothes?

Dobbins: She had on women's clothes.

Liebowitz: What kind of clothes, overalls?

Dobbins: No sir, dress.[124]

Since everyone already knew about the "men's clothes" worn by the accusers, Dobbins's testimony was dismissed. Overalls simply were not admissible as "women's clothes."[125] In Lin Shi Khan and Tony Perez's 1935 book *Scottsboro Alabama: A Story in Linoleum Cuts,* a work that adhered to the Communist Party's defense of the Scottsboro Boys as workers, Bates was depicted in her trademark overalls, elbowing a sheriff in the face.[126]

The accusers' sex work factored even more significantly in leftist discussion about the case. Josephine Herbst reported in *New Masses* that "it is for these women, established as prostitutes, who were not overpowered or hysterical, according to the doctor's report, but merely talkative, that eight Negro boys were legally condemned to die."[127] Langston Hughes, at the height of his Communist period, wrote ironically of the "dumb young blacks—so indiscreet as to travel, unwittingly, on the same freight train with two white prostitutes . . . And, incidentally, let the mill-owners of Huntsville begin to pay their women decent wages so they won't need to be prostitutes."[128] The labor conditions and lack of job opportunities confronting working-class women were critiqued as instantiating a climate where sex work became inevitable and fabricated accusations of assault against Black men proliferated.

Irrespective of their gender presentation or sexual histories, Bates and Price were able to bring down the hammer of injustice on the accused men owing in no small measure to the racist history of lynching in the South that granted them vaunted white-woman status while pathologizing and criminalizing Black male sexuality. Of Ruby Bates, Hollace Ransdall, an activist and writer, wrote in disbelief, "[A]s a symbol of the Untouchable White Woman, the Whites held high—Ruby. The Ruby who lived among the Negroes, whose family mixed with them; a daughter of what respectable Whites call 'the lowest of the low,' that is a White whom economic scarcity has forced across the great color barrier."[129] The weird status upgrade afforded to poor white women by virtue of having charged Black men with rape was further commented upon by Hughes. "Dear Lord," he famously wrote in *Contempo* in 1931, "I never knew until now that white ladies (the same color as Southern gentlemen) traveled in freight trains . . . Did you, world?"[130]

The Scottsboro stories confirmed the racist terrorism that already had been a central target for Communist organizers. Black men were routinely accused of sexual assault to uphold racist laws and practices and as a pretense for disciplining Black bodies. Animated by the Black-led organizing already under way in Alabama, leftists took up the Scottsboro case as an opportunity both to bring to light this disturbing history and to frame Jim Crow laws as tools for maintaining racial inequality. The analytic favored by leftists highlighted the ways sex could be instrumentalized by white bosses invested in driving a wedge between Black and white workers, and part of that defense relied upon "libidinizing white woman" who were also marked as gender nonconforming. Leftist discussion of the Scottsboro case acknowledged how accusations of rape leveled at Black men represented an effort to control Black male workers, preserve white women's chastity, and maintain discord between races. While this critique tended to steer somewhat clear of more-nuanced intersections of race and sexuality that appeared in other contexts, it did suggest how leftists appealed to sexual and gender normativity even as they mounted their vehement opposition to racist laws criminalizing Black male sexuality.

Though the Left did not offer a consistently articulated politics around sexuality, neither was the subject of sex verboten in leftist print culture. While seeking to express their political convictions, many of the same actors who built a revolutionary movement aimed at the liberation of the international working class also puzzled through the intersections of class, race, and sexuality. Adhering to an expanding repertoire of positions on sexuality became a frequently contested benchmark of radical commitment, and a fearlessness around addressing sexual matters was a valued—and much maligned—characteristic of leftist culture. The emphasis upon exposing lynching and racism in the South further introduced a site of critical inquiry for leftists to examine societal assumptions about the relationship between race and sexuality. The broadening of sexual politics on the Left in turn created a foundation upon which leftists constructed a politics of homosexuality.

CHAPTER 3

"To Be One with the People"

Homosexuality and the Cultural Front

On November 3, 1932, the *San Francisco Spokesman,* a Communist-leaning Black newspaper, published an editorial confronting the problem of "prejudice against homosexuals."[1] Founded one year earlier by John Pittman, a graduate of Morehouse College and the University of California Berkeley, with Robert Flippin, director of the Booker T. Washington Community Center, the *Spokesman* had earned some notoriety—on one occasion its office windows were smashed—for its radical perspective on race and class in a city known for its maritime industry.[2] "At that time," Pittman recalled, "there were only twelve thousand Afro-Americans in the entire San Francisco Bay area."[3] Though it was unusual for an outspoken defense of homosexuality to appear in even a radical newspaper, Pittman's editorial adapted the fiery rhetoric, humanitarian concern, and outrage over oppression that were hallmarks of Black and leftist journalism in the 1930s in order to confront the prejudice and indignities faced by San Francisco's many homosexual residents.[4] Pittman indexed his argument through reference to the Black struggle for liberation—a position he had been developing as a leftist during a period when the Communist Party was especially invested in dismantling racist structures.[5]

In affirming the basic humanity of homosexuals and decrying prejudice against them, Pittman's unrepentant polemic resonated with much of the expressive culture found in the Depression-era Left. Even as the Communist Party refused to officially support sexual dissidents, radical writers and artists nonetheless departed from Party policies to articulate leftist perspectives that brought attitudes about homosexuality into conversation with radical positions on class, race, and gender. Pittman's editorial illustrates how some leftists, steeped in the revolutionary language of the Communist Party's Third Period, repurposed resistance to American capitalist institutions and racist structures to advance a radical position on homosexuality.

Readers of leftist publications occasionally acknowledged the impact that radical magazines, newspapers, and novels had on their thinking about homosexuality. In January 1929, *New Masses* published a letter from a San Joaquin, California, man identified only by the initials H.H.C. in its "Workers' Letters" section. H.H.C. recounted the moving story of an eighteen-year-old man's growing consciousness about labor, Bolshevism, and a love that dared not speak its name. "There are many kinds of suffering," H.H.C. wrote in his third-person apologia. "God had created him a little differently from the rest." Describing in romantic language the growth of his relationship with a poet who abandoned him for Italy but left him with "friendship . . . love . . . and understanding," H.H.C. lamented how "the world scorned his love, hated him for it."[6]

Commuting on a train to work, H.H.C. described being overwhelmed by "the faces to whom he desired to give his love" but who "could not accept it." "There is a gate somewhere," H.H.C. wrote despondently, "but he is a coward, and will not open it." Yet the final paragraph of H.H.C.'s letter, to that point a tormented cataloguing of one man's struggle with same-sex desire, struck a more defiant tone. "*New Masses* has helped to show him the gate," H.H.C. declared, announcing that "some day soon he will walk out and find life and be worthy of himself and life."[7] Through *New Masses,* H.H.C. was emboldened to imagine living outside the confines of his rejection and self-loathing. His choice of *New Masses* as a venue for his letter points to the broad reach of this significant leftist publication. It also suggests how the Left provided an important space within which to articulate a defense of homosexuality.

The affective pull of the Depression-era Left has tended to be diminished in favor of historiographic emphasis upon its ideological rigidity and organizational discipline, but H.H.C.'s letter points to a highly individualized negotiation of leftist culture in the twentieth century. The letter also countenances a surprising network of leftists willing to engage questions of homosexuality. Two months after it was published, *New Masses*' editors posted a notice titled "For College Student H.H.C." "A number of letters have been received for H.H.C," the editors wrote. "These will be forwarded on receipt of name and address."[8] Evidently H.H.C.'s roll of the dice paid off, perhaps more than he anticipated since he shrouded his letter in anonymity. H.H.C. articulated a narrative of solidarity with others confronting estrangement from American narratives of belonging that equated his same-sex desire with the proletarian populism espoused on the Left. "Oh, to be one with people, to feel them, know them, love them," H.H.C. effused in his letter.[9] Within the pages of *New Masses,* he could at last feel known and loved. Yet he still could not be named.

Especially within print culture and proletarian literature, leftists navigated complicated questions concerning homosexuality and radical politics. Unpacking leftist discourse concerning homosexuality corrects lingering associations of the Old Left with unrelenting antipathy to homosexuality, suggests common themes spanning twentieth-century radical culture, and establishes a foundation for understanding why sexual dissidents were attracted to the Left even when official policies and organizations rejected them.

ENCOUNTERING SEXUAL CONSERVATISM ON THE LEFT

Homosexuality was widely understood as deviant in the United States during the 1920s and 1930s. Leftists often mirrored such attitudes—unconsciously as they expressed generalized distaste for homosexuality, strategically as they sought to legitimize their politics within mass culture, and defensively as they pushed back against police and G-men seeking to discipline them. The persistence of sexually conservative attitudes on the Left reveals the degree to which radical culture imbibed and echoed mainstream cultural norms and practices concerning sexuality and contextualizes counternarratives that embraced deviance and promoted alternatives to stigmatization and repression.

Though European models of Marxism competed for dominance in the early twentieth century, the Bolshevik Revolution of 1919 cast all eyes on Russia to determine proper revolutionary stances toward sexual matters.[10] In 1928, German sexologist and homosexual advocate Magnus Hirschfeld's Scientific-Humanitarian Committee sought information on Russia's treatment of homosexuals.[11] Hirschfeld had visited the Soviet Union in 1926, returning to Germany disappointed by the lack of energy around politicizing homosexuality. Many leaders of the Russian Revolution, echoing Marx and Engels, dismissed the politics of sexuality in the new revolutionary society as a bourgeois concern. Vladimir

Lenin himself conceived sexual questions to be superfluous matters of little interest to those building a revolutionary society. "However wild and revolutionary the behavior may be," Lenin reportedly stated, "it is still really quite bourgeois."[12]

The decriminalization of sodomy by the Soviet Union in acts passed in 1922 and 1926 provided an opening for admitting diverse perspectives on homosexuality, especially as the newly Communist nation was in the throes of building a collectivist society. In 1927, E. P. Frenkel', a Soviet jurist, defended the decriminalization of homosexuality by tracing lingering vestiges of cultural conservatism to prerevolutionary society. Frenkel' determined that "intrusion of the law into this field is a holdover of church teachings and of the ideology of sinfulness."[13] Similarly, in his entry for homosexuality in the 1931 *Great Soviet Encyclopedia,* a massive volume edited by Vyachelav Molotov and Nikolai Bukharin among others, M. Sereinski, himself a homosexual, wrote that the USSR "goes beyond prophylactic and curative measures to create the indispensable conditions under which the everyday interactions of homosexuals will be as normal as possible and their usual sense of estrangement will be resorbed in the new collective."[14] This position was confirmed in a 1932 publication in Germany by the Russian graduate student Grigorii Batkis, who stated that homosexuality in Russia was comparable to "so-called 'natural' intercourse."[15]

Yet the lived realities in the USSR did not always match up with Soviet ideals, as contradictory as the latter were. In 1922, two Russian "Trials of Homosexuals," one concerning a masquerade attended by "pederasts," ended in arrest under charges of "hooliganism."[16] Then, in 1933, the Soviet Union reversed course entirely and recriminalized sodomy, introducing prison sentences for such offenses.[17] This abandonment of an earlier, more sympathetic position impacted the degree to which sexually dissident leftists could look to a Soviet utopia as a model for homosexual decriminalization.[18] Scholars looking at the Left in the United States cannot ignore the impact of statements such as Maxim Gorky's famous admonishment to "eradicate the homosexuals"—a chilling command that effectively eliminated room for disagreement about the intention of the Soviet officials on matters of sexual diversity.

The recriminalization of sodomy in the Soviet Union precipitated a quiet but significant international response. In 1934, Scottish Communist and self-identified homosexual Harry Whyte, editor of the *Moscow News,* wrote a letter to Joseph Stalin offering a defense of homosexuality as adhering to "the principles of Marxism-Leninism." Whyte argued that "the condition of homosexuals under capitalism is analogous to the condition of women, the coloured races, ethnic minorities, and other groups that are repressed for one reason or another." He also distinguished between causes of homosexuality: those among the bourgeoisie who "take to this way of life after they have sated themselves with all the forms of pleasure and perversity that are available in sexual relations with women" were distinct from—and inferior to—"constitutional homosexuals" who "exist in approximately equal proportions within all classes of society." Whyte further observed that there were already homosexual Communists who were crucial to the Party. Pointing to open homosexuals such as André Gide, he noted how "the fact that Gide has joined the revolutionary movement has not hindered its growth or the support of the masses for the leadership of the communist party." Whyte imagined sexuality as part of the revolutionary charge. "I have always believed that it was wrong to advance the separate slogan of the emancipation of working-class homosexuals from the conditions of capitalist exploitation," he wrote. "I believe that this emancipation is inseparable from the general struggle for the emancipation of all humanity from the oppression of private-ownership exploitation."[19] Despite Whyte's rhetorical flourish and strategic reframing of official Communist policy to buttress his argument, Joseph Stalin was not moved. He simply archived Harry Whyte's letter under the heading "an idiot and a degenerate."[20]

In contrast to Whyte's distinguishing bourgeois homosexuality from "constitutional homosexuality," representations of homosexuals in leftist magazines in the United States frequently depicted both as reactionary. Radical artists routinely produced work that cast homosexuals as political enemies and caricatured political enemies by depicting them as homosexual. Much of the representational shorthand for signifying homosexuality had taken root in the early decades of the twentieth century: images of effeminate men with upturned noses, fashionable coifs, and pruned eyebrows drew upon long-standing ideas about male homosexuality as a form of gender inversion. These tropes were circulated by leftist publications without interrogating their underlying politics. Images of pansies and fairies were mobilized as a lingua franca among leftists who sought entry into American political discourse. These representations aligned the Left with mainstream attitudes dismissing sexual dissidents and recast leftists as themselves normative through their rejection of sexual deviance.

Homosexuality understood as gender inversion precipitated leftist anxiety most often when it feminized male workers who incongruously

William Gropper

FIGURE 5. William Gropper, untitled,
The Liberator, April 1922, p. 25.

"Paul, isn't it horrifying that the perfume makers'
strike is still on?"

favored the capitalist system that oppressed them. A 1922 *Liberator* cartoon by the influential leftist artist William Gropper depicted two sulking pansies with hands on hips, crossed legs, pronounced lashes, and heavily painted lips. "Paul," one whines, "isn't it horrifying that the perfume makers' strike is still on?" (figure 5).[21] The reactionary complaint of Gropper's natty figure suggests how the putatively feminine tendencies of the male homosexual prevented him from exhibiting solidarity with the workers who manufactured his queer accoutrements. The particularities of this figure's elocution serve reactionary purposes here as well: in contrast to the bold proclamations characteristic of a dedicated leftist commitment ("Strike!"), Gropper's affected fairy blithely drops camp hyperbole ("[I]sn't it horrifying") and exposes his antiworker bias through a femininely rhetorical question. That these men are animated by consumption, redoubled through the signifier of fashion, rather than production further distances them from the producerism of the leftist labor movement. They have no interest in controlling the means of production, only in unobstructed access to the trendiest eau de toilette. Homosexuals are depicted as gender transgressive, materialistic, and ill-suited for the revolutionary charge, too busy camping and disapproving to join the picket line.

A 1926 *New Masses* cartoon by Sandy Calder advanced a similarly flippant critique of reactionary homosexual inversion, depicting an effeminate man sitting at a table marked as "reserved for ladies" (figure 6).[22] "I cahn't see the teensiest, weensiest reason why I shouldn't sit here," the man drily remarks as a beefy attendant attempts to eject him from his table. Calder depicts the invert in a feminine posture with one elbow on an armrest, his opposite hand perched daintily on his thigh as he looks away with long-lashed, downturned eyes from the robustly masculine host in a coquettish gesture that is the clearest expression of actual desire in the cartoon. Calder reifies homosexuality as gender inversion and articulates leftist anxiety around femininity through his depiction of a man who simply cannot distinguish himself from the ladies who frequent the establishment. The speech pattern in Calder's caption further suggests a bourgeois affect that reads as effeminate: his soft *a* in "cahn't" reeks of the Harvard affect leftist writer John Dos Passos mocked in his 1936 novel *The Big Money.* "Harvard stood for the broad *a*," Dos Passos wrote, "and those contacts so useful in later life and good English prose."[23] Gender inversion transitioned seamlessly into bourgeois affect and betrayed a failure to adequately speak the language of the working class.

The slipperiness between femininity and bourgeois style allowed pansies to stand in for capitalists within leftist representations. In his 1939 proletarian novel *Christ in Concrete*, Pietro Di Donato painted a vivid portrait of male bricklayers who enjoy the homosociality of the manual labor that defines them. They work together, visit prostitutes together, and live alongside one another in the city's tenements. "Did they not all live one atop the other and feel and taste and smell each other?" Yet this richly democratic working-class community does not extend to the bourgeois bosses who mete out these jobs. Bosses embody characteristics more commonly found among fairies and pansies. The men who "owned the great building and the city" are "glaze-skinned, soft, white-fingered men who looked like painted mustached women dressed in tailored men's clothes"; they are "dainty pink-cheeked perfumed dolls of men who gave out the awards and spoke tired high-class talk."[24] By aligning the proletariat with normative gender and sexual practices, and by contrasting bosses as affected gender inverts, Di

DRAWING BY SANDY CALDER

"Hey, don't you see that sign: 'Reserved for ladies?'"
"I cahn't see the teensiest, weensiest reason why I shouldn't sit here?"

FIGURE 6. Sandy Calder, untitled, *New Masses*, November 1926, p. 21.

Donato distanced workers from competing accusations of their own deviance.

The smear of homosexuality structured leftist disavowals of the upper class and religious conservatives. A 1925 article in the *Daily Worker* charged that "certain forms of sexual perversion" were "practiced with impunity by the British aristocracy." Another in the same year claimed that "religion has a tendency to incite those suffering from it to sodomy."[25] But it was not only bourgeois reactionaries who were disparaged as queer. The manly denizens of the Communist Party distinguished themselves from Socialists by characterizing sectarian opponents as feminine and queer, and thus ineffectual. In 1926, the *Daily Worker* lambasted Socialist partisans by denouncing the "respect some unsophisticated workers still hold for the sadists, Lesbians, disciples of Oscar Wilde and other perverts of the ruling class."[26] This article was unusually direct in naming "lesbians" and "perverts," as well as offering a winking nod to "disciples of Oscar Wilde," the latter doing double duty by signifying Wilde's weak-willed Socialism as well as his homosexuality. Socialists were dismissed as weak, inauthentic frauds holding insufficient dedication to Marxist principles.

Because homosexuality was broadly understood as connected to gender inversion during this period, special scorn was reserved on the Left for liberal politicians, whose weakness was rendered visually as feminine and whose attempt at compromise with conservatives was cast as an illicit form of desire.[27] *New Masses* cartoonists often depicted enemies of the Party in drag. A 1934 cartoon by Jacob Burck, captioned "The Seventh Veil," depicted Franklin D. Roosevelt as Salome just as she approached the denouement of her striptease (figure 7). Roosevelt was routinely targeted in *New Masses* during the Party's Third Period for his reformist dedication to preserving capitalism. That lack of resolve branded FDR as a "social fascist," but his conciliatory attitude toward the free market also suggested he was politically weak. In Burck's cartoon, Roosevelt stands next to a discarded veil emblazoned "PWA," naked but for one remaining veil labeled "CWA" (Civil Works Administration). Though the standard leftist critique of FDR's accommodationist liberalism was clearly the target here, Burck produced a sexually charged image that envisioned Roosevelt as both a woman and an object of queer desire. The veils marking his New Deal programs render FDR female, but they also visualize him as a temptress. Burck's striptease maligns FDR's purported political spinelessness as well as his irresistible appeal to the masses he holds in his seductive thrall. Burck's cartoon of Roosevelt's Salome performance spoke to the collapsing of gender and sexual dissidence in leftist cross-dressing cartoons; he was depicted as a feminine and a sultry (if awkward) sex object whose seductions were of biblical proportions.

FDR cross-dressed again in a 1935 Gropper cartoon, this time to fawn amorously over pictures and other mementos from his lover, Wall Street (figure 8). In this cartoon, Roosevelt's gender inversion is literalized as sexual deviance. FDR both dresses in drag and pines for another man, surrounded by the trappings of queer domesticity that allow viewers a glimpse of their untoward relationship. The queer affection between liberals and bankers was depicted in *New Masses* as the kind of illicit homosexual tryst readers agreed had no place in a Communist vision for the United States. Failing to commit fully to the Communist revolution besmirched Democrats as hopelessly feminine and placed them on a slippery slope to a homoerotic boudoir scene.

The logic connecting decadent homosexuality and reactionary politics was repeated in leftist literary texts that imagined queer desire

THE SEVENTH VEIL.

Jacob Burck

FIGURE 7. Jacob Burck, untitled, *New Masses*, April 3, 1934, p. 3.

impelling capitalist excess. Kenneth Fearing, a leftist writer whose singular voice privileged tough characters, urban settings, and directness across genres, published *The Big Clock,* a noir novel, at a time when tough-talking detectives were becoming literary best sellers. *The Big Clock* describes Earl Janoth, the homosexual CEO of Janoth Enterprises, a fictitious publishing powerhouse with insidiously fascist connections to social engineering. (The company is designing a plan for "Funded Individuals" who represented a kind of über-race.)[28] A series of homosexual revelations between Earl and his girlfriend, Pauline Delos, result in Pauline's murder at the hands of Earl and expose the craven extent to which he will go to protect his corporation. After dis-

FIGURE 8. William Gropper, untitled, *New Masses*, June 25, 1935, p. 8.

covering that Pauline is having an affair with another man, Earl sharply comments, "[A]t least, this time it's a man"—a barbed reference to Alice, Pauline's earlier lesbian paramour. "She's a part-time Liz," Earl announces later to a friend, "did I ever tell you that?" Pauline's bisexuality is connected with her bourgeois sensibility. Later in the novel, Louise Patterson, an artist modeled on social realist painter Alice Neel, declares that Pauline "was beautiful if you like Lesbians in standard, Park avenue models."[29]

After Earl throws her past same-sex lover in her face, Pauline fires back accusations of his own barely repressed homosexuality, noting how he is always "camping" about with Steve Hagen, a "fairy gorilla" who is Earl's business associate and confidant.[30] Thrown into a homosexual panic at his exposure, Earl furiously beats Pauline to death with a glass decanter—a murder itself embodying high camp through Earl's use of a decorative object made of material typically signifying fragility as a brutal weapon. Fearing's villainous capitalist is thus depicted as a secret queer engaging in a campy relationship with his second-in-command, and his icy, wealthy lover is an acknowledged bisexual.

Fearing's novel demonstrates how leftist writers instrumentalized dominant representations of homosexuality to critique capitalist perversion. The depth of Earl Janoth's corruption is revealed through his murder of Pauline, but a sordid web of queer desire and disgust foreshadows both Pauline's tragic end and Earl's malevolence. Fearing ultimately suggests how the world of high-stakes capitalism, complete with fascist overtones, incubates the debauched behavior that poisons Earl and Pauline's relationship and scrambles their ability to distinguish good from evil. Rabid capitalism, corporate publishing, overconsumption, and social engineering were linked to homosexuality as behavior and identity, and the excesses of American capitalism were represented as masterminded by the perversity of same-sex desire.

COMMUNISTS AND SEX IN PRISON

Though representations of male effeminacy and queer capitalist decadence were common in leftist venues, discussions about situational homosexuality in prisons and other sex-segregated institutions provided another occasion for launching radical criticism of homosexuality as debased and disgusting.[31] "It is a place of terror," a writer in the *Liberator* wrote of Leavenworth Prison in 1923, characterizing it as a "headquarters of intrigue, pederasty, secret dope deals and drunken 'favorites' of the internee's homosexual harem."[32] In a 1928 exposé of conditions inside a reformatory, *New Masses* writer David Gordon observed that "there's a lot of homosexuality, and some things even worse," though what could possibly be worse was not specified.[33] A 1934 *New Masses* article confronting the hideous conditions at the Welfare Island prison bemoaned the "indiscriminate commingling of prisoners" in an institution where "lip-sticked homosexuals are numerous and unsegregated." The author proposed a policy separating homosexuals from the general prison population to protect heterosexual prisoners from unwanted advances by their cellmates.[34] Radical outrage over queer commingling in prisons demonstrates how sexual perversion functioned in 1930s leftist culture as a vehicle for advancing ideas about egregious and unwarranted violations of nature's laws.

Communists became particularly concerned about homosexuality in prisons following the arrest of Angelo Herndon, a Black Communist organizer, in 1932.[35] Herndon was convicted on charges of insurrection stemming from an organizing effort in Atlanta that ran afoul of anti-Communist authorities. In March 1934, *New Masses* published an alarming editorial. "News comes from Atlanta that Angelo Herndon, young Negro organizer of [the] unemployed, framed 'for distributing insurrectionary literature,' is about to have another tormented inflicted on him," the editors reported. "In addition to the constant torture and unbearable conditions in the Fulton Tower death-house, sexual perverts are to be introduced into his cell." Herndon's torment was vigorously opposed by the International Labor Defense (ILD), the Communist-sponsored legal-defense organization most famous for wresting control of the Scottsboro defense from the liberal NAACP. The ILD's efforts on behalf of Angelo Herndon included urging sympathizers to "flood Gov. Talmadge" with "protests demanding that Herndon be given the rights of a political prisoner."[36] Five months later, Peter W. Madison updated *New Masses* readers on Herndon's prison conditions, complaining that officials "regularly threaten to put sexual perverts in the cell with him."[37] Exposure to sexual perversion—even the very suggestion of it—represented just one more form of abuse the state was inflicting on Herndon, whose purported lawbreaking was directed against the state rather than against nature.

In 1937, Random House published Herndon's memoir, *Let Me Live*. In this book, Herndon attempted, in part, to legitimize his principled lawbreaking by contrasting it with the homosexual practices he observed in Fulton County Jail. *Let Me Live* did not mention the threat of perverts being introduced into Herndon's private cell. Instead, Herndon detailed the disturbing prevalence of homosexuality among inmates, invoking the terrifyingly public nature of same-sex contact during times when free movement was permitted. "Every day at nine o'clock the cells were opened by the turn-keys, and the men circulated freely in the entire prison block for the rest of the day," Herndon wrote. "This made it possible for the prisoners with homosexual inclinations to go prowling around for their private pleasures. However, these pleasures could not be very private in a place like a prison . . . . 'Love making' was carried on in full sight of everybody. (Frequently I had to turn my eyes away in disgust and pity.)"[38]

In a significant departure from the narrative articulated by his advocates and defenders, the specter of private perversion was replaced in Herndon's autobiography with an unconfined homosexual menace assaulting fellow inmates with terrifyingly public displays of lovemaking that were threatening in direct proportion to their uncontainability. Herndon's reading of prison homosexuality through a narrative of disgust ironically aligned him with the long arm of the law. In his 1934 study *Sex in Prison,* for example, Joseph F. Fishman noted that "the average prison guard has no understanding of the natural or environmental factors which make for homosexuality. To him the congenital homosexual of the passive type is simply a 'dirty punk' who has no actual right to exist."[39] Herndon echoed this unsavory association of homosexuality in prison with dirtiness as he literally turned away from sex acts, unable to stomach such a spectacle.

Though he was most displeased by the explicit homosexuality he encountered in prison, Herndon also described the gender transgression among the "Old Ladies" he encountered in Fulton Tower, many of whom were "second offenders who, during their previous imprisonment, had been initiated into homosexual practices." Herndon confirmed a slipperiness between gender transgression and homosexuality, yet in his narrative the mode of inversion was reversed: homosexuality was imagined to have produced gender inversion, rather than the opposite. "The little boys wore girl's pink bloomers," Herndon complained. "The men who 'kept' them bought them girl's clothing and forced them to wear it at every opportunity."[40] In his manuscript's original draft, Herndon used "obliged" rather than "forced" in this sentence, suggesting a softer relationship. In either case, Herndon confirmed gender transgression as a form of prison humiliation.[41]

An earlier draft of *Let Me Live* offered additional material regarding homosexuality. In one excised section, Herndon not only expressed distaste for homosexuals, but also foregrounded his naivete around such matters. "I have always been unsuspecting of sexual degeneracy whenever I have met with it," Herndon writes.

> My apparent innocence in this matter might largely be explained by the fact that I have an abhorrence of all that is unnatural and decayed. My thoughts I usually concentrate on more wholesome and constructive subjects than

sexual perversion. But the carryings on in Fulton Tower were so open and unashamed that even I could not help but notice them.[42]

In this omitted passage, Herndon again established his own innocence in contrast to the "decay" of homosexuality. His performance of "wholesome" distance from homosexuality advanced a version of leftist uprightness that foreclosed solidarity with sexual dissidents.

Herndon's distaste for the homosexuality he encountered while in prison aligned him with other political prisoners who shared similar experiences. Elizabeth Gurley Flynn, who was incarcerated five times, complained that "the vile language, the fights, the disgusting lesbian performances were unbearable."[43] Flynn's complaint, of course, must be taken with a grain of salt, given that she was likely involved in her own disgusting lesbian performance for the better part of a decade. In part, the fascination with homosexuals in prisons resulted from the fact that Communists often found themselves running afoul of the law. "All inmates have one thing in common," wrote Communist prisoner Frederick Vanderbilt Field in his autobiography. "They all think they are victims of a lousy society. All have been mistreated by the police[,] the judge, the jury."[44] Once incarcerated, Communists found themselves among precisely those elements of the population toward whom they felt the strongest pull. The attraction of Communism was initially, for many members, born out of, or at least impelled the pursuit of, a spirit of solidarity with the downtrodden. Prison cells were heavily populated with members of the lower classes, toward whom Communists often held more sympathy than they did for those who put them there.

In his 1940 memoir, Benjamin Gitlow, a former Communist who had twice been the Party's vice presidential candidate, only to become "America's first Communist prisoner in Sing Sing," recounted interactions with a cross section of Americans that included "tramps, hoboes, cranks, workers, students and professional people, all representing numerous nationalities." In his travels among the proletariat, "I found that men in rags could be profoundly philosophic and far from ignorant," Gitlow reported. "I learned from the lips of men themselves how they lived, how they felt about life."[45] Once in prison, "men in rags" were men with whom Gitlow shared uniforms, meals, and sleeping quarters. Leftist prison memoirs often drew sympathetic portraits of fellow inmates—in contrast to the brutality and inhumanity of the guards, who deprived them of their dignity. In his own memoir, Communist John Gates wrote that "the fact that we were unpopular with the government made us popular with the prisoners. Every prisoner in the place had been put there by the government and this established a common bond among us all, despite the great variety of reasons for our incarceration."[46]

Yet the prevalence of homosexuality in prison disrupted halcyon memories of life among the masses. Gitlow dedicated an entire chapter in his memoir to homosexuality in prison, even though he apparently did not engage in any of the sex he described. Though he adhered to a standard script detailing fascination, disappointment, and distaste for the homosexuality that surrounded him, Gitlow adopted a tone of sociological objectivity that stopped short of the kind of condemnation found in other leftist accounts. He did not display any particular affection toward homosexuals in prison, but he did analyze their practices neutrally, without presenting them as inhumane features of the penal system—save for one particularly gender-transgressive prisoner about whom Gitlow confessed to "the revulsion he aroused in me" before acknowledging that he was, nonetheless, "a favorite among the inmates" (110).

Gitlow was particularly interested in cataloguing the varying terms used to characterize those who engaged in homosexual acts in prison: wolves, kids, pansies, fairies, sweethearts, husbands (108). He also recounted anecdotes concerning several "degenerates," including Princess, Cleopatra, Nellie, and Lizzie, who were with him in Sing Sing (109). As their names indicate, Gitlow detected a particular play with gender categories in the prison—a topic he collapsed into his discussion of homosexuality. "Their mannerisms were feminine," Gitlow noted; "so was the inflection of their voices. They had high heels attached to their shoes, powdered their faces and rouged their lips and cheeks. They remade their shirts to give them a blouse effect and embroidered hearts around the kerchief pockets" (109). Culturally, the homosexuals Gitlow encountered in prison adopted many of the practices associated with gay men on the outside. They "engaged in amenities of repartee and exchanged darts of vulgar wit," and they "called each other, 'hussy,' 'cat,' 'lady bum,' and similar names" (110).

Though his memoir explored many themes that appeared in other leftist narratives about homosexuality in prison, Benjamin Gitlow's discussion complicated this narrative in three ways. First, he emphasized the social backgrounds of inmates to contextualize their same-sex desire. Gitlow acknowledged that homosexuality was particularly common in prison because for "many youngsters" with whom he was incarcerated, "state prison is not their first experience with institutional life.

They have grown up in either religious or state reformatories from which they graduated into the penitentiaries, finally completing their development in a state prison." These youngsters' relationship to sexual dissidence, then, had a social explanation rooted in early experiences of falling outside normative familial and housing structures. Gitlow found a continuity with their experience in institutions where "they look upon abnormal sex relationships as perfectly normal and proper" (108). Even if his final analysis emphasized the strangeness of sexual abnormality, Gitlow acknowledged the significance of social context for establishing sexual values.

Second, Gitlow unpacked lived experiences in prison to understand how deviance scrambled the dominant logic of capitalism. In his description of an inmate named Hoosier, normatively described as a "country lad from the farm," Gitlow emphasized how he was presented with all manner of presents from "wolves" seeking his affection: "soon he sported a wrist watch, new shirts, a nice new sweater." Rather than succumbing to the indignities of prison life with an air of defeat, Hoosier "walked around with a happy air of satisfaction and self-assurance." In contrast to "his father's farm," Hoosier was now "not only at home in the society of the prison big shots, but he was actually one of them" (112). Prison, then, offered opportunities for those who pursued homosexuality to fit into a social environment where they could seek pleasures that might have been denied them outside and to access economic advantages that otherwise eluded them under capitalism. Sexual dissidence upended the political economy, transforming a farm boy into a "big shot."

Finally, Gitlow attended to the pressures of racism—a central topic of concern among Communists. Within prisons, racial categories seemed to matter more than sexual identities. Incarceration seemed to invert the racial hierarchies structuring American life. Recounting the story of "two blond fellows" admitted into Sing Sing, Gitlow noted how these men passed over the white inmates, instead "attach[ing] themselves to a group of Negroes for whom they did washing, cooking, errands and the most menial work thrown upon them." The response of other prisoners to this arrangement played out along racial lines. "The white inmates were not angry with them because they were perverts— not at all," Gitlow wrote. They were angry with them "only because they did not yield their pervert favors to the white men" (109).

Prison broke down and confirmed racial hierarchies in complicated ways. Gitlow was especially intrigued by the relationship between a "Jewish lad" and an "arrogant Negro," the latter named Big Bill Jew.

"The Jewish lad was his kid," Gitlow wrote in an especially charged passage, "but he was more than that. He was his slave" (112). Again, the racial hierarchies marking American history were inverted through prison homosexuality. Gitlow's interest in intersections of race and sexuality complicated his dissection of homosexuality in prison, foregrounding the ways that categories of marginalization both incorporated and resisted American demands for normativity. Homosexuality in prison, ironically, presented an occasion for undercutting white supremacy.

Gitlow's analysis of homosexuality in prison suggests how leftists alternately replicated and pushed against the politics of deviance on the Left. Narratives detailing homosexuality in prisons functioned negatively on the Left to align radicals with dominant gender and sexual values in the United States and to discredit foes with the smear of homosexuality, but they also offered an opportunity to explore the social context of deviance. Some leftists affirmed sexual normativity as a tool for asserting their belonging within American culture, whereas others, such as Gitlow, undermined the idea of sexual pathology by placing it within a social context that was discontinuous from dominant social practices. The limits of Gitlow's sexual progressivism were most evident when he dissected racial categories during his incarceration. Though his analysis was clumsy and problematic, other leftists attended more carefully to intersections of race and sexuality.

INTERSECTIONS OF RACE AND SEXUALITY ON THE LEFT

Even as narratives by Communists such as Angelo Herndon suggest how progressive race ideology and restrictive narratives about sexual dissidence could coexist, other leftists attempted to connect homosexuality with Black liberation. Leftist organizing within marginalized communities, Communist theories of racism as a tool of capitalism, and Marxist theorization of dispossession as a catalyst for resistance brought sexual dissidence and leftist antiracism into conversation. In this respect, the Left of the 1930s represented a departure from earlier iterations of working-class radicalism that theorized race in only the most cursory fashion. Anarchists such as Emma Goldman had been willing to accept homosexuals as fellow humans, but she was not especially invested in race politics.[47] She conceived working-class politics as primarily connected to class difference irrespective of race. Her defense of sexual diversity represented a broader commitment to free love and skepticism about regulatory mechanisms dictating moral and social behaviors. Yet as with her perfunctory perspective on race, Goldman's understanding of sexual difference conceived homosexuality as a biological variation that deserved personal autonomy. Like many anarchists, Goldman believed strongly in equality, boldly affirming in 1909 that "all human beings, irrespective of race, color, or sex, are born with the equal right to share at the table of life." Yet race, as with sexuality, was secondary in Goldman's thought. "It is present," Kathy E. Ferguson writes of Goldman's politics, "yet in a way that obscures rather than clarifies racial power."[48]

"Until recent years," Otto E. Huiswoud wrote in *The Communist* in 1930, "the Negro question and its relationship to the revolutionary working class movement was practically unnoticed, almost completely ignored."[49] By 1932, when the *San Francisco Spokesman* ran John Pittman's editorial on prejudice against homosexuals, a more considered and centralized theorization of race had developed on the Left to such a degree that it informed an emerging critique of sexual hierarchies.[50] The *Spokesman*'s publishing Pittman's piece on an editorial page more typically devoted to columns on the Scottsboro boys and James Ford's vice presidential campaign—Ford was the first African American candidate to appear on a national Communist Party ticket—is less surprising when one takes into account the remarkable flexibility and expansive reach of Black internationalism in the 1930s. "As Harsh as Truth and as Uncompromising as Justice" read the motto atop the *Spokesman*'s banner, and the newspaper frequently made good on this promised temerity by pursuing topics that pushed against respectability and extended radical discourse to communities neglected by other periodicals. Neither did the editors shy away from discussing controversial topics, including those concerning sexual assault. An article titled "Soiled Goods," for example, appeared several months before "Prejudice against Homosexuals" and offered Cora Ball Moten's oral history of Melanie Bruce's rape and abandonment, indicting the culture of sexual violence that permeated the "New South" for perpetuating "white supremacy" and "sex slavery."[51] Pittman also used his platform to lift up Black women, noting in another *Spokesman* editorial that "women get things done" whereas men are "either jellyfish or asses, and in most cases, both."[52]

Though the *San Francisco Spokesman* did not have a formal relationship with the Communist Party, Pittman was himself a Communist, which he attributed to a visit from Angelo Herndon, and he later edited the *People's World,* the West Coast Communist newspaper that employed Jim Kepner as a writer. Pittman's opinion pieces tended toward militancy with an explicitly Marxist perspective. In a September 1932 editorial on Scottsboro, Pittman rallied readers with the rousing conclusion that "in every city in the world where the doctrines of Karl Marx have won converts, there will be parades and gatherings of determined men and women, symbolizing revolution and the rise of the masses."[53] It was, in fact, Pittman's boldness that had provoked a friend to complain, of his *Spokesman* editorials, that "the discerning mind at once detects an undercurrent of despair, bitterness, sarcasm, humor without the savor of a sense of fun."[54]

The *San Francisco Spokesman* had the added benefit of being published in a city with a long history as a "wide-open town," where, as historian Nan Alamilla Boyd has written, "queerness is sewn into the city's social fabric." "Queer communities took up residence in waterfront bars," Boyd writes, "in the theater district, along market street, among labor activists and communists, in Chinatown, along the old Barbary Coast, among the city's Beat artists and poets, in bohemian bars and taverns."[55] Though drag bars and same-sex gathering spots were sometimes aggressively policed, the overarching history of San Francisco suggests a tradition of acknowledging sexual diversity as a fundamental feature of the city's character, and reports on the prevalence of vice often served to attract visitors seeking out pleasure.

In "Prejudice against Homosexuality," Pittman marshaled all three of these local factors—sexual openness, radical working-class culture, and Black cultural and political institutions—to produce a critical document illustrating how Black Communism shaped a radical homosexual critique. Though Pittman's editorial was hardly the first instance of a political radical standing up for the dignity and common humanity of homosexuals, his article represents a critical moment in politicizing homosexuality from a Black radical perspective. "It is idle for Negroes to preach against race prejudice," Pittman declared, "as long as they themselves practice another kind of prejudice."[56] Pittman's editorial responded to the tittering that erupted following a gathering of homosexuals in Berkeley the previous month, wherein "a group of young men entertained themselves" through drag. "Some wore female attire," Pittman observed, and "some danced and talked as women do."[57] This affair's precipitating moral condemnation from the public spurred Pittman to speak out against prejudice and insist that despite their outward differences, "all" those at the gathering "acted normally and without restraint." Emphasizing by turns the sheer banality of the party, which Pittman referred to as an "ordinary occurrence in the lives of human beings," and a challenge to the presumed heterosexuality of his readers—"EVERY MAN AND WOMAN IS POTENTIALLY HOMO-SEXUAL," Pittman advised—the author chastised those "men and women, apparently intelligent and kind," who "are using the incident as a subject for parlor conversation."

Pittman's article was published during the Communist Party's revolutionary Third Period. "Prejudice against Homosexuals" extended an expansive approach to Black internationalism that Pittman had been developing in his *San Francisco Spokesman* editorials for months leading up to the November 3 issue.[58] In an "analysis of communism" from June 1932 Pittman had acknowledged that "for the American Negro, there is no immediate solution. If he repudiates Communism he will turn his back on the one doctrine which offers substantial hope for the future. On the other hand, to champion Communism is to double the weight of his already heavy cross." Pittman recognized the difficult position in which Black San Franciscans found themselves: they were being drawn into a fight for justice that would exacerbate their own stigmatization and deepen their struggle. "And yet," Pittman offered, "martyrdom is a glorious calling!" Pittman recognized that joining a radical movement would subject African Americans to further violence and marginalization while acknowledging that the unfair burden placed upon people of color in a revolutionary movement would bring them closer to liberation.

A similar spirit of empathy for those seeking social justice while confronting political obstacles informed Pittman's editorial on prejudice against homosexuals. Taking antiracism as de rigueur, Pittman appealed to his primarily Black readership by asserting that "both race prejudice and the prejudice against homosexuals are bolstered and maintained by social taboo and the law." Third Period Communism had no space for law and order. The Black Belt thesis proposed that disenfranchised Black Americans needed nothing less than anticolonial revolt. "Only in this way, only if the Negro population of the Black Belt wins its freedom from American imperialism," the resolution stated, "will it win real and complete self-determination."[59] Adherence to law was further suspect to Black Communists opposing lynching—a practice substantiated under the guise of punishment for breaking the taboo against Black sexual contact with white women. Lynching of African Americans represented a subject of high concern within the Communist Party, and the failure of the US government to pass antilynching legislation represented a key factor in the Party's advancing a revolutionary agenda.[60] "Both prejudices make life in this world a living hell for men and women whose only crime is that of being DIFFERENT from the majority," Pittman continued. "Because of the stupidity and malevolence of 'normal' men and women," he wrote,

> a DIFFERENT color of skin than white is a badge of inferiority, the possessor of which may be outraged or outlawed as the whim of the "normal" person decides. Because of this same stupidity and malevolence of "normal" men and women, a DIFFERENT form of sexual expression than with persons of opposite sexes is symbolic of a "curse of God," the victim of which may be jeered, hooted, and shunned as the self-righteousness of "normal" people permits.

For Pittman, the binary of "different" (stylized "DIFFERENT") and "normal" categorized people in order to buttress inequality and perpetuate marginalization of the minority. It was "social taboo" and "the law"—both instruments of oppression—that created categories that instantiated prejudice. Pittman's frustration with the powerful wielding bludgeons against the powerless connected his radical critique of American racism with his defense of sexual dissidents.

The bracketing off of homosexuals as "abnormal" by heterosexuals was further described by Pittman as connected to the characterization of Blackness as itself deviant. Though Pittman allowed that "the riddle of homosexuality is yet far from being explained," he noted of heterosexuals that "only by chance have they themselves escaped the penalty of being DIFFERENT from the great majority—just as intelligent white people know that it was accident alone which saved them from being Negroes." A radical position on race, then, led Pittman to a radical conceptualization of homosexuality. In both cases, the dominant group—white and heterosexual—maintained their power through appeals to normativity. Rejecting blanket dismissals of any minority group undermined the foundation of white heterosexual supremacy.

Pittman concluded his editorial by critiquing the language of liberalism. Not content with tolerance, Pittman demanded a radical reorientation around human difference that tilted toward self-determination. "This is no plea for sympathy for the homosexual," Pittman declared.

> To sympathize with a person because he or she happens to be homosexual is as little appreciated and as much insulting as to sympathize with a Negro for being black. What Negroes and homosexuals both desire is to be regarded as human beings with the rights and liberties of human beings, including the right to be let alone, to enjoy life in the way most agreeable and pleasant, to live secure from interference and insult.

Following Pittman's argument, the "rights" to pleasure, security, and liberty marked the aspirations of both Black Americans and homosexuals. The chief impediments to realizing these goals were interconnected: the persistence of prejudice, stigmatization of difference, discipline by the state, and liberal sympathy. Pittman demanded that readers recognize the fates of African Americans and homosexuals as intertwined, but he also suggested how the American tradition of maligning "difference" pushed marginalized Americans outside mainstream politics. Rejecting compulsory normativity connected Pittman's leftist antiracism with the struggles of sexual dissidents to produce a more just society. Rather than imagining homosexuals and African Americans as united through their shared experience of victimization, Pittman positioned them as equally equipped for revolt against the stifling normativity of the white and straight state through a countermodel of liberation, resistance, and the pursuit of pleasure. In short, he demonstrated how the logic of a leftist critique of American racism could inform radical sexual politics that drew on the rhetoric and discursive possibilities of self-determination.

Though Pittman was unusually forthcoming in his connecting race and sexuality in a leftist frame, other Black radicals pursued similar work. The bisexual Trotskyist writer Claude McKay developed, as Gary Edward Holcomb has written, a "queer black Marxism" in both his fiction and nonfiction.[61] Within published work such as the autobiographical *A Long Way from Home* and novels including *Banjo* and the unpublished manuscript "Romance in Marseille" (which Holcomb describes collectively as "the queer black Marxist novel ménage a trois"), McKay explored Black transnational communities where queer characters engaged the world surrounding them.[62] McKay's leftist sympathies informed his interest in the Black proletariat, whether he described the working ports of Marseille or the streets of Harlem, and he found sexual dissidents wherever he turned his attention.

Though he included homosexual characters in his work, McKay bristled at those who assumed that his queerness made him into a sympathetic ally for white homosexuals. In 1938, Charles Henri Ford—a poet, editor, and noted aesthete whose politics skewed to the left without ever dipping into Party membership—sent a letter to McKay. The two had exchanged earlier pleasantries and occasional camp correspondence in a relationship facilitated in part by a mutual acquaintance—the French Communist photographer Henri Cartier-Bresson, who, Ford informed McKay, was "disappointed because the Surrealists aren't Communist enough."[63] Ford, who edited the literary magazine *Blues,* had written a queer modernist proletarian novel with Parker Tyler, a gay film critic, titled *The Young and Evil* in 1933. In that novel Karel, a character who hangs out "at the communist cafeteria in Union Square," embodied queer possibility through his stubborn refusal to "act straight": "[S]omeone had told him don't purse your lips, but he had said where would I be if I had never pursed my lips?"[64]

In an attempt to curry favor with McKay, who was by that time a well-regarded writer and political radical, Ford enclosed in his letter a poem that he hoped McKay might help him publish. The poem was dedicated to "a young man who introduced himself to you one afternoon at the Harlem recreational center"—an encounter that suggests the overlap between Black and queer spaces in the 1930s.[65] The poem, titled "Not Allergic to Miscegenation," represented an ill-fated attempt by Ford to produce work consistent with the kind of social themes favored by radical Black poets such as McKay and Langston Hughes, while infusing his work with a blues-influenced aesthetic that had impelled Ford to begin editing *Blues* when he was sixteen years old. The apparently interracial same-sex encounter between McKay and this "young man" was foregrounded in Ford's poem. "Not Allergic to Miscegenation" injected elements of social concern into the cruisy introduction to which Ford had born voyeuristic witness: "in one / a priest with his own idea of heaven, / the other: communist: but his own ideas of earth." Ford included some exoticizing references ("mixed them in a chinaberry breeze") and a crude meeting of worlds apart ("from bushman to Washington") to produce his weird paean to queer miscegenation.

McKay was far from impressed. "I do wish you would not oblige me to endure the affliction of your prose in every letter you write," he began his reply two weeks later, a prelude to the breathtaking scorn that followed. "I don't like your verse," McKay offered. "It resembles a loathsome white worm trailing its slime over the body of life." Though McKay did not specify which features of Ford's poem set him on edge, he seemed especially upset by Ford's phoned-in radicalism. "You try to hide your real self," he wrote, behind "a radical formalism precisely as the South tries to hide its hideous inhuman face behind vaporings of chivalry." Additionally, the presumptuously licentious content of Ford's poem seemed to particularly rankle McKay, who complained that "there is the thick homosexual veil over your eyes, blinding you to everything else," before suggesting that "it is something worse which is wrong with you. Edward Carpenter was homosexual, as was Oscar

Wilde." If those homosexuals—both notable for also being Socialists—offered a counterpoint for McKay to the particular stink of homosexuality embodied in Ford, that odious quality of Ford's was painfully discernable to McKay as "the excrement of homosexuality which exudes from your pores and stinks all through your essays of versification."[66]

McKay's response to Ford suggests how the meaning of the "homosexual" for leftists was fraught with associations that did not necessarily line up neatly with the pursuit of sexual partners. For McKay, homosexuality was more than the parlor game and trifling affair Ford's poem seemed to suggest. As a queer Black Marxist, McKay well understood that sexuality meant nothing if it ignored race. Similarly, Black lived experience did not graft neatly onto white conceptualization of a homo/hetero binary. On Ford's end, McKay's letter evidently came as a bit of a surprise. The magnitude of his shock is difficult to overestimate: in the deep wells of rejection letters received by poets, Ford's scolding by McKay must hold a special pride of place. Indeed, Ford commented—albeit without ascending to the piques of graphic disgust McKay so colorfully articulated in his letter—that he found McKay's letter "insultingly gratuitous to a degree bordering on hysteria." Ford dug a deeper grave for himself when he brought a racially charged dismissal of McKay's aesthetic authority into play, asserting that "you yourself, by universal standards, are non-existent as a poet—it is only because it is so unusual that a member of the black race should write even second-rate verse showing the influence of the classics that your work has been noticed at all." If this wholesale dismissal of Black aesthetics as "second-rate" were not enough, Ford continued his retaliation by comparing McKay's "intellectual content" to "that hysterical race-hatred found in the minds of the people who lynch Negroes in the south," declaring that McKay's criticism "reeks of the most primitive 'Stalinist' thinking to which you have apparently fallen victim. Your charge of homosexuality," he concluded, "with moral implications, only corroborates the Stalinist 'puritan' complex—with all its persecution mania."[67]

The exchange between McKay and Ford clearly demonstrates how entangled questions about homosexuality were with discussions about race, aesthetic politics, and the Left. What began as a mildly homoerotic exchange rapidly escalated into a furious standoff in which Black poetics, homosexuality, Socialists, and Stalinists quickly entered onto the scene. Ford's assumptions about race (Black aesthetics were "second rate") and politics (McKay's "Stalinist 'puritan' complex") were met with McKay's radical riposte. McKay lobbed the final volley with a letter to which he could not have expected to receive a reply. "I was not resentful because you imagine yourself so patronizing," McKay offered, "but because spiritually you are so utterly disgustingly ugly!" McKay was particularly incensed by Ford's wading into red-baiting, vigorously retorting, "[W]hy meddle in politics since your brain is too puerile for comprehension?" Finally, McKay concluded in a burst of profoundly deviant politics, declaring that "I prefer a thousand times to belong to an oppressed race, sure and proud of what I am, than to be anything like you, a vile loathsome pathetic crawling filthy worm of the world of oppressors."[68] McKay's conclusion, then, meets Ford's charges of "Stalinism" with a defiant Black nationalism. It is noteworthy that McKay does not *deny* being a Stalinist, even though his Trotskyist leanings might have impelled him to clarify his position, but rather suggests that Ford's red-baiting simply reveals he is out of his depths. McKay attacks the immaturity of Ford's political orientation. His response asserts his pride in belonging to an "oppressed race" and refuses Ford's attempt to shame him. McKay's oppression becomes not merely a historical circumstance, but a declared preference, a source of energy that takes strength in its distance from the distasteful "world of oppressors." Even without naming his sexual dissidence, we might understand McKay's deviant politics as profoundly intersectional and a proud declaration of DIFFERENCE. The structure of his response to Ford's cheap accusations and racist insults rests on his embrace of deviance. An exchange that might be dismissed as hostile to homosexuality, then, was transformed into a performance of political deviance that confirmed McKay's queer Black Marxism.

RESISTING THE STATE

Though resistance to social prejudice represented a significant site for linking Black liberation and sexual dissidence, other leftists capitalized on their shared opposition to state surveillance and disciplining of Black and homosexual subjects. The theme of Black sexual dissidence in opposition to the state was developed extensively in James T. Farrell's short story "Just Boys." Published in 1934, "Just Boys" introduced an intersectional analysis of Black homosexuality, exploring interactions between Black and white homosexual characters against the backdrop of state repression. Farrell departed from Pittman's rhetoric of unity by introducing a stinging indictment of racism among and against sexual dissidents. Though his work did not adhere as closely to an official

Communist Party position on race as did Pittman's—Farrell was, like McKay, a Trotskyist—his expansive leftist vision did imagine an intersectional critique of race and sexuality that placed Black homosexuality at its center.

Farrell's story drew on the intertwined histories of race, sexuality, and the Left in Chicago, a major center of Communist activity in the 1930s. Historian Randi Storch describes a Depression-era Communist Party that particularly appealed to Chicago's "African Americans, ethnics, students, artists, writers, workers, and women."[69] The Popular Front saw even more Black Communist cultural activity in Chicago flashpoints, including the *Chicago Defender*'s turn to the left, Richard Wright's ascendance as a proletarian writer of note, and Gwendolyn Brooks's profound poetic explorations of Black Chicago—all of which converged to produce a major Black-Left cultural center.[70] This was also a city with a highly developed homosexual subculture that attracted much interest from those both within and outside its borders.[71] Sex districts in the city intersected with Black and interracial residential arrangements and labor practices that produced spaces of unique possibility for developing a radical critique of homosexuality and race.[72]

Harlem Renaissance depictions of Black gay identity also informed Farrell's story.[73] As William J. Maxwell has convincingly argued in his discussion of African American writers between the wars, New Negro Black nationalism was inextricably tied to Communism, particularly vis-à-vis literary production. Black literature of the Harlem Renaissance was an important and central antecedent to—and was sometimes indistinguishable from—the 1930s literary Left.[74] Claude McKay, as discussed above, published novels that were connected with both Harlem Renaissance aesthetic politics and 1930s proletarian literature. They featured working-class subjects, centralized race as a category of analysis, discussed radical themes, represented labor agitation, and pushed against the boundaries of middle-class respectability. They also incorporated Marxist principles of labor and value, and they adhered closely to Richard Wright's famous "Blueprint for Negro Writing," which influenced both Black writers and proletarian novelists.[75]

In fact, many queer writers played a central role in shaping Black literary culture in the 1920s and 1930s. Influential Harlem Renaissance figures such as Richard Bruce Nugent and Wallace Thurman openly depicted sexual dissidents in their fiction. Nugent's influential short story "Smoke, Lilies, and Jade" explored an explicitly homosexual fantasia set in Black New York. Thurman, who primarily slept with men, was married for six months to Louise Thompson, who became a prominent figure in the Communist Party. In his outrageous satire of the Harlem Renaissance, *Infants of Spring,* Thurman's autobiographical double, the Bohemian intellectual Raymond Taylor, reveals his desire to join the Communist Party. "I'd like to help disseminate communistic propaganda among the black masses," he announces.[76]

Black writers distributed Communistic propaganda among the masses of Chicago in particularly high numbers during the 1930s and 1940s. The Black Communist writer Richard Wright, perhaps the most successful proletarian writer of the 1930s, became a best-selling writer with his 1940 proletarian novel, *Native Son,* which grappled with the relationship between race, sexual dissidence, and the state. In an early scene in the novel, Bigger Thomas and his friend Jack masturbate in the darkened Regal Theatre before a film begins. This section was excised from the novel upon publication at the urging of the Book-of-the-Month Club, not known for tolerance toward sex or communism.[77] "Within the polymorphously perverse environment of 1930s Chicago," Roderick Ferguson writes, "the scene straddles the line between homosexual expression and heterosexual perversion."[78] Indeed, though it functions primarily to accentuate the spectacle of white female desirability informing the relationship between Bigger Thomas and Mary Dalton, the white woman whom he murders in a gruesome episode later in the novel, it is nevertheless impossible to ignore the same-sex eroticism implicit in Wright's characters' mutual masturbation. "I'm polishing my nightstick," Bigger says when Jack notices him "slouched far down in his seat," suggesting a commentary on police suppression that borders on camp. "I'll beat you to it," Jack replies, infusing what might have been a scene of solo sex with homoeroticism that again camps on the nightstick's intended purpose.[79] The triple meaning of "beat" in this context—as masturbation, competition, and the function of a nightstick as an instrument of police violence—reinforces the libidinal pull of undermining state repression through homoerotic desire.

Though Bigger resists Jack's efforts to make this a shared experience, Jack refuses to let Bigger masturbate alone, inciting him to narrate the experience for their mutual enjoyment. The sex scene thus becomes a discursive event, reinscribing state surveillance of Black male homosociality into a narrative of erotic play. "I'll bet you ain't even hard yet," Jack says to Bigger, who replies, "I'm getting hard." Later, Bigger narrates Jack's orgasm: after seeing him "lean forward and stretch out his legs, rigidly," Bigger asks, "You gone?" Jack's orgasmic reply—"yee-eeah"—

meets with Bigger's observation that "you pull off fast," suggesting possible disappointment at the scene's brevity. Shortly thereafter, Bigger himself "leaned forward, breathing hard," and intones his own orgasm for Jack's benefit, "I'm gone. . . . God. . . . damn. . . ." [80] Following this shared sexual experience, the two men move to different seats in the theater, where they reorient themselves into a properly heteronormative relationship with the cinematic text and, as it happens, the Left: a discussion about Communism ensues between the characters two pages later.

Wright later makes explicit the state violence against Black homoerotic desire that was made into an object of play in the theater. After the police finally catch up with Bigger in connection with Mary Dalton's murder, the state attorney says to him, "I know about that dirty trick you and your friend Jack pulled off in the Regal Theatre," emphasizing state surveillance and tauntingly employing a vernacular expression for masturbation. "I know what boys like you do," David Buckley, the state attorney, says.[81] The precise meaning of "boys like you" is left vague. Boys who masturbate? Homosexuals? Black boys (as Wright titled his memoir in 1945)? The diminishing term "boys" seems to collapse all these meanings by emphasizing the disposability of each category in the eyes of the state—a usage that Farrell similarly critiques in "Just Boys." That it was a fantasy of police overinvestment in Black bodies that instantiated the homoerotic dimension of Bigger's masturbation through his speaking of his "nightstick" is not incidental here, either. Wright's novel suggests how proletarian fiction imagined homoeroticism as part of the vernacular for describing Black working-class lives and critiquing police violence against Black men. The excising of Bigger and Jack's public masturbation from the published novel confirms the threat to bourgeois values posed by leftist representations of Black working-class sexual dissidence in modern American culture.

James T. Farrell managed to largely avoid such censorship, likely because he was a white writer whose books were consistent best sellers. Yet he still faced occasional suppression of his books, impelling him to declare that "the danger of censorship in cultural media increases in proportion to the degree to which one approaches the winning of a mass audience."[82] Farrell's "Just Boys" appeared in *Calico Shoes,* the author's debut collection of short stories, and was published by the leftist Vanguard Press. By the time of the collection's publication, Farrell had achieved no small amount of literary success. *Young Lonigan,* the first volume of his *Stud Lonigan* trilogy, was published in 1932 and secured Farrell's place at the top of a pantheon of noteworthy naturalist writers.

The obscenity of *Young Lonigan* was both signified and suppressed in a disclaimer issued with one edition of the novel: "the sale of which is limited to physicians, social workers, teachers, and other persons having a professional interest in the psychology of adolescence."[83] As befitting a book advertising its own obscenity, *Young Lonigan* was also a success with popular audiences, attracting a broad cross section of readers who eagerly consumed Farrell's gritty and often salacious book.

Written between 1931 and 1934, *Calico Shoes* was published at the height of Farrell's "revolutionary socialist years," extending from the 1920s to the 1940s, when he both immersed himself in Marxist and Leninist writings and developed a sophisticated literary theory, published as *A Note on Literary Criticism* in 1936.[84] Farrell articulated a theory of the novel that incorporated a vast archive of radical ideas and criticism, proposing that "in the field of literature the formula 'All art is propaganda' be replaced by another: 'Literature is an instrument of social influence.'"[85] Though "Just Boys" meandered too far from a strictly Communist Party line or revolutionary theme to function as propaganda, its work as an instrument of social influence nonetheless demands serious critical consideration as a radical critique of the state surveillance of race and sexuality.

As with Farrell's novels, *Calico Shoes* contained a variety of homosexual characters that passed through urban life with greater or lesser ease. One story in *Calico Shoes,* titled "Looking Them Over," was set in Chicago and concerned an interaction between a "purse-lipped" character ("the Pole") and the young man he seduces. "Dey all queer here," the Pole reports of a crowd gathering at State and Quincy Streets. "I got a nice place," he offers. "You sure you wouldn't like to come to my place a little while?"[86] Farrell's proclivity for depicting homosexuals attracted the attention of at least one leftist critic. In an overwhelmingly positive *New Masses* review, Herman Michelson noted that *Calico Shoes* included "stories of homosexuals, of decaying old women, of dumb, beaten old men, and frustrated adolescence."[87] Though Michelson perhaps unfairly catalogued homosexuals alongside the other, more tragic figures in the collection, his review serves as an important reminder that homosexuality was far from invisible to Depression-era readers, and its prevalence was often observed even in Communist publications with understated neutrality.

"Just Boys" details a sour love triangle between a "white boy," Baby Face; his Black ex-lover, Kenneth; and Sammy, a Black man whom Baby Face meets in Washington Park and brings to a party to make Kenneth jealous. The story is set in urban Chicago, carefully mapped by Farrell with settings conforming to actual geographical markers: a rendezvous occurs "at the Blue Eagle Cabaret on South State Street"; a party is thrown "a few doors north of the Prairie Theater at Fifty-eighth and Prairie"; characters interact in the red-light district "down around Forty-third and Grand Boulevard"; the meeting between Baby Face and Sammy occurs while they are cruising in Washington Park and is followed by a dinner at "the Golden Lily on Garfield Boulevard" (81–87). Farrell makes use of familiar sites in lived Chicago, eliminating the distance between his fictional characters and their real-world setting. Farrell also offers readers a virtual tour of queer interracial spaces in Chicago, providing a narrative guidebook of places where such connections might be found.

Similarly, Farrell's story documents queer fashion of the 1930s, attentively detailing Kenneth's "blue velvet coat, a red-and-black checkered lumberman's shirt, and an orange tie"; a "mulatto boy" wearing "wide bell-bottom trousers, with a red patch of flannel and pearl buttons just above the pants cuffs"; and party host Princess Amy's "trailing green formal dress and artificial breasts" (88–90). Farrell also carefully catalogues queer interior design—an important signifier of homosexuality in the 1930s. The Princess's apartment epitomizes piss-elegant style, featuring "shaded lamps, a plush carpet wine red in the lighting, a large overstuffed divan, several wing chairs with leather seats and claw feet, an electric victrola, and red satin pillows that had been scattered indiscriminately about the floor" (88). The Princess's "high poster bed" sits against "green lizards painted over the wall paper" (95, 97). This detailing of camp design reinforces the intimacy of Farrell's account of Chicago's Black gay subculture.

At the same time, Farrell embodies the tactic of "queering the underworld" that literary critic Scott Herring identifies as a tactic used by modernist writers to resist the exoticizing excesses of slumming literatures by "thwart[ing] classificatory knowledge about the mysteries of homosexuality as an 'unveiled secret.'"[88] When a character in one scene describes a sexual tryst, he only gets through the line "Well, you see, it was thissaway" before he is interrupted with laughter. He then squeaks out, "I done stand up and . . ." before again being interrupted (91). The reader has a clear sense of the character's remarkable sexual acrobatics without the author's making them truly explicit.

From the start, the dynamic between Baby Face and Sammy is structured by class, racial, and sexual difference. Baby Face is fully invested in racial categories that alternately express hatred and desire. Kenneth is a "black bitch" and a "black trollop"; Caesar is a "magnificent-looking coppery brown boy"; Princess Amy is "a coal black, corpulent, perspiring Negro" (82–88). "Just Boys" begins as Baby Face emerges from the Public Health Institute in Chicago's "black belt" after receiving treatment for syphilis. He is immediately identifiable as an urban fairy: he "had a thin, sensitive face, with deep blue eyes, a short nose, powdered cherry-red cheeks, and thin, artfully rouged lips"; later Farrell describes "his thin, effeminate hands, with their tapering fingers, and long, polished finger nails" (82–83). In order to exact revenge on Kenneth, Baby Face cruises Washington Park, the same park where he and Kenneth first met, to find "a big, husky black boy who would cause Kenneth to squirm with spite and envy." Baby Face picks up Sammy Lincoln, a "muscular and broad-shouldered Negro of about twenty." Though Sammy was hoping to find a girl in the park, he recognizes immediately upon seeing Baby Face that "this flapper of a white boy was queer" (84). "Sammy," Baby Face reveals, "with me it's searing purple passions" (87). Sammy knows from another friend that "white boys" can be good for "clothes and liquor" as well as "good times at cabarets." Baby Face's feminine features also appeal to Sammy, who recognizes that "he was as pretty as a girl with skin as tender" (88).

A few days after their meeting, Baby Face and Sammy attend a party at Princess Amy's apartment, where Amy's guests dance to "the sounds of hot Negro jazz," play bawdy games such as "kiss-the-pillow," and delight in "every insult, every smutty joke, every sexual reference" (89, 92, 93). Things grow uncomfortable after Kenneth reveals to Sammy that Baby Face has syphilis, which Sammy realizes he has now risked contracting. This discovery meets with Baby Face's rage ("Kenneth, you're just a jealous, viperfish no-account lying bitch"), and the situation escalates to campy violence as Baby Face, donning one of the Princess's dresses, scratches at Kenneth until Princess Amy, "fearful of his dress," splits them apart (92, 94). Soon, however, the violence becomes far more serious, and Sammy, "almost paralyzed with fear," slashes Baby Face's throat with a razor, leaving his head "half-severed" (96, 97). Baby Face's murder is met with "an uproar of shrieks, outcries, and fainting boys," provoking attention from the police, who announce that the commotion is nothing more than "a nigger fairy party," remarking that "one of the shines slashed a white pansy's throat. Christ, you should have seen them when we broke in. Like a regiment of hysterical old women" (98).

From the moment they arrive, the police are far more interested in arresting Black homosexuals than investigating a murder. They immediately dehumanize Sammy, inserting him into a racist narrative that follows a script set in place long before the crime occurred. One officer blithely comments that he will "make nice frying on the hot chair." "The boys are getting rough," another detective observes. "Yeh, just boys," a policeman replies—a phrase that collectively dismisses the actors in language resonant with Wright's "boys like you" (98). Farrell acknowledges Black sexual dissidents as disposable to the agents of state capitalism.

Farrell's story functions equally as an indictment of Baby Face's racism, Sammy's homosexual panic, and police disregard for the Black, poor, and queer. Though Farrell invokes the trope of the tragic homosexual—venereal disease, public sex, relationship dysfunction, violence, and death all make appearances—and veers toward crass stereotyping of Black criminality, he pushes beyond the political anomie animating such narratives by foregrounding structural racism and an unforgiving state apparatus, suggesting how these symptoms of American injustice inevitably lead to violence and bad policing. Farrell makes no gestures toward eradicating homosexuality, instead foregrounding the deleterious effects of racism within queer communities and indicting police as agents of state-sponsored injustice.

Marc Blitzstein envisioned homosexual cruising as itself a form of resistance to the state. Blitzstein, a gay composer with strong ties to the Communist Party, explored the slipperiness between sex and politics in his 1937 WPA play, *The Cradle Will Rock*—a Brechtian allegorical musical depicting the unionization of workers in "Steeltown, USA" as they await their big boss, Mr. Mister.[89] The latter character was first performed by the queer leftist Will Geer, who was also Harry Hay's boyfriend and, at least in Hay's telling, responsible for Hay's joining the Communist Party. (Geer is more famous for playing Grandpa Walton on the 1960s television series.) Just before its premiere, authorities concerned about Communists infiltrating the Federal Theatre Project shut down the play's opening-night performance, spurring an enthusiastic audience to walk twenty-one New York City blocks to a new venue, where the production was restaged. To avoid violating union rules, actors performed their roles from within the audience, the stage occupied only by Blitzstein and his piano.[90] Transgressing the space of the audience became a signature feature of this production, the populist message and proletarian themes of which seemed to resound even more strongly when performed alongside the people paying to see the show.

Yet the narrative in *The Cradle Will Rock*, which drew inspiration from Clifford Odets's *Waiting for Lefty* and Bertolt Brecht and Kurt Weill's *The*

Threepenny Opera in roughly equal measure, was also groundbreaking when it appeared, cleverly integrating Blitzstein's sexuality and leftist politics into a narrative of radical lawbreaking and state resistance through the act of distributing political pamphlets. In the play's second act, protagonist Larry Foreman is hauled into night court after having been arrested for leafleting a park under the cover of night—a crime that shared many features with sexual cruising. Leafleting was a form of social exchange between strangers acting in collusion through a shared narrative of deviance that was closely monitored and subjected to surveillance, harassment, and entrapment by the police. Similar to seeking public sexual contact, distributing political propaganda required a form of intimacy that threatened to spark either a climactic political conversation or verbal, physical, or legal retribution. Blitzstein incorporated the overlap between these crimes—and the pleasure they evoked—into his script.

The song "Leaflets" is performed in a night court surrounded by sex workers and other undesirables. Carefully stacking his lyrics with double and triple entendres, Blitzstein turns the subversive act of leafleting into suggestive camp:

> Ain't you ever seen my act?
> > *He goes into it.*
> Well, I'm creepin' along in the dark;
> My eyes is crafty, my pockets is bulging!
> I'm loaded, armed to the teeth—with leaflets.
> And am I quick on the draw!
> I come up to you—very slowly—very snaky;
> And with one fell gesture—
> I tuck a leaflet in your hand.
> And then, one, two, three—
> There's a riot. You're the riot.
> I incited you—I'm terrific, I am![91]

Though he exploits the uncertainty of his narrative by ironically invoking potential violence (the narrator's being "armed"; the "fell gesture") alongside the dominant meaning of leafleting, Blitzstein's shadowy "creepin'"; bulging pockets; and slow, "snaky" approach point to the slipperiness of sexual and political incitement. His wildly campy turn of phrase from "there's a riot" to "you're the riot" suggests a shift admitting that in addition to a politically motivated riot, a sexual liaison might also be incited in poorly lit parks. It is in these spaces where illicit contact—same sex, interclass, politically radical—occurs, and that contact is easily repurposed as resistance to the state.

The ambiguity of the city park allowed multiple readings of "Leaf-lets." Early recordings of the song played up this ambivalence by camp-ing its more indeterminate lines. The first recording, in 1937, seemed to encourage audiences to read the sexual subtext, especially when Howard Da Silva leered his suggestive "You're the riot." Later performances downplayed this salacious reading by replacing its sly lasciviousness with an aggressive masculinity. Yet especially before its camp elements were downplayed, "Leaflets" offered a compelling narrative of sexual and political deviance that produced ambiguity around the homosexual-Left axis in public parks and imagined resistance to the state as always/already embedded in queer cultural practices. As enemies of the state, sexual dissidents had a world to win and little to lose.

POLITICIZING HOMOSEXUAL VICTIMIZATION

In 1945, Edwin Seaver, a leftist writer and editor who had made a splash with a 1935 *Partisan Review* article laying out his definition of proletar-ian fiction, edited the second annual volume of *Cross Section,* an anthol-ogy of previously unpublished fiction he inaugurated the year before to showcase "a whole sector of writing that cannot find publication else-where, for reasons other than merit." Seaver attempted with this publi-cation to collect those stories that had failed to find a publisher because of their racy subject matter and radical politics. "The magazines still have their taboos," Seaver cautioned, recounting as an example a "highly successful editor who breathlessly confessed" that he "had once had the daring to accept a story about a girl who *considered the possi-bility* of having an abortion."[92] Work containing radical content— sometimes even *actual* abortions—was too often relegated to a handful of left-wing publications, and most of them, *New Masses* included, had limited space for publishing fiction. *Cross Section* gathered in one place a variety of contraband fiction that readers could consume en masse.

In its 1945 edition, *Cross Section* included pieces by established left-ist writers such as Gwendolyn Brooks and Richard Wright. The volume also included a story by Donald Vining, a gay writer of limited success whose realist fiction delved into the shadowy world of the urban homo-sexual. "Show Me the Way to Go Home," Vining's disturbingly frank depiction of violence in the sexual underground, represented an arche-typical narrative detailing homosexual victimization within the prole-tarian urban landscape. Though his story stopped short of representing sexual dissidents as emboldened radicals, Vining's emphasis upon the suffering of his subjects legitimized homosexual claims to victimhood and emphasized queer grievances as political.

"Show Me the Way to Go Home" narrates the story of Einar Hoag, a "tall, towheaded soldier" seeking to jackroll "a queer" at a gay bar, reasoning that "they deserved to be beaten up anyway."[93] After teaming up with another soldier entertaining the same plan, the pair targets an older man, Mr. Listenwalter, who, seduced by the attention from these young and attractive men in uniform, falls prey to their advances. After successfully soliciting the man, the soldiers pull him into an alley where Einar "banged the old man's head against the wall" and knocked him unconscious. After stealing his wallet and dividing his money, Einar walks away, only to find himself pummeled by the same soldier with whom he hatched the plan, who then takes his share of the remaining cash. "Can't trust anybody," Einar concludes as he slips out of consciousness at the story's end.[94]

When Mr. Listenwalter threatens Einar with the police, the latter replies, "[I]f you report this to the police, you'll wish you hadn't. We'll tell them you're queer, that you tried to—." The police, armed with legal restrictions on homosexuality, are as threatening as the violent offenders themselves. In contrast to the police who target them, the gay bar's habitués stage small performance of resistance against the constant threat of violence by enacting gestures of solidarity incubated within their sexually dissident space. After one patron suspects Einar of being "rough stuff," Einar worries (correctly, as it turns out) that "word would travel now among all 'the boys' in the bar," and he finds himself ignored by most of the clientele in spite of his alluring sailor's uniform.[95] The network of support claimed by gay barflies within this counterpublic space provides a mechanism of safety from the effects of prejudice against homosexuals that runs counter to police aggression.

The title "Show Me the Way to Go Home" referenced a comic song that recounts a drunken man's efforts to get home to bed while inebriated. In an ironic turn, Vining repurposed the amusing song to foreground the yearning for safety and security that eluded his homosexual victim. Further, his casting of a soldier in the role of double-crosser—even edgier given the context of World War II, when the story appeared—pushed against more sanguine representations of servicemen as martyrs to the state. The predations of the servicemen were indistinguishable from their quest for cash, and the gay men in the bar were made into easy targets by their positions on the outskirts of society.

Vining's story confirmed a narrative of homosexual victimization that had been incubating on the Left since the 1920s. Though Vining did not offer an explicitly revolutionary message, his narrative drew on the formal structures and thematic interests of proletarian literature— poor urban dwellers; unseemly vices; desperate acts by the underclass; skepticism toward police—to draw his portrait of a social stratum victimized by its own marginalization. His story's inclusion in an anthology of radical fiction suggests how writers incorporated homosexual-victimization narratives into existing structures of proletarian literature. In part, representations of homosexuals as victims of American cruelty brought into stark relief the violence undergirding capitalist social structures. Representing homosexuals as victims pushed against the bourgeois values that proletarian writers sought to challenge.

William Rollins Jr. dissected the relationship between the homosexual victim and proletarian fiction in his 1935 *New Masses* article "What Is a Proletarian Writer."[96] Rollins's article made explicit the connection between his writing proletarian fiction and his inclusion of a homosexual character whose victimization at the hands of the police instigated a working-class rebellion in one of his novels. "Of my four important strikers," he wrote, "the organizer was a neurotic (to a lesser degree), the girl betrayed a man to sleep with a scab, a third was a dipsomaniac, and the fourth a homosexual."[97] Rollins's catalogue strategically placed his homosexual victim alongside others who were too often left out of the radical imagination. As a radical writer, Rollins refused to represent an idealized working class to elicit sympathy from middle-class readers. Rollins surmised that it would not occur to a reactionary critic "to protest that he knew lots of workers and they weren't homosexuals," because "they were workers" and therefore "aliens."[98] Homosexuality functioned in Rollins's work to undo the bourgeois respectability demanded by critics, and representing a homosexual victim was a vital component in constructing a proletarian literary tradition that deviated from middle-class literary expectations. Rollins knew homosexuals because he knew workers.

Both Vining and Rollins foregrounded the physical violence faced by homosexuals. Yet many leftists, attuned to the multiple registers of working-class oppression, were no less attentive to the psychological impact of cultural conservatism on sexual dissidents living under a violent system. Ivan Beede balanced physical and psychological victimhood in his 1926 story "Bertie," which appeared in *New Masses* alongside Max Eastman's translation of Alexander Pushkin's "Message to

Siberia."[99] Beede was an occasional *New Masses* contributor and associate editor of the *transatlantic review,* a disproportionately influential modernist literary magazine that launched and folded over twelve months in 1924. During its short life, the little magazine managed to publish work by luminaries including James Joyce and Gertrude Stein. Having steeped his readers in both a radical and transatlantic modernist milieu, Beede achieved the height of his literary success when his first novel, *Prairie Women,* praised by the Federal Writers' Project for "picturing the disillusion and frustration of Nebraska life in the post–World War period," was published in 1930.[100] Beede's celebrity quickly dissipated, however, and by 1934, *Prairie Women* was named by Nathan Asch as a "neglected book" in the pages of the *New Republic.*[101]

"Bertie" was also set in a Nebraska prairie town where the landscape echoed the title character's isolation and loneliness. "There was a quality of eternal sorrow about the earth," Beede writes, and "watching the red sky" leaves Bertie "feeling lonely and blue." Bertie lives "alone in a pink house with lace curtains where he had his own world: his diary, his flowers, his maltese cat and his dreams."[102] A working-class queer who dropped out of school in the tenth grade, Bertie is hopelessly in love with Paul Moon, whose yearbook picture hangs above Bertie's bed and who is heading off to war. Bertie fantasizes not only about having and loving Paul, but also about a conversation the two might one day share in which Paul embraces Bertie's homosexuality, one in which Bertie

> would twist his mouth up in a pained smile and tell Paul what a funny fellow he was. Paul would listen with a compassionate light in his eyes, a regard like that of Jesus, and then he would say something or other like this: "I understand. We are different, as different as the sun is from clouds, but we can be friends." (9)

Bertie imagines a solidarity that readers of *New Masses* would likely have recognized as a staple in proletarian fiction: the utopian possibility of forging friendships that emerge out of difference. The radical vision of Beede's story also hinges upon Bertie's envisioning a form of confession through which Bertie finds not love, but affirmation. Beede invokes Jesus as a radical whose openness encompasses Bertie's sexual difference, conforming to a leftist tradition of figuring Christ as both a martyr and an advocate for the working class.

Though Bertie stages this halcyon coming-out in his head, he can hardly muster the courage to actually address Paul in public. Yet knowing that Paul is heading off to war, Bertie gathers the strength to finally ask him out for a ride in his Ford truck—a butch signifier in striking counterpoint to the camp signifiers of queer domesticity in his home—a proposition to which Paul hesitantly agrees. Bertie engages Paul in banal conversation, advising him expansively that "everybody isn't alike. It takes all kinds of people to make up a world." This articulation of human diversity allows Bertie to affirm his homosexuality as a dimension of himself he chooses to embrace. "I guess I was made like I am," Bertie declares, adding that "I'm different. I want to be different" (10).

Bertie's confession is met by Paul with a violent reaction: he punches Bertie from his seat in the truck. But this physical violence is fleeting, and Beede immediately probes the act's emotional and affective dimensions. Bertie "was not angry," Beede writes, "somewhere inside he was hurt." Bertie does not deny the reasons for his having been attacked. "He was queer, and he knew it," Beede tells us. Yet more than the sting of rejection by a man whose picture hangs in his bedroom, or the physical pain he experiences from enduring this assault, Bertie fears Paul will reveal his sexuality to the town, about which Paul suggests Bertie need not worry. In an ironic turn, Paul assures Bertie that "I have some sense of decency" (10).

Nonetheless, Bertie descends into self-loathing and torture: "[H]e called himself unspeakable names" and imagined a future forestalled by public knowledge of his shame. As his panic grows, Bertie resolves to behave in a more heterosexual way. He stops for a cigar because "he could think of nothing more masculine." He enacts a vision of a future in which he becomes normative. "He would think and feel as they did. He would chew tobacco and swear and chase whores, and marry the first woman who'd have him." Yet as the story concludes, Bertie finds himself bound in his impossible circumstances. "He dropped to his knees at the dainty pink counterpane," Beede writes, "and raised his falsetto voice to Heaven, praying God to help him be a man" (30).

Beede's story recapitulates a classic mode of tragic-homosexual obsession. Rather than finding love or satisfying his desire for closeness and intimacy, Bertie finds himself alone, despondent, possibly suicidal, in physical pain from a violent attack, and wholly rejected. His desire victimizes him. He "wished he could have been in Paul's place and hit himself, as Paul hit him!" (30). Yet, constrained as Beede's narrative is by these narrative limitations, he nonetheless reframes a familiar gay-victim story as a narrative of social concern. Bertie's tragedy is unambiguously painted as having been produced by the stigma of homosexuality, rather than as an inevitable conclusion to homosexual disappointment. Bertie glimpses an alternative world governed by empathy for those who are DIFFERENT, throwing the suffering of homosexual victims into stark relief against Bertie's fantasy of a more just world. Prejudice against homosexuals is represented as cruel and unnecessary. Neither is the physical violence against Bertie the cruelest form of antipathy to his homosexuality in the story. The trappings of manliness and masculinity are represented as imprisoning rather than liberating. Bertie's pathetic efforts to pray that God change him, even as his domestic trappings and feminine voice betray him, provides a counterpoint to the earlier vision of Jesus as radical, compassionate, and embracing. The homosexual victim of conservative sexual values, like the working-class victim of capitalism, elicits sympathy while offering a glimpse of a better world.

The relationship between homosexuality and the Left was never easy. The vigorous opposition to homosexuality in American culture was often recapitulated on the Left, and at times leftists seemed to take a special interest in marginalizing homosexuals. Yet neither was the Left—or even the Communist Party—defined entirely by cultural conservatism. Efforts to politicize homosexuality and envision homosexuals as part of a radical community disrupt notions of the Left as overly invested in disciplining gay women and men. Through representations of Black solidarity with sexual dissidents and interracial resistance to police oppression, Communists marshaled leftist race politics to address homosexuality. Within representations of prison, modern sexuality was acknowledged as a feature of the dispossessed. By acknowledging the disposability of homosexuals within the eyes of the state apparatus, leftists imagined homosexuality as a site of radical resistance. And by foregrounding homosexual victimhood, leftists admitted homosexuals into the panoply of the proletariat. Each of these strategies pushed against the dominant narratives of homosexuality as pernicious within the Left and capitalized upon broader characterizations of sexual dissidents as socially deviant within American society. The more they were rejected by mainstream American culture, the more homosexuals had to gain by aligning themselves with a revolutionary movement that sought to overthrow its systems of power. Still missing from this piece, however, was the significance of labor in structuring the meanings of the Left. The next chapter foregrounds work as a central concern among leftists that produced important tools for representing homosexuality and admitted sexual dissidents into the radical labor movement.

CHAPTER 4

"If I Can Die under You"

Homosexuality and Labor on the Left

In August 1928, *New Masses* published a first-person narrative recounting the well-known hobo George Granich's harrowing escape from a New York county jail. Granich, the younger brother of Michael Gold and a Communist Party founding member, was an established writer in the leftist press, having first published an article describing his experiences inside a Yuma, Arizona, hobo jungle for a 1922 issue of the *Liberator*.[1] More recently, Granich had been arrested for vagrancy by a "a handsome brute with the eyes of a mad dog and the fist of a pile-driver." When he was hauled before a "fat slob of a judge," Granich was cleared of the vagrancy charges, but the "book of poetry" he carried among his belongings incited the judge to sneer, "Not very practical are you? Thirty days." Finding himself locked "in jail with idiots," one of whom "achieved idiocy through excessive masturbation," Granich reported that he "felt myself slipping," and he plotted his successful escape.[2]

As he fled from the authorities who were trailing him, Granich sought refuge in a Buffalo clothing shop he assumed would offer brief asylum because a poster in the shop's window advertised a speech by August Claessens, a popular Socialist speaker and organizer. Claessens was a New York assemblyman and a supporter of progressive sexual ethics who endorsed the Socialist sexologist William J. Fielding's book *The Sanity of Sex* upon its publication in 1920.[3] Fielding, who wrote for the *New York Call* and attended classes at the Rand School of Social Science, was also the author of *Homo-Sexual Life,* a publication in the

"Rational Sex Series" of Haldeman-Julius Publications' "Little Blue Books" series of pamphlets. Upon entering the shop, Granich recalled, "the boss, an old German Socialist, sized me up with a queer little smile. He called me into the back of his store and gave me a suit of clothes. I was so grateful I almost kissed him."[4] From there, Granich's freedom was assured.

For readers in 1928, the idea of a "queer little smile" making an appearance in a clothing store would likely have raised few eyebrows. The association of tailors and clothiers, like poets, professors, and actors, with homosexuality was deeply engrained in American culture, exacerbated by the burgeoning "pansy craze" that saw representations of fussy decorators and fashionistas reaching critical mass.[5] Clothing both signified perversion and functioned to mask it: in the 1926 recording "Masculine Women! Feminine Men!," Merritt Brunies and His Friars Orchestra had lamented "knickers and trousers baggy and wide / nobody knows who's walking inside / those masculine women and feminine men!"[6]

Granich's additional detail that his almost kissable worker-savior was a German Socialist might seem only slightly more unexpected than the insinuation leveled at tailors and poets. Those ethnically demarcated Socialist factions were, by 1928, being rendered increasingly passé as the revolutionary internationalist movement dispensed with the older generation's demographic determinants and envisioned an internationalist uprising modeled on the Bolsheviks' successful Russian revolt. In spite of their occasional support for sexological inquiry, Claessens's ilk typically drew association with decades-past radicalism that was nearly quaint in its idealism, incremental politics, and staid sexual uprightness. Yet German Socialists still registered as deviant even alongside the flashy style of the avant-garde Communists coming out of the woodwork and taking over Bohemia. Granich's story helpfully connects the queer intimacy cultivated through shared radical politics with the sexual frisson imbricated within sexually demarcated labor.

The connection between occupational lives and queer identities only intensified over subsequent decades. In his *Psychology of Sex,* first published in 1933, another socialist sexologist, Havelock Ellis, noted that inversion "is more frequent among literary and artistic people, and in the dramatic profession it is often found. It is also specially common among hairdressers, waiters, and waitresses."[7] Twenty years after Granich's harrowing escape and sensational near-kiss, Alfred Kinsey, a gallwasp expert and burgeoning sexologist with socialist political leanings, published his massive and shocking report *Sexual Behavior in the*

Human Male. As he tracked all manner of sexual contact between men, Kinsey disaggregated orgasm-producing same-sex contact according to occupations distinguished by "the prestige of the work in which [the worker] is engaged." Kinsey's men followed an upward movement from "dependents" to the "extremely wealthy group," traversing along the way through "day labor," skilled labor," and several other class categories.[8] Because Americans tended to socialize with individuals in their own class, their sexual practices were observed by Kinsey to follow patterns similar to those preferred by their fellow workers.

Kinsey dutifully documented how the lowest classes had the most incidents of homosexuality, followed by the "lower white collar" group, for whom homosexual orgasms were less frequent but still common.[9] Class ascendance, the trajectory Kinsey found most worthy of examination in a postwar period defined by upward mobility and the rabid pursuit of the American dream, was facilitated in part by conforming to sexual practices within one's aspirational class: if one wished to move from "underworld" to "lower white collar," one would have to adopt the practices treated as routine within the lower-white-collar repertoire. Larger jumps from one's class origins required greater sexual discipline to adhere to the racier or more abstemious standards that united one with one's fellow workers. "It is as though the bigger the move the boy makes between his parental class and the class toward which he aims," Kinsey suggested, "the more strict he is about lining up his sexual history with the pattern of the group into which he is going to move."[10] Class, evidently, was deterministically sexed, and sex was a vehicle for class mobility. Working people's class position was thus inextricably connected to their sexual practices.

As Kinsey's clinical investigation into the intimate lives of workers and Granich's retreat into a queerly smiling Socialist's back room suggest, from the Depression era forward, the overlap between working-class identities, labor politics, and sexual dissidence was a topic of intense interest in both leftist and mainstream culture. Interior decorators, professors, and entertainers were commonly represented as transgressing borders of gender and sexuality, just as Communists, Socialists, and anarchists were imagined to be deviant radicals transgressing sexual norms, in large measure owing to their proximity to these illicit occupations. The world of work was a critical site for puzzling out ideas about sexuality in American culture.

Because the Left was so intimately connected with labor, and because labor was inextricable from class, homosexuality was itself indexed through reference to the laboring class. Even within leftist organizations that failed to sketch out an explicit position on sexual dissidence, the inflammatory potential of a radicalized working class occasionally slid into representations of a sexually revolutionary avant-garde. Though the Left failed to fully theorize the connections between sexual dissidence and labor, radicals did grapple with complicated questions about work and sexuality in ways that cannot be reduced to sexual conservatism. Revisiting these sites of struggle reveals how the relationship between homosexuality, work, and the Left continued to resonate in later decades of the twentieth century.

This chapter considers the relationship between homosexuality, labor, and the Left in the 1930s and 1940s, focusing particularly on four critical points of intersection between sex and work. First, particular industries—especially maritime industries, where workers lived and worked in homosocial spaces at sea—incubated radical labor organizations that acknowledged sexual dissidents among their rank and file. Second, labor was represented as a site where bodies were placed on display, thus opening visual culture to a wide range of sexual depictions. Third, prostitution represented an important feature of the urban landscape that connected working-class communities with sexual transgression. Though leftists tended to conceive sex work as debased and exploitative, they also recognized the essential humanity of those involved in the sex trade and acknowledged the economic motivation that made sex work into an object of broader social concern. Finally, the occupational and professional lives of workers were conceived as indicative and instrumental features of sexual identities and political movements. The workplace was, within leftist culture, a sexed environment. These sites of connection between homosexuality, labor, and the Left admitted sexuality as a relevant topic within leftist discourse about labor in American culture, and working-class sexual dissidence was conceived as a subject of interest on the Left.

QUEER LABOR AND THE MARINE COOKS AND STEWARDS

The Marine Cooks and Stewards Association of the Pacific (MCS) was organized in 1901, ostensibly to improve conditions for low-status workers on ocean liners. In fact, the Marine Cooks and Stewards quickly became an all-white union that explicitly sought, in the words of its constitution, "to relieve ourselves of the degrading necessity of competing with an alien and inferior race."[11] The "inferior race" alluded to here were mostly Chinese, Japanese, and Filipino workers who had recently secured long-sought-after employment opportunities in the maritime industries, with the MCS constitution specifying that "we have concluded to form a union for the purpose of replacing Chinese and Japanese now on the Coast by American citizens or by those who are eligible to citizenship."[12] Though the broader labor movement in the early twentieth century was wracked by racism, white workers in maritime jobs were especially rabid in their demand that nonwhite workers be excluded from employment in waterfront trades. As a port city attracting large numbers of Asian immigrants, especially after an immigration station opened at Angel Island in 1910, San Francisco housed large numbers of Asian Americans seeking entrance into the labor market. Their success at this endeavor precipitated a backlash from white workers, who organized against them. Within the MCS, restrictions on Asian workers extended as well to Black workers, making them one of the most doggedly Jim Crow unions of the early twentieth century.[13]

Following an intense strike in 1921, a rival union, the Colored Marine Employees Beneficial Association of the Pacific (CMBA), was formed to organize workers excluded from the MCS.[14] The distinction between the two unions, split along racial lines, brought the racism within the Marine Cooks and Stewards into stark relief. The CMBA and MCS, both of which represented cooks and stewards on ocean liners, competed for jobs and control over maritime workplaces until 1934, when a general strike of maritime workers, centered in the San Francisco waterfront, resulted in their merger as a newly radicalized MCS.[15] The racial intolerance that had brought the MCS into being was abandoned in favor of a reconstituted union advancing a pluralistic vision of interracial solidarity.

Following its reorganization in 1934, the MCS began a slow, painful transformation into one of the most progressive labor unions in the United States. Leftists gained control of the union's leadership after 1935, mirroring a hard-left turn in American political culture and the labor movement more generally following the formation of the Congress of Industrial Organizations (CIO) in the same year. Though they did not change the culture of the union immediately, radicals in the MCS pushed against the racism that stained its history. "Gradually, as Communists became the leading force in the union," Bruce Nelson notes, "the MCS began admitting nonwhites," and by "1950 the membership was approximately one-third white and 45 to 50 percent black, with the remaining 15 to 20 percent drawn from other minorities."[16]

Revels Cayton, a radical Black labor activist, was elected as the MCS's representative to the Maritime Federation of the Pacific Coast—an organization founded in the wake of the 1934 strikes to bring together various maritime unions—alongside a leftist slate of candidates in 1937, ushering in a period of progressive politics for the MCS that brought it into closer alignment with the Communist Party.[17] By the 1940s, the rank and file had elected many Communist leaders, and the union was positioned on the front lines of radical race, class, and sexual politics. It amended its constitution to ban racist hiring practices, aligned closely with other radicals seeking social transformation, and positioned itself at the vanguard of union-building efforts that advanced greater gender equality in the maritime industries.[18]

Black leaders such as Cayton, a straight Communist who was also a vocal champion of gay MCS members, became notable spokespeople for antiracism, mobilizing members to see racism as a singular obstacle to working-class revolution and opening up the union to articulate a broader platform of resistance to various forms of hatred and bigotry. The MCS developed a reputation for attracting members whose transgressions crossed racial, political, and sexual boundaries. "On the San Francisco waterfront in 1941," one member recalled, "the word was that the Marine Cooks and Stewards Union was a third red, a third black, and a third queer."[19] Those categories sometimes overlapped: gay Black Communists joined the union, and members marginalized from normative strains in American society were often among the most militant. This is not to suggest that the union dispatched its entire racist history. In fact, many of the most desirable union jobs continued to go to white workers even during the union's most radical period. Yet the perception that the union was deviating from stifling normativity in American society shaped the perspective of its members regardless of whether they themselves belonged to marginalized groups.

Stephen Blair, a gay radical MCS member in the 1940s, recalled the taunting by longshoremen that sometimes greeted cooks and stewards upon arriving back in port. "You should've heard them," Blair recalled of one hostile reception after returning to the shore following a stint at sea; "they were like animals, the sons of bitches." The cries Blair heard harked back to deep strains of American violence that touched on each of the associations drawn with the MCS: "Lynch the sons of bitches! Kill those commie cocksuckers! Look at that fruit!"[20] Racial, sexual, and political violence represented interwoven strands of rage that the MCS marshaled by developing radical policies, advocating militant politics, and acknowledging the multiple prongs of oppression confronting its membership. The union also invited these epithets by resisting racism, refusing to condemn its homosexual members, and aligning itself with Communists. The tendency of members to associate with the dispossessed rather than aspiring to respectability suggests how tightly deviant politics were stitched into the fabric of the union's culture.

The labor movement had long maintained silence on matters concerning homosexuality, instead focusing energy on workplace matters that especially foregrounded salary, benefits, inequality, and safety issues. The MCS was unexceptional in this regard. Even though the union attracted a sizable gay membership and quietly sanctioned same-sex intimacy on the boats where these workers spent long periods at sea, homosexuality was not typically addressed in public. Instead, sexual dissidents affected the MCS in two key ways. First, members of the MCS who were attracted to the progressive politics within the union repurposed its radical rhetoric to address homosexuality, especially claiming the language of dignity and equality to advance positions advantaging gay members. These efforts in turn precipitated representations of homosexuality within the MCS that pitted less-radical unionists against their militant comrades, in the process bringing to the forefront sexual dimensions of labor that might otherwise have been foreclosed. Second, the open secret of MCS sexual dissidence opened the union to incorporating queer representations into the vernacular graphics of the union. MCS radicals produced representations of same-sex intimacy that offset depictions of proletarian perversion.

The National Union of Marine Cooks and Stewards was sometimes referred to as "Marine Cocksuckers and Fruits" by its own members—a campy play on the union's name that highlighted the sexual behaviors ("cocksuckers") and subcultural communities ("fruits") that were trademarks of the maritime workers. The fact that the MCS was based in San Francisco added to its queer flavor: the free availability of sex brought throngs of homosexual workers to the Bay Area, many of whom found work on the city's thriving waterfront.[21] As a port city with a sizable working-class population, San Francisco housed a vibrant leftist community that was particularly centered in the maritime trades. Though it was not the radical center that New York became in the 1930s, San Francisco hosted a series of important Communist-led general strikes in 1935 that offered a model for the nation's radicalizing labor movement, and its working-class communities were known nationally for their leftist bent.[22]

Though the MCS primarily organized men, the vigorous masculinity that was a hallmark of longshoremen was less instrumental to the work of cooks and stewards on boats departing from the Bay Area. The familiar history of gay men working in "feminine" jobs such as waiting tables, cooking, and cleaning was repeated on ocean liners, where cooks and stewards worked alongside ship mechanics and crews.[23] When MCS efforts to secure women's employment on ocean liners achieved greater success in the 1940s, women and men were revealed to possess similar abilities in occupations that became associated with an uncharacteristically visible gender neutrality.

The cramped sleeping quarters and pockets of privacy at sea also facilitated erotic intimacies. Whereas workers in most industries had to negotiate daily between their work and domestic lives, ocean liners required laborers to spend extended periods at sea, where they lived among their fellow workers. As Nayan Shah has described in a different context, homosocial labor that collapsed workplace and living quarters produced a form of intimacy that incubated sexual dissidence.[24] The unavailability of a range of normative sexual outlets on ocean liners facilitated sexual contact between male workers and introduced a specter of homosexuality that permeated the culture on ships.

Historians Jo Stanley and Paul Baker write that "for gay seafarers in the mid-twentieth century such vessels were one of the only places where they could be open about their homosexuality."[25] Even on land, the argot of homosexual "cruising" tacitly acknowledged the quasi-utopian space for developing same-sex intimacy in seafaring culture. "Hello, sailor" became a recognizable camp entrée both on- and off-shore, turning on the open secret that men resorted to, or took advantage of the relaxed prohibitions on, same-sex intimacy during lengthy bouts at sea. Though sexual liaisons between men were often dismissed as situational, they also pushed against sexual identities that demanded a homo/hetero binary. The pressure to find sexual partners on boats created a curious form of visibility for those who sought to make their sexual availability known, effectively shifting the coded performances governing everyday life once a ship departed from shore. Ocean liners represented spaces where rules for sexual contact were rewritten even when homosexuality was officially prohibited, and homosexual contact was widely available to those who sought sex between men.

The racial politics of labor further inflected the culture of the MCS in ways that amplified the union's queer dimensions. Black workers in San Francisco were increasingly organized between 1920 and 1940. Los

Angeles eclipsed San Francisco as home to California's largest Black population, still relatively small by national standards, but a rich history of cultivating Black institutions and progressive race politics shaped the Bay Area's political and cultural landscape. San Francisco became especially amenable to the wave of Black radicalism sweeping across the United States in the early decades of the twentieth century. The formation of the CMBA had represented an important moment when Black workers organized to compete with white unions. By the 1920s, both the NAACP and the Universal Negro Improvement Association had San Francisco branches, and the Communist Party had a growing presence in Black neighborhoods. As in most American cities, Black San Franciscans were disproportionately poor and working-class. Consequently, they were particularly drawn to movements calling for racial and economic justice. Left-wing political parties and radical labor unions appealed to Black residents who were shut out of mainstream unions and liberal political organizations that discouraged Black workers from joining their ranks. The Communist Party's outspoken antiracism spoke directly to Black workers.[26]

The overlapping realities of Black, gay, and radical San Francisco converged in the post-1934 MCS. Drawing on his deep knowledge of the Black organizing and radical labor movement, Revels Cayton articulated an explicit form of deviant politics. "If you let them red-bait," Cayton recalled, "they'll race bait, and if you let them race-bait, they'll queen-bait. These are all connected, and that's why we have to stick together."[27] Paul Brownlee, an MCS worker, further articulated the stakes of deviant politics: "If you were in the Marine Cooks and Stewards, you were automatically gay. So fuck you!—we didn't pay any attention to that."[28] The deviant practices of interracial organizing, Communist association, and homosexual intimacy marginalized MCS workers to such a degree that respectability was hardly operative, impelling a movement toward militancy that capitalized on the organizing potential of dispossession. "Merchant seamen were considered trash! We were considered outcasts," Stephen Blair recalled. The MCS "was a place where you lifted your head out of that sewer and said, God, I can make it this day."[29]

In some instances, white MCS members drew parallels with the Black liberationist movement that drew African Americans to the Left. Ted Rolfs offered that "there were a great many homosexuals who were drawn to the party, I knew them, but they were drawn to the party as maybe a Black person was. They felt that there was a fair shake there."[30] The idea that radical movements offered a "fair shake" was often enough to bring sexual dissidents into the orbit of the Left. With that empowerment came a great deal of freedom to distinguish the union through its militancy and to refuse to submit to characterizations of the union's queer dimensions as anything other than a source of strength.

Paradoxically, the MCS was moving toward Communism at precisely the same moment that the Communist Party was adopting official policies clamping down on "degeneracy" among its members. The 1940s represented a period of retrenchment when, primarily in response to the encroaching threats to Communism from forces seeking to squelch un-American activities, the leadership sought to purify its ranks by implementing rules that rejected elements that could be used by enemies to smear or indict the Party. Yet within the MCS, those restrictions were largely ignored. According to Miriam Johnson, an MCS cook in the 1940s, the antigay policies of the Communist Party had little impact on the actual beliefs and practices of members. "The official position, the party line is one thing," she noted. "The guys around the waterfront were different, that's all, it was just a much more acceptance of differences among people, and I reflected that. I didn't reflect the party attitude, I reflected the waterfront attitude."[31] The "waterfront attitude" allowed greater latitude in admitting diverse behavior along sex, race, and gender lines. Though the Communist Party supported militant MCS workers with political resources and organizational structure, the "waterfront attitude" allowed maritime workers to carve out a relationship with the Party that channeled its revolutionary spirit while refusing to capitulate to Communist anxiety about homosexuality. "Marine Cooks and Stewards," one member recalled, "yes they were gay, but goddammit they stood up."[32] The MCS represented a radical space from which to harness the militant energy harnessed by the Party while adapting it to foreground the experiences of sexual dissidents.

Still, the anxiety that precipitated Communist Party discipline was not entirely imaginary. The encroaching Cold War logic of containment made it risky to openly declare Party membership in the postwar years without finding oneself accused of anti-Americanism. Ted Rolfs, a MCS member, claimed that

> the tragedy was that gay people I knew who were Communists, lesbians and men, homosexuals, were afraid to come out and have it known that they were Communists, and yet they were drawn too like a moth is drawn to fire. They were drawn to it and yet they figured it'd be their death if they really were themselves.[33]

Rolfs's recollection is particularly revealing in its imagining Communism as a form of identity about which one might "come out." Closeting was a familiar feature in the 1940s United States, but it was not necessarily sexuality that was shuttered away from the public eye. The Communist Party attracted sexual dissidents who found themselves in the awkward position of tucking away another socially shunned piece of their lives, but it nonetheless represented a prized tool for dismantling structures of oppression.

This is not to suggest that the MCS was entirely consistent or forthcoming in its support for homosexual members. In a 1943 letter to the *MCS Voice*, for example, member Joseph O'Connor attacked the National Maritime Union, accusing it of attracting "glamour boys and publicity hounds, which the N.M.U. has quite a reputation for."[34] O'Connor's easy dismissal of "glamour boys" suggests how antipathy to homosexuality could emerge even from within a radical union. Yet in spite of occasional slips, the MCS was less inclined toward these public expressions of sexual conservatism than its rivals. O'Connor's insinuation paled alongside the blatant attack by the American Federation of Labor (AFL) on the radical tendencies of the MCS that painted its members as queer. "The Communist Party [is] gamboling in gay debauchery under the guise of organized labor," wrote one critic in a 1940s AFL editorial. "The witching-hour has arrived and the masks are off. . . . [T]he smudged mascara—the smeared lipstick—stand out in garish proof of too much kissing in cozy trysting places."[35] This accusation drew explicitly upon the common knowledge of "trysting" on MCS ocean liners, invoking the established tolerance of homosexuality within the union to disparage its radical elements. The Communist Party's involvement in the MCS became a kind of drag, a form of perversion that the stalwart AFL boldly sought to unmask. The representational slipperiness between homosexuality and radicalism confirmed the deviant politics of the Left.

The radical labor movement's calls for solidarity appealed to working-class sexual dissidents who often found themselves alone and adrift in American society. "In the National Marine Cooks and Stewards—this was the first time for me and I'm sure for other people too—there was an affiliation and camaraderie of tenderness, a certain amount of sex, a great deal of identification," Stephen Blair noted. "No leaders or followers. You and me. Us. We used 'us' more than anything you could possibly think of." The particular intimacy that developed between workers on the ocean liners bled into the solidarity that spurred the working class into radical associations. Blair attributed the success of the leftist union to the presence of so many homosexuals; the closeness of men seeking same-sex affairs produced an intimacy that informed a version of solidarity that admitted "a great deal of identification." "Most seamen—in fact a whole lot of heterosexual seamen—would get closer to a gay man than anybody, as friends," Blair recalled, "because there was such loyalty, such devotion."[36] Labor solidarity offered a solution to social isolation, a function that dovetailed with community practices among sexual dissidents, and in turn, the homosexual members in the MCS strengthened the solidarity and militancy that defined the union.

MCS workers also privileged a particularly playful form of camp that introduced the vernacular practices of urban gay culture into the radical labor movement. Miriam Johnson recalled discovering that Paul Boyle, a Communist and MCS member, was gay. "Once I went to the soup kitchen where the strikers went and sat down and joined them, a number of guys, and any excuse to mention Paul Boyles' name I did. And the guys around said, 'Paul Boyles? You mean—Helen?'"[37] Adopting the name "Helen" allowed the striking workers to both identify Paul as queer and admit Miriam into the community's camp practices. "In the Marine Cooks and Stewards and on the [SS] Lurline," according to Johnson, "it was no question about the femininity, the homosexuality, the talk, the conversation, the appearance, the gestures, the stories that they told you." The sexual dissidence available at sea was indistinguishable from the vernacular performances of gay counterpublics that were becoming visible in cities like San Francisco. MCS ships were not only sites of sex; they also cultivated queer community.

The structure of camp solidarity was further reflected in the visual culture produced within official MCS materials, most notably the *MCS Voice,* the official newspaper of the union. Frank McCormick briefly assumed editorial control of the *Voice*'s launch in 1943 until 1944, at which point E. F. Burke took the reins and transformed it into a popular weekly publication. As a gay Communist MCS member, McCormick was especially attuned to the structure of deviant politics. "Red-baiting will not be permitted in the *Voice,*" McCormick announced in his inaugural issue. "Red-baiting has actually become nothing less than profanity, an obscenity."[38] The melding of anti-Communism and obscenity in McCormick's editorial reframed the discourse of censorship to single out red-baiting as objectionable content. Under McCormick's editorship, the *Voice* introduced a sensibility that balanced radical militancy and queer subtext.

Images played an essential role in mediating between these positions. The *Voice* peppered its radical editorial content with incidental graphics, often unanchored to their surrounding text, that were expected to resonate with members and hold their interest. They appeared alongside radical critique that espoused Marxist analysis and reported on Communist Party politics. Sharing the page with reports from the front lines of the labor struggle, as well as columns such as a feature serving dishy gossip about social affairs by the "the Port Hole Peeper" ("I'm only the Port Hole Peeper. I'm only to peep what I see and tell you all about it one way or another"), these images suggest how the culture of the MCS linked radical labor graphics with queer visuality.[39] Rendered in an offhanded visual vernacular that was more whimsical than militant, the illustrations cued members to the offbeat sensibility of the MCS. Though they were typically unsigned and uncaptioned, the images bore characteristics that defined the aesthetic of the union and introduced a unique site of overlap between political and sexual dissidents.

Many of the illustrations printed in the *Voice* fit into two general categories: images of queer solidarity and depictions of male femininity. Many of these unsigned images were drawn by leftist artist Phyllis "Pele" Murdock de Lappe (also known as Pele deLappe), a San Francisco–based artist who joined the Communist Party and participated in the San Francisco waterfront strikes that radicalized the MCS. Her whimsical illustrations were found in many leftist publications.[40] Pele was enlisted to draw for the *Voice* in 1934, and she described her cartoons as "pretty crude." She continued to produce drawings for the publication into the 1940s, even after John Pittman recruited her to write and illustrate for the *People's World*.[41] Though she was not gay, Pele did, at least later in life, affirm gay rights, eventually publishing, in 1980, an article in the leftist *People's Daily World* about homosexuality in Cuba.[42] In her *Voice* graphics, Pele favored a jaunty style that featured figures in casual poses, often with joined hands and decidedly feminine features. Her commitment to worker solidarity informed her style, which softened some of the masculine iconography typically found in union graphics in favor of gentler images of solidarity.

A typical Pele image from 1945 features three smiling men holding hands, the central figure's arms crossed in a kind of self-embrace that also joins him to his fellow workers (figure 9). This scene imagines solidarity between workers of different races. Yet Pele's illustration urges a specifically queer solidarity that foregrounds casual forms of intimacy. DeLappe's slight figures enjoy one another's company, smiling

FIGURE 9. [Pele deLappe], untitled, *MCS Voice*, April 28, 1948, p. 4.

comfortably in a scene that connotes companionship. The image illustrates the MCS goal of bringing workers together in radical friendship.

Whereas much labor and revolutionary imagery of the mid–twentieth century accentuated depictions of physical might, MCS images framed radical solidarity through quiet moments of same-sex affection and the pleasures of collective bargaining and union participation. The expressions on Pele's figures' faces convey joy and contentment, and their enjoyment of one another offsets representations of labor as drudgery and organizing as tedious. The figures depicted in these incidental illustrations are further stylized as feminine, their hair coifed and their physiques slim. The space for queer intimacy in the workplaces and living quarters on MCS ships was redoubled through vernacular images that visualized union camaraderie as sites of interracial and same-sex intimacy.

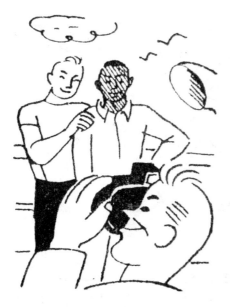

FIGURE 10. [Pele deLappe], untitled, *MCS Voice,* ca. 1948.

An interracial pair in another Pele graphic poses cozily together for a photograph on a ship—the melding of domestic, tourist, and work spaces on ocean liners visualized as a site of solidarity between differently raced workers (figure 10). A smiling figure, toned and adorned in a simple T-shirt, casually drapes an arm over the shoulder of his Black comrade. The latter's arched eyebrows project confidence as he perches his hand on his hip in a modestly camp posture. The cheerful men in the image are depicted engaging in leisure, the unique space of cooks and stewards on boats opening up opportunities for homosociality that replicates the kind of coupling that might occur among travelers on cruise ships. A Pele image of three men camping in a choreographed dance routine (singing waiters, perhaps) again suggests how queer solidarity facilitated enjoyment of homosocial intimacy (figure 11). Even as these workers are defined by labor, work does not come at the expense of pleasure. The associations of the image with forms of work drawing close associations with gay men—waiters, performers—further suggests the insistent queerness of the MCS.

Humor and irony have sometimes been imagined as anathema to radical labor politics, but the camp sensibility commonly found among MCS members spilled over into the graphics of the *Voice.* One image that appeared in several issues from 1945 through 1947 illustrates this radical camp style. The image depicts a handsome marine cook with

FIGURE 11. [Pele deLappe], untitled, *MCS Voice*, March 8, 1945, p. 7.

high cheekbones, parted lips, and carefully coifed bangs, looking side-
long at an ocean liner perched behind him (figure 12). The liner's prow
has been caricatured as a face with feminine lashes, painted lips, and a
wide-open mouth. The oversize features and camp aspect in the illustration veer into a drag affect. The interaction between the boat and the
MCS worker might be summed up in a single double entendre: cruisy.
The shared glances between the figures are both bold and furtive, a
public flirtation that stops short of explicit intimacy. The libidinal
energy of the wide-open mouth of the boat redoubles the sexual frisson
of the image. The cook's features also conform to the typical iconography of the rouged, mascaraed, lipsticked midcentury fairy. This image
was drawn by the Italian American labor artist Giacomo Patri, president of San Francisco's Local 88 chapter of the United American Artists
and a contributor to many San Francisco newspapers. Patri was no
stranger to depicting challenging themes in his art: *White Collar,* his
wordless book of linocuts from 1940, included, in addition to images of
labor and union activities, a depiction of a woman's abortion.[43] Yet the
Voice image represents a departure from Patri's usual style, which typically featured serious subjects rendered in a humorless idiom. The infu-
sion of exuberant camp suggests how the MCS impelled an engagement
with queer cultural signifiers that were legible to the sexual dissidents
who sought refuge in, and shaped, the union.

The combination of political deviance, sexual dissidence, interracialism, and queer domesticity on ocean liners combined to create a unique
space within the MCS for developing radical sexual politics and queer

FIGURE 12. Giacomo Patri, untitled, *MCS Voice*, August 23, 1945, p. 7.

labor aesthetics. The MCS's "waterfront values" did not always square with hard-line Communist ideology, though some members avowed, as we have seen, that sexual dissidence was inseparable from leftist politics. The association of the MCS with sexual dissidence shaped the Left by drawing on Communist organizing and ideology while repurposing labor politics to address the uniquely queer dimensions of maritime life, and the visual culture associated with the MCS *Voice* connected queer visuality with radical labor struggle in ways that corresponded to the vogue for social realism in American painting.

PINKISH VISUALITY

At the end of the 1930s, *Life* magazine commissioned several American artists to pictorially document a series of recent historical events for their predominantly middle-class readers. Among the artists solicited for this project was Paul Cadmus, a young New York painter and close confidant of Lincoln Kirstein, Cadmus's brother-in-law, a gay leftist with close ties to the Communist Party who championed the work of sexual dissidents in the visual and performing arts.[44] Cadmus had achieved notoriety when his satirical painting *The Fleet's In* (1934) was removed from an exhibit at the Corcoran Gallery for depicting the navy in an unsavory light.[45] The painting provoked controversy for its ribald depiction of lusty servicemen, but also because Cadmus depicted a variety of sexual dissidents in his Riverside Park scene. Cadmus's work completed after that controversy confirmed his interest in themes connected to the public spaces familiar to gay New York, bearing titles such as *Greenwich Village Cafeteria* and *YMCA Locker Room*.

Whereas many of Cadmus's paintings from the 1930s explored vernacular subjects broached decades earlier by the "ashcan artists"—city life, cafeterias, and inebriated women and men—Cadmus departed from his urban antecedents when he selected from *Life*'s list of historical events the Herrin Massacre, a horrifying labor dispute from 1922 (figure 13).[46] Labor violence was a familiar subject for leftist artists of the 1930s, and choosing this topic placed Cadmus closer to their inner circle.[47] Cadmus's pursuit of a social viewpoint in his paintings, depiction of working-class subjects, and interest in labor violence suggests how leftist art shaped queer representations during the Depression era.

The bloody conflict just outside Herrin in Williamson County, Illinois, began with a clash between striking members of the United Mine Workers and strikebreaking workers brought in to cross the picket line at the Lester Strip Mine. On June 22, 1922, the situation escalated, and apocalyptic violence broke out when a mob of union workers beat, shot, and hanged scabs and guards in a local cemetery. Twenty-one people died there. Unlike more familiar flash points such as the galvanizing 1929 Gastonia Strike in North Carolina, the Herrin Massacre complicates the narrative of heroes and victims. The inevitability of violent conflict as a result of hiring scabs for union jobs has typically been imagined as a righteous threat rather than literalized in representations of conflict. Though Paul M. Angle wrote a sensationalistic account of the event in 1952, the Herrin Massacre has been largely forgotten—so much so that Philip Eliasoph's description of the event in his discussion of Cadmus's work in his 1977 catalogue of Cadmus's work got nearly every detail wrong.[48] Still, Cadmus's depiction of the episode was apparently faithful to the event in at least one respect: the art critic, Emily Genauer, referred to *Herrin Massacre* in *Art Digest* as "unspeakably bad and gory."[49] Though it had commissioned the piece, *Life* magazine declined to publish Cadmus's painting. It was not reproduced until it appeared in *Art Digest* in 1942.

FIGURE 13. Paul Cadmus, *Herrin Massacre*, 1940. © 2020 Estate of Paul Cadmus / Artists Rights Society (ARS), New York.

Though the image might yield a reading as reactionary—union members are depicted as unruly perpetrators of violence while scabs are treated as sympathetic—the broader context of both 1930s labor politics and Cadmus's history as an unaffiliated leftist invites a more nuanced reading. Cadmus traveled in left-wing circles in the 1930s. He trained at the Arts Students' League and, like many leftists, matured as an artist on the WPA's Public Works of Art Project. He was employed by the WPA when he painted *The Fleet's In,* and he considered this period foundational to his identity as a painter. Cadmus fraternized with leftist artists such as Philip Evergood and Raphael Soyer, and he absorbed the energy of Popular Front–era New York by joining the Artists Union, a leftist group, formed out of the John Reed Clubs in 1933. He signed on to the call for an American Artists' Congress, a Popular Front group founded in 1936 in response to the rise of fascism in Europe and the antifascist struggle in Spain.[50] Though Cadmus never identified as a Communist, Kirstein characterized him as "a fellow-traveling socialist agnostic."[51] Cadmus later referred to his own politics as "pinkish," a clever collapsing of the red and the queer.[52]

Well-attuned audiences detected the ways Cadmus's style and subject matter aligned with leftist visual culture. His scrapbook contains a nasty piece of hate mail he received at the height of the controversy surrounding *The Fleet's In* that included the red-baiting and anti-Semitic inscription "Is this a sample of Communist/Jew culture?"[53] Though it was framed as smear, the letter nonetheless suggests how audiences associated Cadmus's lumpenproletarian subjects with left-wing visual culture. Throughout the 1930s, Cadmus's work echoed that of his social realist compatriots in both subject matter and style, especially when placed alongside satirists such as Reginald Marsh. Leftist representations of muscular workers also allowed Cadmus to indulge his fascination with the male form. "The idealization of labor accelerated in the thirties," Jonathan Weinberg writes, "so that the muscular body of the industrial worker became a central icon of American culture."[54] Cadmus insistently employed an iconography of queer embodiment that was permissible because of the representations of labor that were being produced on the Left. His work comprises a veritable orgy of male flesh, homoerotic scenes, and queer cues.

Herrin Massacre employed the palette of social realism to broaden the artist's subject matter. The image features a crowd of workers in a cemetery, two of whom are depicted in the midst of attacking, with metal pipe and pitchfork, several men who are already injured and bleeding. Behind them, facing in the direction of the painting's viewer, a group of men watch and carouse. One of the victims in the foreground reaches a hand toward his attacker, apparently pleading for mercy. The colors in the image are bright and garish, and the figures on the ground are chiseled as though in marble. The victims are depicted as highly idealized specimens of the male form, while the central figure standing in the rabble, laughing with a cigar in his mouth, boasts a big, full belly. Next to him, a slump-shouldered man aims a pistol at men who appear mortally wounded. Farther in the background of the painting, far to the right and in the top corner of the canvas, another group, this time an interracial and mixed-gender group, hangs a man from a tree, while a second man lies on the ground with a bloodied face. Taken as a whole, *Herrin Massacre* is a spectacularly bloody, vicious painting, shocking in its subject matter and unyielding in its portrayal of mob violence. The tensed arm of the man wielding the metal pipe in the center of the picture plane imbues the image with a kinetic energy that suggests the scene will only become gorier, frozen in a macabre mise-en-scène that has not yet become an aftermath.

Though the violence of *Herrin Massacre* takes clear precedence over other details, the painting is imbued with insistently homoerotic overtones that suggest it might properly be read as allegory. The wounded men in the foreground are represented in various states of undress, their bodies exposing sculpted torsos and highly eroticized anatomy. Though no victim looks directly at the viewer—that gaze is reserved for a young man, modeled on Cadmus himself, bearing witness with a pained expression—their faces are chiseled in accordance with classical standards stretching from Michelangelo's *David* to the photography of F. Holland Day. The anatomical details favored by Cadmus further connect him with a queer visual style: the buttocks on a figure lying facedown are rendered in a shapely form common to Cadmus's work, and two men lie on their backs, propped on their elbows, with their trousers unbuttoned. A third man's pants have been torn off him, and blood is visible between his thighs, suggesting possible sodomy, perhaps by the large-bellied man bearing a long, phallic pipe whose gaze is directed toward this figure.

The title of the painting leads viewers to read it as a representation of the Lester Strip Mine disaster, but the visual cues in the image suggest its sexual dimension—a reading that is reinforced by observing the insistent eroticism of Cadmus's preparatory sketches for the work, one of which included two men in a "69" position. The muscular bodies of the victimized men might render them sympathetic as workers, but it also invites audiences to eroticize them.[55] The interlocking bodies of the disaster's victims also suggest that this scene might be read as a depiction of sexual terror, as though the horde has stumbled upon an orgy and responded with violence. Cadmus's downcast expression while observing the massacre introduces further ambiguity into the painting. He is figured amid the masses, a visual analogue for his solidarity with union workers, but his gaze projects empathy with the victims of the attack. Violence appears in this scene as a baroque spectacle with sexual dissidents cast as martyrs, but Cadmus's self-portrait positions him as both perpetrator and victim.

Herrin Massacre's fetishized violence is redoubled as the viewer looks deeper into the picture plane, in the background of which Cadmus depicts a presumably white man being hanged from a tree. This gruesome detail relates an actual event from the Lester Strip Mine disaster, where a hanging did actually occur. Still, Cadmus's decision to depict that detail connects the massacre with a practice well understood to be closely associated with racist terrorism and violence. Cadmus was familiar with this history, having supported antilynching efforts, including contributing a drawing, *To the Lynching!*, to the 1935 exhibition "An Art Commentary on Lynching."[56] Cadmus was aware at the time when he produced *Herrin Massacre,* then, that lynching bore a particularly odious set of cultural meanings in American culture, and he had incorporated themes relating to racial violence into his career as an artist.[57] Yet the lynching scene in *Herrin Massacre* includes a Black man among the spectators, with a white body hanging from a noose. If *Herrin Massacre* is to be read as an image critiquing violence as a product of labor struggle, and further as a commentary on violence against sexual dissidents, it bears noting that Cadmus flattens the racist targeting of Black men living under Jim Crow by instead depicting eroticized white victims. Further, while he represents a racially diverse mob, his victims adhere to white standards of male beauty. Cadmus invokes signifiers of sexuality, race, and class, but he instrumentalizes racial violence and whiteness to a symbolic end that avoids confronting the deeper history of white terrorism in US history.

Herrin Massacre reflected Cadmus's ambivalent engagement with sexual dissidents, labor politics, and the Left in the 1930s. As an artist, Cadmus was well enough attuned to leftist art practices and politics to draw upon familiar themes emerging from within radical circles through both the selection of his topic and the details of its execution. By repurposing the social perspective favored on the Left to explore sexual dissidence, he was able to articulate a viewpoint that connected his pinkish social critique to the concerns of the leftist cultural front. While he productively incorporated sexuality into his exploration of working-class visuality in *Herrin Massacre,* he stopped short of embracing a full-throated leftist critique in favor of an image that traded on ideological ambiguity and racial ambivalence.

SEX WORK

In US cities, homosexuality was intimately connected with sex work. Havelock Ellis observed in 1933 that "the importance of homosexuality is, again, shown by the prevalence of homosexual prostitution."[58] Thomas Painter, a sex researcher who was particularly interested in male prostitution, estimated in 1941 that "surely ten thousand *normal* boys are male prostitutes, a vicious, criminal social life, while the number who casually prostitute themselves now and again to homosexuals must number several million."[59] The availability of sex in exchange for cash drew men seeking same-sex intimacy into the nation's metropolises, shaping the sexual geography of urban spaces and frustrating associations of sexual acts with identities. Male hustling had long attracted the attention of vice agents, many of whom were convinced that homosexual contact served chiefly as a replacement for female prostitution when the latter was unavailable, or simply inconvenient. As historian George Chauncey has noted, many men seeking female prostitutes were at least putatively willing to engage the services of "fairies," even if they were not actively seeking sex with men. One New York official discovered that a number of sailors had hooked up with male prostitutes because "they might be able to get a girl if they went 'up-town' but it was too far up and they were too drunk to go way up there."[60] Yet prostitution also provided opportunities for those intentionally seeking out same-sex contact to find outlets for their desire under the cover of convenience. Because it opened a number of interpretive possibilities ranging from substitution to last resort, soliciting male hustlers provided opportunistic channels for men wishing to engage in same-sex affairs without attaching those acts to a fixed identity.[61]

Male hustlers explained their participation in sex work in a variety of ways: as a dire circumstance owing to the unavailability of other employment, as an enterprising means to capitalize upon sexual pleasure, and as an expression of homosexual desire. Urban male prostitution offered a space where homosexuality was not discernably devalued in relation to other forms of sex: sex for money was sex for money, and within that hermeneutic, queer sex was, at least on some level, treated as a benign variation on the dissident act of solicitation. In Ralph Werther's 1918 book *Autobiography of an Androgyne,* a meticulously detailed recounting of the author's "sexual abnormality," class struggle appeared at least as often as sex acts, and sex work was positioned as work as much as sex. Werther, a trans sex worker, described prostitution as the "satisfaction of strong instincts, which unsatisfied would make practically impossible the higher life I regularly lived."[62] Though Werther presented sex work as a way to realize her sexual desire and contrasted it with her aspiration to respectability, she also offered explicit descriptions of the violence she confronted at the hands of both the police and the men who solicited her on the street. The labor conditions of hustling—"my career around the military posts," in her phrasing—were inextricable from the violence she encountered.[63] Werther was not a radical, but inasmuch as her narrative sheds light on the labor conditions of sex work, it represents a naturalist depiction of lumpenproletarian life and exposes the conditions experienced by queer sex workers.

Indeed, the entire urban sex industry, such as it was, seemed to invite queer associations, even when it was presumptively heterosexual desire that was being satisfied. Within her decidedly straight "disorderly house," Polly Adler, New York's most famous madam, incorporated all manner of gay culture through both her high-camp persona and her promotion of drag entertainers. One typical evening's entertainment at Adler's establishment included, in her spirited description, "three queer boys who were completely in drag, with wigs, false eyelashes, high-heeled pumps, and beautiful evening gowns," as well as "Mabel, a big fat colored girl clad in white tie and tails, who flaunted a key ring on which was inscribed 'With love' and the nickname of a well-known Park Avenue matron."[64] Prostitution brought sexual dissidents together in ways that pushed against a neat distinction between homo- and heterosexual. Audiences for Adler's entertainments included men seeking sex with women, women selling sex to men, and promiscuous nightlife habitués who were open to anything.

Cabarets, another significant site of queer urban entertainment, were often targeted by antivice forces, in part because their mode of nightlife was perceived as too close to sex work and thus prone to illegal violations of decency.[65] Historian Nan Alamilla Boyd notes that in the theaters of San Francisco, "prostitutes mingled with queers" while "female impersonators transported the language and gestures of a nascent queer culture to the popular stage."[66] Urban speakeasies also harbored homosexuality and sex work, particularly in the nation's mixed-race "black-and-tan" saloons. In Chicago, historian Kevin Mumford notes, "although speakeasies represented only 9 percent of the total number of institutions investigated" by the city's notorious Committee of Fourteen, "they accounted for 78 percent of all legal violations of prostitution that the committee uncovered."[67] Homosexuality, prostitution, and performance went hand in hand, and the slackening of puritanical values attending to soliciting and selling sex allowed for a wide range of queer opportunities for workers to make money. It also introduced labor into discussions of homosexuality.

Yet in spite of the implicit narrative about work that attended to representations of prostitution, the cozy alliance between sex workers and homosexuals seemed by some also to bespeak a shared antagonism toward labor radicalism. In 1934, *The Organizer,* a local publication of the Minneapolis General Drivers' Union, published a cartoon satirizing mayor A. G. Bainbridge, who had allied with a group called the Citizens' Alliance against the city's labor unions. In this image, the artist depicted Bainbridge as a highly feminized pansy clutching a buxom sex worker ("prostitute press") in an alliance with capitalism against the "just men" representing the union boys.[68] In this cartoon, the artist embellishes Bainbridge's thinning pate with a towering blond coif—a flourish that caricatured the detested mayor with a common signifier of the urban homosexual. Prostitutes and pansies were natural bedfellows, and they were rarely allowed to be on the same side as the "just men" at the vanguard of the labor movement.

Leftist writers more often invoked prostitution as a metaphor for the excesses of capitalism.[69] In a memorable 1922 attack on the consumerist horrors he found in the *Saturday Evening Post,* Michael Gold characterized the emblematically middlebrow magazine as a "filthy lackey rag, so fat, shiny, gorged with advertisements, putrid with prosperity like the bulky, diamonded duenna of a bawdy house."[70] Especially noteworthy in Gold's vivid description is his suggestion that the fundamental problem of capitalism was that it was *tacky*—a critique that both confirmed Gold's privileging of the proletarian milieu and functioned to distance leftist culture from the faux elegance of a bordello. By the time he published *Jews without Money* in 1930, the Communist Gold had changed his tune significantly: in an early scene, the young narrator is scolded by his mother for taunting Rosie, a neighborhood prostitute, in the streets with his friends. "Murderer!" his mother berates him, "why did you make Rosie cry?"[71]

One by-product of the proliferation of homosexuality and male hustling in American cities was an increased visibility for homosexual contact among the lower and working classes. Writers and artists depicting urban life routinely foregrounded the prevalence of such vice not only in order to control it, whether out of moral objection or because it seemed exploitative to workers, but also because it was impossible to entirely avoid acknowledging its undeniable visibility among the proletariat. Leftist writers, whose aesthetic ideology prioritized "honest" depictions of poor and working-class neighborhoods, many of which overlapped with red-light districts, took ample note of this stalwart feature of the urban landscape. Yet in some instances, radicals allowed for a more capacious representational politics through their depictions of sex work as a form of labor.

On March 13, 1934, Albert Maltz, a young Communist writer who is best known as a screenwriter and playwright—and, later, as a blacklisted member of the Hollywood Ten—published a short story titled "Onward Christian Soldiers" in *New Masses*. Maltz's first-person narrative describes two men, the narrator and his friend Ed, observing an older, wealthy man soliciting a street hustler. Lurking within the corners of a darkened city street—at one point the narrator pulls his friend deeper into the shadows to avoid detection—the men watch as the older man makes "a gesture of disgust" and rebuffs the advances of a female prostitute in favor of a "nice-looking boy with a clean-cut, bony face and a square jaw." Maltz describes in meticulous detail the encounter between the hustler and his client, noting how the wealthy man offered him a cigarette and lit it for him, made cruisy conversation ("a cigarette's good once in a while, isn't it?"), and "touched his arm with the gold head of his cane." As the hustler proceeds to the older man's apartment for a promised meal and, readers come to understand, paid sex, the narrator observes the young man crying. After seeing the scene through to its conclusion, the narrator and his companion bemoan their powerlessness to help the dispossessed boy, noting that "there are sixteen million like them." As they listen to a Salvation Army band playing in the distance, "[H]ell," Ed declares, "what this country needs in a good revolution."[72]

"Onward Christian Soldiers" suggests how Depression-era leftists responded to male hustling as a site for exploring economic relations through sexual dissidence. By emphasizing the exploitative dimensions of sex work between men, Maltz was able to bring together long-standing anxieties about homosexuality and capitalism as entwined sites of perversion, sexual as well as economic. Indeed, the term "perversion" appeared far more frequently within leftist publications as a description of capitalism than it did referring to homosexuality. The overlap between capitalism's fundamental immorality and prostitution's craven disregard for human intimacy produced ambiguity that leftists invoked in order to emphasize the debasement of the United States. Capitalism and sex work were represented as intertwined symptoms of a culture in the throes of greed, self-interest, and commodification. On its most basic level, male hustling seemed to represent the purest distillation of capitalism's most exploitative excesses. It cut to the core of capitalism's rapacious nature, and it functioned as a shorthand for an entire system gone off the rails.

Yet even Maltz's moral outrage did not satisfy all *New Masses* readers. In April 1934, the magazine published a letter from Barney Conal, a subscriber who was later named as a Communist during the Cold War House Un-American Activities Committee (HUAC) hearings. Conal struggled "to understand why the *New Masses* printed" Maltz's story. Conal distilled the narrative to its fundamentals: "[T]wo young men, at first inferentially and then obviously, class-conscious, watch a starving kid being exploited by a rich pervert." This latter character, also described by the letter writer as a "fat pederast," clearly symbolized "the degenerate capitalist viciously exploiting" a young man, yet Conal bemoaned how the narrator and his companion "stand there immune to the stench, sheltered from it, watch the crime, shrug their shoulders, emit a few fulsome verbal (social democrat?) squibs, and go their way, wearied by it!"[73] Though Conal rejected the possibility of reading male hustling as anything other than exploitation, his frustration suggests how Maltz's ambivalence about a proper leftist response to sex work failed to satisfy some radical readers. The "social democrats" observing the transaction yearned for a revolution, but, paralyzed by the current system, they allowed for the liaison to proceed.

In spite of persistent representations of prostitution as exploitative, male hustling also introduced a novel site for leftists to imagine prostitution as an industry where workers controlled their means of production. Conceived in economic terms, that is to say, and represented unapologetically within a naturalist literary form, male hustling created space for acknowledging same-sex desire that failed to entirely negate the mutuality of transactional sex. If sex was conceived as work, and if work represented an essential component of human existence, male hustling represented a backhanded form of sexual and economic liberation. These concerns were on prominent display in a controversial chapter from Tom Kromer's 1935 novel *Waiting for Nothing*. Kromer was a twenty-eight-year-old hobo who spent over a year working for the Civilian Conservation Corps (CCC) before writing a book about his experiences on the road. As historian Margot Canaday has noted, the CCC "saw its mission as saving young unemployed men from ruin, including sexual degeneration, and the CCC was regularly credited with keeping boys off the road." Many features—homosociality, transience, and dispossession among them—were shared among CCC workers and vagrants.[74] Kromer occupied both those social positions.

When Kromer published his autobiographical working-class novel, he could not have expected his readers to look too kindly upon the risqué content he included throughout. In fact, by his own admission, Kromer did not anticipate his book finding an audience. "I had no idea of getting *Waiting for Nothing* published," he wrote in an author's note to the book's British edition; "therefore, I wrote it just as I felt it, and used the language that stiffs use even when it wasn't the nicest language in the world."[75] How Kromer "felt it" was spelled out especially clearly in his fourth chapter, where Kromer vividly described having sex with men for money. That section, according to a review in the *New York Times* when the book was published, "describes the most terrible and most degrading of [his] experiences."[76] In fact, the British edition of *Waiting for Nothing* replaced the racy chapter with an insert explaining that the publisher had excised this "particularly terrible experience of Kromer's," which they cut "with reluctance and with shame, merely consoling ourselves with the thought that fortunately the continuity of the book is in no way affected."[77]

Though Kromer was begrudgingly tolerant of the men who paid his bills and provided him shelter, he treated his sex work as indifferently as he did the rest of the train hopping, flopping, and jackrolling that he matter-of-factly detailed in his picaresque novel's other eleven chapters. Kromer begins as an indolent observer, watching "a guy" who "twists and wiggles with mincing steps"; taking note that "his eyelashes are mascara'd" and "his lips are flaming red with lipstick"; and registering that "he smells pretty good" with nearly sociological detachment.[78] "Oho," Kromer laconically comments, "this guy is queer, and he doesn't care who knows it." Kromer, evidently, both knew it and was prepared to act on it, and though he does prickle at the reactions of passersby to his john—"[I]t is misery for me to walk down street with this queer," he writes, because "people stop in their tracks and watch her wiggle"—he nonetheless pursues the queer connection (48). Absent from this account is any threat of violence or overarching squeamishness around sharing the details:

> He lays his hand across my leg. I must not jerk my leg away. He is feeling me out. If I jerk my leg away, he will see that he is not going to make me. This queer will not put out for a meal until he sees that I am a good risk. I leave my knee where it is. These pansies give me the willies, but I have got to get myself a feed. I have not had decent feed for a week. (44)

Though he admits his displeasure as the tryst proceeds, Kromer none-theless acknowledges that his sex is there for the taking if money is there for the making. He is waiting, evidently, for nothing. Even as he refuses to concede any reciprocal desire, Kromer narrates the proceedings in a matter-of-fact style that emphasizes his disinterest far more than any blanket disapproval.

The transactional nature of Kromer's hustling allows him to freely acknowledge the banality of homosexual contact among vagrants. "You can always depend on a stiff having to pay for what he gets," Kromer notes after having sex with another man. "It is chilly here, and I am sleepy. I will have to go to bed sometime" (53). The bed of Kromer's john serves multiple purposes: as a place of rest, a site for work, and a sexual scene. In *Waiting for Nothing*, sex work stripped homosexuality to the barest exchange theory of capitalism: same-sex prostitution signi-fied nothing more complicated than a form of labor and a transfer of money and services, and homosexual desire registered as unremarkable. "This guy is my meal ticket," Kromer blithely notes. "I will go right to his room" (48).

While leftists struggled to connect male hustling and labor politics, the routine appearance of prostitution in leftist writing points to a lin-gering interest in admitting sex work into the purview of radical con-cern. These representations participated in a narrative marginalizing sex work as a form of exploitation and perversion, but also as a fact of proletarian life. Though same-sex prostitution was generally regarded as abject even on the Left, attending to the conditions under which sex workers worked, and positioning hustlers as workers, offset some of the puritanical strains found in antivice crusades. Imagining sexual dissi-dents as workers presented a lens through which leftists might envision them as members of the proletariat—which, even outside the sex indus-tries, harbored enough homosexuals to structure other representations within proletarian literature.

SEXUAL DISSIDENCE AT WORK

The conventions of proletarian literature offered an important site for thinking through how sex and labor were intertwined. For some leftist writers, work was imagined to be inextricable from homosexuality, even when it did not take the form of prostitution. Radical writers rou-tinely represented labor as a highly sexed enterprise, detailing incur-sions of sexuality into the world of work and envisioning labor as a signifier of sexual identity. In some instances, sexing labor allowed left-ists to reinforce recognizable tropes of particular professions as indica-tively gay. Professors, for example, were represented as a profession that seemed especially attractive to homosexuals. In his 1932 novel *Beyond Desire,* Sherwood Anderson, a highly regarded leftist writer, depicted a professor as gay and described his attraction to Red, one of his students. "He might have been a trifle on the queer side," Anderson writes of the professor, who "had spoken of the beauty of [Red's] body. . . . [H]e always seemed about to caress Red with his hands." Alone in his office, the professor's eyes "became suddenly, strangely, like a woman's eyes, the eyes of a woman in love," which "had given Red a queer uncertain feeling sometimes in the man's presence."[79] H. T. Tsiang similarly represented an intellectual professor as sexually dissi-dent in his 1935 novel *The Hanging on Union Square.*[80]

Other jobs seemed to invite associations with sexual dissidence even if the occupation was not itself connected with homosexuality. In Dan-iel Fuchs's proletarian novel *Summer in Williamsburg,* a character named Cohen tries to get directions from a cab driver. "He saw Cohen's splotched face, the goggles, the plastered hair, and the strange expres-sion. He must be one of these guys, the driver said to himself. 'Are you making passes at me, dearie?' he said with hard sweetness."[81] In a *New Masses* article from 1926, David Gordon, a semiregular contributor to *New Masses* who wrote another piece that got the magazine censored, recounted a variety of experiences working as a messenger for Western Union. During one of his deliveries, Gordon found himself in the office of a man who had more on his mind than sending a telegram. "It seemed as though the sender was not particularly anxious to have the message sent immediately," Gordon wrote. "He invited me to a seat; told me to throw off my rain-cape and offered me cigarettes." The two exchanged some benign repartee: "Do you think that cigarettes are harmful for a boy?" Gordon asked as he took one from the pack. "Why no. There's nothing like them to steady the nerves," the client replied before he "asked me to stay a little while." Though he did not welcome these advances, "a twenty-eight cents tip didn't so poorly cover the time I spent with that man."[82]

William Rollins Jr.'s 1934 proletarian novel *The Shadow Before* was one of several fictional works appearing in the 1930s that were modeled on the 1929 Gastonia Strike. (Anderson's *Beyond Desire* was another.) The uprising served as a flash point for leftist labor organizing through-out the Depression era. Rollins signaled the convergence of homosexuality and labor at Gastonia's Loray Mill—refigured in his novel as Baumann-Jones—through his character Olsen, a heroic gay mill worker and unapologetic femme who illustrates how leftists imagined labor as a site of queer possibility.[83] Barbara Foley describes the work as an emblematic "'collective' strike novel."[84] As discussed in the previous chapter, Rollins emphatically defended his pluralistic vision of the proletariat in a 1935 *New Masses* article titled "What Is a Proletarian Writer?," where he specifically named "a homosexual" as one of the characters driving the action in *The Shadow Before*.[85] Olsen was that homosexual.

Even before Olsen is introduced, the specter of homosexuality looms over *The Shadow Before*. In an early scene, a character's thoughts drift into a daydream where he will "walk home through Sundaydeserted streets and sit by my window and watch the ferries and the fairies—. That's something!"[86] Rollins introduces Olsen, a "squeaky-voiced" worker whose "fat buttocks jerk up and down as he walked away," using the same language as in his descriptions of the bobbins in the Baumann-Jones textile mill's machines: "UP; down. UP; down." Olsen's walk conforms to a common understanding of homosexuality at the time. "The homosexual, typically, has a peculiar walk," Thomas Painter wrote in his study of homosexuals,

> walking so that the ball of the foot, and not the heel, strikes the ground first and then the heel, as if one were almost walking on tip-toe, but came down lightly on the heel at every step. With the resulting hip-swinging and shoulder-swaying motion of the body, this is the typical homosexual glide.[87]

UP; down. In *The Shadow Before*, Olsen's legibly queer body becomes a literal embodiment of mill's machines.

Even more pronounced than Olsen's feminine walk is his same-sex desire, which is primarily directed toward his fellow worker Doucet. Olsen's coworkers at the mill constantly tease Owen about his infatuation. "Doucet's got the prettiest blue eyes!" a fellow worker, Bozo, camps in imitation of Olsen's fawning affection: "*[O]h, dearie!*" Bozo repeatedly refers to Olsen as a "goddamn fairy" (101). Rollins's familiarity with gay argot—*dearie* was high camp, and *fairy* was a common term at the time—suggests his sensitivity to the homosexual signifiers that later impel Olsen to militancy. Bozo connects Olsen's gender transgression, work, and sexual desire. After Olsen is offered a drink, Bozo again mocks Olsen: "That liquor ain't made for no lady, man! Oh, dear! dear me! . . . It'll kill her!" before adding, "[T]hen what'll Doucet do when he's hard up?" (99, 98, 99).

For his part, Doucet also recognizes Olsen's desire for him. "He had seen Olsen peer at him," Rollins writes; "felt the boy thinking of him, even when those fishy eyes, entombed in their opaque lenses, were turned away" (100). While Doucet does not desire Olsen, neither does he feel the antipathy toward him that other workers, especially Bozo, do. In fact, Olsen's moving deeper into the labor struggle impels Doucet to commit himself more fully to the movement. In part, this turns out to be because Olsen's sexual dissidence proves to be a source of strength. His sexuality overlaps with his radical labor politics in two registers. First, it is within the workplace that he experiences intimacy with another man, producing a space to indulge his same-sex desire. Second, by committing himself to labor radicalism, Olsen is able to channel his desire for Doucet into a broader working-class solidarity that reaches a crescendo when the strike turns violent.

Rollins represents Olsen's radicalization as emerging from the same impulse as the pursuit of his queer sexuality. After he witnesses some thugs throwing rocks at the novel's labor organizer, Marvin, Olsen approaches Doucet to offer his services as a volunteer guard for the workers. Olsen imagines getting closer to Doucet as they move deeper into radical labor militancy. These fantasies do not oscillate between sexual and political desire as much as they intentionally confuse these categories:

> "Doucet I—" Olsen cleared his throat. "I want to be a guard," he said, looking down at the gun.
> (As he dreamed his way along the streets toward the hall, Doucet's dark face had lit up with a smile. He clamped his hand on Olsen's shoulder. "That's the stuff, Olsen," he said. "I knew you had it in you!"
> (Or, Doucet had laughed mockingly. "*You* be a guard? What the hell can *you* do?" And Olsen, looking him in the eye, had said, simply: "I can die—if I can die under you." And Doucet gazed at him a moment, incredulous; and then slowly held out his hand and gripped his own.) (222)

This passage is rich with sexual imagery and tension that is overtly homoerotic: readers can hardly ignore the libidinal force of Olsen's longing gaze at Doucet's gun, Doucet's suggestive hand clamping Olsen's shoulder as he voices his gruffly masculine approval, Olsen's loving commitment to "die under" Doucet, or Doucet's momentary gaze and comradely handshake. Yet the scene also imagines Olsen's radicalism as the staging ground for his queer subjectivity, imagined here as a form of futurity.[88] The inextricable knotting of sexual dissidence and leftist politics constitutes the essence of Olsen's subjectivity and a signature feature in Rollins's radical novel. The scene conflates Olsen's sexual and political desire, in effect suggesting that one form of liberation begets another. Olsen's queer desire is not sacrificed to his politics. His politics are, rather, a natural outgrowth of his queerness.

The theme of martyrdom explored in Cadmus's *Herrin Massacre* also appears in *The Shadow Before*. In one of the most dramatic scenes of violence in the novel, Olsen, arrested for participating in the strike at the mill, is beaten in jail as Gomez, the attending officer, tries to extract information from him. Rollins again highlights Olsen's queer desire as he is beaten, his mind repeating "Doucetdoucetdoucet*doucet.*" Yet even as the officer tries to beat information out of him, Olsen "remained quiescent, silent, upheld by one word" (238–39). The "one word" maintaining Olsen silence is the name of his beloved Doucet. Olsen simultaneously becomes a martyr to both the labor movement and his sexual desire. His silence becomes a vehicle of his sexual dissidence and his militant political stance.

Olsen comes to understand the complicity of the state in targeting him as a worker and homosexual. As he lies on the floor of his jail cell, an officer taunts him as "the fat little fairy that used to be down the Baumann-Jones." The comment initially punctures the radicalism that had been swelling in Olsen: "[T]he pride was gone like a burst bubble, leaving only overwhelming pain, weakness, unendurable heaviness" (239). But just then, the strikers assemble outside. "And suddenly," Rollins writes, "that group was a long line, snakedancing hand in hand in front of the dark massive courthouse," the sound of their songs and chants resounding with such force "that the echoes came back from the greystone wall" (240). In this moment, Rollins swaps out Olsen's individualized narrative for an image of collectivity that mobilizes the mill workers in support of the strike. Olsen's abjection thus serves as a catalyst for the movement and the transformation of Rollins's narrative from a character study into a collective labor novel.

In *The Shadow Before,* William Rollins Jr. drew on an emblematic Depression-era labor struggle to connect radical direct action to sexual dissidence. Doucet's sympathetic response to Olsen's queer desire facilitated his labor radicalism, just as Olsen's sexual dissidence, which made him an enemy of the state, was inextricable from collective forms of resistance. Rollins's sexual politics cannot be extracted from his leftist sympathies, and his depiction of a sexed workplace as a vehicle for solidarity between workers demonstrates how the form of proletarian literature, especially in its demand for a denouement absorbing individual struggle into collective resistance, offered a useful genre for connecting homosexuality and radical labor politics. Olsen's sexuality both informs and announces his labor radicalism, but it is only against the backdrop of collective protest that his individual victimhood can be understood as the engine that drives the labor movement.

The Left in the 1930s and 1940s, overwhelmingly concerned with labor and class, adopted a militant stance that pitted workers against bosses. The Marxist principle that workers should own the means of production precipitated an intensive reexamination of what constituted work, whose work was valued, and how the principle of solidarity expanded the definition of a worker. The building of a radical working-class movement pushed leftists to adopt an antagonistic position toward the state, in the process producing overlap between workers and other groups discarded by normative politics and the dominant culture. While the distinction between sex and labor was often understood as discrete, leftists could not entirely ignore their frequent overlap both in the workplace and in cultural representations. Leftist organizers, writers, and artists invoked labor as a vehicle for advancing a radical politics of sexuality. Sexuality further intruded on work in ways that frustrated efforts to conceive radicalism as disconnected from sexual dissidence. Labor politics on the Left were increasingly inextricable from sexual politics.

CHAPTER 5

"Socialism & Sex Is What I Want"

*Women, Gender, and Sexual Dissidence in
the 1930s and 1940s*

In April 1934, Maxwell Bodenheim, a leftist Bohemian writer, published
his poem "To a Revolutionary Girl" in *New Masses*. "You are a girl,"
Bodenheim announced in direct address, "a revolutionist, a worker."
While, "like every other worker," the revolutionary girl was "sworn to
give the last, undaunted jerk" of her body to fight "against the ruling
swine," she also "long[ed] for crumpled 'kerchiefs" and "nonsense understood / Only by a lover." In his attempt to laud the revolutionary women
animating working-class radicalism, Bodenheim stumbled upon ideas
about gender that highlighted a perceived pull between Marxist militancy
and girlish crushes. This tension was resolved for Bodenheim by pointing
to a utopian, postrevolutionary future where he envisioned a "time of
violets" marked by "less impeded tenderness." Until that point, save for
"an hour, now and then," girls were expected to tuck away their decidedly feminine need for love, intimacy, and "ribboned sleeves," and instead
were encouraged to fight for the eventual freedom to prioritize their normatively gendered desires.[1]

Around the time when Bodenheim was crafting his influential paean
to revolutionary girls, Betty Millard "became caught up in the social
movements of the day and went to work for the Labor Research Association," following which her name was added to the masthead of
New Masses. Though she did not publish her most famous work—a
Communist tract titled *Women Against Myth*—until 1948, Millard
had already joined the antifascist movement in support of the Spanish

Republic while an undergraduate at Barnard, and she soon traveled to Cuernavaca with Hope, a woman who, to that point, "was clever, poised, and sexy, and she intended to get married and have children as soon as one of her boyfriends said the word." During the trip, Millard fell ill, and as she struggled with fever, Hope "seized the thermometer from me and put it in her own mouth—she said she wanted to catch whatever I had and she didn't want to live without me." Rather than waiting for her time of violets, Millard connected her revolutionary politics with her pursuit of sex and intimacy with women, dedicating remarkable energy to building a movement that refused to forestall her impeded tenderness. "I was in love with her, partly because she was charming and partly because I had wrested her away from Bobbie, a very cute lesbian with curly hair. But I was conscious of my inferior position; I was lacking a most important thing and I've lacked it all my life: self-confidence. There's nothing more sexy than self-confidence, or at least the appearance of it. Hope had plenty of it. Maybe it was basically that she had options sexually and I see now that I never really had any."[2]

Millard adopted a butch style ("I was very comfortably uncomfortable in my black tie & men's jacket"), and, despite misgivings about her self-confidence, she was bold in her pursuit of other women. "Socialism & sex is what I want all right," she wrote in a 1934 diary entry after enjoying dinner with a male comrade; "I just didn't happen to explain to him which sex."[3] The revolutionary woman, if one takes Millard's life over Bodenheim's prescription, was perfectly apt at bringing her sexuality and radicalism into alignment, and pursuing sexual pleasure was inextricable from the here and now of radical struggle.

The tension women on the Left confronted through their status as women impelled many to bring together feminist theorizing, class militancy, and leftist movement building. At times, these efforts took the form of pamphlets, articles, and books that addressed women's role in the Communist Party and broader society. At other times, leftist women called out men who diminished their revolutionary work. When *New Masses* published a note to readers in 1947 that named eleven male editors and staff members but listed no women, Elizabeth Gurley Flynn, an important Communist Party activist who had an extended affair with fellow radical Marie Equi, sent a letter to editor Joseph North, warning him that "the women are on your path again!" "For heaven's sake," Flynn wrote,

> when you list an editor's meeting of eleven men, couldn't you name a couple of women? It would make my life easier and yours too, I suspect. . . . Are

your meetings all stag? If I become a rip-roaring feminist, you'll be partly to blame on N.M.'s staff. Please show this to the boys next time they meet. Surely one among you must become woman conscious or at least have us on your conscience.[4]

North sent an apologetic reply. "I don't know how the devil to explain the editors' meeting of eleven men without having mentioned any of the gals involved," he wrote. "I guess the best explanation is the real one: the staff, all of us, are not conscious enough of the question you pose." North's awkward mea culpa suggests an obeisance to women that undermines generalizations about their sublimated role in shaping the Left.

Among themselves, women vented their frustration with male leadership and built a collective response by writing criticism and formulating Marxist analyses of women and society. Jeanne Vermeersch, a French Communist, sent a clipping of the *New Masses* article to Betty Millard, underlining the list of men and adding a note: "Where is the other half of the population?" In an homage to radical collage, Vermeersch also clipped an advertisement for a forum on the question "Are Progressive Men Progressive about Women?" and pasted it below what had been a solicitation for new subscribers with the heading "Here's my answer."[5] Women were on the path, and their commitment to liberation determined their own involvement within the Left while pushing men to make space for their voices and ideas.

For sexual dissidents on the Left, women's struggles were even more pronounced and complicated.[6] Pursuing socialism and sex sometimes demanded ambiguation around which sex one wanted, as Betty Millard experienced, but at other times the leftist emphasis upon militancy, solidarity, and bold action allowed for a performance of butch toughness and cultivated female intimacy. The gender politics of the Left intersected with homosexuality in uneven ways, and thinking through the relationship between sex, gender, and revolution often fell upon women whose sexual dissidence informed their relationship to the Left. Radical women demanded—and created—opportunities to put queer women on the front lines of revolution and to expand the forms of sexual and gender expression that leftists could embody. Further, the deviance of the Communist Party attracted women who imagined their sexual dissidence as consistent with, and even essential to, revolutionary struggle. Queer women were both drawn into and played a vital role in defining the Left.

WOMEN, SEX, AND THE LEFT

Socialist women between 1870 and 1920, Mari Jo Buhle has written, "demonstrated that the prospect for a new civilization rested upon broader principles than class struggle."[7] Particularly among immigrant women, Socialism offered a form of politics and a set of principles that challenged patriarchy while pushing against capitalism's excess. Working women, who confronted limited job opportunities, workplace discrimination, low wages, and gendered forms of precarity, advocated for strengthening labor laws and building a more just economy. They also connected economic factors to their status as women, both demanding recognition of household labor as work and noting how the structure of capitalism relied upon women's continued marginalization in a society where they made up half the population. Prominent advocates for women's rights such as Jane Addams and Margaret Sanger connected feminist concerns with class analysis. At the same time, Socialist women failed to fully connect race and sex, as evidenced in, most notably, Sanger's support for eugenics. The settlement-house movement's efforts to eradicate prostitution further stigmatized women's sexuality even as it confronted their oppression.[8] Though Addams shared a life with Mary Rozet Smith, sexual dissidence was never her public concern.

The Bohemian dimensions of Socialism in the 1910s and 1920s allowed for a playful relationship to sexuality for leftist women, emblematized in the vibrant culture of Greenwich Village. Mabel Dodge hosted heady salons to bounce around ideas about "sex, penology, anarchism, birth control, poetry, and modern art," as Daniel Aaron writes, among "notorious radicals who were happily subverting the social order by word and deed." Antibiotics for treating syphilis were the cost of entry into this raucous vanguard.[9] "Nearly every thinking person is in revolt against something," Dodge declared in 1913, and revolution touched every dimension of human experience.[10] As the song "The Greenwich Village Epic" described, "Here the modernist complexes, / And the intermediate sexes— / Fairyland's not far from Washington Square."[11] Neither were the headquarters of the Socialist Party, or, later the Communist Party.

Leftist writer Tess Slesinger's satire of socialist intellectual culture in her 1934 novel The Unpossessed deftly captures the sexual charge infusing a group of radicals seeking to create a socialist magazine, including representations of the queer dynamics animating the central players. While adherence to Marxist principles impels the self-described Black

Sheep's creation of a magazine along the lines of *The Masses,* the legendary publication that balanced radical politics and sexual libertinism from 1911 to 1917 (and attracted the attention of censors who eventually shut it down) by aiming, in the words of John Reed, "to everlastingly attack old systems, old morals, old prejudices—the whole weight of outworn thought that dead men have saddled on us—and to set up new ones in their places," the sexual affairs, liaisons, and sociality among the so-called Black Sheep in the novel speaks to the spirit of excitement and energy that linked socialism and sexuality among radicals.[12] Women such as Slesinger were animated by the thrill of building something new, and while this might have put them in the company of men, it also created space for women to enter into the vivacious conversation.

The ascendance of the Communist Party presented an opportunity for activists to reframe women's place on the Left and demand that sexism be made a key part of the platform. According to Rosalyn Baxandall, "more females joined the CP than any other socialist party, and especially in the 1930s and 1940s engaged in workers' and community struggles."[13] While the Party grappled with the role of women in a movement that struggled to connect class and gender, the radical energy of the Depression years galvanized women to push against male leaders who minimized their concerns and relegated them to roles as, in leftist writer Meridel Le Sueur's words, the "Party's housekeepers."[14] The alcohol-and-rage culture of radical men especially frustrated queer leftist writers such as Josephine Herbst. In 1931, Herbst complained to Katherine Anne Porter about a man who left a meeting where women's issues were raised. He stormed out "full of a masculine importance you and I will never know, alas, and came back somewhat boozy but so far as I could see with not one idea the smarter." Herbst was frustrated by her male comrades' refusal to listen to women's critique, trying to explain that "as long as the gents had bourgeois reactions to women they would probably never rise very high in their revolutionary conversations," but finding that "said remarks rolled off like water."[15]

Communist women theorized women as a key group in class analysis and pointed to the model society in the Soviet Union both by coming into contact with revolutionary women in their travels and through writing and representations of Russian women. Ruth McKenney, a columnist for *New Masses* beginning in 1940, noted in a piece titled "Women Are Human Beings" that "nobody can write about the 'woman question' today in good faith without stating the fact that women have been completely and unconditionally emancipated in the Soviet

Union."[16] To write, perchance to dream—but it was a dream many leftist women shared. As Sheila Rowbotham writes, "[T]he immediate task of creating a communist society from the chaos of the Soviet Union in the twenties required a great effort of self-discipline—in fact the good old virtues of the bourgeoisie in early capitalism: hard work, abstinence, and repression."[17]

In the 1930s and 1940s, the Left's gender politics became a focused site of analysis, both within women's actual lives and in the representations that were centralized within the cultural front. As Michael Denning has written, "[T]he period between 1929 and 1948 marked a moment of crisis and transformation in the sexual organization of work, in gender relations, and in household formations."[18] The Communist Party responded to that crisis by publishing the *Working Woman,* a publication of the Party's National Women's Department (figure 14). Beginning as a newspaper in 1929 and transitioning to a magazine in 1933, the publication changed its name to the *Woman Today* in 1936 as it adapted to the Popular Front. Though its editorial content shifted somewhat over the years, the magazine consistently foregrounded women's issues and was produced by a majority-female staff of journalists and illustrators. The *Working Woman* positioned itself against splashy women's magazines such as *True Story* and the *Woman's Home Companion,* which "appeal to the women on the basis of petty clothes, cooking recipes, care of skin, cosmetics, etc.; all of the points which shove women into the position of making her feel that she has only certain interests in life, that her main tasks are that of a home maker. That her chief desire should be to get a rich man and be a parasite, and that she should ape the rich and forget her class interests."[19] Articles in the magazine frequently took aim at the schlock pushed by romance magazines. Complaining about *Serenade* in 1935, Barbara Alexander trenchantly observed that that magazine's

> tales are calculated to lull the reader into believing that; (1) there will most certainly come a fairy prince who will sweep into one's life and drive all the nasty old bill collectors and landlords away; (2) that there is not one, but maybe two or three such attractive men with good jobs aching to meet you and you only; (3) the Woolworth stores are betting that having read this tripe, you will be standing in line to buy "Tattoo" for eyelashes and brows (on sale at all toilet goods counters) and "Irresistible" perfume, powder, paint and "Lip Lure," also on sale, and that then, you will surely meet your strong, broad-shouldered, silent, witty, clever, adoring ONE. (Who has a good job.)[20]

FIGURE 14. Untitled, *The Working Woman*, November 1930, p. 8.

Nonetheless, the conflicted gender politics of the Communist Party remained on occasional display, as in a 1935 subscription drive for the *Working Woman* that awarded its winner a "choice of LENIN—Complete Set of His Works, or, Cast aluminum cooking pots, two of them, guaranteed for long wear."[21] What did Communist women really want?

The iconography of protest produced a road map for radical women's activism. One typical cover of the *Working Woman* from July 1935 featured a cluster of picket signs that includes slogans such as "Fights against War and Fascism," "Reduce Meat Prices," "Free Birth Control Clinics," and "Equal Pay for Equal Work for Women." The signature antifascism that dominated the Communist Party in the mid- to late 1930s was paired with household economics, reproductive choice, and income equality. While the *Working Woman* focused primarily on American labor issues, the internationalist orientation of the Communist Party, even outside the broadening antifascist movement, also created space for covering pressing topics such as "Bermuda Women Denied Vote" and "Turkish Women Strike."[22]

The intersections of race, class, and sex were also regularly discussed among leftist women. The triple oppression faced by Black working-class women was raised as an issue of paramount concern among women on the Left. As Erik S. McDuffie writes, "[B]lack left feminists countered prevailing assumptions within the CPUSA and the black Left that constructed the 'worker' as a white male factory laborer, the 'working woman' as white, and the shop floor as the determinant of class consciousness."[23] A 1930 article in the *Working Woman* acknowledged that "Negro women are being exploited under the worst conditions," and another announced that "the Negro women in the mining section are just as militant as the whites in the picket line. They fight shoulder to shoulder down in Powhatan, are out every morning at four to fight oppression."[24] The *Working Woman* regularly published articles about lynching, including extensive coverage of the Scottsboro case, and confronted Jim Crow segregation. When these articles appeared, they most often proposed greater attention to interracial organizing rather than identifying multiple forms of oppression. More intersectional analysis tended to appear in the streets, which, Irma Watkins-Owens notes, "became the most viable location for an alternative politics," and in private gatherings hosted by Black women such as Grace Campbell, a friend of Claude McKay and Elizabeth Gurley Flynn who joined the Workers Party in 1927. Spaces controlled by Black women such as Campbell, McDuffie argues, incubated "a revolutionary black nationalist, anti-capitalist outlook that was open to sexually transgressive ideas and practices [and] informed black Communist women's burgeoning black left feminism."[25]

A broad social demand that women were destined for marriage connected gender and labor politics. Women who worked outside the home confronted an unequal status whereby they were branded as temporary workers while waiting for a husband—a situation remarked upon in a 1931 article in the *Working Woman* about women advocating for fair wages in Chicago. These women faced a limited repertoire of career options: "Quit, get married, or die."[26] The magazine's editors opposed "forced marriage," pointing to instances when, for example, "the Kansas City Power and Light Company tells its young women employees to hurry up and ask this question ["Will you marry me mister?"] of the first man they can grab if they wish to keep their jobs." In contrast, in the revolutionary society, "women work as the men do, earn salaries as the men do, and can marry or stay single if they please, and there is no time limit."[27]

When sexuality did appear in the *Working Woman*, it was most often in the context of exploitation. The particular problem of sexual harassment in the workplace was occasionally discussed, as in an exposé written in 1934 by "a Hollywood extra girl." Recounting life on the set, she recalled how women pursuing such work might expect to "stand humbly by, listening to a dance director call you every filthy name invented by modern language, while an assistant director snoops about the lot, seeking to interest visiting firemen and Rotarians in your well-advertised physical charms."[28] More frequently mentioned was prostitution, which was understood through a Marxist lens as a form of capitalist exploitation. In a cartoon from September 1931, for example, a shame-faced woman with head hanging down and face in her hands stands on a pedestal surrounded by the usual caricature of cigar-chomping fat cats with self-satisfied grins (figure 15). "The pedestal is but an auction block," the cartoon announces, drawing parallels between the trafficking of women and slave auctions. The closed factories in the background of the image further suggest how the economic crisis precipitated by the collapse of capitalism "forced" women into sex work. While the cartoon suggested a leftist critique that resisted shaming women for sexual choices or circumstances, the bracketing of prostitution in the framing of capitalist exploitation also advanced a narrative of the fallen woman that worked against more-Bohemian celebrations of women's sexual agency. "Working mothers, your daughters are not to blame," the publication announced. "You are not to blame. Capitalist society creates prostitution as a solution to unemployment and then in true hypocritical fashion acts outraged and throws the burden on its victims."[29] This, too, had a racial dimension. One article profiled a Black woman arrested for prostitution, who explained to a white woman sharing her cell, "[M]ostly why more of us colored girls are in here is because the white girls get more money, and so can bribe the police, while we do not get enough to buy ourselves off."[30] Lesbianism rarely appeared at all, and when it did, as in a review of *These Three*, an adaptation of Lillian Hellman's *The Children's Hour*, it was dismissed as "unnatural love for one woman by another."[31]

Finally, birth control and abortion were discussed openly in the *Working Woman*. In a 1933 issue, a woman described her abortions due to lack of access to birth control. "I can't afford more children," she wrote. "I have practiced home-made methods to no use, and I average at least two abortions a year, which I do for myself, and which are ruining my health." Meanwhile, an unemployed male worker complained that "I've tried hard to find out about birth control, but people put you off with stuff that's no good, and where I live they say it's against the law. I bet my boss who laid me off gets it all right from his private doctor and his wife doesn't have to go through such hard times."[32]

Perhaps most significantly for queer women on the Left, radicals challenged the notion that indecency pertained to sex rather than to class exploitation. Sasha Small, writing in the *Working Woman*,

FIGURE 15. Untitled, *The Working Woman*, September 1931, p. 3.

complained that "the church at this moment is on a crusade against the indecent movie. Indecent, meaning, love affairs between unmarried people, the birth of illegitimate children and kisses that last longer than a certain number of seconds." In contrast, "no one has begun a crusade against the poisonous anti-working class propaganda in the movies."[33] In 1928, Elizabeth McCausland, a leftist art critic, journalist, and, later, three-decade lover of photographer Berenice Abbott, submitted an essay, "The 'Blue Menace,'" to WBZ, a Westinghouse-owned radio affiliate. In this eight-page exploration of the deleterious effects of "professional patriots," McCausland articulated a radical critique of the antivice crusaders who united political and moral threats under the guise of preserving American values. Channeling a phrase introduced by the Congregational minister Vivian T. Pomeroy, McCausland railed against the "spirit of intolerance" pervading charges of "moral laxness" that were invoked to silence radical—and often feminist—perspectives from being voiced in the public sphere.[34]

Though the radical gender analysis remained attenuated even within a Communist Party that touted the total equality of the sexes in the Soviet utopia, women on the Left did manage to push for leftist positions that foregrounded their experiences and exposed their social conditions. Through analysis of phenomena ranging from sex work to racism, leftists advanced feminist ideas that both shaped the Left and drew women deeper into the movement. These ideas not only appealed to queer women; they were also shaped by them.

QUEER WOMEN ON THE LEFT

On June 28, 1947, Betty Millard hosted what appears to have been one hell of a party in her West 4th Street apartment. "The people downstairs are going to be away for the week-end," she wrote in her invitation;

> we've got the pedal on the piano tied up again with a hunk of chicken wire, so—you can sing and stomp on the floor and all hell can break loose here this Saturday night if that's the mood you're in. A wonderful trombone player we know is coming over with some of his friends and if you're an aficionado of long-hair, we've got that, and if you're a short-hair they've got that too. If you just want to sit under the plane trees and discuss the relations between the sexes, you can do that in the garden out back.[35]

While this rip-roaring queer party promised to be a good time, Millard was not one to pass up a chance to make her event work for the working class. "The cost of all this is a mere buck, plus some negligible sum if you should find yourself thirsty, and the money goes to *New Masses*." Given that the Left has so often been characterized as homophobic, misogynist, and boring, it is interesting to learn of a party promising whatever you're into alongside dissections of patriarchy and radical fundraising. As Daniel Hurewitz has noted in his study of Bohemian Los Angeles, sexual libertines and radical activists often occupied the same spaces.[36] For lesbian leftists in the 1930s and 1940s, they often occupied the same bodies as well.

Betty Millard was intimately connected to the world of both homosexuality and the Left. For her, liberating the working class was not mere theory. She moved between jobs frequently, from checking dresses at Macy's (six weeks) to operating a turret lathe at Ford (nine and a half months). She worked as a receptionist (four weeks and three days) and night blood-bank manager at the Brooklyn Red Cross (three weeks) before moving into editorial work at *New Masses* (three years, nine months), the *Los Angeles Review of Books* (five years), and Henry Holt and Company (seven months).[37] She traveled widely, including trips to Paris, London, China, the USSR, and British Guyana. She also embraced her sexuality from as early as 1933, when she wrote in her diary, "I took a long step into the dark, toward a dark place from which there is no returning. But I think it was an inevitable conversation which would have happened without the gin, and I think it has been coming for a year, since the 4th of November. Now I am wondering where my 'very good friend' is & how much she knows & how much the others know, & especially how much they are now going to find out."[38]

Plenty of women found out. "Nina's bedroom is getting to be quite an institution in my life," she journaled in 1934. Later, "I'm playing a new role these days and I'm not sure how the part suits me. I am cast as a Corrupter of the morals of the young and I will have to admit that I enjoy it very much except for certain scruples of conscience which are not quite as strong as they should be!"[39] Still later,

> This interesting day in the Millard life began about 10 PM and ended about 8:30 AM with much novel experience in between, supplying valuable addenda to observations of July 3rd. The locale this time was a place in Long Beach called The Paradise. This dive is inhabited by fags as well as spriggins. I had a long conversation with a sweet little fag who didn't like to do drag acts in Miami because it was too much trouble to change and who always wanted to be an actress. The floor show was almost continuous and included Hitler and his storm troopers who captured him a handsome spy, besides the usual Fiesta numbers.[40]

As scholars such as Elizabeth Lapovsky Kennedy and Madeline D. Davis have described, bars represented key spaces for socializing among lesbians that also calcified cultural practices.[41] Developing lesbian spaces was even more important among working-class patrons for whom access to rarified environments harboring homosexual communities such as art museums and opera houses was restricted.[42] Millard's affectionately camp description of the Paradise, which brought together "fags" and "spriggins," suggests a finely tuned acculturation into queer life and an embrace of sexual dissidence in its many splendored forms. Her trip to the Paradise occurred within a couple of weeks of throwing herself into radical antifascism, as she describes in her journal: "Tom McKenna of the League against War and Fascism and the Civil Liberties Union came in and after welcoming me with open arms (they always do) tried to think of something for me to do (they always do)."[43] Open arms embraced Millard whether she was entering into a gay bar or a meeting of leftists figuring out how to assist Republicans in the Spanish Civil War. "I can never forget that wonderful night we spent together when we learned to love each other," a woman wrote her in 1940. "We were both so terribly young and full of beauty, your eyes were like stars and in your tender curls clung the haunting fragrance of hashish. . . . I know ours will be a deathless love, a blue flame suspended in the constellation of the infinite for astronomers to wonder at even as historians are baffled by the magnificence of my novels and your paintings which will be inspired by our love. I like the confession story you sent me too except I think the ending."[44]

As she immersed herself in queer life and relationships, Millard developed her Marxist analysis of women. In a time line she prepared later in life, Millard paired her political work with the women whom she loved. In 1940, for example, Millard joined the Communist Party (after several years in the Young Communist League), during which time she developed relationships with Ruth Lowe and Hope, the latter of whom accompanied her on the trip to Cuernavaca and was a longer-term lover. Millard is best known for her pamphlet *Women Against Myth,* published by the Communist International Press in 1948. In that document, Millard infused her analysis with ironic humor, observing, for example, that "judging from the number of square feet given to the subject in every issue of the *Ladies Home Journal,* the highest ideal of American womanhood is smooth, velvet, kissable hands." The emphasis upon femininity offered by capitalist society as women's "highest ideal" held little appeal for Millard as both a Communist and as a corrupter of morals. In order to combat the allure of consumer capitalism and women's oppression, "it is only the socialism foreshadowed by Marx and Engels, abolishing as it does all forms of exploitation of one human being by another, that can make it possible for women to achieve real equality."[45]

Like many other women on the Left, Millard traveled to the Soviet Union, embarking in 1949. As Julia L. Mickenberg has noted, "Russia and the Soviet Union helped American new women envision themselves, society, and possibilities for the future."[46] Many sexual dissidents were drawn to the Soviet Union due to their conviction that revolutionary principles would liberate them from the strictures of patriarchal capitalism, as well as a sense that women had more opportunities for work and family following the Russian Revolution. In *Moscow Yankee* (1935), Myra Page imagined a Russian woman at odds with an American man who rejects Communism: "So this was what her professor had meant. All those fairy tales and promises they put over on the masses. But was this man so dumb, he couldn't see through them!"[47] The fairy tales of capitalism, including those in which a hapless woman bumbled through life hoping to find her Prince Charming, held no traction in Russia. "Nontraditional erotic relations," Mickenberg writes, "from heterosexual unions defined in terms of 'free love' to homosexual partnerships, often went hand in hand with commitment to social transformation and, by extension, support for the Russian Revolution."[48]

Though they never visited the Soviet Union, Ruth Erickson and Eleanor "Steve" Stevenson spent much of their lives passionately defending it. "The Russians have made many friendly concessions to us," they wrote to their local newspaper in 1947, "but we have been so unfriendly to them that they have learned to fear us."[49] The pair had met in New York City in 1925, when they were both working at the New York Public Library. Stevenson was taken by Erickson, describing her as "a regular Viking with her blue eyes and fair hair; fine mind and big heart, and tastes strangely like mine."[50] Erickson, who grew up in New York, adopted an edgy affect in her personal style, which she curated in defiance of fashion trends and gender expectations. "I have gone through a bob, bangs, side part, shingle, boyish indiscriminate," she wrote in 1926, "and now I am cutting it myself in such original manner I defy copy."[51] Stevenson similarly refused to blend into the crowd: "Ted will hate the hair, and I think Glad will rather envy me while wondering how I can let myself look like that! Two of the Library girls one day, very interested, asked me if I didn't occasionally get tired of looking like a freak. Of making myself conspicuous with clothes and hair and such. Of 'being diff'rent.'"[52] While they might have looked like freaks, Erickson and Stevenson liked it that way. They preferred traveling in Bohemian circles.

As a transplant from Minnesota, Stevenson had been diving headfirst into the scene of the Greenwich Village intelligentsia prior to meeting Erickson. In 1924, Stevenson described how

> I'm getting a real kick out of meeting such widely diverging people as church members, atheists, Reactionary Republicans, Communists, Anarchists, Jews, Romanists, Protestants, orthodox, heterodox, radicals, liberals, thinkers, bankers, intellectuals, artists, social workers, socialists, economists, theologists, Americans of many generations back, Americans of a few days, half a dozen nationalities, nationalists, internationalists, pacifists, military and naval men, failures, successes, business men, dreamers, idealists, realists, animalists, ascetics, ———————— working, along different lines, for the same end: a more human America.[53]

Once the pair began their relationship, likely as "————————s," they enjoyed these things together. They went to Bohemian parties, hung out with Edna St. Vincent Millay, and attended anarchist meetings, the latter an entry point into the radicalism they pursued until their dying breaths. "Wednesday of this week Ruth and I hope to meet Jean Toomer, Maxwell Bodenheim, and perhaps a small scattering of writers, artists, black and white," Stevenson wrote in 1925. "Paul Robeson might easily be there." Neither were their intellectual, political, and romantic pursuits kept discreet. "There have been walks by moonlight and walks in the rain," Stevenson recalled. "Anarchist meetings and suppers with church youth groups."[54]

As their dive into the Left deepened, Erickson and Stevenson moved closer to Socialism and then the Communist Party. "The Anarchists I was interested in," Stevenson recalled, "got too narrow and prejudiced for me."[55] At the core of their relationship was their commitment to social justice. "Gosh darn it," Stevenson wrote, "if America is not what I want it to be it's up to me to stay here and make it so, even if it kills me in the attempt!"[56] By 1925, Erickson and Stevenson were living together in New York, where they stayed for several years before retreating to a country home in New Milford, Connecticut, in 1930. They intended it as a summer home, but they lived there for the rest of their lives. Though they left their scene in Greenwich Village behind, Erickson and Stevenson continued to pursue the radicalism that had energized them there by participating in their local chapter of the League of Women Voters, attending Progressive Party meetings, sending a deluge of letters reading elected officials to filth, studying leftist books and publications such as the *Daily Worker* religiously, and maintaining relationships with leftists such as Grace Hutchins and Anna Rochester, with whom they remained friends for life. In 1947, they visited Hutchins and Rochester in New York, during which visit they also spent time with Elizabeth Gurley Flynn and Clara Bodine, whom Stevenson described as "grand women!"[57] They were also friends with Albert Kahn and Will Geer, both of whom were gay Communists; Michael Gold; and Anna Louise Strong. Like their lefty friends, Erickson and Stevenson shared a distaste for American nationalism. "Look out for the boys who wave the flag too hard," Stevenson wrote in a letter from the 1930s.

> If they are against labor, against some kind of racial or religious minority, always looking under the bed for socialists or communists, against income taxes and for sales taxes, against price control and rent control and subsidies to dirt-farmers, against school lunches, and screaming 'economy' when

someone asks for more money for some social service—you can begin to believe they are against the USA whatever they call themselves.[58]

It is unclear whether they ever joined the Communist Party, but at the very least, Erickson and Stevenson were faithful fellow travelers. "Communists believe in human dignity, that's one reason we like 'em," Stevenson wrote in a 1947 letter.[59] "Communists may bore us and often do," the two wrote in a letter to the New York Herald Tribune that same year. "[T]heir constant 'midnight ride of Paul Revere' warnings may tire us out, we may wish they would laugh more often and preach less, and if we are devoted adherents of capitalist economy they may annoy us by their criticisms and their insistence that a socialist economy would be better, but let's not be scared to death by this tiny group—or rather, by the wholesale lies peddled around about them."[60]

While their public face distanced them from avowed members of the Party, Erickson and Stevenson's sympathetic relationship with Communism was admitted far more openly in their correspondence. "We personally do not believe that communists pose any threat to our country," Stevenson wrote to a US representative in 1947. "Here they consist of a small group, with a slightly larger group of friends who are not actually members, who seem to spend most of their time urging better living standards and more democracy and less race-bigotry within the country, and cooperation for world peace and aid to the victims of Hitlerism abroad: hardly 'subversive' activities, either of them." Whether Erickson and Stevenson were part of the small group or in their circle of friends, they brooked no criticism of leftists' alleged un-American activities. When Communists were smeared with labels such as "subversives," Stevenson noted that "no one has ever suggested that a gangster, a bigot, a war-monger, a purveyor of any form of indecency, is a communist."[61] Erickson framed her Communist defense through reference to antifascism. "We fought a war against fascism, and Communists proved good fighters in that war," she wrote in 1947. "The people abroad learned the hard way that the 'red scare' was Hitler's weapon to divide and conquer the people. Veterans should not forget who the enemy is. Schools should tell the truth about people. Lincoln was not afraid of the Communists, he corresponded with Karl Marx and appointed a Communist a general in his army."[62]

While they were openly supportive of Communists, Erickson and Stevenson were sympathetic to their desire to remain discreet. In a 1947 letter to a friend, Stevenson noted that "we yell at Communists because they don't 'admit' they are Communists and then crucify one when he says he is one."[63] Erickson echoed that concern in a letter the next day. "Our Communist friends always have something to offer," she wrote.

> Of course there are individuals who dare not come out openly because prejudiced people who don't know what they stand for would immediately think they were devils and they would be fired from jobs, barred from appointments and hounded in many ways. . . . When Communists are assured of a fair deal, constitutional rights, equality under the law, cooperation for humanitarian work they will all come out openly. If you like progressives, liberalism, and freedom of speech then you should demand it for others as well as yourself and here is a good chance to defend the rights of a minority group as well as the rights of other liberals.[64]

The proximity of Erickson's and Stevenson's letters suggests the kinds of conversations that were unfolding in their shared home, particularly around the trepidation Communists felt about openly discussing their Party membership and their status as a "minority group" that was justifiably anxious about "coming out." On many occasions, Erickson and Stevenson jointly signed their letters, especially the ones they sent to politicians. On at least one occasion, this led to some confusion. "You can imagine our surprise when we got a letter on a senator's stationary which began 'Dear Ruth and Steve'!" they wrote in 1945.[65]

Stevenson went by the name Steve privately, and Erickson consistently referred to her partner this way. The gender nonconformity they valued in their relationship was confirmed in a poem Ruth wrote for Steve's birthday in 1961, where she catalogued her various pet names for her partner:

Here's to Eleanor
Here's to En
Here's to B
And here's to Ken
Here's to Steve
(And here's to Son)
Here's to neighbor
And here's to friend
Here's to labor
to help defend
Here's to Sister
And here's to Cousin
Here's to mister
E. Stevenson
Here's to One
Who seems to be many
People to whom we say Yes![66]

Erickson connected Stevenson's many nicknames—and genders—to their leftist politics, culminating with a Popular Front allusion to Carl Sandburg's Depression-era poem "The People, Yes!" Stevenson left few documents articulating their own feelings about their sexuality or gender, but the poem Erickson dedicated to Stevenson after sharing an intimate partnership for more than three decades suggests how gender, sexual dissidence, and radicalism were interwoven in their lives. Negotiating gender was a significant feature in the pair's relationship, and it was construed on their own terms as relational, fluid, and playful.

Neither their partnership nor their politics was a secret. "All last spring and summer, when we'd go to the village (5 miles away) for supplies," they reported to their friends in 1954, "the boys hanging around the streetcorner would whistle and yell at us, even once breaking into 'The Campbells are coming, hooray, hooray', but substituting 'commies' for Campbells!"[67] Though they rarely discussed their sex life in their letters, one addressed "Dear girls" detailed a European cruise they took together in 1926. "Some of the passengers really dress up in dinner gown," they wrote; "part of the time we had no wraps on deck."[68] In the copy of the letter preserved in their papers, the latter detail is typed over to near illegibility.

Though Erickson and Stevenson adopted a wide range of progressive positions, they were acutely aware of the particular pressures they confronted as women. "A woman may lead a most exemplary life, standing head and shoulders above the average mortal," they wrote in a 1946 letter; "yet if just once she takes a gun and shoots someone through the heart she is done for: all the past record goes for exactly nothing; she is considered all the more to blame because there was no previous warning she might act so."[69] Far be it from Ruth and Steve to hold one act of retribution by a woman against her. Certainly there were times when their own anger at injustice drove the two to piques of righteous anger. "Indignation . . . " Stevenson wrote in 1947; "Well, it's better than indignity!"[70] As sexual dissidents and Communists, Erickson and Stevenson remained conscious of the ways mainstream society smeared them. "It's not 'realism' for reactionary writers to portray Communists as devils: neither is it realism to portray them as all-wise, all-strong, all-good," they wrote, perhaps thinking about their own legacies. "Isn't it better all around to portray them as most of them really are, human beings with the human faults and failings and shortcomings BUT human beings dedicated to the greatest cause in the world today, and therefore struggling against overwhelming odds with a courage and devotion rarely found elsewhere?"[71]

Intimate bonds between radical queer women struggling against over-whelming odds were common throughout the 1930s and 1940s. Eliza-beth Gurley Flynn "strictly confidentially" joined the Communist Party in 1926, and she soon after became a well-known and public figure in the movement.[72] Years before she became the Communist Party's resi-dent "rebel girl," Flynn had involved herself in labor radicalism, particu-larly throwing herself into work with the Industrial Workers of the World and the Sacco and Vanzetti case—activities that, Flynn wrote in her autobiography, "led me, to my mind logically and irrevocably, to apply for membership in the Communist Party."[73] Around this time she became sick, and she was tended to by Marie Equi in her Portland, Ore-gon, home, binding the two in a community of care—albeit somewhat dysfunctional care—that extended for nearly a decade, during at least some of which time the two shared a bedroom. "Sometimes she wrapped a towel around [Flynn's] head," Equi's daughter recalled, "grabbed a cane, and sang 'Johnny Comes Marching Home Again.'"[74] Equi's sexual dissidence was not strictly confidential; she had been in long-term rela-tionships with Harriet Speckart and Kathleen O'Brennan prior to meet-ing Flynn, and she was widely recognized as a lesbian with an investment in queer radical community. An attorney publicly attacked Equi's radical community of "long-haired men and short-haired women."[75] She was also known as "Queen of the Bolsheviks." While Equi and Flynn shared a home and a bedroom, they also joined in leftist movements. In 1929, both spoke at a meeting in support of convicted labor leader Tom Mooney, and in 1934 they each contributed articles for the *Voice of Action,* a labor newspaper in Seattle, in support of waterfront strikers.[76] Their partnership was built on a foundation of shared radicalism.

A similar radical orientation bonded the photographer Berenice Abbott and Elizabeth McCausland, same-sex lovers who met in 1934 and remained partners for three decades. Abbott had entered into the orbit of the Left following her move from Ohio to New York in 1918, where she joined the vibrant Greenwich Village scene and became friends with Hippolyte Havel, a close ally of Emma Goldman and an unabashed anarchist. She hung around with the bisexual poet Edna St. Vincent Millay and cultivated an alliance with the queer modernist writer Djuna Barnes.[77] She immersed herself in queer leftist culture through her friendships with Lincoln Kirstein, Claude McKay (who enjoyed "her crazy personality"), the gay radical poet Hart Crane, and André Gide.[78] When McCausland and Abbott moved to Paris, Abbott expanded her repertoire by taking photographs of butch women in stately portraiture, and when she returned to New York in 1929, her passport photograph depicted a solemn figure cloaked in gigantic fur-trimmed outerwear, her hair a sternly angled pageboy. While Abbott and McCausland did not have a strong network of lesbian radicals around them, Abbott's connection to the Photo League, a Popular Front photography group, did bring her close to the lesbian photographer Angela Calomiris, who joined the Communist Party in 1942, and whose Village studio was secretly financed by her work as a spy for the FBI.[79]

Elizabeth McCausland was a journalist in Springfield, Massachusetts, who had a distinctly radical orientation, partly informed by her coverage of Nicola Sacco and Bartolomeo Vanzetti's highly publicized trial and execution. After McCausland met Abbott at the Museum of the City of New York in 1934, the two struck up a correspondence.[80] Their relationship grew into an intimate partnership, as well as a creative and political one. In 1936, McCausland moved to New York to settle into a new apartment with Abbott and collaborate on a book of photographs and essays. McCausland wrote articles about Abbott for *New Masses* (under the pseudonym Elizabeth Noble), the *Daily Worker,* and *Forward,* a Jewish Socialist newspaper. Abbott's images explored proletarian themes, incorporating gritty scenes and urban landscapes. Abbott showed her work at a group show featuring works by members of the American Artists' Congress and wrote about photography for *Art Front,* a leftist magazine to which McCausland also contributed. The couple sponsored a dance by the Artists League of America in 1941. They collected records that included Paul Robeson's Popular Front anthem "Ballad for Americans," and a recording by the Soviet men's chorus. "Among her very favorite films," biographer Julia Van Haaften writes of Abbott, "was the 1943 American-made *Boy from Stalingrad,* in which the lone girl in a pack of orphan partisans decries as 'reactionary' her exclusion from a mission, 'Girls are just as good as boys!'"[81] Fellow artist Barnett Newman believed Abbott to be a member of the Communist Party, and Louis F. Budenz named her as a "concealed Communist" after he left the *Daily Worker* and began his second career as an FBI informant. In its report on Abbott, the FBI noted that she "wears slacks constantly." The FBI noted Abbott and McCausland's "homo-sexual affair for a number of years."[82]

In 1940, McCausland wrote a poem, "There Shall Be Day," in which she articulated a bold vision for a utopian future boasting wheat, banners, and erotic awakening. "Bright dawn shall flood the earth," she wrote,

The night was dark, but day
　　　is bright with hope
Take heart, my love.
We live at history's dawn
　　　to watch the sun come up
Within myself I know
　　　The dawn.
The life that stirs in me
　　　the tides, the
　　　growing wheat
Are proof that day is
　　　here
The hidden joy within my
　　　flesh is answers
Crying life
will not be denied forever[83]

For queer women on the Left, intimacy was connected to political struggle and the hope that lovers "live at history's dawn." The bonds created
through radical activism, the "hidden joy within my flesh," strengthened
personal connections, and the experiences of women aligned with the
Communist Party put them into a joyous space from which they could
raise issues specific to their sex and align themselves with other women
in the movement. Many of the most important documents articulating
leftist feminism in the 1940s were written by queer women. They were
outsiders who developed a revolutionary vocabulary from which to
challenge the structure of a society that could not contain them.

QUEER WOMEN AND PROLETARIAN LITERATURE

Agnes Smedley published her influential proletarian novel *Daughter of
Earth* in 1929.[84] Smedley was deeply attracted to other women throughout her life, especially her close friend Florence Tenenbaum, with whom
she lived in New York in 1919. The two enjoyed a relationship that
included touching, such as "a sort of massage" administered routinely
by Tenenbaum "to take the kinks out."[85] While she was not entirely
open about her desire for other women, in 1927 Smedley wrote a piece
for *The Nation* that, biographer Ruth Price writes, "apparently contained a discussion of her lesbian tendencies."[86] In that same year,
Smedley submitted to *New Masses* a piece including material detailing
their relationship, titled "One Is Not Made of Wood: The True Story of
a Life." Though the magazine ran the piece anonymously in August

1927, the editors both excised the word "lesbian" from the piece and omitted a paragraph delving into the subject.[87]

For the most part, Smedley stopped short of fully embracing homosexuality in public. When she was planning a birth-control committee with Margaret Sanger, Smedley resisted their Communist comrades who wanted to include Magnus Hirschfeld in the conversations. Though she supported his work, Smedley reported in a letter that she would "like to see the clinic under the care of physicians, pure and simple, with no homosexuality or venereal diseases or tubercular appendages." She was quick to note that she had "nothing against him at all," but for Smedley, birth control "and homosexuality are two different things and must not be confused in the minds of the public." In another letter to Sanger, Smedley was more direct referring to homosexuality as a "form of perversion."[88] Though sex between women did not figure explicitly in her work, Smedley's explorations of female intimacy emblematized a queer feminism that appeared routinely within proletarian literature. Smedley had turned to Communism following her tour of the Soviet Union. Her friend Emma Goldman was not especially sympathetic to Smedley's fidelity to the Bolshevik Revolution, writing to a friend in 1939 that it had "killed all other feelings in her, as it does to everyone who is infected with the virus."[89] Yet Smedley's autobiographical novel, rife with all kinds of feelings, nonetheless spoke to the experiences of many women who, like her, found themselves on the vanguard of class war, sexual liberation, and rejection of patriarchy.

Paula Rabinowitz has argued for "a reading of women's revolutionary novels as a genre marked by the relationships of gender, class, and sexuality in its narratives."[90] For leftist writers like Lillian Hellman, exploring same-sex desire offered a lens into sexual perversion, albeit with some titillating lesbian content along the way. For others, such as Josephine Herbst, coding a lesbian relationship drawn from her own life as a straight one offered an opportunity to truly explore queer women's relationship to radical politics.[91] Barbara Foley argues that "women's proletarian novels frequently foreground the relation of sexuality to political conviction, thus developing the notion that class emancipation is both a premise to and an outgrowth of personal liberation."[92] Though radical fiction never developed a vocabulary for exploring lesbian desire that was as fully developed as that pertaining to gay male desire, it did offer a venue for exploring female intimacy in ways that pushed against both sexism and heteronormativity.

While *Daughter of Earth* has been upheld as a signature proletarian novel, Smedley centralizes love and intimacy throughout her narrative, which Paul Lauter describes as a "record of Smedley's recurrent struggles to transform herself."[93] Part of that transformation involves Smedley's narrator, Marie, learning that "the way to love lies through suffering" (33). It also involves coming to terms with the complex of desire that structured women's relationships with one another. Describing Marie's Aunt Helen, Smedley details how "awkward, ugly girls who might have easily hated her for her beauty, stood gossiping with her over the back fence, and when she came darting in at the back doors their eyes were wistful and hungry" (43). The line between hungry desire and envy was so thin.

Though Smedley prioritizes female toughness and structures desire through relations between women, she also defines women in contrast to weaker men. In one childhood scene from the novel, Marie describes a conflict with a boy whose effete lawyer father looks down on hers hauling bricks. "We used our sling-shots on such sissies," she notes (51). Yet she also rejects her father's tough masculinity, expressed most viciously through his shaming Marie's sister's sex life ("'Annie in a rooming house all night . . . ' that meant sex. My father and mother on the verge of beating her for it." [72]).[94] Masculinity always seemed to end in violence.

As she moves into the world outside her home, pursuing sex with various men, Marie becomes immersed in a messy world of sex and secrecy. "Had all these people known that I had love affairs," she observes, "they would not have respected me." This double standard plagues her: "[W]hy should [men] be so care-free, so happy, while women must submit to other standards?" (346). Ultimately, this bind convinces her to fight for liberation. "Freedom is higher than love," she determines. "At least today. Perhaps one day the two will be one." Smedley's playful repurposing of "two becoming one" points to her rejection of superficial romance in favor of a more radical gesture toward women's liberation. "There is sex, to be sure," she tells one male interlocuter, "but the thing I call love does not exist." Asked to define love, she replies, "[U]nderstanding, tolerance, freedom—all combined." (357).

Freedom was foreclosed through secrecy around sex: "[B]ecause we maintained secrecy, there seemed something poisonous about it; natural and beautiful things do not need to be kept secret" (347). It was also limited by the demand for heterosexual conformity from which Marie seeks to be freed. "I had a shrinking, fearing attitude," Marie recalls, "toward sex expression" (361). That attitude connects to the cultural restrictions placed on American women. "I have the atmosphere of America," Marie observes, "the unnatural, Puritanical attitude, to thank for this. Against this shame stood my intellect, knowing my life was my own, knowing the standards about me were hypocritical" (348). Smedley imagines sexual conservatism as an "unnatural" byproduct of Americanism, wholly outside intellect and entirely hypocritical. "I have no desire to submit to the life that most women live—darning socks, cooking, cleaning, depending on a man for my living," Marie declares. Indeed, "the world was filled with women who weep, enslaved by the institution of marriage and by their love for men" (365).

Smedley's narrative resolves in a short-lived marriage, but on the road to that place, Marie understands her relations with men—reduced, for her, to "sex experiences"—to have been almost an experiment: "not so much a physical experience as an adventure." (350). In contrast, Marie's relationship with her friend and roommate Florence, likely modeled off Smedley's own with Florence Tenenbaum, speaks to a different, arguably deeper, form of intimacy. "Once she said: 'I love you as I have loved no other,'" Marie reports in one such domestic scene. The two spar over the projections they place on each other's future, bounded within society's heterosexual expectations. "You are the type of girl who will someday fall in love and get married," Marie charges, to which Florence retorts, "I don't value men enough to think that they are worth fighting against all the time" (352). Though Marie eventually marries, she conceives her heterosexual coupling through the lens of solidarity rather than romance—"all that comradeship seemed to mean in work and in life, all that friendship means" (365).

Daughter of the Earth does not detail lesbian relationships or explicitly mark same-sex desire. In her rejection of male–female relations under patriarchy, however, and through her meticulous discrediting of the naturalness of gender roles, Smedley produced a key text in queer leftist literature. Her narrative represents a woman who seeks liberation from, in equal measure, sexual secrecy, presumptive heterosexuality and its prioritizing of opposite-sex relationships, control over women's bodies, and lifetime monogamy. That Smedley was herself involved in physical and intimate relationships with women further suggests how leftist women's writing allowed queer women to push against both the expectations of heterosexuality and the narrowing of women's potential under capitalism.

In those aspects, Smedley's novel might be placed alongside a number of other works of radical fiction written by queer women including Josephine Herbst, Gale Wilhelm, Jo Sinclair, and, later, Lorraine Hansberry. Herbst's Trexler family trilogy of novels, which were published between 1933 and 1939, were significant in representing both how, as Mary Ann Rasmussen has written, "a collective sense of the inherent instability of the subject is critical to dismantling the power and authority of the ruling class" and "that the uneven and unfinished business of subject formation is a key battleground of revolutionary struggle."[95] Herbst had intimate relationships with both women and men. Her sexual partnership with the artist Marion Greenwood, biographer Elinor Langer writes, "is the personal secret at the heart of Josie's life and she did not speak of it herself."[96] Perhaps not, but the two certainly shared intimacies in private, and Herbst's husband at the time of the affair, John Herrmann, was evidently aware the affair was happening. Herbst met Greenwood in 1932 as the writer was drawing closer to the Communist Party and completing work on *Pity Is Not Enough*. Writing to Greenwood when the two were apart, evidently after her previous missive went unanswered ("So, bitch, you did not write me even a line for today"), Herbst observed to her "awfully sweet delicious" "tadpole," "Here we are, in bed, but not in bed, alas, together. Could anything be funnier than the lives of women?" Funny, perhaps, but also difficult: "[I]n our next lives," Herbst continued, "let us be males. At least one of us." Herbst imagined how, were they together, she would "dress [Greenwood] in a grass green dress," allowing that "I'd rather get on to the undressing." Greenwood replied with her own romantic sass, addressing "my blue-eyed buxom bitch" before announcing cheekily, "I'm going to get hard—females, women have to be *hard* in this world, I'm going to think of pain and get hard—write me soon."[97] The playful gender play in Greenwood's reply, which resonates with Herbst's envisioning their same-sex relationship as a straight one, repurposes women's struggle into a highly eroticized expression of queer desire.

Though she was not herself a Communist, the queer writer Carson McCullers was drawn to the Left early in her life. Edwin Peacock, her best friend, was a gay man who introduced Carson to the work of leftist contemporaries such as John Dos Passos and James T. Farrell, as well as to the writings of Karl Marx. He also introduced Carson to his leftist comrade Reeves McCullers, whom she eventually ended up marrying. The three frequently discussed Marx "as rapt new disciples," and after Peacock met his eventual partner, John Zeigler, they talked frequently with Carson about the Spanish Civil War.[98] "Black and white people in those days rooting in garbage cans," Carson recalled of the Depression years. "People, kind, sweet people who had nursed us so tenderly, humiliated because of their color. I do not wonder now, as my father used to wonder, why I was a great believer of the Communist Party when I was seventeen, although I never joined it."[99] McCullers later lived in a house with W. H. Auden, the gay poet who famously supported the Republicans in the Spanish Civil War; Benjamin Britten, a gay composer and Communist; and Richard Wright, the Black radical author of *Native Son*. Her own relationship to the Left was no less complicated than that of her illustrious roommates, nor that of her friends Gypsy Rose Lee (with whom McCullers once claimed to have had sex), Paul and Jane Bowles, Newton Arvin, and Erika and Klaus Mann, all of whom were either gay or bisexual and linked more or less closely with the Communist Party.[100]

McCullers's debut novel, *The Heart Is a Lonely Hunter*, took cues from the Popular Front's demand for celebrating pluralism and lifting the downtrodden. While the novel is commonly read as an emblematic "southern gothic," McCullers's insistence upon marking her characters' minoritized positionality suggests her attentiveness to the struggles of those exiled from the promise of capitalism. Her characters include Jake, a gay Communist; Mick, a gender-nonconforming girl too easily dismissed as a "tomboy," who, like McCullers herself, desires to be a pianist; and, modeled off Edwin Peacock, John, a mute character— McCullers often depicted people with disabilities in her work—entangled in a loving relationship with his male roommate. Neither is the time setting of her novel incidental: McCullers attends to the Great Depression's impact on characters already laboring on the outskirts of society. Mick is forced to work at a department store when her dreams of an artist's life are shattered by the reality of her social conditions, and her failure seems benign compared with fates of the other characters populating the novel. "The bastards who own these mills are millionaires," Jake says as he tries to make the townsfolk understand. "So when you walk around the streets and think about it and see hungry, worn-out people and ricket-legged young'uns, don't it make you mad? Don't it?" For McCullers it certainly did, and for her and many other queer women, radical fiction offered an essential platform for directing their fury at the capitalist, patriarchal, and heteronormative society surrounding them.

QUEER MASCULINITIES AND REVOLUTIONARY WOMEN

As art historian Melissa Dabakis has documented, the Left often valorized masculinity at the expense of women. The strong bodies of male workers functioned as a metonym for espousing the values of a working-class movement, and masculine embodiment became the archetype for visualizing revolutionary commitment.[101] "Muscular male proletarians routinely appeared on the covers and in the pages of the *New Masses*," Barbara Foley writes; "if a female member of the working class was featured, she was usually at the side of her husband."[102] Such representations paralleled structures of inequality within leftist organizations, which struggled, in turn, to bring their ideological commitment to equality of the sexes into alignment with lived practices that often fell short of such goals. Although women played important roles in shaping and building the Communist Party, as we have seen, the Communist Party leadership rarely took issues concerning working-class women as seriously as they did when the same problems confronted men.[103] The particular concerns of women were often subsumed under the larger and more urgent "class struggle," diminishing attention to the particular ways sexism structured women's repression and experiences of liberation. The marginalization of women on the Left resulted in an almost entirely male leadership, persistent inattention to women's issues, and a general culture of masculinity that permeated everyday life and cultural representations.

Yet leftist fetishization of masculinity sometimes opened new opportunities for women, allowing for a broader palette of gender performance than has typically been admitted. Jack Halberstam positions female masculinity as "a queer subject position that can successfully challenge hegemonic models of gender conformity."[104] Lillian Faderman attributes the lesbian butch as emerging from theories of homosexuality as gender inversion.[105] More recently, scholars have acknowledged a longer history of "transing gender," which, in Jen Manion's framing, describes "a process or practice without claiming to understand what it meant to that person or asserting any kind of fixed identity on them."[106] Transing gender was closely aligned with sexual dissidence in the 1930s and 1940s, and for many radicals, that was understood as a source of empowerment rather than something to be rejected.

While it was by no means consistent, female masculinity was often extolled on the Left, and bourgeois women were frequently represented as overly feminized. The overdetermined heterosexuality implicit in patriarchal gender roles was imagined as counterrevolutionary, as in a cartoon from the *Woman Today* depicting a gathering of women in elegant dress extolling Mussolini as "SUCH a man!" (figure 16). The exaggerated bosoms, elegant posture, and fawning affect of the bourgeoisie reinforced the notion that femininity was inextricably linked to

"Mussolini is SUCH a man—he sees something he wants
and he just takes it."

FIGURE 16. A. Redfield, untitled, *The Woman Today*, June
1936, p. 24.

capitalism. Another cartoon from the same year features a similar caricature coming up against a domestic worker, depicted in aggressive posture, defiantly resisting her demands (figure 17).

In leftist representations, radicalized women were often depicted
throwing off the trappings of bourgeois femininity. A two-page cartoon
in *The Liberator* from 1921 depicts a butch woman labeled "Communism" (figure 18). Dressed in a rugged uniform of short pants with
patches on the knees, a shirt opened to the waist with rolled sleeves, and
an unstylish cap, Communism, depicted as a strapping butch, builds a
strong, solid wall. Though her clothing is functionally androgynous, her
partially exposed breasts suggest a concerted effort by the artist to depict

"I am a woman of few words," announced the haughty mistress to the new maid. "If I beckon with my finger, that means come."

"Suits me, mum," replied the girl. "I'm a woman of few words myself. If I shake my head, that means I ain't comin'."

FIGURE 17. Untitled, *The Woman Today*, December 1936, p. 27.

her as a masculine woman. Holding a brick in one hand and a mortar spreader in the other, Communism advises "Capitalism," the latter represented as a heavily made-up woman in restrictive, elegant dress, "You can't do it in those clothes, you know." The heavily rouged cheeks and outsize feathers in her cap suggest Capitalism likely would have been read as a prostitute. Her hunched posture, hopelessly compromised by girdle, bustle, and train, frustrates her half-hearted efforts to build her own wall, which clumps and falls in an embarrassing and pathetic heap. Communism's outfit here even outbutches the revolutionary dress designs of Soviet constructivists Liubov Popova and Varvara Stepanova,

"You can't do it in those clothes, you know."

FIGURE 18. Untitled, *The Liberator*, August 1921, pp. 18–19.

the latter of whom wrote in 1923 that "fashion, which psychologically reflects our everyday life, habits, and aesthetic taste is giving way to clothing organized for working in everyday branches of labor."[107] In *The Liberator*'s cartoon, female masculinity is conceived as revolutionary, while femininity is unsentimentally rejected. Work, it seems, represents a masculine space that women enter by shucking the conventions of patriarchy, which, in turn, frees them from the demands of fashion and makes of them ideal architects of revolution.

Representations of proletarian butch cut both ways: on the one hand, celebrations of female masculinity promoted women to equal status in a political movement dominated by men; they also sometimes perpetuated a historic valorization of masculine bodies that veered on coercive. Nonetheless, the emergence of proletarian butch style created space for masculine women to see themselves represented and for queer women to push the boundaries of their critique of patriarchy.

For some writers on the Left, the image of the working class as a masculine woman bespoke radical potential on the cusp of leftist revolution. Communist poet H. H. Lewis, in a poem titled "The Man from Moscow," envisioned the radicalized American working class as a strong butch:

> The American working class is a big-boned working-woman
> Muscled like a man,
> Simple-hearted, direct and vulgar
> Sweaty and stinking from the vulgarity of it—
> An Amazon
> With great waddling dogs and obscene capabilities.

For Lewis, female masculinity, with all its "stinking vulgarity," deviated from American normativity. Further, Lewis depicts the true Communist as appreciably more masculine than "the queer Socialist," for whom Lewis adopted a femmy affect: "[T]sk, tsk, shame forbid!" In contrast, "the MAN from Moscow" was "the International hero," against whose formidable force "the Impotents sulk off into the background and lurk forlornly."[108]

The labor militancy extolled among leftists favored iconography featuring women in defiant postures: fists raised, jaws clenched, chests puffed grandly, hands sternly on hips (figure 19). The revolutionary costume for labor strikes and picket lines necessitated a rejection of the trappings of modern femininity. In a 1936 article detailing a Wisconsin strike, Lola Bullard reported, "Today I am wearing a pair of low-heeled shoes. All my life I have worn teeter spike-heeled pumps of shiny patent leather or kid." In contrast, "[m]y new shoes are not pretty: Flat heels, stubby round toes, heavy brown calfskin built up sensibly high around the arch. No, one couldn't call them gay shoes, nor frivolous shoes." Labor radicalism shifted both Bullard's sense of fashion and her sense of self: "[T]hese 'sensible' shoes are a symbol of what has happened to me and to the men and women I work with. *We are down to earth at last!*"[109]

The butch performances of radical women did not demand a total rejection of all feminine fashion influence, which could sometimes be repurposed to militant ends. "Strong and masculine though she appears," Helen Morgan wrote of a French radical feminist, "Mme. Weiss is not at all ignorant of the advantages that lie in stressing strictly feminine weapons." When the police attacked Weiss during a protest, she forced "a score of those brass-buttoned gentleman [to] run for shelter, sneezing and coughing and half-blinded by a sudden barrage of heavily perfumed face powder."[110] Repurposed by strong and masculine women, high-femme trappings could make effective weapons against the state apparatus.

FIGURE 19. Untitled, *The Woman Today*, May 1937, p. 6.

The physical demands of strikes and radical direct action—marching, rock throwing, resisting arrest—demanded a new posture from women that allowed for a capacious rejection of gender norms in favor of a tough masculinity, no longer reserved for the male sex. A photograph from the *Working Woman* of a woman arrested in a Detroit auto workers' strike in 1933 suggests the gender trouble inherent in radical protest (figure 20). In this image, a woman wearing a skirt, stockings, and pumps twists her arm disobediently as she is manhandled by a police officer. Her strong stance and stern expression, coupled with her short hair and chiseled jaw, cut a striking image of female masculinity that pushes against many of the images of feminine decorum found in other media outlets. That this woman is portrayed as a heroic outlaw demonstrates how leftist militancy opened space for a broadening repertoire for butch women in the 1930s.

FIGURE 20. Photograph, *The Working Woman*, April 1933, p. 9.

The Soviet Union was invoked by leftists as a utopian society free from the constrictions of capitalist demands for femininity. A March 1935 photograph in the *Working Woman* of the Soviet women's basketball team depicts an intimate line of women who "don't have to worry about their next meal as you can see" (figure 21). The women adopt a range of gender presentations, the legs of each straddling the woman in front, hands around one another's waists. Contrasted with familiar depictions of sexually titillating lines of American chorus girls—a veritable trope in US representations of women whom, notably, leftists insistently portrayed as workers (figure 22)—the image of these young women preparing for their basketball game conveys a breezy, playful intimacy that allows for masculine camaraderie in the interest of revolutionary sport.

Just Working Women — Out for Fun

Look around you and see if you can find a crowd of city women that look like this in the United States. These young women live in the Soviet Union, in fact, they live in Moscow. They are ready for a game of basket-ball. They don't have to worry about their next meal as you can see. With spare time because of short working hours, and no fear of losing jobs they have peace of mind and there are plenty of wonderful things for them to do.

FIGURE 21. "Just Working Women—Out for Fun," *The Working Woman*, March 1935, p. 3.

Though most leftist representations of female masculinity asserted the unassailable femaleness of butch workers, in some instances they deftly dismantled essentialist gender categories by explicitly transing gender. "The Red Commander," a 1928 *New Masses* article by noted leftist Joseph Freeman, celebrated a female soldier passing as male to fight for Communism in Russia's Red Army.[111] The Red Commander's desires begin long before their revolutionary commitment, suggesting that trans-ing gender could catalyze leftist militancy. Freeman describes a "frail and precocious child," who, at age six, "began to have daydreams of becoming a soldier, especially a cavalryman." By age sixteen, the child was "rather boyish," even if "there was profound feminine charm" in their "soft eyes and clear voice." After joining the Communist Party in Budapest, the Red Commander became committed to the Russian Revolution, and after they "shaved her head and bandaged her breasts so they would not be noticed," they joined the Red Army in Ukraine.

FIGURE 22. William Gropper, untitled, *The Working Woman*, May 1935, p. 5.

Upon meeting a girl in a village where "all the village girls thought she was a young man," the Red Commander "took the girl for moonlight walks, bought her sunflower seeds, and kissed her."

The Red Commander stopped short of having sex with this female paramour, but Freeman acknowledges a relationship between their transing gender and sexual desire. The Red Commander's masculinity also cast them as a successful and esteemed comrade; Freeman notes that they were "known as the coolest 'man' in any situation." Though his narrative resolves with the Red Commander returning to civil society and discovering that "in the army uniform she had felt like a man," whereas in their "new skirt she felt like a woman," Freeman's article celebrates revolutionary commitment as it was embodied in an episode of transing gender. His sensitivity to the Red Commander's childhood fantasies suggests their transing gender was animated by more than militancy, and their ability to "feel like man" indicates a decided versatility around exploring gender on the Left. Masculinity was a prized attribute for revolutionaries even when it pushed against the Communist Party's celebration of male bodies and tipped precariously into queer erotics.

For some radicals, transing the Left was a matter not of instrumentalizing gender expectations, but rather of living out a deeply held identity. Foremost among these was Pauli Murray, a trans Black civil rights activist who pursued sexual relationships with women. Murray began to develop a radical consciousness in 1934 while staying at Camp Tera, one of the camps set up for women by Eleanor Roosevelt during the Depression as an alternative to the all-male Civilian Conservation Corps. Murray was forced to leave Camp Tera, which was suspected of incubating Communists, when a copy of *Das Kapital,* purchased for a course at Hunter College, was found during a cubicle inspection shortly after his arrival at the camp. Murray had little interest in the book until it was marked as contraband, and thus began a period of autodidacticism in both Marxism and sexology. Murray's reading list included works by Magnus Hirschfeld and Havelock Ellis.[112] His radical awakening, then, was deeply interwoven with gender and sexuality.

As a worker in the Works Progress Administration (WPA), one of the important initiatives of Franklin D. Roosevelt's New Deal and an incubator for many radicals, Murray moved further to the Left, aligning with the Lovestoneites, a group of former Communists and fellow travelers who opposed Stalin. While Murray held deep skepticism about Communism—informed, in no small measure, by a growing perception that Black women were underrepresented in the rank and file and, even more so, in the Communist Party's leadership—he was spurred by his experiences on the Left to commit his entire career to civil rights activism, particularly among the working class.[113]

Within leftist literature, female masculinity was employed as a signifier of political deviance. A signature moment in the evolution of proletarian butch occurred with the publication of Jo Sinclair (Ruth Seid)'s *Wasteland* in 1945.[114] Sinclair was a leftist writer who was radicalized while working on the WPA. She began contributing to *New Masses* that same year.[115] *Wasteland,* which won the Harper Prize for a novel by an "unnoticed" writer, generated a fair amount of attention (including a blurb from Richard Wright), owing in no small measure to the novel's important lesbian character, Debby. Sinclair's Debby is a soft butch who, like Sinclair, works on the WPA and writes a story "about colored people" for *New Masses*.[116] She is a well-adjusted and confident gender-nonconforming woman who provides the moral center of the novel. *Wasteland*'s author was suspiciously similar to her protagonist: when the *Cleveland News* announced Sinclair's award, they described her as "a straight-haired boyish looking blond who has been bobbing in and out of Cleveland newspaper offices for the past couple of years."[117] In addition to generating book sales and controversy ("[D]on't read *Waste-*

land," a "very elegant" woman advised fellow attendees at a dinner party; "it *looks* sordid"), *Wasteland* also precipitated an avalanche of correspondence to Sinclair from women and men who saw in her character signs of a fellow same-sex lover.[118]

Sinclair might have been largely unnoticed prior to writing this novel, but she was hardly unknown. Her work already had been published in leftist literary and political magazines. Sinclair's debut novel represented a culmination of stories, poems, and essays of social concern that had guided her radical perspective on American culture for years. *Wasteland* was viewed somewhat askance on the Left, culminating with Albert Stevens's caustic review in the *Daily Worker,* where he charged that, though Debby guided her brother deeper into the Left, she did so "at the cost of her having to assume the masculine paternal role in which her father and brother have failed, sacrificing her femininity and becoming a Lesbian."[119] The distaste Stevens expressed was shared by more-reactionary and anti-Semitic audiences, such as a reader who wrote a letter to Sinclair offering that "you should have called it Wastepaper or just Waste—human waste. Even as an instrument to solicit sympathy it failed utterly. The book has one thing in common with the race of people you write about—they both stink."[120]

For Sinclair, the character of Debby, both lesbian and Jewish, represented a source of moral authority who challenged lingering anti-Semitic attitudes in American culture and, at the same time, suggested homosexuals as legitimate victims of hatred who bore a particular responsibility to help others similarly stigmatized. Debby's experiences as a Jewish lesbian awaken deep feelings of solidarity with African Americans and people with disabilities. "I'm part of a person they call nigger, or dirty Jew, or cripple," Debby says. "Maybe it takes hurt to understand hurt, I don't know. But it's like I can understand all kinds of hurt now. Every kind there is." Having herself encountered a number of incidents in which she was targeted for her butch presentation, as when she passed four women who were "pointing at her, and all of them had turned from their babies and were laughing," Debby seeks to eliminate multiple forms of prejudice. Her knowledge of individual pain generates a moral imperative to align with other movements for social justice.[121]

Debby literalizes her humanitarian solidarity through the act of giving blood for the war. She "gives as a way of warding off, and fighting, evil: the sins of society against minorities, the evil of society's segregation of Jew, Negro, homosexual. Her blood is offered up against ghettos of any kind, physical and spiritual."[122] In this respect, Sinclair shares a vision with Carson McCullers, whose *The Member of the Wedding*, also published in 1946, included a similar Popular Front fantasy of commonality through blood donation. In McCullers's novel, Frankie Adams "decided to donate blood to the Red Cross; she wanted to donate a quart a week and her blood would be in the veins of Australians and Fighting French and Chinese, all over the whole world, and it would be as though she were close kin to all of these people."[123] For both Sinclair and McCullers, wartime blood donation was envisioned as a metaphor for highlighting points of commonality across difference. When one was bleeding, differences were reduced to common humanity. Yet this was also a utopian vision: in reality, American blood was segregated by race until 1950.[124]

Jo Sinclair's sensitive portrayal of Jewish and gay characters might be seen as a legacy carried over from earlier working-class Jewish fiction. Gay writer Myron Brinig's 1929 novel *Singermann*, written when he was aligned with the Left and writing labor novels, included two homosexual characters, brothers Harry and Michael Singermann.[125] Addressing subjects such as prejudice, assimilation, and identity, Brinig repurposed familiar tropes to draw his portrait of Jewish homosexuals discovering both their subjectivity and the intolerance of the society surrounding them.[126] Sinclair's characters were similarly invested in questions of subjectivity. Initial descriptions of Debby highlight the peculiarities that set her apart from others in her family: her brother Jake recognizes she is "different, entirely different" and puzzles over how "she was so damn odd." Yet Sinclair also connects Debby's difference to her radical politics, suggesting how marginalized ethnic and sexual identities were imagined to impel leftist identification. Her deviance from mainstream American norms as a Jewish lesbian radical butch confirms Debby as a model revolutionary—a framing that positions minoritized subjects on the front lines of a progressive vanguard. "Maybe she [is] the one destined to lift up this horrible, hard-luck family of [ours]," her brother muses upon discovering Debby's work in *New Masses*. "Maybe this queer, not-to-be-understood girl [is] finally the one to do it."[127]

Though her fashion and friends mark her as queer, the most significant feature Jake puzzles through is Debby's "secret." That word appears obsessively in Jake's description of Debby: even as he acknowledges her gender transgressions—"the way she looked like a boy, her hair cut short that way," and how "she'd always worn pants around the house"— Jake ultimately concludes she "was a secret, half like a man and half like a woman." Jake makes her secret into a metonym for her person: she does not have a secret; she *is* a secret. Jake also notices that Debby, far from following the tragic homosexual trope, is surrounded by a community of women with similar "secrets," many of whom gather at her and Jake's house on weekends, including "a girl they called Toby" who "looked kind of like a happy, smiling boy," and Barbara, Debby's boss on the WPA. In spite of all signs pointing to Debby's relative peace with herself and her community, thinking about Debby invokes in Jake "a feeling of shame," as though she were "the symbol of all the strange and distorted aspects of their family.[128] Though Sinclair's representation of Debby's gender nonconformity suggests an urgent engagement with female masculinity in the 1940s, the idea of a "secret" that precipitates "shame" points to a liminal moment for sexuality in the postwar period. Sinclair displaces precisely those concerns instrumentalized against homosexuals—secrecy and shame—onto their families. In *Wasteland,* it is Jake whose analysis is incomplete, and it is his burden that Sinclair documents in order to replace stigmatized queer pathologies with a new politics of representation. After he goes through psychoanalysis, Jake no longer sees Debby as "a degenerate," but only "as Debby. I don't think, she's a man, or she's a woman, or what in hell is she?"[129]

Readers closed the gap between literary representations of homosexuality, gender nonconformity, and real-world struggle in the letters they wrote to Sinclair, whose connections to Debby were assured by her own author photo.[130] Had Sinclair wished to mask her own masculine presentation, which she shared with Debby, one reader offered, "it would have been so easy to conceal this fact from them. It wouldn't even have been necessary to avoid putting your picture on the book jacket, since the style of your dress and hair were dead give-aways from the very start when compared with your description of her."[131] Sinclair was moved by the letters she received—decades later, she reported that she "felt—my god, the responsibility a book can create—aside from the writing—for people, people. All readers are people!"[132] Sinclair's masculine appearance encouraged readers to see her as the inspiration for Debby. "After finishing 'Wasteland' and seeing a picture of you," one woman wrote, "I feel that you will understand."[133]

Correspondents referred to themselves as "Debbies," sought to determine if the author was, as they suspected, herself a "Debby," and expressed particular interest in the character of Debby, even when they stopped short of explicitly connecting those dots. One letter writer in 1946, for example, began her correspondence with Sinclair by sending a benign fan letter praising her representation of Jake, only tentatively mentioning Debby in a short postscript. A second letter, however, arrived two weeks later in which the writer admitted her fascination with Debby and segued into a defense of Sinclair's sensitive portrayal: "Your 'Debby' is a very interesting character. . . . [W]hen one says lesbian people get a horrified expression and look so shocked, but your dealing with the subject is so understanding."[134] *Wasteland* brought homosexuality into the public sphere and created a counterpublic united through their reading of the novel and shared investment in Jo/Debby. "All of us will benefit by 'Wasteland,'" another reader wrote. "I can still scarcely believe that there is a bestselling novel on the market for anyone to read, with a lesbian as the only dependable decent driving force (or possibly 'support' would be a better word) behind a group of unhappy and bewildered people."[135]

In 1946, Leo Bergman, a rabbi in Rockford, Illinois, wrote a letter to Sinclair describing the scandal he triggered by advocating for homosexuals after reading her novel. Though Bergman was an admirer of *Wasteland,* his letter wasted little time on literary analysis, instead positioning the rabbi as an outspoken champion of sexual diversity. At a recent service, "I blew the roof off the Temple," Bergman wrote.

> I went off on a discussion of Lesbians, Homosexuals, and all people who are assigned to ghettos by the smug, complacent, dominating bourgeois Babbitts of the middle class, who cover their vicious subtle vices by condemning others who differ from them, as a means of warding off judgment and guilt from themselves. Spontaneous reaction should be "So What"—to realization of emotional differences among people. A person is a Lesbian or a Homosexual or this or that—"So What." And that blew the roof off![136]

Bergman's letter gestures toward Sinclair's radical perspective through his dismissal of "bourgeois Babbitts." Sinclair's bold lesbian character also attracted notice from her fellow leftist writers. Chester Himes, for example, sent a letter to Sinclair in 1945. "I always knew you'd do it when you got around to being honest with yourself," Himes wrote. "Perhaps I might do it myself someday when I can afford to be honest with myself— or perhaps Dick [Richard Wright] will do it when he gets honest again."[137] The slipperiness of Himes's "honesty" leaves open multiple interpretations: was he praising Sinclair's inclusion of a lesbian character that resembled herself? Was he attracted to her fearlessness in exposing various forms of social prejudice, especially American racism? Himes's use of "honesty" is particularly evocative given the emerging psychoanalytic understanding of homosexuality that saw repression as a form of victimization. Himes was not likely homosexual, and neither was Richard Wright, though the playwright Theodore Ward, who wrote *Big White Fog*, called Wright a "third sex man,"[138] and Margaret Walker insinuated his possible queerness in her biography, noting that "he discussed homosexuality in males almost obsessively."[139] But Himes did routinely represent same-sex eroticism, especially in his 1952 novel *Cast the First Stone*, based on his experience in prison. Perhaps that novel indicated Himes's eventual "honesty with himself" as he explored, through a semiautobiographical fiction, the complicated erotics of race and homosociality through the lens of Depression-era incarceration.[140] Regardless, his praise for Sinclair's honesty certainly indicates an acknowledgment of the slippery relationship between her biography and her work.

Sinclair's radical embrace of homosexuality resonated with readers. It also documents an instance of vernacular resistance to cultural prohibitions on homosexuality that points to an emerging politics of homosexuality outside large urban centers in cities like New York and San Francisco. "A few are chosen," wrote a reader in a poem she sent to Sinclair,

> To light the way
> A few are given
> The words to say
> And you are one
> Of the chosen few
> Just you.
>
> And countless thousands
> Will read your book
> And see the blinding light
> And countless thousands
> Will inward look
> And strive to find the might
> To down the prejudice
> Hate and fear
> That is ever with us
> Far and near.
>
> So—onward Jo
> You've work to do
> For you are one
> Of the chosen few
> Just you.[141]

Of course, it was not just Jo Sinclair who downed prejudice far and near. An entire network of leftists throughout the 1930s and 1940s took pen to paper, picketed in the streets, and threw boisterous parties as they clamored to free themselves from the oppressive constrictions on their personhood that the capitalist patriarchy insisted were natural. By building networks within the Left and pushing the limits of what leftist politics looked like, sexual dissidents created new spaces for fighting against misogyny, heteronormativity, and coercive femininity. The Left might have been dominated by men, and the narrative of social reproduction advanced by leftists might have continued to dullen the impact of their movement, especially within the Communist Party. But the rebel girls, queer women, and fearless revolutionaries who transed gender instrumentalized the tools of the Left to develop feminist critique, create intimate partnerships, and put some notches in their bedposts. They all had work to do.

CHAPTER 6

"Playing the Queers"

Homosexuality in Proletarian Literature

The Federal Bureau of Investigation's file on the writer Willard Motley meticulously tracks the places of residence, social calendar, and living habits of a subject whom the agency repeatedly branded "an eccentric." Given Motley's status as a best-selling novelist and a Black gay leftist, it is unsurprising that his perambulations caught the attention of J. Edgar Hoover and his snooping G-men. "In June of 1942," the FBI reports,

> WILLARD MOTLEY tended bar at the Sky-Hi Dance sponsored by the Workers School. Informant advised that this Party was held at 228 South Wabash Avenue, Chicago, Illinois. Informant further advised that after this dance a party was held in WILLARD MOTLEY's room, 1261 South Halsted Street.

Throughout the 1940s, Motley, whom the FBI also identified as "a homosexual," "generally hung around Maxwell Street, which is one block away from 1261 South Halsted, and . . . during this period he was hanging around with bums and prostitutes." Yet for all the insinuation in which this dossier trades, the file acknowledges that Motley "did this to obtain background for the book he was writing."[1] Ever attentive to lived experiences on the Left—perhaps even more attuned to its social and cultural dimensions than the typically dour caricatures found in mainstream representations—the FBI revealed in its report on Motley how his social life engaged deeply with working-class spaces, leftist cultural practices, and socialization with the dissident and dispossessed. His activities frustrate broad characterizations of the Left that paint individual radicals as joyless automatons doggedly carrying out Soviet directives. Further, the act of writing proletarian fiction offered Motley cover for pursuing unsavory activities that otherwise might have aroused even more aggressive state curiosity. Producing literature on the Left demanded all manner of lurid contacts. Motley's literary output, then, confirms his placement within a broader radical milieu that refused to distinguish between politics and sociality; art and life; sex and radicalism; or observation and participation.

Many leftist writers of the 1930s and 1940s similarly threw themselves amid the proletariat, engaging directly with social geographies where radicals encountered those whom they in turn depicted in their fiction. H. T. Tsiang named his central character in *The Hanging on Union Square* Mr. Nut; the FBI, describing the author, noted that "he has rather 'queer' ideas and is somewhat 'nutty.'"[2] Tsiang wandered the same streets as his protagonist, hand-selling copies of his self-published book. If the proletarian writer has been defined by an unwavering commitment to realism—perhaps most succinctly described by cultural historian Walter Rideout as one who "must set down ugly detail after ugly detail out of what he has learned of the present [society] until every shocking thing has been told"—this cultural perception might be partly attributable to the nearly clinical precision with which radical novelists grafted their fictions onto spaces familiar to both leftist and working-class readers.[3] "We are scientists," Michael Gold wrote in *New Masses* in 1930; "we do not have to lie about our hero in order to win our case."[4]

Of course, telling the truth about proletarian heroes demanded that writers move among them, lurking in shadowy corners on Maxwell Street or hawking books in New York's Union Square. Willard Motley threw his radical parties, hung around, and set his first novel in Chicago's slums. In 1949, the *Daily Worker* reported that he was arrested when he "had simply been standing on the corner of Huron and St. Clair Streets at 2:30 AM after he had seen a friend to his car from the author's home nearby."[5] As leftist writers depicted proletarian lives, they also constructed critical maps of working-class, radical, and homosexual interzones that impelled a nuanced engagement with sex, race, and class in urban spaces. Their interest in foregrounding experiences among the dispossessed folded neatly into a bold representational strategy that incorporated sexual dissidence into leftist literary forms.

The working-class and proletarian communities represented by writers on the Left rarely adhered to bourgeois literary standards that were hallmarks of middle-class respectability. "Proletarian realism deals with the real conflicts of men and women who work for a living. It has nothing to do with the sickly mental states of the idle Bohemians, their subtleties, their sentimentalities, their fine-spun affairs," Michael Gold wrote in 1930. "The worst example and the best of what we do not want to do is the spectacle of Proust, master-masturbator of the bourgeois literature."[6] Yet proletarian writers' interest in pursuing radical modernism also pushed them to exhibit broad license in their sexual depictions. Leftists seemed suspiciously eager to acknowledge sex as a site of pleasure that existed outside consumer culture, and they pushed against capitalist commodification while also acknowledging the economic motivations that informed many sexual relationships. The outer limits of Gayle Rubin's famous "charmed circle" of sexuality, which describes behavior outside what is conceived as normative and thus acceptable in American culture, might just as easily function to describe the characteristics of radical fiction's sexual depictions: proletarian literature had no shortage of "bad, abnormal, unnatural" sexuality that was sought "in the park," "non-procreative," "for money," "promiscuous," "cross-generational," and so on down the list.[7] The pursuit of sexual pleasure was conceived as inextricable from radical politics, and the impulse to incorporate sexuality into proletarian literature introduced an expanding range of spaces for producing intersectional leftist politics where sex was central.

The demands of literary naturalism emerged alongside a compelling interest among leftist writers in situating performances, both vernacular and theatrical, as urgent sites for developing modernist aesthetics. The insistently realist marching orders issued from the Soviet Union to American writers at the 1930 Kharkov Conference were met with some derision within the United States. The perpetually disillusioned writer Max Eastman, for example, complained in 1934 that "enthusiasm at its best is a poor cloak for incompetence, but enthusiasm over a detailed, itemized, rolled-out, hammered-in and nailed down *demonstration* of your incompetence is certainly as shaky a foundation for the building of a revolutionary art and literature as its worst enemy could devise."[8] Even as pitched debates over the proper literary form for proletarian writers roiled, the collapsing of high and low, reality and representation, and labor and pleasure within American leftist culture instantiated a perverse engagement with sexuality that met generic promiscuity with political deviance. "The conjuncture of popular culture and left politics," Walter Kalaidjian writes, "fostered an alternative discourse of racial, sexual, class, and transnational experience."[9] Drama, dance, and burlesque captivated audiences in ways that both competed with and overlapped with popular literatures, and fidelity to realism clashed with modernist demands for fragmentation, experimentation, and irony as soon as actors, dancers, and artists entered the stage. Before he settled into his career as a writer, Willard Motley blurred the line separating life from art as a member of the Stage for Action, described by the FBI as "a Communist dominated group which frequently puts on plays, shows, and rallies for the Communist Party."

In this chapter, I consider the relationship between homosexuality, urban geographies, and proletarian fiction by considering two leftist writers of color whose work pushed in distinct formal directions. Willard Motley's novels represented an emblematic contribution to literary naturalism, depicting the poor neighborhoods of Chicago with a bold enthusiasm for exploring sexual undercurrents while working within a realist tradition. The unpublished drafts of his novel *Knock on Any Door* further demonstrate how intentionally he attempted to bring homosexuality and radical fiction into alignment. H.T. Tsiang, on the other hand, wrote strange and surprising novels, drawing on the experimental spirit of high modernist writers such as Gertrude Stein to explore sexuality in proletarian New York. Both writers engaged directly with leftist literary cultures, and both brought to their work an interest in depicting sexual dissidence from a radical perspective. Attending to their literary contributions suggests how leftist writers engaged with homosexuality within the realm of representation, incorporating queer themes into their work in ways that challenged both popular understandings of urban homosexuals and prevailing ideas about the literary Left. In a description of Depression-era proletarian fiction, Barbara Foley notes that for leftist writers, "the key issue to be addressed was not the knowledge or theory of class struggle, but practice: would the reader take sides and get out into the streets?"[10] The range of representational modes through which Motley and Tsiang produced their work demonstrates how the breadth, rather than the limitations, of leftist literary forms allowed for a capacious sexual dissidence that both reflected and expanded the sexual politics playing out on the streets of Chicago and New York.

WILLARD MOTLEY'S QUEER RADICALISM

Willard Motley broke onto the American literary scene when, in 1947, he published his first novel, *Knock on Any Door*. The extraordinarily successful novel, which was quickly adapted into a successful Hollywood film starring Humphrey Bogart, explored the slums of Chicago in exacting detail, launching Motley's literary career with frank, often vulgar, depictions of poverty, depravity, and the usual contours of a hard-knock life. Motley's debut novel appeared at the tail end of an American vogue for literary naturalism, a formal style that dovetailed with radical interest in social realism during the Depression era. While naturalism was not inherently opposed to modernism, it took cues from sociology to develop a literary form that foregrounded social critique by attempting to faithfully represent existing social conditions. The radical political commitments of leftist writers impelled their deep dives into a social milieu where poverty inflected every aspect of existence. Though his novel comfortably fit into the naturalist form, Motley experimented more in the draft of his novel, which was heavily edited for publication.

Despite vigorous debates about how proletarian literature should be defined, artists and writers on the Left largely agreed that realistic depictions of proletarian life should include raw, honest representations of sex as a routine feature in urban slums. Their efforts to acknowledge the depravation of poverty coexisted uneasily with representations of sexual license that seemed to offer an attractive alternative to stuffy American puritanism. Motley struggled to resolve that tension, as evidenced in the conflicted title he gave an unpublished book of short stories in the 1940s: "Desire Is Sad."[11] Even as authors of radical works opposed the social conditions that impelled their narratives, readers of proletarian fiction found within the pages of leftist novels the steamy excess of characters unconstrained by the banality of bourgeois discipline. Michael Gold's *Jews without Money* (1930) might have been upheld by many writers on the Left as a major achievement in Depression-era proletarian fiction, but that endorsement seems unlikely to have been a major consideration when Tower Books reprinted a pulp edition of his influential work in 1961. Tower excised from that printing Gold's final paragraphs, where the protagonist joins the Communist Party, and replaced it with an advertisement for "the best in Dynamic, Virile Fiction." The novel's reissue by "a firm that specialized in pornography and shock fiction" suggests how even novels of social concern could serve to titillate audiences who might or might not have been interested in fomenting revolution.[12]

Willard Motley was unabashed in his commitment to dissecting sexual mores in urban life—a calculation that nearly cost him his book contract and stalled his career in the 1940s. Much conflict emerged between Motley and his editors around his insistence upon infusing his sexual scenes with rich, gritty detail. This inclination was particularly pronounced with respect to homosexuality—a dear topic for a gay writer who included unvarnished depictions of same-sex affairs in each of his works. Some of these representations were decidedly rough, as when the jackrollers in *Knock on Any Door* targeted homosexuals; others were campy, as when a character in *Let No Man Write My Epitaph* (1951) drily announced, "Respect the opposite sex. Respect all the gay bitches!" In notes for an uncompleted story, Motley envisioned how "a girl, boy-ish, marries and now listens to the dirty stories married people tell. She is a very nice and decent girl but is delighted to hear these stories for she has always had a boy-complex and this makes her feel that she is behind the scenes."[13] Throughout his career, Motley grappled to represent sexuality, and especially homosexuality, in all its spectacular variety, employing a naturalist form that provided cover for his lurid interests.

At the same time that he expanded his repertoire of explicitly gay characters, Motley's commitment to the Left similarly deepened.[14] He was involved in Chicago's Progressive Party and in the National Council for the Arts, Sciences, and Professions, both closely associated with the Communist Party. He was a conscientious objector in World War II, and he threw parties for Communist comrades.[15] He routinely socialized with leftists, which was noted in a newspaper account reporting on one such gathering that "joined together the cream of the reds and pinks."[16] The connection between Motley's homosexuality and his radicalism was noted in his FBI dossier, which tracked Motley from the 1940s until his death in 1965. By 1951, an FBI informant reported hearing Motley "and eight of his black and white friends toast the Communists and cry 'down with the United States.'" The agent further noted that "he is currently living with a blond white boy 'companion' whose name I do not know." The FBI was less interested in Motley's aesthetic investments, barely commenting on his novels. The attention to Motley's interracial companions, both political and sexual, further suggests how his race and sexuality were policed. He was, the FBI concluded, a "Negro writer with Leftist and homosexual tendencies who has lived in Mexico for a number of years."

Setting his novels in poor and working-class neighborhoods allowed Motley to straddle the line between exposing the struggle against dispossession and reveling in the temptations of the urban sexual underground. Motley also possessed a deep understanding of American racism, his impassioned resistance to which likely impelled his radicalism and informed his sensitivity to prejudice against homosexuals. "Economically the Negro has been pushed into the lowest paying and most menial labor bracket," he wrote in an unpublished essay from 1940, around the time he wrote some of his earliest stories. As a Black man, Motley was well attuned to the pressures of American racism. Motley foregrounded the economic impact of racism in his social analysis, which he also connected to the development of urban slums: "He has been shoved into slum neighborhoods where the housing sanitation and even the policing of the streets are the poorest. If he wanted a decent place to live there were other neighborhoods—colored neighborhoods where the rent was always at least double that paid in white neighborhoods of the same status. But all this was bosses, corporations, cities."[17]

As Motley struggled against American racism, prejudice against homosexuals, and class inequality, the Left offered him a political and literary vocabulary for confronting multiple and intersecting sites of oppression. He included in his personal library copies of books such as Ann Petry's *The Street,* Jack Conroy's *A World to Win,* and V. F. Calverton's *The Making of Man,* suggesting an abiding interest in race, proletarian fiction, and sexuality that was reflected in the themes he explored in his novels.[18] He was similarly embraced by the literati as an important Black writer, about which Motley was somewhat conflicted. Carl Van Vechten had him sit for photographs, which he hated. "I didn't like them at all," he wrote in his diary. "Don't think they look at all like me. Had to write him that I thought they were swell."[19]

Though leftist commitment to depicting truthful accounts of working-class life gave radical writers some latitude to avoid censure, Motley's particular insistence upon foregrounding homosexuality within his literary output pushed against the uneasiness many editors felt about publishing queerly erotic proletarian fiction. In a cataloguing of topics, generated in the late 1940s, that he sought to highlight in his work, Motley listed "prostitution, rape, hunger, theft, homosexuality, relief, housing, clothing, work, illegitimate children, children, and social disease."[20] This was a commitment for which he endured tremendous criticism. After reading the manuscript for *Knock on Any Door,* a literary agent pleaded with Motley to "please forget about tavern wenches, dying men, half-breeds, and tramps. . . . Write about the middle classes as much as possible."[21] Motley refused, risking his reputation by resisting pressure to compromise on sexual matters.

Motley's deep investment in Chicago's slums precipitated his interest in depicting sexual dissidence. "Sex is loose and easy in the slums," he wrote in an unpublished essay likely written around the time he was drafting *Knock on Any Door,* "and the young boy and girl soon discover both the pleasure and attitude."[22] Though Motley was committed to progressive social change, he also delighted in the slums' energetic embrace of sexual dissidence and wholesale rejection of bourgeois values. "The slums have given us the most vicious words in our language: 'pimp,' 'fairy,' 'hop head,' 'fence,' 'racketeer,' 'hi-jacker,' 'moll,' 'killer,'— to name a few," he wrote. Yet as a proletarian writer, he found great freedom in adopting these vicious words, his usage of which both connected his writing with the downtrodden characters he represented and pushed against the demand among middle-class audiences for reading about more-respectable topics. "The slums are the black apostle of tolerance, sympathy and understanding," Motley wrote. "The slums have a mission."[23] Motley's mission was to align himself with the residents of Maxwell Street, bringing the dispossessed into his readers' living rooms without apology.

Part of what attracted Motley to the slums was the slackening of restrictions on sexuality he found there. His defiance around sexual matters was common among midcentury American radical writers. This abiding interest in depicting sexuality dated to at least his high school days. He had achieved some renown by that point as the author of a weekly column in the *Chicago Defender,* a Black newspaper with national circulation. Beginning at age thirteen, Motley contributed a popular column under the pen name Bud Billiken, for which he was paid three dollars a week.[24] His early connection to the *Defender* might also have informed Motley's interest in the Left. As scholars such as Bill V. Mullen have noted, the *Chicago Defender* had achieved broad notice for engaging with leftist politics and culture.[25]

Though his Bud Billiken columns steered clear of sexual content, Motley wrote a racy story titled "Leo Clayton, Waterboy Substitutes" while he was still a student at Englewood High School. The story describes the titular character, who has a crush on a football player named Bert. "Maybe Bert did and maybe he didn't notice the yearning in Leo's eyes," Motley wrote, capturing the familiar frisson of gay adolescence. In another scene, Motley described how Leo, sandwiched between two football boys, felt his "heart beat fast. He held his breath and didn't dare say a word."[26] Though this might have been intended as merely a story about a quest for high school popularity, it seems Motley was testing the waters of homoerotic intimacy before his career as a proletarian writer had truly begun. Motley struggled in these formative years to bring his interests in dissecting the Black urban milieu and probing same-sex desire into alignment. Bud Billiken publicly wrote about the former, while Willard Motley privately wrote about the latter.

That bifurcation in Motley's literary politics changed in the Depression era, when he delved deeper into the cultural front after becoming involved in the development of *Hull House Magazine*.[27] Though he drifted away from the reform elements of Jane Addams's work, Motley cut his teeth in an institution that foregrounded the experiences of sex workers and was located in the slums, where he felt most at home. Motley further developed his literary voice after signing on with the Illinois Writers' Project in 1940, which put him into contact with writers who were developing incipient ideas about labor, literature, and the Left. Beginning in the early 1940s, Motley wrote a number of short stories, most of them dealing with proletarian life, that he submitted to magazines including *Accent* and *New Anvil*. Many of his stories contained homosexual themes set in Chicago's interzones.

"Boy Meets Boy," rejected by *Accent* in 1940, concerned "one of those charming, delicate, artificial young men who had a lot of batty, neurotic male friends hanging around." The story centered on a drifter who, after he "hopped off a freight," found a home within Chicago's gay male subculture, navigating between his hard life as a vagrant and the effete, cultured group of aesthetes whom he met on West Madison Street.[28] The story failed to resolve the tension between these worlds, falling occasionally into a well-trod alignment of homosexuality with bourgeois decadence. But Motley's attentive depiction of the intersecting hobo and homo cultures in Chicago suggests an early attempt to highlight the circles through which he himself passed.

Placing the story for publication proved more challenging. "I don't object to homosexuality as a subject," *Accent*'s editor wrote to Motley in his rejection letter, "but it isn't enough in itself to carry a story." Still, the editor assured Motley that the submission "shows competent writing, and we'd like to see more of your work."[29] Unwilling to put the story to bed, Motley sent it to *Esquire*, where it was also rejected. The editor noted of the story's central character that "his 'simply adoring' nature doesn't come within our scope."[30] Though "Boy Meets Boy" never found a home, Motley's persistent efforts to get it into print suggests his growing confidence in the queer direction of his literary pursuits.

"The Beautiful Boy," drafted around the same time and also unpublished, delved into similar themes, many of which were later incorporated into *Knock on Any Door*. The story is written in the voice of a first-person observer of a "handsome hoodlum" named Mike, who possesses "the same subtle harmony of features; the ivory loveliness of complexion; the gentle and utterly bewitching personality of an enchanting girl." The queer signifiers attached to Mike's androgyny are redoubled through the narrator's observation that "he might have been Oscar Wilde's Dorian Gray." Though Mike is not explicitly described as gay, his experiences with heterosexuality are marked by failure. "Aw," he complains when being teased about his lack of experience, "they all tell me they feel like my big sister."[31]

The narrator in "The Beautiful Boy" follows Mike through the pool halls and taverns around West Madison Street in Chicago, observing as he falls deeper into the rough life of the urban jackroller. The narrator's descriptive gaze often lingers on Mike's handsome features, which are connected to his aura of danger. "If he was the finest looking youth I have ever seen," the narrator remarks, "he was also the most dissolute and licentious." The narrator becomes especially concerned when he finds that Mike has been "playing the queers and luring them to a spot where he could jack-roll them," noting that Mike attracts his targets by wearing "tight-fitting trousers" through which "the outline of his loins and his large calves could be traced." Mike frequents homosexual haunts along West Madison Street. "He became increasingly depraved. He knew a good looking boy could get along on West Madison and he knew every flicker of an eye-lid. He could pick out the homos at a glance."[32] Motley's insistence upon navigating class, sexuality, and urban geography anticipates the more tightly constructed narrative in *Knock on Any Door*. Though neither story made it into print, "The Beautiful Boy" and "Boy Meets Boy" explored the themes that later defined Motley's career: class antagonism, homosexuality, insolent youth, Chicago streets, and the pursuit of sex both for pleasure and for profit.

These themes were fully realized in Motley's first published novel. His working title, "Leave Without Illusions," signified the hard realism animating his tough proletarian aesthetic while signifying his commitment to representing slums with honesty and frankness. "I don't know whether Leave Without Illusions is a good book or a bad one, an obscene book or an 'artistic' one—whatever that means," he wrote of his manuscript.[33] His dissatisfied publisher proposed to Motley a number of terrible (and roundly rejected) alternative titles, each of which avoided the hard realism announced in Motley's. "Waste No Tears" was especially odious to Motley. "I cannot too strongly say how much I dislike WASTE NO TEARS," he wrote to his editor. "To me it sounds like Fannie Hurst or a drug store novel title."[34] Ultimately Motley settled on "Knock on Any Door," a compromise that softened the programmatic reading instructions in his working title but retained the voyeuristic slice-of-life tenor of his original.

Motley's editor at Macmillan remained anxious about the number of doors upon which Motley insisted on knocking. In 1945, Ted Purdy, Motley's editor, suggested he travel to New York for a week of intensive editing. Purdy had decided that Motley's painful excision of many sex scenes did not cut deeply enough to allow for publication. "Macmillan wants the book cut considerably," Purdy advised. "They also want it 'desexed' to some extent." But Purdy seemed most concerned about Motley's homosexual content. "I have told them that in my opinion Owen [the sympathetic gay character] must stay in," Purdy wrote, "but that some of the other homosexual episodes could be cut or elided. I think we can work out a compromise about this. You can say a lot of things by suggestion and indirectly, if necessary."[35] Motley seemed disinclined to speak indirectly. He compiled a lengthy index of obscenity used in his manuscript, with entries that included "ass," "sucking ass," "show him your ass," "uck-fay," "fuck," "cunt," "prick," and "piss."[36] All were deemed unacceptable.

After months of extensive edits, George P. Barrett, Macmillan's director, issued Motley a final cautionary letter. "I have been in this business for thirty-three years and have had a voice in the editorial policy for more than a quarter of a century," he wrote, "and I think I can tell you without danger of contradiction that LEAVE WITHOUT ILLUSIONS has created more controversy, more indecision, and has taken up more time of our editors, our editorial board, than any book that it has been our privilege to consider at any time." In particular, Barrett complained that the book "seemed to all concerned to be far too long, to go far too much into detail, and to dwell too much on sex, especially on homo-sexuality."[37] Motley's refusal to pacify Macmillan by excising his book's "homo-sexuality" threatened an ignominious end to his literary career before it had really begun.

Appleton-Century eventually published the book, and Motley managed to attract a large enough audience to warrant publishing three subsequent novels.[38] While his published book was stripped of many queer scenes, homosexuality nonetheless pervaded Motley's exploration of "the Skid Row of the mind."[39] The novel follows the life of Nick Romano, an Italian American, from his sensitive boyhood through his move into the slums and deeper into the world of crime, ending with a lengthy trial and Nick's execution for killing a police officer. Some vindication for Motley's bold themes arrived in the form of a letter from Christopher Isherwood, who wrote to Motley, "I would like to tell you how deeply [*Knock on Any Door*] moved me, both as a work of art and as an act of human decency."[40] That Isherwood chose "decency" as a description signals his refusal to capitulate to the critics who rejected Motley's narrative frankness as unseemly, a refusal Motley surely appreciated.

The specter of homosexuality emerges as a constant theme throughout Nick Romano's development, and his ability to read sexual cues from men allows him to exploit their desire for material gain. His initiation begins with a boy flirting with him in reform school. After moving to Chicago, where he walks through the slums, Nick observes a group of "young Italian boys, fourteen to eighteen years old," clowning around at a dance hall together. "The boys each grabbed another boy," Motley writes, and they "protruded their rear ends. They kicked their toes against the street. Some postured like girls, smirking, touching their hair, putting their cheeks up against their partners'."[41] As a high school student, Nick encounters Reggie, the owner of a lunchroom that attracts a range of queer customers, who "looked like he was poured into his sweater and tight-fitting pants." Nick scores free drinks when he knowingly "widened his clear, innocent brown eyes with his head half down" (110). Nick not only learns to recognize homosexuals as part of the broader urban milieu, but also instrumentalizes same-sex desire to his own advantage.

As his friends move deeper into adolescence, they begin to participate in more homoerotic play, as when Nick's friend Jinks "wrestled with Stash on top of the Maxwell stand and got him down and got on top of him, forcing his legs out. Then Jinks, with his face down next to Stash's kidded him and pushed his body down tighter and tighter on Stash's" (117). The homoerotic charge of adolescence represents a nonthreatening form of sexuality that runs in stark contrast to the fearsome threat of heterosexuality, anxiety around which brings Nick tremendous shame. It also represents a liminal moment when sexual expression remains unfixed to identity, the latter of which Nick passionately resists. After his first brush with a girl on the streets, Nick "was disgusted with himself. He'd be ashamed to even look at himself in the mirror. He kicked at the sidewalk. He sneaked along. His head was down. Way down" (121).

Though he learns to pursue sex with women—a process that Motley carefully maps as a form of education rather than a natural inclination—Nick's resistance to heterosexuality structures his desire to connect emotionally with other men. He "knew girls and women on the street glanced at him curious-like. And men, too, in a sort of admira-

tion" (128). He also performs his seductiveness, practicing "the innocent stare" because you "got to make them notice you." Yet Nick also
recognizes that arranging himself to attract attention from homosexuals
brings him into their world. "He saw himself standing in front of the
discolored mirror practicing to make the phoneys look at him," Motley
writes, and "walked out of the poolroom fast, ashamed" (139).

In part, Nick's anxiety around heterosexuality is connected to his
being cast as a uniquely sensitive child. At key points in his development,
Nick's sensitivity is directed toward animals. His mother proudly repeats
a story about his having saved a mouse from an attack by a cat as a
young boy; Nick winces "scared and with pity" when he helplessly witnesses a puppy struck by a car on his first visit to Chicago; and he
responds to a classmate torturing a fly "with most of his sympathy on
the fly's side" (85, 102). Motley depicts Nick, even when prone to criminal acts, as a sensitive soul who is redeemed by his caring nature, the
latter of which offsets generalizations linking crime with rough masculinity. Even in prison, awaiting execution for the murder of a police
officer, Nick returns to thoughts of the animals who made an impression
on his youth. Just before he walks to the electric chair, Nick's "eyes
slanted across the death cell to the floor. Suddenly, where he looked he
saw the dog" (495). Vulnerable animals are more meaningful to Nick
than the police—a sympathy that, while perhaps hyperbolic, it is not difficult to imagine Motley might have shared. Empathy with weaker beings
humanizes Nick, and it emerges from his experiences among the poor.

Nick also craves intimacy with other boys. He collects a series of
close male friends including Don, who "looked like a sissy"; Jesse, who
"was handsome like a brown, smoothly built race horse"; and Vito,
who "was a husky guy who wore a chauffeur's cap pushed back on his
head and had a sloppy way of walking" (94, 37, 101). Nick's craving
for same-sex intimacy is facilitated by the specificity of the urban milieu.
In the slums, the rules governing American sexual values slacken, creating spaces where homosexuality is undisciplined and intersections of
communities of color, sex workers, and gay men are commonplace.
"West Madison Street hides many things," Motley writes. "Night and
West Madison hide them all. Jackroller. Crooked cop. Whore. Dope
fiend. Thief. West Madison puts them away in secret cubbyholes. West
Madison puts them all to bed and blankets them over with darkness
and secrecy" (336).

It is within this darkness and secrecy that the intersections of race,
class, and sexuality pull Nick deeper into that world. He had first

learned of the slums in reform school, where a visitor told him about Chicago. "Oh, it's big and it's dirty and there are a lot of slums there," he reports having heard. "But it's a great town. It's a man's town. It's alive." When he arrives in this great town shortly thereafter, Nick encounters an interracial space where characters easily cross the color line. "Negroes in flashy clothes—high-waisted pants, wide-brimmed hats, loud shirts" travel the same streets as a "Mexican boy watching a crap game in the middle of the street" and "two gypsy women" who "wore several different colored skirts." The diversity of people in the slums impresses him immediately: "[Y]es," Nick observes, "they were smart down there" (83, 86, 83, 86).

One of the most important lessons Nick learns in the slums is how to read signs of homosexuality in order to single out targets for jackrolling. This begins by identifying bars where gay men hang out: the Long Bar, the Nickel Plate, and the Pasttime Poolroom. The visibility of Chicago's sexual underground is made explicit when a patron of the Pasttime Poolroom describes how a man "came up to me and asked me if I wanted a room. You know what that means on Madison Street." Cafeterias like the Nickel Plate accommodate "bums, tramps, drunks, panhandlers, jackrollers, road-kids, a few phoneys, and—at night—no women." Sexual dissidents freely cavort with other undesirables. In one scene, Vito suggests the pair visit the Paris, a movie theater across the street from the Pasttime, because "there's always a lot doing there." In the balcony, a man "moved over next to Nick," slowly "edging over in the seat as close to him as he could get" (139, 140).

Once inside a queer establishment, the process of jackrolling requires Nick to cruise for signs of both money and sexual availability. These signifiers sometimes blur: in his first such outing, Vito advises him to "look for creases in their pants and shines" (133). That process drifts into actual sexual cruising, as Nick frequents gay male hangouts and lures targets into dark spaces where he might steal their money. In one scene in the Pasttime Poolroom, Nick begins his seduction ritual by leaning "against the Coca-Cola case, half-sitting." He then plays a couple of games of pool with a man whose "timid eyes went away fast, fluttering down." After attracting the desired attention, Nick leaves, walking "slow, pretending to be interested in the store windows." He turns into an alley, "as if he were going to take a leak." When the "phoney" follows him, Nick grabs the "sonofabitch," cautioning, "[D]on't you know it's one to thirty for fooling with a boy?" (136–37). The man hands Nick five dollars. The sequence of this encounter ends with a threat of violence where a sexual encounter might have been the expected outcome, but the process otherwise follows the rules of cruising: mutual recognition, furtive following into a dark space, assumed intimacy.

Jackrolling, like gay cruising, requires an intimate knowledge of urban geography, particularly through identifying the places where "phoneys" hang out. Motley's casting of homosexuals as "phoneys," a term he had likely heard on the same streets where his novel is set, suggests the oversignification of masculinity required to survive in the slums. Homosexuals make good targets because they are not real men—a mark that Nick's posturing carefully avoids. After they hit their target, Nick and his friends "walked, feeling their manhood, squaring their shoulders, eyeing the broads, throwing their legs in long, ungainly strides, tightening their belts and cocking their hats over their eyes" (136). Their socially deviant and explicitly homoerotic activity is infused with a sexual energy that produces a strident masculinity. Nick's physical attractiveness also works to his advantage. When his friends see how much money he has made playing the homosexuals, one comments, "[T]hey *all* go for Nick!" (156). After Nick is arrested for killing a police officer, the newspapers brand him "Pretty-Boy Romano."

Nick's jackrolling further depends upon a broad recognition that homosexuals are unable to appeal to the law when a crime has been committed against them. When Vito worries that one "could turn us over to the cops" because "he saw us pretty good," Nick reassures him by asking rhetorically, "[H]ow the hell can they squeal?" (138).[42] This observation, which was familiar to Black Chicagoans who were justifiably suspicious of law enforcement, echoes Nick's own distaste for the police beginning in his early adolescence, when a prostitute saves him from a police officer who is chasing him ("[C]ome see me and I'll make it up to you"), moving into resolute hatred of even the officer who attempts to save him from arrest ("I ain't taking no favors from any goddam cop!") (24, 100). The criminalization of homosexuality thus facilitates Nick's targeting of sexual dissidents, while his sympathy toward lawlessness in the slums allows him to move through the queer subcultural spaces with remarkable ease.

Though *Knock on Any Door* frames Nick's movement into the gay underworld of Chicago as a descent from which he cannot escape, Motley's indulgent descriptions of the slums' allure registers an investment that also rewards him financially, emotionally, and sexually. The pleasures of the slums receive far more attention than their pernicious social ills. Even when Nick is sentenced to death in the electric chair, what stands out in his trial is the cast of characters who leap to his defense because the slums care for their own: a Black man named Sunshine who invents a cover story for him; a "Mexican boy" named Juan who vouches for him as well; and Grant Holloway, a white sociologist who is attacked by the prosecution as a Communist "opera lover and socialite," and who associates with "bums, panhandlers, degenerates and all-around thieves" (458). Perhaps the most famous line from *Knock on Any Door*, made iconic in the novel's 1949 film adaptation, is Nick's frequently repeated motto: "[L]ive fast, die young and have a good-looking corpse!" If readers were expected to read the novel as a morality tale, that possibility was offset significantly through Motley's steadfast refusal to affirm law enforcement as a social good and slum life as a social ill. Nick's fast life offers a lengthy menu of pleasures that Motley rarely avoids an opportunity to taste. For audiences seeking sexual dissidence, *Knock on Any Door* presents a remarkably wide array.

Though jackrolling provides the opportunity for many homosexual near misses, Nick also engages in hustling. His first such encounter occurs with Barney, who runs the Pasttime Poolroom. Desperate for money, Nick follows Barney to his apartment. Motley does not describe their sex, instead emphasizing Nick's fixation on Barney's male embodiment, especially his arm, which he imbues with phallic signifiers. "Heavy-veined. Hairy. Muscular. The hairs black, stiff, curling." Similarly, Motley describes Nick's discomfort through language that suggests oral sex: "[T]o keep from bawling, to stop his bottom lip from trembling, he put his teeth over it and fastened down" (147). Though he works through his initial disgust, Nick remains conflicted about having sex with men for money, which he seeks out and then often regrets: "[H]e did it for money anyway, the shame becoming more and more intense" (151).

Nick's primary point of entry into the homosexual world in Chicago comes through his movement into the slums and pursuit of petty crime, but that connection is strengthened through his intimate relationship with Owen, an "unhappy man" he first meets at the Nickel Plate. The man has "loose blond hair and gray-blue eyes that had a sad look in them, deep down and way back" (156). Later, after Nick is hurt in a scrap, Owen brings him to his home near Henry Street, marked by any number of midcentury queer signifiers: a "big-flowered cretonne slip"; a "flower-pattern rug"; "flowered cretonne curtains"; a "*swell* bathroom" with a "fancy toilet mat" (171). Nursing his wounds, Owen affectionately comforts "Nicky," offering him soup and covering him with a blanket when he falls asleep on the sofa. Though Nick does not spend the night, he returns after being beaten by his father. Again, Owen cares for him, his empathy offered in distinct counterpoint to Nick's rejection by his father. "You can stay here," Owen offers in a demonstration of the tenderness Motley repeatedly finds in the slums of Chicago (182).

Nick slowly realizes Owen is a homosexual. Though he routinely "played the queers" on the streets, he does not initially take Owen's kindness for sexual interest. The signifiers of his homosexuality suddenly dawn on Nick, who "stared at Owen" intensely, resolving to treat him like the phoneys at the Pasttime Poolroom. "The sucker!" Nick thinks. "I'll take him for all I can!" (183). Yet his affective investment in Owen prevents Nick from treating him as a target. Though his "lips were drawn back in a tight-skinned sneer," his "eyes were wide and innocent" (184). Nick becomes vulnerable—"[H]e forgot to be hard-boiled and don't give a damn"—and resolves that Owen is too good for him: too good to jack-roll, too good to exploit for money, too good to abandon. "You're all right," Nick tells Owen. "I don't care what you are. You're all right" (185). Between them, "a certain liking and friendship had grown." Though Nick occasionally reminds Owen of the difference between them ("Aw, go on, you phoney," he tells him on one drunken occasion), he nonetheless opens up to Owen in a way he cannot with the toughs on the streets. "I tell you things I wouldn't tell anybody," he reveals (189).

Nick's relationship with Owen develops into a queer intimacy nurtured by their shared lives on the margins of society. "Owen was somebody who understood Nick," Motley writes, "because Owen, in his way, lived outside the law, too." Their bond emerges, then, through their shared lives as social and sexual dissidents. Owen despairs that the relationship will fade when Nick turns to a more socially acceptable lifestyle. "What's going to happen when you get married?" Owen asks. "Well," Nick replies, "we'll be good friends like we are now." The slums incubate spaces for friendship that falls outside the strictures of law, society, and identity. "Nick doubled his fist and playfully rubbed it against Owen's jaw," Motley writes. "You're all right with me" (189).

The ethics of "You're all right with me" provide a through line in Motley's novel, marking the slums of Chicago as a unique space where intimacy was not contingent upon socially acceptable forms of sexual and emotional expression. Motley never fully details the extent of Owen and Nick's sexual relationship, but he strongly suggests such a connection. When Nick arrives drunk at Owen's doorstep one night, Owen attempts to send him home:

> "Go home, Nicky," Owen said.
> "*No.*" Nick pronounced it slowly, echoing it in the emphatic open circle of his lips.
> Owen drank his wine. (296)

The section ends here, but Nick's "emphatic open circle" leaves little doubt as to what happens in the omitted scene. Owen is among the last to visit Nick in his prison cell before his execution. "Why do I like Owen?" Nick asks himself after he leaves Owen for the last time.

> Because he was always decent to me no matter what I did. And liking, love, being pity, sympathy, half-understanding; liking being the recognition of faults along with the good; liking, love, being the circle that ties all things together, Nick went and sat on the bench with his hands at either side of his face. (481)[43]

The concept of "liking" strikes a note similar to the principle of solidarity that animated leftists. While Nick remains acutely aware of the differences between himself and Owen, they have no impact on his "liking" him, and he comes to see his relationship with Owen as central to his understanding of himself and society. Though Motley's novel departs from some of the proletarian literature that dominated the 1930s by omitting a Communist revolution or labor strike, Nick's gradual understanding of the value of his connections to dispossessed lives in the slums brings him to a self-awareness that deviates from personal enlightenment to instead privilege a form of queer intimacy that refuses categorization. Tellingly, the state attempts to use Nick's closeness to the dispossessed to discredit and shame him. The lawyer hired to prosecute him "called bums, hoboes, hostesses and prostitutes, tavern owners and panhandlers" to testify (393). Yet each of them confirms Nick's uprightness, and while the state wins its case, the prosecution comes off decidedly worse than the defense. Motley's novel, then, while acknowledging the social problems incubated in poor urban neighborhoods, nonetheless admits a radical perspective that affirms not only the humanity, but also the potential for solidarity, that was unique to lives and spaces on society's margins.

The unpublished manuscript of *Knock on Any Door*, ruthlessly edited for publication, reveals even more explicitly how Motley drafted a queer radical novel that engaged carefully with Chicago's gay culture, interracial politics, and a total rejection of American capitalism. The demotic language Motley privileges in his draft refuses to distance his narrative from either his characters or their social context. In an early scene where Nick discusses jackrolling queers with men at Pasttime Poolroom, one remarks, "I met some guy the other night who wanted me to do the 69 with him."[44] This level of detail and rough language was smoothly edited out of the published version.

Similarly, some key markers of gay social spaces were removed from Motley's manuscript. In his draft version, a campy scene sets the stage for readers to understand the gay culture inside a cafeteria, detailing patrons whose "faces looked slightly powdered and their lips looked too red. They moved their lips emphatically as they talked; their heads bobbed up and down with their words. They talked with their eyes and their eyebrows. And they talked fast, in whole streams" (371–72). Another bar scene describes a "fruit convention" where one patron asks another, "[A]re you gay?" (578).

Though the published version of *Knock on Any Door* made it clear that Nick was visiting spaces shared by homosexuals, these unpublished passages carefully detail the pleasurable interactions taking place inside them. Motley further describes Nick's interactions with "fairies" not only as a predator, but also as a willing participant in their camp culture. In one scene, a man wearing a "white scarf" asks him, "'Why are you so quiet? Don't you like my company?' '*Sure* I do,' Nick said; and with bravado he reached over and pulled the 'girl's' cheek" (560).

Motley's cataloguing of queer signifiers demonstrates both his facility in depicting gay culture in exquisite detail and contextualizes Nick's introduction to it. Patrons at Reggie's, the lunchroom Nick first encountered as a high school student, explain the queer underworld to readers who might have encountered gay Chicago for the first time. While the published version glosses over these details, Motley's draft includes extended dialogue, with customers describing "Blue Monday parties" where "all the sisters come in drags. . . . This fellow I went with took me into a room and I asked him 'Where's the party?' and he told me 'We'll be the party.' Then he got drunk and took off his clothes" (374). Nick takes pleasure in hearing about such things. "It was fun standing around and kidding with Reggie and Gene," Motley writes, "and it was fun listening to their dirty talk and dirty jokes" (375). Further, Reggie's represents a racially mixed space where a "couple of colored fellows from the school with big-brimmed hats pulled over their foreheads, with high-waisted pants, with loud, tricky jackets, put the palms of their hands over the flies of their pants and, one arm held out stiffly, danced across the floor alone, dipping with the beat and slide of the music" (384). Gay socializing was also a site of queer interracial intimacy.

Motley's unpublished draft also enlists Nick in conspiring with Reggie to resist policing of queer spaces. When Reggie offers Nick a cigarette, "Nick put his head close to Reggie's and said in a whisper, 'You better be careful about selling the guys cigarettes. A goddamn cop offered to pay me if I bought a smoke from you.' Reggie's hand closed in soft fingers over Nick's and pressed a minute. 'Thanks, doll!' he said" (383). Nick was invested in challenging the authority of the state along with his fellow sexual dissidents—a critique that, for Motley, linked policing sexual dissidence with race. In a handwritten glossary, Motley defined "lily law":

> Uncomplimentary term used for any segment of law and order. ("Here comes the Lily Law"—actually making fun, implying "that one's queer too." "Mother Harrison," a divisive term for Captain Harrison—Chicago police station). This term sometimes abbreviated to "Lily" ('you better wipe of that powder, kid, because Lily Law walks in here pretty regularly.')[45]

Motley's embrace of queer argot suggests a deep connection between his political and sexual deviance.

Similarly, Nick's motivation for hanging out with homosexuals is far more ambiguous in Motley's draft manuscript, where Nick has sex with men for money, but also for pleasure: "[I]t was a way of loosening the tenseness that was knotted up inside him. A way of spreading out the dirty thoughts he had about girls every few days" (564). Nick's relationship with Owen, lightly coded to be read more along the lines of a queer friendship in the published version, is also drawn more explicitly in the unpublished draft as a mutual relationship. In his first sexual encounter with Owen, the published section that cut off abruptly plays out to its conclusion:

> They went toward the bedroom door. Owen put his arm around Nick's hip. They went in. The light faded out behind them. Only a small angle of it, growing dim, followed them into the bedroom. Owen stood close to Nick. His weight was against Nick, pressing him back against the bed. Nick sat down on the edge of the bed, not caring. His lips were drawn back in a sight-skin sneer, showing hard white teeth. But his eyes were wide and innocent.
> "Nicky!—Nicky—!"
> Nick lay back on the bed, stretching out.
> "Nicky—I had to have you. I couldn't bear it any longer."
> Then he was kissing him on the mouth, first gently, then harder and harder with his loose, damp lips. (753–54)

The next chapter begins the following morning, when Nick wakes up, noticing that "all of his clothes were off. Owen rouses next to him, and "leaned over, gently, and kissed Nick." While Nick remains conflicted about his sexual relationship with Owen in the draft version—"Don't talk about it!" he cautions Owen when the latter begins describing a previous relationship "with another boy" who "looked like you"—he continues to see Owen. "I guess everybody wants to be loved by someone, Nicky," Owen says. "I'll see you Saturday," Nick says as he walks out the door (755–58).

Perhaps most significantly, the published version of *Knock on Any Door* omits both Nick's class consciousness and the intersections of explicitly queer-Left geography in Chicago. In the draft manuscript, after Nick marries and returns to Owen, drunk, to have sex, he wanders for the first and only time in the novel outside the slums. Nick observes the crass excess that provides a counterpoint to the neighborhoods of Chicago that he calls home, and his interior monologue registers his disgust with conspicuous wealth that depends upon poverty to be maintained—a consciousness that emerges only after he has accepted that he cannot give up his sexual relationship with Owen. Nick "walked, blindly, not knowing where his feet took him," Motley writes.

> He came down off the bridge at the other end along the high wall of the Civic Opera House. Taxis were drawn up at the curb. Chauffeur-driven Cadillacs and Pierce-Arrows. Bitches in their five and ten thousand dollar furs with layers of pearls strung around their neck and dirty rich bastards in tails and high hats were getting into the cars. Nick stared at them. He bared his teeth as if he were going to spit. His nose curled. These bastards and bitches here while right down the street the bums and hoboes and drunks were walking, staggering along West Madison. Nick pushed through the rich bitches and bastards. He turned, angrily, and shoved back through them, pushing a woman with his shoulder and making a top hat go slantwise on some old pot-bellied guy's head. And west and south beyond West Madison there ain't nothing but slums. The slums stretch in frame shacks and tenements far as you can see—or even imagine, goddamn it! Greeks. Dagos. Spics. Niggers. Kikes. Jumbled up. In their little shacks without anything to eat or nothing to wear. (1163)

In the published version of the novel, Nick's world is hermetically sealed inside the slums. He moves through these spaces with ease, exploiting those he can and making alliances with those he desires. In this excised passage, Nick draws a contrast between the world he inhabits and the one that lies beyond his reach. Yet rather than yearning for that other world, Nick kicks against it, literally pushing against the wealth he reviles. He observes how race and ethnicity structure the inequality that surrounds him. The slurs that conclude the paragraph, delivered in a list of punctuated fragments, invoke all that he loves about the slums while announcing the language that keeps the "Greeks," "Dagos," "Spics," "Niggers," and "Kikes" separated from the "other end" of the West Madison bridge. Nick's relationship with Owen opens his eyes to the realities of injustice and allows him to develop a sense of solidarity with the dispossessed.

Though Nick stops short of formally joining a left-wing movement, he recognizes, in the draft manuscript, the overlap between the organized Left and the queer underworld of Chicago, particularly in Bughouse Square, where he encounters "soap boxers preaching the gospel, shouting politics, talking Communism, red-baiting." Moving deeper into the park, he "went over to the bench near the toilet and sat down to see if he could still work it," watching the cruising men "furtively and seeking." When he is pursued, Nick accompanies one "close to the bushes where it was dark," and where "the man moved closer to him and put his hand on Nick's leg." Throughout, the two hear "the soap boxes in the street" where "the speakers shouted democracy, religion, Communism" while the homosexuals around continue "talking in the voices of women; calling each other, 'Miss Hartford, Mrs. Jones, Queenie, Bubbles, Josephine, Madame Aldridge.'" (1244).

While *Knock on Any Door*, in both its published version and its unpublished drafts, revealed Motley's interest in bringing his radicalism, desire to faithfully represent life in the slums, and familiarity with homosexuality into conversation, his manuscripts reveal a far more nuanced understanding of sexual dissidence than what appeared in the version that made it onto best-seller lists. Rather than crudely representing homosexuality as a form of abjection and Nick's same-sex affairs as linked to his criminal activity, Motley attempted to depict the slums as a unique space where undesirables could find one another. Those efforts did not end with the book's publication, shortly after which Motley moved to Mexico, presumably owing to the encroaching McCarthyism and growing racism in the United States. He did not return. In the 1950s, Motley noted that he intended to subscribe to the homophile publication *ONE*.[46] By 1961, he was plotting a "HOMO BOOK," through which he aimed to depict "such people through a novel, describing their frustrations, their attraction, their hatred, their misunderstanding, their guilt, and their love."[47] Motley maintained a robust glossary of homosexual argot that paired terms such as "rim," "fish queen," "golden stream artiste," and "goop-gobbler" with equally in-the-know definitions ("vulgar term for mouth sex"). He was also concerned with detailing "homos as to profession," compiling a list that included "male nurses, beauticians, window trimmers, interior decorators, clerk in men's shops and music shops, masseurs, actors, artists, musicians, poets, writers, singers, priests, athletes." [48] He passed away before he could begin that work, but much of what he was plotting had been seeded in both the published version of *Knock on Any Door* and the drafts his publisher rejected.

Motley's radical fiction explored sexual dissidence with great sensitivity. He refused to produce a work that centralized sexual identity, instead meticulously representing a social context that offered explanatory potential for understanding both the possibilities and slights confronted by sexual dissidents in urban slums. His characters led robust sexual lives that included homosexuality and prostitution. They lived, worked, and played in neighborhoods marked by conflict, but also shaped by a shared experience of dispossession. Nick Romano was Italian American, but the circles in which he traveled crossed lines dividing sexuality, race, and ethnicity. Literary critic John C. Charles describes how "Motley valorizes the crossing of all social borders as a way to resist the manner in which dominant culture notions of identity functioned as a mechanism of social division and control."[49] As a radical writer, Motley critiqued systematic inequality by depicting the struggles he observed in the slums of Chicago. Yet he also allowed space to represent the intimacy, camaraderie, and solidarity uniquely available to those who inhabited the public and private spaces of the urban underworld. He left no illusions about the misery inflicted by capitalism's cruel designs, but he identified deeply with those on the margins. His work suggests how leftist writers probing the sexual underground could find lurking in the shadows an army of undesirables anxiously waiting for their moment to rise up.

H. T. TSIANG'S PROLETARIAN BURLESQUE

In January 1941, novelist, poet, performer, and playwright H. T. Tsiang wrote a letter to the leftist artist Rockwell Kent on a roll of toilet paper from an Ellis Island deportation cell where he was being detained on immigration charges.[50] Tsiang, a Chinese American writer who had achieved some notoriety following his publication of three novels and a volume of poetry, was biding his time while the judicial system decided whether he was eligible to stay in the country where he had resided since 1926. Tsiang's detention was hardly unique; the Johnson-Reed Act of 1924 had sent many of his fellow immigrants to meet a similar fate, and restrictions on Chinese immigration had been central to US immigration policy since the Chinese Exclusion Act passed in 1882. Yet his unorthodox response to his conditions was a typically bizarre supplement to his offbeat literary career: in spite of his vulnerable circumstances, Tsiang refused to behave as a model US citizen, offering friends and colleagues evidence of neither his respectability nor his decorum. Instead, Tsiang sent his letter to Kent on the most vulgar signifier of his conditions imaginable, his small cell transformed into a stage upon which he could perform his radical gesture of refusal. As though to reinforce the intentionality of his scatological performance, Tsiang also included a traditional typewritten transcript of his letter. The enjoyment of low culture was always at the forefront of Tsiang's economy of pleasure.

Tsiang's profane scroll stands as a testament to his transgressive literary performances. His letter recounts the banalities of life at Ellis Island with a sharp sense of humor and quirky eye for irony. Tsiang remarks upon how he created a writing table by folding blankets atop his toilet; his discomfort having to interact "with all white people"; and his endless amusement at a photograph Kent sent of himself, in response to which Tsiang tabulated the number of hairs he could count on Kent's balding pate. Yet language constituted but one aspect of Tsiang's artistic expression, and his correspondence having been written on such foul parchment was as significant as any of the mundane tales he recounted. Throughout his career as a writer and actor, Tsiang's cultural production, both public and private, emphasized performativity as much as description. In Tsiang's hands, a letter could be transformed into a pungent performance of insubordination, just as under his pen a novel could become a dramatic production of proletarian burlesque, a peculiar sexual radicalism that combined a commitment to leftist politics with a perverse celebration of sexual misbehavior's revolutionary potential.

Six years before sending his letter to Kent, Tsiang had surprised leftists and writers with the self-publication of a queer proletarian novel that he later transformed into a stage production. *The Hanging on Union Square* suggests how Tsiang used artistic techniques drawn from performance to articulate leftist politics while refusing to meet heteronormative expectations. His profound sense of the ironies in American life was uniquely attuned to the difficulties confronting those who wished to challenge the repressive sexual mores, oppressive economic conditions, and racial and ethnic prejudices that made a mockery of American life. "Everything is fine and gay," Tsiang wrote on his toilet-paper scroll, "but the locked door, guard and uniform." Rather than attempting to participate in an American conversation built upon exclusion, Tsiang disclosed the deviance at the heart of the sexual economy, the illogic of US capitalism, and the complex ways in which performance could both shape and shed light upon the curious practices and queer pleasures of everyday life in the United States.

Even within the annals of modern literature, *The Hanging on Union Square* is a peculiar text.[51] Tsiang foregrounds fragmentation, bad taste, minimalism, and campy humor. The novel is divided into sections; each section is further divided into chapters that begin with a short rhyming verse repeated throughout the section. Characters are named for central attributes, stereotypes, or social locations: the main character is a confused man named Mr. Nut; a defiant Communist organizer is named Miss Stubborn; a prominent capitalist goes by Mr. System. *The Hanging on Union Square* follows the unemployed Mr. Nut's travels throughout New York and traces his initial revulsion toward and eventual commitment to Communism. The story culminates with Nut's staging of his own hanging on Union Square in order to draw attention to the plight of the unemployed. Tsiang's is a bawdy, raucous novel that depicts all manner of sexual scenarios. The rhythmic style of the narrative and his overtly radical politics place it firmly in the category of modern proletarian fiction.

Tsiang's work embodies an underexamined tendency in radical fiction toward the proletarian burlesque, engendering elements of performance and perversion to challenge, assault, and bait readers. Robert C. Allen characterizes burlesque performance as "grounded in the aesthetics of transgression, inversion, and the grotesque." Such performances, Allen argues, are useful for mobilizing "the 'low other': something that is reviled by and excluded from the dominant social order as debased, dirty, and unworthy, but that is simultaneously the object of desire and/or fascination."[52] Lucinda Jarrett adds to this explanation by noting how burlesque "offered promiscuity and expressed a sexual and economic independence."[53] It is difficult to imagine a more fitting description for *The Hanging on Union Square,* where Tsiang's characters are seduced into radicalism by experiencing the pleasures of capitalism's unregulated red-light district and find within the dirty bedsheets and naked glare of the stage lights a seductive alternative to capitalism's dreary ennui.

The proletarian burlesque could be found in Depression-era radical literature ranging from Samuel Ornitz's *Haunch, Paunch, and Jowl*—a fictionalized autobiography later adapted as a "drama in two acts and seven scenes" that included a preposterously staged drag show performed in "mincing steps and squeaky voice" and included a vulgar song "that couldn't bear repeating even in a frank book" performed "down among the audience"—to Michael Gold's whiteface drama *Hoboken Blues*.[54] It combined five features: an emphasis upon performance and performativity; an interest in sexual dissidence; a critique of capitalism; a vicious use of vulgar humor; and a reliance upon overtures toward realism as license to depict explicit and lurid sexual scenes to challenge the audience's detached spectatorship by both exciting and affronting them with blatant perversity.

Though each of the five features making up the proletarian burlesque could be found in fiction preceding the 1930s, they were particularly prominent within Depression-era proletarian literature, and they combined to reframe radicalism in several significant ways: by incorporating marginalized sexual subjects into the radical project; assigning agency to working-class subjects; and reframing the project of literature to break down the inequality transmitted through power dynamics between subject and object. Tsiang's proletarian burlesque assaulted his audience by frustrating their narrative expectations, foregrounding a surfeit of obscene content, wallowing in low culture, depicting slapstick comic scenes, portraying outlandish violence, describing vulgar floor shows in exquisite detail, and confrontationally defying good taste. Tsiang reimagined proletarian literature to make it perform important political work by pushing readers into unexpected thematic, stylistic, and sexual territories. Though he was not alone in this endeavor, his work is unusually bold in this direction.[55]

That performance should play a particularly prominent role in radical art and fiction has seemed counterintuitive, given the emphasis upon realism and a "documentary impulse" that motivated mid-twentieth-century leftist cultural producers such as Willard Motley. The mass of critical work studying radical fiction has turned on the notion that the primary relationship between cultural producers and their subjects was marked by efforts to connect representations with real-world circumstances: art called attention to material conditions so that they would be changed. Social problems were best described by those who sought to break down the line between representation and reality; and efforts to sway public opinion, policy, and society could do so most efficiently by confronting audiences with scenes reflecting the power of the masses in unequivocal, legible terms. Yet rather than rejecting the world as a stage, radical writers often produced a peep show for the proletariat.

For Michael Gold, the proletarianization of American literature could be described only through a theatrical metaphor: "The People

Come on Stage."[56] Performance, Jill Dolan argues, "provides a place where people come together, embodied and passionate, to share experiences of meaning making and imagination that can describe or capture fleeting intimations of a better world."[57] This "embodied and passionate" space was the foundation upon which the proletarian burlesque was constructed. Within 1930s and 1940s radical fiction, everyday performances were set up as sites for radical "intimations of a better world." Ann Petry, in her 1946 novel *The Street,* set in New York, describes her protagonist Lutie Johnson's visit to a cheap 116th Street apartment building where "the tenants . . . would sit on the stairs just as though the hall were a theater and the performance about to start."[58] Claude McKay offers his meditation on similarly vernacular performances in a 1938 poem, "Lenox Avenue," in which he describes the famous Harlem street:

> The mummers mass in Lenox Avenue,
> A Negro theater by night and day,
> In accents strong and colors of every hue,
> A race enacts its passionate play.
> . . . .
> Here is a vaudeville that never stops![59]

Even those rare radical authors who did not include so much as a cursory scene featuring dramatic production or everyday performance still performed important work through their untoward provocations directed at readers, disregard for politeness, fetishization of social problems, and prurient obsessions. They effectively made their middle-class readers into consumers of working-class amusement and reorganized their working-class readers into aesthetic arbiters.

Much of the untoward provocation in *The Hanging on Union Square* derives from its unabashedly queer aesthetic. Though details about Tsiang's life suggest he had a strong interest in sexual dissidence, his work was not strictly autobiographical.[60] Nonetheless, he often drew on his life to produce his art. He was born in China in 1899 (though he preferred to claim his birth year was 1906) and immigrated to the United States to attend Columbia University. He moved in leftist circles and participated in classes at Erwin Piscator's dramatic workshop, immersing himself in the world of avant-garde drama and absorbing the tenets of epic theater. His failure to find a supportive political, literary, or theatrical community impelled him to forge an independent path and to endlessly promote himself with limited success. He claimed to have attracted luminaries such as Orson Welles and Rita Hayworth to his performances, and his books were read and occasionally praised by many leading figures in the literary Left. Tsiang expressed his strong physical attraction to Rockwell Kent, and he was quite forthcoming about articulating his deep love for Kent in his letters; one of these included a sketch of Kent by Tsiang that sports a remarkably tumescent endowment.[61] Tsiang's advances were never acknowledged by Kent directly, and the two were not particularly intimate outside this correspondence. In a letter to the publisher Richard J. Walsh, who had rejected a Tsiang manuscript that Kent had sent him, Kent referred to Tsiang as "emotional and unstable" and indicated his wariness around the offbeat author. The fact that his books were self-published, his theatrical entrees were self-directed, and the publicity surrounding his artistic output and his reputation as a cause célèbre were self-generated suggest how Tsiang blurred the line between autobiography and performance. His life was inextricable from his work.

Tsiang's leftist attachments are more easily established. He supported the reformations of the conservative Kuomintang in China before emigrating for the United States, where he lived on a student visa and later as a political exile. In a 1935 *New Yorker* profile, Tsiang wryly noted how his move to the Left inverted the Chinese government's rightward turn. During his time as a student at Columbia University, Tsiang became committed to radical politics within the United States, especially through the Communist Party, which he openly supported. It is unknown if he joined as a card-carrying member, but he attended meetings through at least 1952. In addition to his leftist fiction and poetry, Tsiang wrote regularly for the *Daily Worker* and *New Masses*. He sold his books on the street at a 75 percent discount to members of the Communist Party, and he playfully referred to the publishing time line of his first three books as his "Five Year Plan."[62] When a man at a store accused him of being "pink," Tsiang reportedly replied, "Pink!—Hell, I'm as red as that."[63]

When *The Hanging on Union Square* was self-published in 1935, Tsiang's novel mystified critics, readers, and publishers, most of whom were unprepared for the task of evaluating such a formally inventive, politically outspoken, and scandalously sleazy work. Tsiang conceived his novel as a piece of modernist, experimental writing put in the service of a radical political position. In the 1935 *New Yorker* profile, he declared his allegiance to the queer modernist writer Gertrude Stein.[64] The precariousness of this allegiance was made into reflexive fodder when Tsiang mocked his critics for having "condemned the book with 'he is not much of a writer and his chief literary influence is the decadent Gertrude Stein,'" highlighting the charge of "decadence" that was sometimes used by leftists to condemn reactionary literature while also connoting sexual libertinism.[65] Yet despite his aspirations to high modernism, especially in its more perverse and experimentalist mode, Tsiang was equally drawn to the "low other," incorporating the generic conventions, sexual appetites, violent outbursts, prurient obsessions, and sensational plot contrivances of the dime novel—a debt he signifies throughout his novel's lurid story and winking innuendo.[66] Several scenes in *The Hanging on Union Square* involve actual dimes: in the opening scenes as the price of a cup of coffee; as a prop in a sexual performance later; and as the cost of admission into a sleazy movie house called the Dime Hotel, where Nut is finally radicalized. The working-class appeal of the dime novel is signified each time one of Tsiang's characters finds through this common currency a new form of radical pleasure. Tsiang interweaves sexual desire, working-class amusements, and mass culture to produce his proletarian burlesque, and if his novel's political work is occasionally difficult to piece together as it is washed out in the blinding light of his sparkling language and the shadows of his seedy sex scenes, Tsiang's privileging of pleasure and transgression as sites of ideological investment offers a striking corrective to representations of working-class identity exclusively seen through the lens of hardship, frustration, and want.

Before the narrative even begins, *The Hanging on Union Square* contains eleven pages of material that catalogues the rejection of Tsiang's manuscript by mainstream publishers and the support he procured among prominent radicals of the day. Though the imprimatur of these noteworthy radical writers undoubtedly widened his readership, Tsiang's eagerness to broadcast his rejection established him as a writer working outside the literary establishment. One editor at the John Day Company refused to even correspond with Tsiang, complaining to Rockwell Kent that "he has a bad habit of quoting publishers' rejections in his books."[67] At the same time, Tsiang's inclusion of a bizarre array of endorsements, disclaimers, notes, and other preliminary material enhanced his star turn as author, narrator, editor, publisher, publicist, and salon host extraordinaire to the fanciest personalities on the Left. His novel was a glamorous rehearsal for his one-man show.[68]

The publisher feedback Tsiang excerpts ranges from the banal to the prescriptive. "The idea of the book is an interesting one," one editor writes, "but we are afraid you are never going to be able to get it published as long as it remains in its present form. We suggest that you re-write the story in straight-forward terms as a realistic novel."[69] By reproducing this suggestion, Tsiang invites his reader to share in his deviant pursuit of pleasure and filth. As it happens, Tsiang was not entirely opposed to social realism on either aesthetic or political grounds. In a scene from *The Hanging on Union Square,* Tsiang describes a man marching in a demonstration carrying a sign reading "We Want Milk for Our Baby." "It was not artistic," Tsiang writes, "but [he] knew that their baby needed milk."[70] Yet the inclusion of such dismissive editorial advice did the dual work of both identifying Tsiang with other radical writers who more comfortably fit this mold and disidentifying him from leftist critics' generic commands.[71] Tsiang's performance thus passes from one of mere refusal to a staging of curious, even queer, attachment, where his own refusal to follow good advice becomes a site of pleasure, play, and campy theatrics. Readers are encouraged to read the book as forbidden contraband.

Tsiang also includes a short foreword by the critic Waldo Frank that both celebrates and criticizes the novel. Though he applauds its "flashing counterpoint of almost savage sensuality and delicate pity," which Frank imagines might emerge when proletarian writers are freed from the "straightjacket of what calls itself 'Marxist realism,'" he also concedes that the book "contains passages that may offend by their crudity and by the *naiveté* of their presentation."[72] Still, Tsiang includes a note at the bottom of the page objecting that as a matter of fact he "employed the method of 'Socialistic Realism and Revolutionary Romanticism' when [he] wrote the novel."[73] Tsiang's insistence that his novel actually *does* employ social realism, all evidence to the contrary, ironically aligns him with the aesthetic model his most prominent champion dismisses as retrograde. Tsiang's authorial performance takes pleasure in adopting the role of a tragic comedian—a staple of the 1930s burlesque—who secures his own marginalized fate and enjoys some dark gallows humor on his way to the noose.

Though its narrative is set in apartments, cabarets, burlesque houses, movie theaters, and cafeterias and on the streets of New York, Tsiang's novel is structured as a literal performance. The book is separated into four "acts," and the minimalism of Tsiang's language suggests that much of his narration might be imagined as stage notes. In fact, Tsiang later adapted *The Hanging on Union Square* into a performance featuring himself as writer, producer, and star. The novel follows Mr. Nut as he evolves from a cranky reactionary into a full-blown Communist revolutionary. This transformation is aided by the gender-ambiguous Miss

Stubborn, a variety of humiliating or upsetting experiences, and a nameless movie-theater masturbator; it culminates when Nut double-crosses Mr. System at the well-attended event that was supposed to stage his own hanging. The novel is loosely plotted, mostly consisting of scenes featuring Nut's thwarted attempts to secure food, sleeping quarters, and, eventually, the love of Miss Stubborn. The novel's second half largely concern's Nut's "coming out" as a Communist.[74] Most of the hanging on Union Square is less dramatic than the hanging that occurs in the final section of the novel; instead, the characters indulge in a good deal more hanging out.[75] Tsiang's book drifts between class, sexual, and ideological polarities in a cruisy narrative of pleasure seeking and active spectatorship that assaults its audience with a catalogue of disgraceful scenes. The novel refuses to distinguish between staged or theatrical performances and the vernacular performances of everyday life. An intimate sexual act in the privacy of a bedroom follows the same stage directions as a public performance for an audience assembled to watch a show.

The novel opens with a snappy dissection of American life in which Tsiang distills the variety of human experience under capitalism to its bare economic motivations. Within this exposé of the performances in everyday life, Tsiang introduces his proletarian burlesque through an appearance of his first floor show: "The girls in the next door burlesque show with nothing on except their natural skins. Shaking breasts. Moving hips. Sparkling eyes. Front going up and down. Before a lip-parted and mouth-watering audience. Making money" (14). For Tsiang, the burlesque represents an important site of pleasure, but it also reveals the machinations of the political economy. "The fellow writes sex stories," Tsiang writes with a wink. "Sex is depression-proof" (15). Of course, Tsiang is writing sex stories of his own. *The Hanging on Union Square* contains more sex than labor; more burlesque than grotesque; more sexual dissidence than straight decorum. Much of the novel describes wild sexual scenes: homosexuality, masturbation, striptease, sodomy, and cruising abound; some scenes are so shocking, so mind-bendingly filthy, it is difficult to even decipher what is going on. Yet throughout, sexual acts are also conceived by Tsiang as sites ripe for a Marxist interpretation. "He is a nice looking fellow. Has he any money?" (13). A materialist critique of the sexual economy allows Tsiang to describe sexual dissidents in terms that are both revelatory and witty, and the proletarian burlesque is celebrated for its potential for fun as well as its radical sexual implications.

The opening striptease is but one example of Tsiang's burlesque writing performances. In another bizarre scene, Mr. Nut finds takes a job as a "rabbit" for a tough who goes by the name Mr. Ratsky—a gangster, a capitalist, and a sadist.[76] When he orders Nut to perform a striptease—more strip than tease—in his apartment, Ratsky calls out a series of salacious commands that seem to equally describe Tsiang's poetics: "Take off your hat! Take off your overcoat! Take off your coat. Take off your shirt. Take off your trousers. Take off your underwear! The room is warm, it'll do you no harm. Stay where you are without moving!" (83). The minimalism of Tsiang's language performs the dual work of revealing the raw sexual energy in Ratsky's forceful demands and signifying the performative impulse of excising descriptive language and all elements of romanticism from Tsiang's novel. For Ratsky, these demands become themselves sites of pleasure. These commands function also for Tsiang to direct his readers by sanctioning his obscenity and presenting a stage for producing a pornographic-realist narrative. Tsiang transforms the demand that radical writers truthfully record social conditions into permission for chronicling sexual escapades with a raw edge and a smutty abandon. "If the Communists don't shout," one character asks, "how can they make a revolution?" (18). Tsiang's performance shouts from every page.

Tsiang opens his narrative in a Communist cafeteria in Union Square—a space that signifies both the robust urban sexual underground and a hot zone of working-class radicalism. One character complains of the square that "there are so many Reds, so many Socialists, so many Anarchists and so many 'What-Nots'" that "every inch of the ground [is] deeply cursed" (197). Cafeterias were similarly well-known sites for both queer and leftist gatherings.[77] The area around Union Square was particularly rich with cafeterias that were patronized and managed by radicals, and they were well-known sites for queer cruising and radical soapboxing.

Though homosexuality is only one form of sexual performance Tsiang includes in his novel, his interest in prurient themes is such that none of his characters engage in missionary-position, heterosexual intercourse. Tsiang casts his perversion as a radical position. "I don't believe in what is called disgrace and what isn't called disgrace," a Communist character declares before making a radical proposition: "Politically we should form a United Front, for the benefit of both our classes" (188–89). Even a seemingly heteronormative love story between Mr. Nut and Miss Stubborn is made queer through Stubborn's initial appearance as a butch Communist who passes as male. Nut mistakes her for a "young fellow," eventually realizing that "that young fellow was not a *fellow* but a girl. A girl in a certain kind of uniform" (20). The uniform of the Communist Party broke down gender categories and opened up new forms of sexual desire. Stubborn "becomes" female only when she announces to her comrades that "we have to be at the meeting earlier so the boys can not say we girls are inferior." Her female identity is less a matter of biology and more the product of a performative utterance. "Being able to stand up and become 'She,'" Tsiang writes, "was a joy, a privilege, and a human right" (175).

Yet Stubborn's radicalism is also signified through her refusal to participate in socially constructed performances of femininity. When Mr. System instructs her to "use lipstick to make her lips redder and use powder to make her face whiter," she initially relents. Soon, however, she cannot subject herself to such demands; she strikes Mr. System, who is stunned that "so delicate and so soft a hand could make his fat, rubber-skinned face feel so hot with pain" (28, 29). Though Tsiang resolves Nut's initial confusion about Stubborn's sex, she continues to exhibit tough characteristics that resist feminization: she wears a leather jacket and a "little button with Lenin's picture on it"; she puts herself on the line for workers; and her "boldness" had "acquired the confidence of her union" (105).

The union of Nut and Stubborn never quite occurs, but readers are led to understand that it is, in part, their curious love that brings on a revolution. The androgynous Miss Stubborn declares that "to love whom she wanted to love and to express her love—express it openly—that was a revolution" (175). It bears noting, then, that within Tsiang's fiction, all sexual performances are depicted as queer insofar as they resist straight readings, regardless of the sexual or gender taxonomies of the characters. "There was love for the biological reason," a character opines within the novel's pages, "for the artistic reason, and for the political (revolutionary) reason." Stubborn decides that "if a girl was not governed by the ideas of a cheap movie and was not dreaming of marrying the boss for money, she was not so bad" (175, 176).

In *The Hanging on Union Square*, homosexuality particularly surrounds Tsiang's protagonist, Mr. Nut. He generally rebuffs such advances even though he is described as having an "artistic temperament"—a common reference to homosexuality during the 1930s.[78] Still, gay sex is widely practiced and discussed by the working-class heroes who eventually spearhead Mr. Nut's radicalization. When one female character kisses another on the mouth, the second responds diplomatically. "That wasn't so good. I didn't like it," she says. "But my dislike is just a matter of personal taste. It has nothing to do with our political opinions. We should form a United Front always!" (189). Tsiang's sexual underground might be subject to taste and preference, but it refuses explicit judgment. Sex is always a tool for revolution, and the language of the Left provides an ideal framework for bringing together sexually diverse populations under the uniting banner of the red flag.

The most pronounced channel for describing the revolutionary implications of queer sexuality is articulated in Tsiang's alignment of writing and reading with sexuality. Tsiang was forthcoming about the intimate relationship between literary and sexual radicalism. "Poetry seemed to him," he writes of one of his reactionary characters, "to be no more than the yearning of a sex-starved idiot" (34). Yet for Tsiang, the theme of writing as both a surrogate for sex and as an indicatively sexual performance recurs with great frequency, and the "sex-starved idiot" turns out to also be the agent of revolution. A parallel depiction of sexuality and writing appears when Mr. Nut meets a gay poet at the corner of Eighth Street and Sixth Avenue and, as can hardly be read as coincidental, on page 69 of the self-published book. Tsiang's description of the poet immediately identifies him as a queen: his hair was "richly oiled and it was carefully scissored along his neck"; his "eyebrows were poetically arranged"; and "the lips of the young fellow were painted and his tongue went out just a little bit and made his tiny mouth more noticeable." Nut accompanies him to his studio—"[D]on't say flat," the poet advises, "it isn't poetic"— where Nut is seduced and engaged in campy repartee. Upon finding that he has never met Nut before, the poet drily remarks, "Oh, what's the difference? Strangers this time. Acquaintances the next" (69, 71, 70).

After enjoying some food and drink in an apartment appointed with a photograph of the poet's mother inscribed "[T]o my dear son—from his lonely and affectionate mother," Nut declines the poet's persistent offer to "read you some poetry." He instead retires to the sofa, where he sleeps with "his legs stretched out and his body relaxed." Very soon, however, he finds himself awakened by "the young fellow . . . running his hand through Mr. Nut's hair" and kissing "Nut's forehead, cheeks, and lips." Though Nut decides to leave, he remains polite, thanking the poet for the bread. The "young poet" finally gets to recite a piece of verse as Nut turns to leave his studio: "*I wish your taste would be like mine—We could just be sixty-nine*" (73). The poet's act of transubstantiation, where poetry both stands in for and articulates queer sexual performance, presents a scene in which the performance, narration, and formal innovation are symptomatic of the same sexual economy.

Nut then moves into the next scene, titled "Artist and Uniform," which immediately introduces an additional sexually dissident character for whom reading and sexuality are inextricable. The character has "the appearance of a professor," and his comportment is contrasted with the poet's: he wears a "small beard"; his "hips were steady"; and he "had no powder on his face and no lipstick on his lips" (75). The man reveals himself to be a radical intellectual and writer, and he describes traveling to the Soviet Union—a standard pilgrimage among 1930s radicals.[79] "In Moscow, 'Artist in Uniform!'" the man exclaims "triumphantly" and "somewhat Max-Eastman-ly" (75). Tsiang's joke about Max Eastman's famous "writers in uniform" also offers a pun on "manliness" that highlights Tsiang's self-consciousness about defying the demand for rugged masculinity expected of Depression-era radical novelists.[80] The polemical writings of literary figures such as Eastman, a curious advocate of manly writing whose work teems with sublimated homoeroticism, and Michael Gold advocated a tough realism that confronted social problems with open eyes and furled fists. As *The Hanging on Union Square* illustrates, Tsiang rejected the demand for toughness among radical writers and refused to write in a "man-ly" or Eastman-ly fashion.

The professor's masculine performance, incorrectly read by Nut as heterosexual, is undone through his decidedly bold advances when the two share a bed. The professor orders Nut to share his bed; to sleep on the "inside," where he will presumably be more sexually available; and to remove his pants, each of which demand Nut obeys. Nut is awakened when he "felt something uncomfortable touching the lower part of his back. It was not the old man's hand. Nor was it the old man's finger. Of course, Mr. Nut knew what it was" (78). This passage's slippery signifiers slide between embodiment, perversion, and the pleasures of words, speculating on the notion that linguistic indulgence might signify sexual dissidence and revolutionary performativity.

The idea of an active audience, be it at a burlesque show or movie screening, in a library, or at a labor-union demonstration, implicates readers of Tsiang's novel. Each performance in *The Hanging on Union Square* assumes an audience that does more than just sit back and enjoy the show. The audience frequently takes orders from the performers, becoming themselves agents of change in the text and society at large. Mr. Nut stops inside a movie theater to take a short nap only to find himself subjected to a musical soundtrack that encourages cruising and sex among the audience while anticipating the cataclysmic act of revolutionary violence that concludes the novel:

If you want to have your fun,
You can play with your gun!
If you want your heart to spring,
You can pull your string. (118)

This song evokes a cry of "Jesus!" from one audience member; another "began to follow the instructions of the romantic music and started showing some action." Nut's mixed-up experience in the movie theater becomes the catalyst for his radicalization. "Theoretically," Tsiang informs readers later, "Nut, ever since he had stepped into . . . that ten cent movie-house, was a Communist" (119, 132).

We might consider Nut's hanging on Union Square as itself a final sexual performance. Nut's plan is to hang himself so he can create a spectacle and reduce the number of unemployed. The autoerotic possibilities in self-hanging offer further motivation. The performance is staged as a dancing extravaganza—as another performance of racy proletarian burlesque. In one rehearsal, Nut is squeezed so hard by his instructor that he spontaneously ejaculates on the floor in a scene foreshadowing the erotic potential of strangulation that the hanging similarly promises to deliver (200). Tsiang thus transforms the spectacle of political protest into a burlesque performance where the audience for the hanging is depicted as deriving no small sexual thrill from Nut's coming performance: "Here's a kiss!" one girl calls out to Nut as he ascends to the stage. "Isn't he cute? He's smiling," another announces (206). The staging of the performance also directly parallels an earlier sexual liaison in the novel when a lamp's swaying stands in for the motions of intercourse.[81] The rhythm of sex governs the performance of the hanging; after listening to Mr. System's rich description of the event's staging, the event's promoter, a cynical opportunist named Wiseguy, finds he needs a cigarette (196).

Yet the spectacle of violence is, of course, the other significant draw. As we have seen, Tsiang conceived performance as always demanding direct engagement from audiences; whether this was of a sexual, violent, or utterly banal nature here becomes ambiguous. Violence, however, like sexuality, demands that audiences respond viscerally to their bearing witness—a point Tsiang illustrates by including scenes of beatings, suicides, and brutality. When Nut participates in an earlier racially charged incident that results in police brutality, his inability to attain any critical distance from the warm blood flowing from the body of the beaten activists causes him to realize that "the blood of the colored race and the blood of the white race that fell on the cement pavement were of one color" (59). Nut's hanging is supposed to do similar work on its audience, forcing spectators to adopt a radical perspective on the performance and to conceive the hanging as a vehicle for promoting their own incipient radicalization and union. Whereas solitary hanging represents a social-realist performance, as evidenced in Nut's private suicide attempt earlier, described by Tsiang as having "ended the story literarily, non-propagandizingly, and publishably," a public hanging unequivocally demands an audience (181).

Neither are the deeply racialized and sexualized implications of a public hanging far from Tsiang's narrative. The lynching of African Americans in the South was a widely discussed issue among radicals in the 1930s; Tsiang directly mentions the Scottsboro defense in the novel. "You helped black people," an African American character declares; "now black people help you" (58). Yet for Tsiang, the spectacle of lynching is less analogous to Nut's staged hanging than is the capitalist exploitation of Black cultural performances. Wiseguy's determination to cash in on Nut's public suicide resembles the capitalist exploitation of Black culture by white entrepreneurs that was an all too common feature of the US entertainment industry, from the blackface minstrel stage to Tin Pan Alley. Wiseguy envisions Nut's hanging as a song-and-dance routine where dances correspond to the constricting of oxygen to Nut's brain:

> You know, we Americans like jazz. So the first few minutes, Mr. Nut could have his hands and feet—his whole body—swaying to the rhythm of a waltz. In the beginning, Mr. Nut would go slow—taking things easy. Then a foxtrot would be played—and Mr. Nut would go a little quicker. For his breathing will be shorter and he'll naturally go quicker.—Then a tango will be played and you understand, when Mr. Nut begins to feel pain he will have to go faster and faster. And finally when there is no more breathing and the oxygen in his system is exhausted, he will be at ease and take life just as it is. Naturally, at this time, the "St. Louis Blues" should be the tune. (196)

Tsiang's wry deployment of a Dixieland vision of racial "harmony," where the "ease" of plantation life is signified by concluding the deathly soundtrack with a performance of the "St. Louis Blues," makes visible the violence implicit in US performances of race and racialization. Mr. Nut's performance is scripted by Wiseguy to conform to the racial demands of audiences at hangings and the capitalist interest in both indulging this expectation and exploiting its commercial potential. Wiseguy's demand for Blackness challenges the categorization of racial identity in the United States by treating performance itself as constructing a racialized identity.

Wiseguy's raced demands of Nut—a character with whom Tsiang closely identified, and the role he played in his stage adaptation of his novel—was not incidental. As an actor, Tsiang found himself typecast in roles that demanded he conform to Chinese stereotypes, which tended to be particularly limiting.[82] After he was lauded by critic Edwin Schallert for his portrayal of Quisling in the 1944 film *The Purple Heart,* Tsiang responded by taking out an advertisement mocking Schallert's praise, noting that he appeared in the film with "no pipe, no glasses, no hair, plenty of grinning." Tsiang was equally displeased by those who saw his ethnically charged performances as failures or successes: either he was affirming racist expectations that he rejected, or he was failing as an actor. As a writer, Tsiang was careful to name-check literary models with whom he felt his audience would expect an alliance. In letters seeking a publisher, for example, he emoted enthusiastically about Pearl Buck—an unlikely literary hero for one as transgressive as Tsiang. Buck was a white woman who had grown up in China, and she was popular writer of the day whose novels, including *The Good Earth* in 1931, dissected Chinese culture. Yet in *The Hanging on Union Square* Tsiang adopts the voice of a prostitute to attack Pearl Buck's middlebrow orientalism, imaging himself writing a very different book about China that asks "whether the shape and size of that very thing of men there, is the same as that of the men here" (191). Tsiang preferred to imagine himself sharing more in common with a randy female prostitute, and his novel proposed to replace the good earth with a salacious comparative study of the male anatomy—the research for which, one imagines, Tsiang was prepared to perform with relish. Even if, as a novelist, Tsiang could not risk alienating readers by disavowing the inevitable and distasteful comparisons made between him and Buck, his characters do a tidy job of undermining her literary pretensions and claims to authority.

Of course, the literal hanging of Mr. Nut does not occur. In a scene that refers back to the masturbatory episode at the movie theater, Nut at last "plays with his own gun," turning the much-anticipated performance against its audience when, just before he is supposed to be hanged, Nut double-crosses and shoots Mr. System. "I, a Forgotten Man, a Little Man, an Average Man, a Worker," Nut proclaims, directly citing the language Wiseguy used to promote Nut's hanging, "will this time –doublecross you, Mr. System—the Exploiter, the War-maker, the Man-killer." The hanging turns from a violent sexual spectacle into a radical pageant that is itself imbued with sexual signifiers. The pageant—complete with political speeches and vaguely suggestive ideological pronouncements such as one spectator's exclaiming, "[O]veralls are coming!"—becomes itself a form of proletarian burlesque: rather than a theatrical representation of political realities, politics are enacted through a performances that grabs at its audience (208, 207). The spectators for the hanging produce a discursive frame for making sense of the event that in turn allows Nut's gunshot to acquire meaning. The event works only because the politics of the burlesque are always-already performative; performances are double-crossing acts that threaten the comfortable distance of ideological detachment. The hanging on Union Square thus becomes a self-referential defense of the project of producing radical cultural texts that foreground performativity and a rationale for taking on political commitments. The performance shifts from an act of surrender to a call to arms, and the audience is transformed from witnesses into co-conspirators.

In the final scene we discover that we as readers, scholars, and sleaze-show ticket holders are thrill seekers in Tsiang's audience. Just as *The Hanging on Union Square* begins with a series of critical comments about the manuscript—and even though the words "THE END" appear immediately after the gunshot—Tsiang's novel does not end here. The book concludes with fifteen pages of material in increasingly shrinking type excerpting Tsiang's other books, citing endorsements of those works by similarly prominent critics, and pleading with readers to help reduce the financial burden on future Tsiang novels through subscriptions—an effort that was apparently successful, since his most celebrated work, *And China Has Hands,* appeared two years later. The abrupt ending to Tsiang's novel refuses to fade into the blankness of the book's endpapers; it instead announces an encore performance where Tsiang reminds audiences of his work and that there are always more things that must be done. Tsiang's resistance to easy resolutions, pithy platitudes, and least of all silence sums up his contribution to the history of queer leftist literature. For Tsiang, a novel might end with its climax, but there are always more wicked acts to follow, more wild performances to attend, and more work to be done—vertically, horizontally, and even while hanging on Union Square.

Both Willard Motley and H. T. Tsiang capitalized upon the freedom they found in writing proletarian literature to foreground sexual dissidence within a leftist literary project. Their experiences as people of color well acquainted with American racism informed the circles in which they traveled and the themes they explored in their work. Much of their salacious content brushed against the limitations of publishing, which foreclosed some content from reaching audiences—with extensive revision or self-publishing the only mechanisms available to bring their work to readers. While *Knock on Any Door* and *The Hanging on Union Square* departed formally from one another, each novel carefully navigated urban geographies, finding in city streets the shared spaces and radical gestures that pushed against the bourgeoisie. By exposing social problems, the authors attempted to incite readers to revolution. But their deep dives into the urban underworld also revealed how sexual dissidents could resist the state, threaten capitalism, and offer alternative avenues for pursuing queer pleasure and intimacy.

CHAPTER 7

"We Who Are Not Ill"

Queer Antifascism

Homage to Catalonia, George Orwell's influential 1938 memoir of fighting in the Spanish Civil War, opens in the Lenin Barracks in Barcelona, where an international group of ragtag volunteers set out to defend the Spanish Republic. As he tours the facilities, Orwell encounters "an Italian militiaman," a "tough-looking youth of twenty-five or six," to whom Orwell takes "an immediate liking."[1] Struck by the instantaneous connection between the two, Orwell observes how the solidarity shared among fellow travelers in Spain shifts the rules of intimacy between volunteers united in their willingness to put their bodies on the front lines as soldiers fighting in the antifascist struggle. Some of them are Communists, others anarchists, others liberal or social democrats, but all are connected in some way to the political Left. "Queer," Orwell writes, "the affection you can feel for a stranger!"[2] Indeed, if the Left had in previous decades incubated new forms of intimacy among political partisans united in their shared revolutionary fervor, the growing resistance to fascism, especially as it played out in the battles of the Spanish Civil War, represented a critical site where queer solidarity strengthened those bonds through reference to a common ideological enemy.

As the antifascist struggle consumed and shifted the priorities of the Left, the latter's relation to homosexuality similarly changed. On the one hand, the antifascist struggle opened the Left to a form of democratic pluralism that could be instrumentalized to foreground homosexuals as part of America's national fabric. Radical inclusivity—

a marker of a society free of fascist influence—opened a popular new narrative of Americanness that occasionally extended to homosexuals. This democratic form of antifascism celebrated strength in diversity, allowing gay women and men to envision themselves as fully deserving of a seat at the table. The particularly high stakes for homosexuals became especially pronounced as Nazi antipathy became well known.

At the same time, the structure of 100 percent Americanism that gripped the Communist Party during the mid-1930s replaced revolutionary calls to overthrow capitalism and decolonize the Black Belt with gentler forms of coalition building. The demand for a total rejection of the American state, which structured the political deviance that drew many sexual dissidents into the orbit of the Communist Party, was sidelined in favor of a broader Popular Front that urged working with existing political structures and building alliances between liberals and leftists. Granville Hicks, a former *New Masses* editor, observed that "the American Communist party of the Popular Front period was a long way from the Leninist concept of the disciplined, monolithic party of trained revolutionaries."[3] Absent that revolutionary fervor, the pull of the Left shifted to a more sanguine narrative of shared investment in American political life. This discourse was consistent with emerging ideas about sexuality that framed homosexuality in the language of human rights and tolerance and reconceived American history as a teleological march of progress in which gay women and men could either join in or get left behind. This shift set the stage for the emergence of a national identity-based politics of sexuality that calcified in the formation of the 1950s homophile movement. It also represented a move away from ideological opposition to racial capitalism that had for decades informed the relationship between homosexuality and the Left.

The flash points of antifascism in the 1930s—Hitler's rise to power in 1933; the Comintern's adoption of the Popular Front platform in 1934; and the battles of the Spanish Civil War from 1936 to 1939—fundamentally reshaped the relationship between sexual dissidence and the Left in American culture. "All this was queer and moving," Orwell wrote of the Spanish Civil War, and though the British novelist was not himself especially concerned with homosexuality, other writers on the Left were.[4]

This chapter considers two sites of intersection between sexual dissidence and the Left in relation to antifascism. First, the threat of Nazism precipitated a Popular Front strategy on the Left that proposed alliances across identities and political persuasions as critical to waging a successful war against fascism. The emerging emphasis upon pluralism softened some of the militant rhetoric that had previously defined the Communist Party. Second, fighting in the Spanish Civil War provided an occasion for sexual dissidents to fight alongside one another and create bonds of intimacy that sometimes became sexual. Even Orwell's battalion included "a half-witted little beast of fifteen, known to everyone as the *maricón* (Nancy-boy)"; to him was given the best rifle in the barracks.[5] While the popular image of the nearly three thousand Americans who joined the Abraham Lincoln Brigade (ALB) has tended to favor a manly volunteer, presumably heterosexual, the presence of sexual dissidents within the ALB challenged associations of the revolutionary ranks with straight masculinity. Fighting against fascism demanded fighting alongside, and sometimes even on behalf of, sexual dissidents, and the Left was fundamentally changed by the antifascist struggle.

WRITING SEXUAL DISSIDENCE INTO ANTIFASCISM

In 1934, Edward Dahlberg, a Communist "fellow-traveler" who, according to a reviewer in *New Masses*, "has been constantly drawing closer to the revolutionary movement," published his third novel, a "work of revolutionary fiction" titled *Those Who Perish*.[6] As the author of a semiautobiographical novel, *Bottom Dogs* (1929), Dahlberg had achieved enviable status as a novelist whose work received mainstream notice while also garnering praise from the literary Left. *Bottom Dogs*, an important work of proletarian fiction, established Dahlberg's reputation as a radical writer, and the novel's success emboldened him to expand the purview of his literary concerns.

By 1933, Dahlberg's focus had shifted from the plight of the US working class to the rise of fascism in Europe—a global crisis epitomized by Hitler's ascension to power in Germany. Though antifascism became a familiar fight on the Left as the 1930s progressed and the global threat posed by Hitler became devastatingly clear, Dahlberg was the first writer to publish a novel concerning the rise of the Third Reich. *Those Who Perish*, which earned Dahlberg a paltry $200, featured gay characters animating the struggle against fascism in the United States.[7] In his blurb for the novel, leftist literary critic John Chamberlain described Dahlberg as "a Proust of the lower and middle depths of society."[8] Though Charles DeFanti later complained that "even in a novel of protest [Dahlberg] could create only characters that are composites of himself and his mother," such is the stuff of queer literary history.[9] If Dahlberg's perfunctory plot and lightly sketched characters seemed underdeveloped to critics approaching his work, the urgency with which he rushed *Those Who Perish* to publication spoke to the menacing climate of the moment and the ways leftist writers were uniquely prepared to spearhead a cultural response to the crisis. Despite its grim sales figures and (arguably) solipsistic composition, *Those Who Perish* heralded a new age for radical writers fighting against fascism.

Those Who Perish's publication at a time when Dahlberg was closely aligned with the Communist Party emblematized a key shift in leftist politics that put antifascism at the center of radical art and literature. The formation in 1935 of organizations such as the League of American Writers, a left-leaning antifascist organization of which Dahlberg was a founding member, and the Artists against War and Fascism confirmed opposing fascism as a primary concern of leftist culture workers.[10] The antifascist mood impelled naturalist writers, Dahlberg among them, to create a diverse range of characters occupying vulnerable positions in US society. If the central question posed by American writers observing rising fascism in Europe was "Could it happen here?" leftist writers were well positioned to show what already *had* happened under capitalism and where it would lead if allowed to proceed unchecked.

Fascism in Germany was concerning to American leftists in part because Nazi leaders opposed Communism. "The left wing is bellicose," the *Chicago Daily Tribune* charged in 1938, "and hopes to engage the United States in the conflict to save the world for bolshevism."[11] But this conflict was not reducible to ideological disagreement. Leftists, who had been working to embolden the most vulnerable victims of capitalism for decades, were uniquely attuned to how fascism posed an existential threat to the already marginalized groups the Nazis brutally terrorized. The overrepresentation of ethnically diverse immigrants and African Americans within the ranks of the Communist Party, following a longer history of leftist organizations built by minoritized Americans, further informed the speedy response to fascism by those on the Left.

As Hitler gained strength, and as his terrifying global ambition became clear, leftist writers produced work that directly confronted the rising tide of anti-Semitism and imperialism both globally and domestically, adopting, as Michael Denning writes, "a politics of antifascist and anti-imperialist solidarity."[12] Hitler's violent exercise of power in Europe represented an especially clear and immediate danger to a precarious population that was made all the more urgent to leftists because so many radicals were also Jewish. Many of the most bellicose American radicals had found refuge in the United States after fleeing persecution in Europe.

Though it was discussed infrequently in leftist news outlets, Hitler's regime also threatened homosexuals. By 1934, the *New York Times* had published an article in which Hitler referred to homosexuals as "absurd apes."[13] As many as sixty-three thousand gay men were tried and convicted in Germany between 1933 and 1945, and up to fifteen thousand died in concentration camps. This staggering persecution came on the heels of a growing alliance between gay rights supporters and leftists that had calcified during the Weimar Republic. Germany's Paragraph 175, which had criminalized homosexuality in 1871, was in the throes of being abolished when the Nazis swept into power. The German Social Democratic Party had long opposed the law (an initiative to overturn it was introduced by the GSDP in 1898), and it had rarely been enforced during Otto Braun's term as prime minister.[14] Magnus Hirschfeld's Institute for Sex Research (ISR) was founded shortly after leftists came to power, and prominent GSDP officials openly supported the institute's work.

The Communist Party of Germany also maintained a close relationship with sexologists.[15] Kurt Hiller, a Communist who directed the Party's Scientific Humanitarian Committee, was arrested, beaten, and thrown into a series of concentration camps before escaping to Prague.[16] Hiller stated in 1928 that "a Marxist is making a fool of himself when he tries to connect the homosexuality of the present with the class struggle, by pointing to it as a symptom of the 'moral decadence' of 'a certain sector' of society, namely the bourgeois sector: as though same-sex love did not occur among proletarians of all kinds—among workers, peasants, employees, little people in all occupations—just as much as among the possessing classes."[17] The ISR saw its holdings burned in one of the earliest acts of Nazi purges. The vibrant gay culture in Berlin, which included organizations and publications in addition to a sizable bar and cabaret scene, was also targeted by Hitler's brutes. Gay gathering places were shuttered by Nazis, and homosexuals were placed under intense discipline even before they were adorned with pink triangles and ordered into concentration camps.

While some scholars have focused on homosexuality among the architects of the Third Reich, American leftists showed little appetite for casting Nazis as deviants. "The truth of the matter is that it doesn't really matter very much whether Goering is a dope fiend or Hitler's sex life is peculiar," Ruth McKenney complained in *New Masses*. "Perversion is unpleasant, but not very important. The private lives of fascist leaders may be dull and dirty, but the anti-fascist movement cannot center its attacks on the vicious manners and abnormal appetites of Nazi rulers."[18] Though occasional sport was made of speculation about the perceived homosexuality of some Nazi leaders, it hardly defined the American Left.

Dahlberg was inspired to write *Those Who Perish* after witnessing Nazi terror firsthand during a 1933 visit to Germany, during which he was assaulted and arrested by the Sturmabteilung (SA). He published an article recounting his travels for the *New York Times,* foregrounding the class struggle in a nation where "the swastika has replaced the red flag on every house." His analysis was inflected with an emphatically left-wing viewpoint. "The industrial titans expect to come into the foreground," he wrote, and students, who had "little sympathy for the workers," supported Hitler because "they want to win back class distinction, economic preferment, all the prerogatives of caste that the Hohenzollern empire had previously given them." Witnessing Hitler's brutal regime impelled Dahlberg to note that "Catholic, Jewish, Liberal, Social Democratic and Communist newspapers (with the exception of two or three underground papers which must necessarily have an extremely restricted circulation at the moment) no longer exist." In a chilling prediction, Dahlberg added that "Hitler proposes to keep the Communists and Social Democrats in concentration camps."[19]

In *Those Who Perish,* Dahlberg depicted a wide range of straight and gay characters working in and around a Jewish community center in New Jersey. The novel opens with Regina Gordon, a worker at the center, contemplating how "the whole world at this moment was bursting shells of horror on all sides of her." In particular, "the murders as well as the cold legal pogroms against the Jews in Germany had filled her with fears and forebodings such as no hallucination or fever in the darkest period of her childhood had." Seized with paranoia, Regina sees fascists around every corner. The specter of the holocaust in Germany drives her to madness. Against the backdrop of encroaching fascism, new alliances are forged. Walking by a bookstore window, Regina sees both *Psychopathia Sexualis* and a volume titled *The Communist Party Lives and Fights* on display. The intersection of deviance and radicalism entices her. When she finally gives in to her Communist sympathies—"[I]f you were against murder and war, you were a Communist, a pariah"—she decides, "So be it."[20]

Dahlberg represents sexual dissidents as key figures both building and shaping the antifascist struggle. Moses Kotch, one of the central leftists in the novel, is introduced wearing "a green silk necktie held in place by a woman's gold beauty pin"—an outfit that immediately puts him at odds with the corporate members of the center's board. He is further mapped as homosexual by carrying "a paper edition of the private life of Oscar Wilde" in "the side pocket of his purple suit," and he suggestively asks over lunch if Eli Melamed, a sensitive former perfume salesperson, has "ever read Havelock Ellis." Kotch is the first character in the novel to raise alarm about fascism coming to the United States, suggesting that he heard from a Socialist that "the Ku-Klux-Klan will get together and commence a pogrom" with Hitler.[21] The gulf separating Nazi monoculture from US racism was neither deep nor wide.

Though Eli is not himself homosexual, Dahlberg tenderly suggests same-sex desire as an impetus for building antifascist solidarity. Eli's proximity to sexual dissidence through his queer occupation and dispossession impels him to fight against fascism. Unemployed, broke, and two months behind on his rent, Eli is taken to Childs cafeteria by an ex-surgeon with "tapering, fluent fingers" and "groomed nails and fragrantly soap smelling hands" who speaks in "concert 'cello chords.'" The man, who tells Eli that he "could go on recounting the picaresque escapades of Hazel Dawn, the San Francisco underworld," cruises him "in the park behind the 42nd Street Library." "You know," he says, "your hair reminds me of the Mediterranean around Capri . . . really sensitive and musically impassioned hair." Though Eli rebuffs the man's advances and "hurried off," Dahlberg writes:

> He walked and wept; sobbed to think that any one could want him, could find in him a want and a need, he who was so needy and by now wantless because it had become so futile to want anything at all.[22]

Framed within so explicitly antifascist a novel, this passage is made all the more remarkable. Rather than depicting a homosexual preying on a man who is down on his luck, Dahlberg instead positions their interaction as a turning point in Eli Melamed's radicalization. It is through a same-sex advance that a destitute character finds himself affirming his worthiness as a human being after having been rejected by the capitalist economy and the machinations of a cruel democracy that refuses to stand up to fascism. Dahlberg's foundational text—an early contribution to leftist literature's antifascist turn—relies upon sexual dissidence to produce the solidarity necessary for fighting against Hitler's formidable force. Even at a time when it seemed futile to want anything at all, queer intimacy produced affective bonds that spawned a movement.

While the rise of fascism introduced alliances between sexual and political dissidents struggling against the Nazi threat, antifascism in the United States also produced a discursive slipperiness between Jews and homosexuals. In 1938, Harry Hay, later a homophile-movement founder, wrote an unpublished story titled "Little Jew-Boy."[23] "Little Jew-Boy" follows the title character as his rabidly anti-Semitic classmates mercilessly bully him. Hay writes that "he was a sissy. You could tell to look at him. All black curls, and red lips like on valentines, and skin so white it was blue." In addition to his effeminacy, "when he tried to play ball, or run the fifty yard dash, his behind wiggled just like a girl's." Perhaps most incriminatingly, "little jew-boy never played with little girls, or went down under the bridge and made them pull their dresses up."

Hay's narrator describes the boy's efforts to make friends with new children who have moved into town, each attempt thwarted by the boys who "make fun of the new one and call him sissy-bait" and "show the new one how little jew-boy could only cry and wilt around when he got mad." Little Jew-Boy does have one redeeming feature: he owns a football helmet. The boys scheme to have him play tackle in order to injure him and gain use of the helmet. Again, their cruelty becomes cartoonish: "[W]alking on him," the narrator describes, "was like jumping on an old inner-tube when it's got a leak, and he was so blue-white and prettier'n any girl."

Little Jew-Boy eventually makes friends with a boy named Bill, their relationship becoming so serious that "they were even giving each other presents and stuff on birthdays," precipitating a tremendous backlash. "This going steady stuff," the narrator complains, "wasn't being a decent American." Things come to a head when Little Jew-Boy radicalizes Bill with talk "about Greek religion, and how Saint Paul was only a politician," and how "in Russia the people had torn down all the churches and killed all the preachers." A female character reports this to her family, and her uncle becomes enraged. "I allus thought there was somethin sneaky about that kikey bunch," he fumes. "Dirty foreign trash tryin to teach our kids I.W.W. talk." His rant escalates, and eventually a group of town men with torches go on a midnight raid. "The white folks got to show their superiority somehow," one child's mother observes.

The clumsy narrative of "Little Jew-Boy" suggests Hay's interest in proletarian fiction, having at least absorbed the Jewish cultural signifiers and blunt caricatures of social fascism that characterized much Popular Front literature while demonstrating no absorption of subtlety or modern literary techniques. "Jews are terrible people," the narrator declares at one point, "and shouldn't be allowed to live with other people." At times the narrative's obsession with Little Jew-Boy's genitals seems designed to titillate: "[L]ittle jew-boy is a pig," students taunt in a grimly forced epithet, "he puts it in his hand and makes it big." While it is putatively within the realm of possibility that Harry Hay was thinking carefully about the contours of Jewish struggle as he crafted, or rather drafted, his unusual work of fiction, it seems far more likely that he was drawing on the robust climate of antifascism to expand the Leftist conversation to include a queer victim of American hate. Very little in the story points to stereotypes circulating about Jewish boys, but most aspersions cast on gay boys make at least a fleeting appearance.

In 1945, Richard Brooks, later known as a director of high-profile films including *Blackboard Jungle* (1955) and *In Cold Blood* (1967), published *The Brick Foxhole,* a brutally violent potboiler that, in Judith E. Smith's analysis, "argued for boundary-crossing cosmopolitanism through the moral condemnation of its opposite."[24] The novel was set during World War II, a context that tested the limits of democracy by placing its characters in close quarters.[25] Rather than exploring soldiers on the battleground, however, Brooks's novel was set in the barracks (the "brick foxhole" of the title), an uncompromising domestic setting that introduced everyday homosociality as a political concern. The book raised the ire of the US Marine Corps, who were not permitted to review the book's content before publication and objected to its unglamorous portrayal of American troops.[26] *The Brick Foxhole,* later released in a pulp edition that promised an "outspoken" and "shocking" narrative, detailed the baiting and murder of a homosexual civilian at the hands of military men fueled by masculine sport and antigay foment. ("I ain't beaten up a queer in I don't know how long," one character complains.)[27] This plot point might have heralded the trope of tragic queers that persisted well into the Cold War, and indeed Mr. Edwards does conform to many of the standard representational strategies that presented gay men as disempowered vehicles of American affliction. "I have such a bitchy life," the gay character melancholically complains, further lamenting, in a clunky bit foreshadowing, "I'm so lonely I could simply die."[28] But the ferocious attack on this gentle character also positions him as a sympathetic victim within a narrative of American prejudice: his attackers are also virulently racist and anti-Semitic, and his murder propels a narrative that exposes the wicked core of American hatred that was brought to the forefront alongside the ascendance of fascism. Though the extent of Nazi persecution of homosexuals was not fully understood in the United States until Richard Plant published his exposé on the "pink triangle" in 1986, Brooks's novel did include homosexuals in a moral cosmology that was, at its core, deeply antifascist.[29]

Progressive representations of homosexuality in the wake of World War II tended to highlight points of commonality between racially and ethnically targeted Americans. Brooks's inclusion of a homosexual victim in *The Brick Foxhole* allowed critics such as Sinclair Lewis to admit a social critique that included Jews, African Americans, and "especially homosexuals" as victims of prejudice, ultimately concluding that the true problem for Americans was "hatred finally, for everyone and themselves."[30] Richard Wright similarly praised Brooks's "first public excursion into fierce truth-telling," noting how the novel's foray into "the apartments of men who like to pick up lonely soldiers" allowed him to explore "the noble citizens who inhabit this great arsenal of democracy."[31] In *Crossfire,* Edward Dmytryk's 1947 film adaptation of Brooks's novel, the persecuted homosexual character was easily recast as a Jew.

Within leftist literary culture, resisting fascism offered a critical tool for writers to blur the line separating antifascism from queer militancy. Valentine Ackland was a Communist who both lived and collaborated with her lover, the British novelist Sylvia Townsend Warner, author of the 1936 queer-leftist novel *Summer Will Show*.[32] Ackland had established her own reputation as a talented journalist and poet who wrote for many leftist publications, as well as contributing to more-mainstream outlets such as the *New Republic*. She attended the 1939 Congress of American Writers and threw her support behind the Republicans in the Spanish Civil War. She was also a gender-nonconforming woman who lived in Dorset, England. In a 1935 letter describing her favored attire—corduroy and flannel—Ackland observed that in her village, the "younger people all became friendly to me because, I think, it made me unlike the people who so much oppress them (as you'll find when you talk to them), the 'County' grandees, and the clergy and their wives."[33] Female masculinity connected Ackland with the masses.

In 1943, Ackland published a poem, "Teaching to Shoot," in the *New Yorker*. It appeared at a time when Hitler's atrocities were unfolding in public view and the antifascist struggle had expanded into World War II. In this poem, as advertised, Ackland describes teaching her lover to shoot an unnamed target:

This thing you hold as you once held my hand is ready to kill.
We intend to finish those who would finish us—we who are not ill,
Are not old, are not mad; we who have been young and who still
Have reason to live, knowing that all is not told.

In your hand you hold iron, and iron is too old
And steel, which breaks and shatters and is cold,
And our hands are together as always, and know well what they hold.[34]

Ackland was an antifascist; a Communist journalist and poet who wrote for *New Masses* and the *Daily Worker*. She was also a queer woman who was "not ill," was "not mad," but was angry, militant, and ready to shoot. "Teaching to Shoot," a defiant work that positions radical self-defense at the nexus of queer and antifascist politics, emblematizes the joining of sexual dissidence and antifascist poetics. Though Ackland does not name fascists as the target that she teaches her lover to shoot, the cultural context in 1943 encourages such a reading. Her ambiguous "we who are not ill" and "are not mad" also suggests how Ackland exploited the militant vernacular of the antifascist moment to address both fascism and persecution of sexual dissidents—though it is more the latter that yields the warning that "all is not told." The poem's intensity draws upon the passion of a lifelong political struggle that demands taking up arms against "those who would finish us"—the "us" familiar to both victims of fascism and queer people subjected to unrelenting state repression. Grasping the trigger of a rifle offers a tactile intimacy that calls to mind the joining of lovers' hands and foregrounds the radical potential in repurposing this familiar gesture to take aim at fascists, whatever form they take.

John Malcolm Brinnin, the gay Communist who dedicated his debut poetry collection, *The Garden Is Political,* to Kimon Friar, included in that 1942 volume a short poem, "Waiting," that similarly collapsed the familiar wartime landscape of the antifascist struggle into a defiant narrative of love and militancy during a time when politics intruded upon even those spaces designed to nourish aesthetic pleasure:

What reasons may the single heart employ
When, forward and impervious, it moves
Through savage times and science toward the joy
Of love's next meeting in a threatened space?
What privilege is this, whose tenure gives
One anaesthetic hour of release,
While the air-raid's spattered signature displays
A bitter artistry among the trees?[35]

242 I "We Who Are Not Ill"

Brinnin's poem includes signifiers of pressing social conditions ("savage times"), brief encounters ("one anaesthetic hour of release"), impending destruction ("the air-raid's spattered signature"), and tremendous passion. "Forward and impervious" moves Brinnin's heart toward his lover, or his Party, or his brief encounter with an unnamed Other. Brinnin reimagines the air raid as an illuminating state apparatus that reveals the "spattered signature" of a too-short encounter, equally adaptable to both love in wartime and gay cruising under the sign of state-sponsored sexual repression.

"Love's next meeting" could have meant many things. It might have been a meeting of lovers, or strangers, or comrades. It might have been a singular affair, or a weekly commitment. But when it occurred, it was for one anaesthetic hour; before and after, there was waiting. Love's next meeting might have been held in a smoky room where radicals plotted their revolution, or it might have occurred in the shadows of a park under the cover of trees that ensured none could bear witness. It might have resulted in a release from the oppression under which so many struggled, or it might have resulted in a singular moment when its subjects were released from the pressures surrounding them. As dispossessed people around the world struggled to survive under a fascist threat that seemed too great a force to repel, that one hour offered all the joy of an eternal masterpiece or a perpetual revolution. Love's next meeting, wherever and whenever it occurred, possessed the power to change the world. What bitter artistry leftists displayed during this weighty historical moment.

HOMOSEXUALS AND THE PEOPLE

Edward Dahlberg's antifascist novel anticipated the Communist Party's Popular Front, which shifted the vernacular of the Left to privilege democratic discourse through which political parties and ethnic groups united to affect change. Meeting in Moscow on July 25, 1935, to draft a new platform for the first time since Hitler assumed power in Germany, the Seventh Comintern Congress adopted a series of resolutions that both acknowledged the gathering fascist threat and plotted its opposition. "In face of the towering menace of fascism to the working class and all the gains it has made," the Comintern determined, "it is the main and immediate task of the international labor movement to establish the united fighting front of the working class." The antifascist struggle was cast as the Left's highest priority, "even before the majority of the working class unites on a common fighting platform for the over-throw of capitalism and the victory of the proletarian revolution." This common platform required leftists to join "with the organizations of the toilers of various political trends for joint action on a factory, local, district, national, and international scale." The particular actions required to achieve the goals of unity necessary to repel fascism were wide-ranging: joining with "the social-democratic parties" and "reform-ist trade unions"; participating in elections "to prevent the election of reactionary and fascist candidates"; establishing "a wide anti-fascist people's front on the basis of the proletarian united front."[36] Unity was the word of the day, and the shifting political climate in Europe pre-cipitated a strategy that made strange bedfellows of Communists, New Deal Democrats, and liberal labor unions.

The Popular Front period represented a clear turning point for the American Left. The previous Comintern congress, which met in 1928, had taken a harder revolutionary position, advocating nothing less than "the seizure of power and the overthrow of the bourgeois capitalist order." The "Theses and Programs" adopted at that conference, which had dragged on for almost two months, charted a rising "revolutionary tide"; it was "the task of the proletarian party to lead the masses to a frontal assault on the bourgeois state."[37] This frontal assault curried no favor with those who failed to sign on to the full Communist platform, rejecting claims of solidarity with any organizations or individuals who wavered in their commitment to the "revolutionary ferment." The Par-ty's Third Period dominated leftist politics until the fascist threat became so attenuated as to demand realignment. For those who had fallen in line with the revolutionary Communism of the Third Period, the abrupt shift from opposing all alliances with capitalists to making peace with parties, organizations, and individuals that had been dismissed, to that point, as reactionary enemies of the proletariat caused a fair amount of whiplash.

The impact of the Popular Front was felt immediately. Many fellow travelers who had stopped short of joining the Party welcomed the oppor-tunity to join with, and even lead, a movement that extended beyond revolutionary Communism. The John Reed Clubs, a Third Period organ-ization of artists and writers committed to militarism, disbanded, and in 1935 the American Writers' Congress (AWC), organized by a motley col-lection of Communists, Trotskyists, and liberals, issued a call for political writing that spoke to the working class while resisting demands for leftist purity. Ernest Hemingway was suddenly participating in conversations about literary politics with Communist critic Kenneth Burke. The AWC's

1937 meeting was particularly contentious. Henry Wadsworth Longfellow Dana, a gay Communist who had fallen victim to Harvard's Secret Court, an internal tribunal established in 1920 to root out homosexual students, and been arrested in Boston on a "morals charge," reported that "the critics' commission was getting very dramatic, so I left."[38] John Dos Passos spoke passionately about "the state of mind of freedom," arguing for writing "clean truth and sharply whittled exactitude." Burke pushed for "revolutionary symbolism," replacing "the worker" with "the people." Distinguishing the latter from "the proletarian symbol," Burke suggested, "has the tactical advantage of pointing more definitely in the direction of unity." Langston Hughes encouraged "American Negro writers" to "unite blacks and whites in our country, not on the nebulous basis of an interracial meeting, or the shifting sands of religious brotherhood, but on the *solid* ground of the daily working-class struggle to wipe out, now and forever, all the old inequalities of the past."[39] Freedom, unity, and truth were keywords of the day. Writers and artists were free to pursue individual artistic visions without sacrificing their radical bona fides, allowing a slew of newly radicalized culture workers to align themselves with a leftist movement previously dismissed as dogmatic.

If Communism had been especially attractive to those who wished to overthrow the US government, the Popular Front gave permission for "the people" on the margins to imagine themselves as its protectors. "We are the Americans and Communism is the Americanism of the twentieth century," Earl Browder, general secretary of the Communist Party USA, announced in 1936. "We Americans are a mongrel breed and we glory in it." Though Browder connected Americanism with broader revolutionary struggle—"unless," he noted, "we are ready to agree that Americanism means what Hearst says"—his enthusiasm for celebrating US history, diversity, and freedom coalesced with a desire among less-committed leftists to preserve the fundamental structure of the United States.[40] The "mongrel breed" Browder celebrated looked less like a colonized population and more like Henry Ford's melting pot—or, in Rockwell Kent's analogy, "like a tapestry, woven of brilliant colored threads, every one of which can be distinguished, and keep its own characteristics."[41] Nonetheless, as cultural historian Andrew Hemingway recounts, the "Party convention in May 1938 took place in a hall where the Stars and Stripes mingled with the Red flag, and the proceedings opened with a playing of the Star Spangled Banner."[42] Communism was 100 percent Americanism, and Americanism here meant diversity in its many splendid forms.

The Popular Front's attendant celebration of freedom impelled writers to conceive pushing the limits of free speech as itself a form of literary radicalism, opening radical writing to deeper explorations of sexuality. Whereas earlier leftists had connected antiobscenity laws to US suppression of radicals, Popular Front leftists contrasted American free speech with fascist censorship. James T. Farrell drew a direct parallel between Hitler's censorship of his work and the Canadian government's effort to ban *Young Lonigan* for its obscene content. In a strongly worded letter to the Canadian prime minister, Farrell asserted that "[t]he authorities of the Third Reich have banned the sending of copies of my trilogy, STUDS LONIGAN, to American prisoners of war," suggesting that, if Canada took "a parallel action," it would provide comfort "only to those who hate and who fear to allow the writer that freedom without which a culture will dry up and become mere spiritual rot." Rather than defending his work against charges of obscenity, Farrell defended the obscenity of his work as instrumental to the American democratic project. If *Young Lonigan* were banned as indecent, "then life is going to become increasingly indecent despite all the efforts of all the censors, official or otherwise."[43] The freedom to write openly about sex offered a bulwark against the creep of fascism.

At the same time, celebrations of American diversity were imagined as emblematizing a democratic culture impervious to fascist forces. Leftist composer Earl Robinson's famous "Ballad for Americans," which Paul Robeson debuted in 1939, included a comically exhaustive catalogue of seemingly every marginalized group in the United States ("Czech and double-Czech Americans"). Critics such as Robert Warshow attacked the song as emblematic of the kitschiest elements of the Left (an example of the 1930s "disastrous vulgarization of intellectual life," he wrote in 1947), but the song functioned, Michael Denning has argued, as "an unofficial anthem of the movement."[44] Exuberant celebrations of the American "people" impelled sexual dissidents to produce competing lists confirming American pluralism while pushing against the exclusion of homosexuals from the festivities. Willard Motley, as we have seen, was no stranger to envisioning solidarity among all kinds of undesirables. In a speech written for a World War II–era antifascist rally, he offered his own ballad for Americans, using derisive, rather than inclusive, language to mobilize the masses:

WHORE!
HOMOSEXUAL!
COMMUNIST!

CRIMINAL!
RELIGIOUS FANATIC!
CHRISTIAN!
Damn dirty Jew!
Black nigger!
Greaser!
Dago!
Shanty Irish!
polock!
bohunk!
. . . .
How we love to call names! How we love to hate![45]

Rather than ennobling the toiling immigrants who made America great, Motley took full advantage of his soapbox to remind listeners of the violent language that kept undesirables on the outskirts of society while signifying against their disempowering histories by reclaiming the pejorative usage leveled against them. He carefully employed categories that were offensive rather than inclusive, reimagining exclusion from full citizenship as grounds for resistance. Motley refused to make diversity pretty or celebratory, instead producing a list that instigated and offended, recapitulating a wholesale investment in racial, ethnic, sexual, and religious hatred that demanded a radical alternative. He repurposed the script of Popular Front Americanism to build new alliances among those whose deviance became a means to challenge the state apparatus.

Among those who sought further inroads to participate in populist conversations inaugurated by the Popular Front was Newton Arvin, a gay literary critic at Smith College whose work attempted to establish an American literary canon. This project was, for Arvin, connected to his embrace of Communism—a commitment that began with his left-leaning sympathies in the 1920s. Arvin joined critics such as F. O. Matthiessen, a fellow gay leftist who taught at Harvard, in producing a narrative of America's usable past that provided fodder for radical revisions of US history. Arvin, who wrote an influential book reviving interest in Herman Melville, mined popular writers for radical ideas. Melville was an interesting case study for gay leftists: in 1930, the Communist artist Rockwell Kent produced an illustrated edition of *Moby Dick,* by then a largely forgotten work, for Random House, teasing out Melville's homoerotic themes to fundamentally shift the way readers related to the book. (His illustrated edition remains one of the most popular versions available today.)

Arvin was fired from his position at Smith College in 1960, after his homosexuality was revealed to administrators. Though Arvin claimed to the college's investigative committee that he had not been a member of the Communist Party, he sidestepped his appreciably more complicated history as a fellow traveler, which included signing a letter to the *Daily Worker* in 1940 supporting the Abraham Lincoln Brigade veterans.[46] A great admirer of Walt Whitman, especially the "Calamus" poems—an affection he shared with leftists such as Michael Gold ("A Jack London or a Walt Whitman will come out of this new crop of young workers who write in the *New Masses,*" Gold declared in 1929), as well as with any number of queer literary types—Arvin had drifted further to the left as the rabidly capitalist mood of the United States in the 1920s proceeded unabated.[47] He exerted a gravitational pull among leftists to western Massachusetts, drawing noteworthy scholars such as Daniel Aaron, who joined the Smith College faculty in 1940, into the radical culture of the Connecticut River valley.

Though he acknowledged the frustration felt among many fellow travelers at the dogmatism of Communist Party leaders in the 1930s, Arvin also recognized the need for them to do their work. "It is a bad world in which we live," Arvin wrote to Granville Hicks, an editor of *New Masses.* "I believe we can spare ourselves a great deal of pain and disappointment and even worse (treachery to ourselves) if we discipline ourselves to accept proletarian revolutionary leaders and even theorists for what they are and must be: grim fighters in about the most dreadful and desperate struggle (perhaps) in all history—not reasonable and 'critically minded' and forbearing and infinitely far-seeing men."[48] Like many of his fellow leftists, Arvin understood that the occasionally frustrating positions of Communist Party leaders should not discredit the entire movement. If a revolutionary society was to be built, it require the hands of fighters. The Communist movement's hierarchical structure and unyielding revolutionary politics drew Arvin deeper into its orbit.

Arvin adapted easily to the Popular Front, which presented an opportunity to bring into focus some of the work he had been pursuing for years. The Americanism of the Popular Front allowed Arvin to advocate expanding the literary canon in ways to which he had already been predisposed. "We ought to hear much from left-wing writers," Arvin declared at the Second American Writers' Congress in 1937, as "of Pushkin and of Dostoevski, of Rimbaud and of Proust, of Goethe and of Thomas Mann."[49] The list of writers whom Arvin invoked represented a panoply of forms and nations, and many of them were either known or suspected homosexuals. Though Arvin proposed adding left-wing writers to his list, it is noteworthy that his expanded canon leaned heavily upon writers whose work delved deeply into queer themes, as was true of many of the other writers on whom he expended his critical energy.

At the time Arvin spoke at the American Writers' Congress, he was steeped in work on his monumental study of Walt Whitman, which he published in 1938. His call to expand the literary canon connected with his ongoing project claiming Walt Whitman as an important subject for radical criticism. Whitman had been upheld by many leftists as emblematic of a Socialist celebration of workers that fit neatly into the tongue and groove of the Popular Front. The revolutionary Whitman embraced in the Third Period—"Walt Whitman's a hell of a lot more revolutionary than any Russian poet I've ever heard of," John Dos Passos wrote in 1932—gave way to the radically democratic Whitman.[50]

Most Third Period celebrations of Whitman, even when his romanticism was celebrated, had downplayed the homosexual themes explored in his work. Michael Gold, for example, had characterized his generation of socially minded writers as "Walt Whitman's spawn," which, despite Whitman's never actually having spawned anyone, was, one supposes, high praise coming from Gold. Whitman was a "heroic spiritual grandfather" who had the "faith of a viking" and "feared nothing," bespeaking a vigorous masculinity easily contrasted with someone like Thornton Wilder, whose work Gold elsewhere disparaged as "a daydream of homosexual figures in graceful gowns moving archaically among the lilies."[51]

In recovering a radically gay Whitman, Arvin joined other leftists who, unlike Gold, resisted the urge to transform him into a paragon of heteromasculinity, most notable among them Max Eastman, who wrote a damning review of Emory Holloway's *Whitman: A Narrative Interpretation* for *New Masses* in 1926. Eastman was a case study in leftist contradiction: he was a champion of proletarian literature who popularized the phrase "artists in uniform"; he was a man of means who aligned himself with the working class; he supported Communism yet held iconoclasm as his highest value.[52] Still, Eastman was among the most prominent leftist critics when Holloway's book was published, and his palpable fury over Holloway's straightwashing portrait of the queer poet simmered throughout his review. "The fact he fails to state," Eastman complained of Holloway, "is that Walt Whitman was strongly homosexual." For Eastman, that omission was not incidental to Holloway's failure as a critic. "Without stating this fact," he fumed "and discussing in simplicity its position and importance in his life and poetry, it is foolish to pretend to interpret him or tell the story of him." Not content to merely document Holloway's fatal omissions, Eastman volunteered a likely explanation for "*why* this straight-laced and husbandly person should want to immerse himself in the poetry of Walt Whitman." Framed as an entirely innocent question, Eastman pondered,

> is it because he has in him exactly that thing that he finds so "sentimental" in Walt Whitman, but he has it tightly suppressed and such a solid structure of "permanence and human dignity," and general diffused matrimoniousness, built up on top of it, that it can only creep out through this highly intellectual channel of being a disapproving but very assiduous student of Walt Whitman?[53]

Eastman's scorn for Holloway's rejection of Whitman's same-sex desire might have been atypical in the force with which he suggested the critic's unconscious homosexual motivations and in his outspoken rejection of heteronormativity (framed in the cute neologism "matrimoniousness"), but it did throw down an interesting gauntlet: on the one hand, overly emphasizing Whitman's homosexuality might be read as counterrevolutionary, but on the other, ignoring it could place one under their own cloud of suspicion. By refusing to recast Whitman as a heterosexual Viking, Eastman offered a blueprint for bringing homosexuality and radicalism into conversation. Newton Arvin built his career on it.

Arvin harnessed the democratic energy of the Popular Front to argue for the interwoven radicalism of Whitman's political and sexual themes. *Whitman,* Arvin's groundbreaking study of the poet, sidestepped "the question whether or not Walt Whitman is a 'socialist poet,'" instead emphasizing how his "democratic and fraternal humanism" might "fortify the writers and the men of our time in their struggles against a dark barbarian reaction" and "interest and animate the peoples of a near future in their work of building a just society"—about as clear an articulation of Popular Front values as could be found in 1938.[54] Arvin departed from earlier critics who had dismissed Whitman as insufficiently leftist. Floyd Dell, for example, had branded Whitman as "the most complete and thoroughgoing anti-Socialist in all of literature," and V. F. Calverton discounted Whitman as "a petty bourgeois individualist" and "a believer in private property."[55] The fact that Whitman was not himself a Socialist said little, in Arvin's analysis, about the purposes he might serve for the leftist cause. It was the job of critics to extract the radical potential from texts by authors who did not necessarily align themselves with the Left.

Arvin's *Whitman* acknowledged the ways his homosexuality moved Whitman closer to a radical aesthetic politics. What was most interesting about Whitman was how, "unlike the vast majority of inverts, even of those creatively gifted, he chose to translate and sublimate his strange, anomalous emotional experience into a political, a constructive, a democratic program."[56] Arvin's interest in radical politics and American aesthetics converged with his tentative interest in foregrounding homosexuality as a critical force in articulating Whitman's literary contributions and politics. Still, Arvin took a firm stance against Whitman's failure to condemn US enslavement of Black people and efforts to sidestep its evil in favor of celebrating the "unity" of the nation. Arvin also directly confronted the racism in Whitman's early writings, citing as particularly odious an unpublished sketch that cast a "slave-gang" in egregiously offensive language.[57] Communist Party Americanism opened new democratic vistas, but it had no space for admitting racism under the guise of singing oneself.

The Popular Front moved the Left in a more normative direction by allowing celebrations of American history and democracy to infuse radical culture. Deviating from American exceptionalism was less appealing when articulations of inclusive democracy were newly accessible to leftists. Critical work reflected this move by foregrounding radical approaches to reading a wide range of literary texts, trading demands on the proper form of proletarian literature for a deeply theorized critical approach that placed diversity and democracy at its center. Though squeamishness remained around politicizing homosexuality, the language of difference gained cultural currency, and leftists recast homosexuals as essential to building a radically democratic movement.

HOMOSEXUALITY IN THE SPANISH CIVIL WAR

Frank O'Hara recounts in his "Autobiographical Fragments" the story of his rising political dissidence when he was attending parochial school. O'Hara reports his "revulsion at having been made to pray for Franco's success during the Spanish Civil War."[58] This significant memory awakened O'Hara's sexual, political, and aesthetic consciousness. His aversion to the politics of the Catholic Church was an important precursor to his celebration of gay culture. O'Hara's use of the word "revulsion" repurposes the language typically used to demonize sinners to instead critique the church's support of the fascist rebels in Spain, connecting his Catholic school's sexual repression with the church's fascist sympathies and thereby linking O'Hara's sexual awakening to an implicit alliance with antifascism on the Left.

Much of O'Hara's attachment to antifascism derived also from his attraction to Federico García Lorca, the gay Spanish leftist poet who was killed, presumably because of his antifascist support for the Spanish Republic, shortly after the outbreak of civil war. García Lorca, whose *Poeta en Nuevo York* was particularly popular among the queer literati, was taken up as a hero among American poets across the political spectrum, but his work was particularly attractive to leftists due to his outspoken defense of the Spanish Republic. The work was also, according to Aldon Lynn Nielsen, "prized reading among black poets from [Langston] Hughes to [Audre] Lorde" and others.[59] Hughes was particularly invested in Lorca's work, eventually producing a volume of translations in 1951, for which he consulted the gay Spanish Civil War reporter Stephen Spender. Amiri Baraka wrote a poem titled "Lines to García Lorca," which was selected by Hughes for inclusion in the 1964 anthology *New Negro Poets, U.S.A.*[60] Frank O'Hara's 1957 poem "Failures of Spring" proclaimed, "I'm getting rather Lorcaesque lately / and I don't like it. Better if my poetry were, / instead of my lives."[61]

It was not only New York School poets who indulged what scholar Jonathan Mayhew refers to as "Lorquismo" in their work, indexing the Spanish Civil War as an aesthetic, political, and sexual awakening.[62] Robert Duncan, a radical poet who, in 1944, published an important defense of homosexuality in Dwight Macdonald's radical magazine, *Politics,* declaring in an article titled "Homosexuals in Society" that "only one's continued opposition can make any other order possible," claimed in his 1950 volume *Caesar's Gate* that "the events of history— the actual events of the Spanish Civil War and of Lorca's life history . . . we took as events in a mystery that referred to poetry."[63] The famously gay and radical beat poet Allen Ginsberg wrote a poem titled "Death to Van Gogh's Ear!" that included the lines "The American Century betrayed by a mad Senate which no longer sleeps with its wife / Franco has murdered Lorca the fairy son of Whitman."[64] Ginsberg explicitly connected US anticommunism with the execution of a gay leftist poet during the Spanish Civil War.

The legacy of the Spanish Civil War's queer dimensions, particularly vis-à-vis García Lorca, weaves together many strands of American culture. The struggle to preserve the Spanish Republic cultivated homosocial bonds in an internationalist theater of war that rejected the military's more odious strains of nationalism while initiating a set of political commitments that admitted sexual dissidents as welcome players in the antifascist struggle. Volunteers in Spain came from both Communist and capitalist nations, and while the United States had a long history of instrumentalizing war in order to promote American values, the Spanish Civil War attracted a motley crew bound only through their shared rejection of fascism. The absence of a national interest among the international volunteers pushed against ideas about war mobilization as requiring bonds of nation, sex, or sexuality. As Robin Kelley has written, African Americans were especially inclined to fight in the Spanish Civil War, in part because, in the words of Oscar Hunter, "this ain't Ethiopia, but it'll do."[65] Spanish Civil War volunteers shed demands typically placed upon troops to represent their nations as citizens, and Spain's need for willing fighters, exacerbated by the US government's refusal to involve itself in the conflict, slackened restrictions nations otherwise placed upon soldiers to conform to dominant racial and sexual hierarchies.

Though the Spanish Civil War has often been emblematized through the heteronormative manliness Ernest Hemingway espoused in *For Whom the Bell Tolls,* a love story that drew liberally from Hemingway's experiences as an ambulance driver, the presence of same-sex intimacy, both in Spain and in the antifascist movement more generally, pushed against this particular form of strenuous masculinity.[66] In a questionnaire following his service in the Spanish Civil War, volunteer Will Aalto suggested that the "biggest coward, punks, etc. can be a good fighter if he agrees with goal and has a making strong enough to keep him there," further recommending that "Hemingway should be kept out of this."[67] Gay volunteers were greeted with campy nicknames, sought and found same-sex lovers, and boldly declared their homosexuality. Some of them even experienced the first stirrings of same-sex desire in the war. Donald H., for example, was a twenty-one-year-old presumed-heterosexual man when he first stumbled into the Spanish Civil War. Traveling to Europe from the United States in preparation for his wedding to a woman, he strolled into Spain on "a walking trip to get in good shape."[68] He quickly discovered the country was in the throes of an antifascist struggle that both initiated Donald into the world of radical militancy and allowed him to experience the same-sex intimacy that confirmed his burgeoning bisexuality. "A great deal of affection was shown to me by the rebels in Spain," he recalled of his experience among the defenders of the Republic; "a tremendous comradeship which I wanted and which meant more to me than sex." Following his experience of comradeship, Donald wrote a letter his wife delaying their marriage in order to join the Republicans in the war. "She wrote that if I didn't think enough of her to get married we should call the whole thing off. I agreed on condition that we go back to Spain."[69] Later, while working briefly for the Spanish Loyalists in Boston, Donald had sex with a male soldier, whom he remembered fondly after returning to Spain. Donald H. participated in a study of "sex variants" that was published in 1935. His Spanish Civil War experiences formed the center of his sexual awakening.

For Donald H., the line between political solidarity, homosocial intimacy, and sexual dissidence blurred to the point of irrelevance. The experience of "discovering" one's same-sex attractions when living and fighting in wars was common. One Abraham Lincoln Brigade volunteer worried in a letter home that "the boys are beginning to ogle eyes at each other," expressing hope that having sex with women while on leave might help him and the others "keep from going 'fruit' altogether."[70] Many went fruit anyway. Volunteer David Miller explained in an interview that "there were other outlets for sexual activity, a few men who enjoyed outlets other than brothels, but we don't have to go into that."[71]

Other sexual dissidents joined the Spanish Civil War fully aware of their homosexuality. David McKelvy White taught English at Brooklyn College, where, according to the FBI, he was "a known Communist" who "followed the party line in every respect" before shipping off to Spain in 1937. "He asked for formal leave of absence," according to an FBI informant, "and said it was up to HITLER and MUSSOLINI as to whether he would return for the coming term." (He did not return, but only because he was fired.) White volunteered as a machine gunner in Spain in spite of bearing none of Hemingway's masculine features. The FBI described him as "very thin, sickly looking, with pale, slightly hollow cheeks" and noted that as a child "he was a quiet, reserved type of lad" who was "very studious, spending most of his time reading."[72] He was, according to his student Harold Norse, a "fervent Communist," and he was openly gay long before he embarked for Spain, living in Brooklyn with his boyfriend and fellow Communist, Murray Young.[73] A comrade in White's brigade, Milt Felsen, recalled White carrying the collected works of Shakespeare around with him and "holding his rifle at arm's length and examining it gingerly through his heavy glasses as though it were some rare museum artifact. 'You couldn't hit a bull in the ass with a steam shovel, Dave. Why don't you put the damn thing some place where it won't hurt anybody?'"[74] White brought his camp humor to the battlefield. When a commander, Mirko Markevitch, appeared in his battalion, White demanded Felsen pinch him "so I'll know that Mirko is not the lead tenor, this is not a Bizet opera, we will not sing in the chorus, and Carmen will not come dancing in with a rose in her teeth."[75] After being wounded in battle, White returned home to teach English at Lafayette College, where, the FBI notes, the "Head of [the] English Department [James Waddell Tupper] describes WHITE as a homosexualist" who "lived with a 'male wife.'" White was purged from this post as well.

Also among the Abraham Lincoln Brigade volunteers were Young Communist League members David Gillis Kelly, who was a Communist Party membership director, and Jack Mail, who was a Communist Party educational director. Shipping out of San Pedro together on September 14, 1937, the pair was affectionately known by their fellow volunteers as "the Dolly Sisters," and their comrades noted they were rarely found away from each other's company. Kelly and Mail produced a Spanish Civil War counterestablishment sheet titled *The Undercrust,* and the two participated in forming the "San Pedro Institute of Higher Learning." Kelly was remembered within the battalion for his great appreciation for "concerts, ballets, and Impressionist paintings and savory food." Following the conclusion of their service, Kelly and Mail opened a floral shop together on Madison Avenue.[76]

Will Aalto was another gay Abraham Lincoln Brigade volunteer, an aspiring radical writer who found little success aside from a handful of poems published in *New Masses* after his return. Aalto's refusal to hide his sexual dissidence points to a fiery dissent against normative expectations of the mid–twentieth century. Aalto was not conflicted about his homosexuality, as his fellow volunteer Irving Goff recalled. Aalto "had been actively [homosexual] since his early teens and found nothing repugnant or morally compromising in the fact."[77]

Aalto's relationship to Communist Party was similarly unconflicted. He was an active and exuberant member of the Bronx Young Communist League when he shipped off to Spain at age twenty.[78] His sexual dissidence and leftist politics were both remembered by his friends through one recurring word: defiance. "There was defiance in his bearing and, in his movement, more than a hint of swaggering arrogance," his friend James Foss recalled, "the kind of swagger New York men learn as boys on the streets of their neighborhoods." This swagger might also have helped Aalto survive as an openly gay man in the 1930s. "How could a big, athletic guy like that," Irving Goff imagined others wondering, "a militant communist revolutionary, be one of those?"[79] Yet these twin markers of Aalto's identity—his Communism and his sexual dissidence—were far from mutually exclusive. Irving Goff made the connection between Aalto's bold openness about his homosexuality and his radicalism explicit when he remembered that Aalto's confidently acknowledging his homosexuality "was a not untypical act of defiance on Bill's part."[80]

For Aalto, this confluence of sexual and ideological defiance was not mere metaphor. In a survey he completed about fear among troops in the Spanish Civil War, Aalto's playfulness came through. When asked about the effect of "going into action along with an experienced man," he indicated that such camaraderie produced "a much better soldier." "Boy," Aalto noted in the margins, "you cling to him." Later, when asked in the same questionnaire whether he ever experienced "involuntary sexual emissions" during the war, Aalto scrawled, "only when dreaming of Franco"—a bold reference to his wartime male companion (not to be confused with Francisco Franco, about whom Aalto harbored no such warm feelings).[81]

In 1958, New York poet James Schuyler published his poem "Dining Out with Doug and Frank," in which he eulogized Aalto. Written in the chatty, parenthetical style that typified the practice of "deep gossip" that was traded like currency in midcentury gay urban communities, the poem reflected on art, consumption, love, and the impossible inevitability of death. "I cannot accept their death," Schuyler writes after cataloguing a series of unfortunate and ill-timed passings among his friends, "or any other death."[82] In the middle of this verse, Schuyler meditates on his life with Aalto, his lover, whom Schuyler had met through the tentatively radical and decidedly homosexual British poet W. H. Auden. Auden was, unlike Aalto, uncertain in his commitment to the Communist Party, even as he traveled among leftists. He embarked in 1937 to drive an ambulance in support of the Republicans (the *Daily Worker* reported on the "Famous Poet to Drive Ambulance in Spain"), and while he was never given an ambulance to drive, he did write a piece on the war for the *New Statesman* and, more significantly, his well-known poem "Spain," which was published in pamphlet form to support the Medical Aid for Spain and, nonetheless, dismissed by George Orwell as a melding of "the gangster and the pansy."[83] Where "yesterday" Auden found "the abolition of fairies and giants," today "Our moments of tenderness blossom / As the ambulance and the sandbag; / Our hours of friendship into a people's army," and "to-morrow the rediscovery of romantic love."[84]

Schuyler documents Aalto's tempestuous return from Spain, where he fought valiantly only to see Franco's victory and his own legacy stained by his homosexuality. Aalto's battles with alcoholism, violent outbursts, and persecution were exacerbated by his being exposed as gay by former comrades in the Spanish Civil War, who were by then working alongside him in the US Office of Strategic Services, where Aalto found employment after having been rejected in his attempt to enlist in the US military. "I want to get at the enemy, I'm experienced, but I am a veteran of the Lincoln Brigade and so not eligible," he complained.[85] His commitment to antifascism never wavered, but Aalto was forced out of the OSS when his friends and comrades found him cruising sailors in a public park. His homosexuality, they feared, would make him a security risk and susceptible to blackmail.[86] Milton Felson recalled:

> Irv comes in one day and he says, we've got a problem. What's the problem? Billy Aalto is cruising around picking up sailors in downtown Washington. I said, are you sure? I said, I can't believe it. Billy knows what we are up against in the outfit, and he wouldn't do that. Sure enough, Irv says let's stake it out. Which we did. And there is Billy going through his thing, picking up sailors. So we got together, whoever was there—I don't even remember some of the other guys. . . . And we decide we got to let the outfit know and let them do what they want to do. So we turned him in, to our everlasting shame.[87]

Vincent Lossowski disputed Felsen's account, complaining that in Felsen's recollection, "Bill's homosexuality is treated in a flippant manner and, as a result, a grave injustice is done to Bill Aalto who was a dedicated anti-fascist, who more than paid his dues in the war against Fascism in Spain."[88] James Foss recalled a scene following Aalto's acknowledgment of his homosexuality to Irving Goff: "Bill came in, sat down on the edge of his bed and began to cry. His friend woke up and, feeling terribly awkward and embarrassed and not having the slightest idea of what he might say without sounding a fool, went over, sat by him and put his arm around Bill's shoulders. Bill went on crying but managed to say that no one would ever be able to understand what a man like himself had to endure."[89]

Regardless of precisely how his expulsion from the OSS played out, Aalto's betrayal by his friends ruined him. "He acquired a fearsome reputation, among the expatriate American homosexuals whom he met and the Italians too, for staging operatic scenes in public places," James Foss recalled. "Tables and chairs were overturned. Glasses broken. Crockery smashed and food strewn everywhere amid cries, threats and howls."[90] In a tragically ironic turn, it turned out the FBI became frus-

trated as their increasing pressure on Aalto to name names yielded not
a single revelation in spite of their most diligent efforts. Schuyler writes:

Bill

Aalto, my first lover (five tumultuous
years found Bill chasing me around
   the kitchen table—in Wystan Auden's
house in Forio d'Ischia—with
a carving knife. He was serious
and so was I and so I wouldn't go
when he wanted to see me when
   he was dying of leukemia. Am I
sorry? Not really. The fear had
   gone too deep. The last time I
saw him was in the City Center lobby
and he was jolly—if he just
   stared at you and the tears began
   it was time to cut and run—
and the cancer had made him lose
a lot of weight and he looked
young and handsome as the night
we picked each other up
   in Pop Tunick's long-gone gay bar.
Bill never let me forget that
on the jukebox I kept playing
   Lena Horne's "Mad about the Boy."
Why the nagging teasing? It's
a great performance but he
thought it was East Fifties queen
   taste. Funny—or, funnily enough—
in dreams, and I dream about him
a lot, he's always the nice guy
   I first knew and loved, not
   the figure of terror he became.
Oh well. Bill had his hour: he
was a hero, a major in the
Abraham Lincoln Brigade. A dark
   Finn who looked not unlike
a butch version of Valentino.
Watch out for Finns. They're
   murder when they drink) used
   to ride the ferries all the
time, doing the bars along
the waterfront: did you know
that Hoboken has—or had—
more bars to the square inch
(Death. At least twice when

someone I knew and hated
died I felt the joy of vengeance:
I mean I smiled and laughed out
   loud: a hateful feeling.
   It passes.) to the square inch
than any other city?[91]

Schuyler acknowledges both the heroism of Aalto's service and the bro-
kenness of his life. Aalto's betrayal by the US government as a homosexual and a Communist who fought a war whose veterans received no
national honor fractured his identity, and the shrapnel of his imploding
emotional state ricocheted off his comrades and lovers with a tragic
force. "Ever since Don went off," he wrote in a letter, "I realized that I
had become involved with a great many immature mediocrities who
wanted me to be Poppa. Not a real poppa but either a god or a doll. I've
had it. Unfortunately, they are most of them pretty and available to
yours truly and I don't like to sleep alone. I received your letter in the
midst of the latest one whose bright eyes bore me off to his 'charming'
flat with Callas, record-players and where I was assaulted until I am
black and blue which is nice but it ain't a way of life."[92] So damaged
was Aalto by the end of his life that one close friend and fellow Lincoln
Brigade volunteer, Vincent Lossowski, remembered his death as suicide
rather than the result of the leukemia that killed him.[93]

Yet Aalto's story, like those of so many forgotten and neglected Lincoln Brigade volunteers, is not only one of tragedy; it is also a story of
ideological and sexual dissidence. Aalto's story represents an earlier iteration of queer leftist politics that can be found in traces, in fits and starts,
during the Popular Front, when the Left was uniquely able to appeal to
a broad swath of progressive artists, writers, and songwriters who were
attracted to progressive community and politics in the midst of the
Depression. His commitment to antifascism, shared with other sexual
dissidents who joined forces in the Spanish Civil War, led him to push
against the rise of hateful ideologies while refusing to participate in normative American heteromasculinity. William Aalto's biography defies
historiographic compartmentalization as wholly as does his dissent from
the standard narratives of the closeted, nonpolitical "East Fifties queen"
and the played-out trope of the prudish Communist revolutionary. He
was no less the man hanging out in Pop Tunick's gay bar, poking fun at
the repeated Lena Horne songs on the jukebox, than he was the Spanish
Civil War hero, throwing himself into battle to beat back fascism and
clinging to his sexual partners even when he was beaten black and blue.

The emergence of the leftist Popular Front and the fight against fascism in the United States shifted the Left in significant ways. First, Hitler's rise inaugurated a crisis that leftists responded to by positioning themselves against multiple forms of hate. Second, the adoption of the Popular Front by the Communist Party introduced democratic discourse that foregrounded diversity and identity as tools for repelling encroaching fascism while bringing moderates closer to the orbit of the Left. The cultural texts that emerged during the Popular Front envisioned homosexuals as a discrete group that pushed the limits of American diversity. Finally, the internationalist dimensions of antifascism challenged normative relationships with nations, highlighting the deviance of those who aligned themselves with the Left. Sexual dissidents who fought in the Spanish Civil War found their loyalties tested and their incorporation into American society questioned. Each of these factors provided a backdrop for the realignment of homosexuality and the Left during the Cold War, when a homosexual rights movement took form and leftists found themselves estranged from the growing alliance between homosexuality and Cold War Americanism.

CHAPTER 8

"The Secret Element of Their Vice"

Deviant Politics in the Cold War

While it is true that there is not a Communist under every bed, the Freudians would have a good deal of justification for the claim that there is a bed under the basic emotional motivations of every Communist.

—Morris L. Ernst and David Loth, 1952

I know there is a great desire to shift from Communists to homos.

—Senator Millard E. Tydings, 1950

We aren't Communists, Herb. We're decent people!

—Eva Philbrick to Herbert Philbrick, 1952

In 1960, Countess R. G. Waldeck, a political writer for the conservative Washington, D.C., newspaper *Human Events,* published a report on the ousting of homosexuals from the US State Department. While the purges were, by that point, old news, Waldeck's hot take brought to light a dimension that she argued had been broadly overlooked in initial reports: the Communist undercurrent coursing through gay culture. "Welded together by the identity of their forbidden desires, of their strange, sad needs, habits, dangers, not to mention their outrageously fatuous vocabulary," Waldeck reported, "members of this International constitute a world-wide conspiracy against society." If the capitalization of "International" were not a clear enough clue as to the precise nature of this wide conspiracy, Waldeck made sure her point was made crystal clear by asserting that homosexuals "serve the ends of the Communist International in the name of their rebellion against the prejudices, standards, ideals of the 'bourgeois' world," moving, as they did, "from being enemies of society" to "become enemies of capitalism in particular." Anticapitalism was especially fostered by gay promiscuity, which, because it facilitated interclass sexual relations, produced "fusion . . . between upperclass and proletarian corruption."[1]

While Waldeck was piqued by the refusal of Americans to fully appreciate the immediate threat of homosexual-Left intersections, she peppered her analysis with some choice nuggets drawn from the recent past, noting that "the Homosexual International began to gnaw at the sinews of the state in the 1930s." It was during the Depression, the "dawn of the Pink decade," as she termed it, that "writers, poets, painters and such—discovered Marxism." While "the same sentiments which motivated the Communist conversion of intellectuals in general—such as opposition to Nazism and Fascism, visions of the end of capitalism and the need of a faith—played a part in the Communist conversion of homosexual intellectuals," the latter group's "particular emotions gave it an additional fervor."[2] For one thing, homosexuals' "forbidden desires" impelled them to cooperate "with the Worker's Movement," and "the Communist assumption that the workers represented the future gave a respectable façade to that social promiscuity that is the secret element of their vice." At the same time, however, Waldeck detected a more insidious shared set of political goals between homosexuals and Communists, for both of whom, she wrote,

> the promise of a classless society where everyone would be free appealed to their own need of freedom from "bourgeois" constraint. For, weren't they too an oppressed class? Weren't they too "threatened in their conditions of existence" (Communist Manifesto)? The way they figured it the Communists in fighting capitalism were revenging them for the ostracism which capitalist society held forever dangling over their heads.[3]

It is unlikely that Waldeck had delved too deeply into the history of homosexuality and the Left in American culture before drafting her screed. Her report mostly recycled a familiar narrative circulating during the Cold War about a secret homosexual cabal that overlapped with Communism, making strange but promiscuous bedfellows of equal enemies of the state. And yet, Waldeck correctly diagnosed the historical origins of queer-Left intersections. She perhaps overplayed her hand a bit when she speculated that "the disturbing increase in homosexuality, not to speak of its Marxist accentuation, is the result of a Moscow-directed propaganda expressly designed to corrode the tissues of capitalist society." But the radical belief that homosexuals were "an oppressed class" in need of "freedom from bourgeois complaint" did, in fact, have roots in the 1930s, and in the 1950s, when "the Homosexual International [had] become a sort of auxiliary of the Communist International," that radical belief crystallized, however briefly, in the emerging homophile movement, about which Waldeck offered no comment.[4] "As we read into all this curious talk about a Homosexual International," a columnist complained in ONE Confidential, a newsletter of ONE, Inc., "we expected to come across some mention of the homosexual organizations and publications, but the Countess seemed to be ignorant of these."[5]

ONE had a particular dog in this fight, given their position as an important organization of the homophile movement founded by Jim Kepner, a leftist journalist who wrote for both the Daily Worker and People's World, in 1952. As early as 1943, while he was moving deeper into the Left, Kepner was visiting San Francisco gay bars including LiPo's, Rickshaw, Foster's Cafeterias, Finocchio's, and Mona's 441 Club.[6] Mattachine, meanwhile, had been formed by a coterie of current or past Communists, including the outspoken Harry Hay, in the heady stew of leftist and gay culture that Daniel Hurewitz characterizes as "Bohemian Los Angeles."[7] In spite of, or perhaps because of, this history, reaction to Waldeck's argument within homophile publications was mostly dismissive, the lines between homosexual rights and the Left drawn more starkly as the 1950s proceeded. By 1959, ONE, Inc., was reaching out to prospective members with an unequivocal message: "ONE is not an underground conspiracy to overthrow the government. ONE is in no way connected with communism."[8] The historical overlap between homosexuality and the Left was disavowed within the homophile movement as ferociously as it was touted by more-reactionary forces.

In particular, the fear that homosexuals represented "security risks"—a pretense that was invoked to fire workers in the State Department and cast doubt on the citizenship of gay women and men—permeated Cold War American culture.[9] "The constant pairing of 'Communists and queers,'" David K. Johnson writes, "led many to see them as indistinguishable threats."[10] This fear reached its denouement when William Martin and Bernon Mitchell, presumed gay lovers, defected to the Soviet Union in 1960.[11] Attorney General William Rogers announced that "[t]he Soviets are exploiting sex situations."[12] ONE

Magazine's editors were also outraged—not because homosexuals were security risks, but because it was, by this time, utterly inconceivable that queer leftists could even exist. "The last thing most American homosexual men and women want to do is go to the Soviet Union or adopt any Marxist form of Communism," the editors wrote.

> Communism and homosexuality are contradictory and inimical. One can hardly be a Communist and a homosexual at the same time. The homosexual is an individual, he loves his freedom too much, he is almost a rebel from conformity. He does not merge and jell easily with the masses, nor trust blindly like many homosexuals in communal behavior. Why then would the homosexual want to part with that form of government which offers liberty to choose one's own way of life? If we must choose a sexual preference most likely to produce a Communist, then let it be the heterosexual who may be easily pressured in his wish to survive and conform.[13]

The foundation had been set for the histories of homosexuality and the Left to diverge—a fracturing that was declared essential to the success of the homophile movement, which purged leftists from its own ranks. There were certainly individuals who disagreed with the idea that Communism and sexual dissidence were incompatible. A reader submitted a letter to *ONE*'s editors complaining about the broad brush with which the magazine tarred gay leftists. "You state that homosexuality and communism are inimical," he wrote in 1961. "I disagree most heartily. I think that only when we have a greater degree of socialism in our life with its consequent greater liberty of trying to understand the various sociological problems, will homosexuality have a chance to be understood properly."[14] Yet the homophile movement, detached from its radical history and overly invested in normativity and whiteness, overwhelming suppressed such connections.

The Cold War era represented an inaugural moment when the homosexual rights movement took root both in the United States and internationally. As with much else that transpired during a period marked by HUAC investigations, strategies of containment, racial injustice, and an expansive repertoire of red-baiting, the emergence of the homophile movement in the United States was inextricably linked to both American anti-Communism and leftist history. The postwar period borrowed and departed from the language of the Popular Front, which produced much of the enthusiastically pluralistic framing favored by homophile activists to define their work and facilitate politics organized around sexual identity. As this book has argued, the 1950s were not the first decade when homosexuality was politicized or when sexual dissidents built a social movement. The decade did represent, however, a signature moment in the development of gay politics by both putting homosexuality at the center of activist work and envisioning a movement that treated homosexuals as citizens who could uphold the status quo. Not incidentally, this was also a critical moment in US history when a broadly conceived Left, including its radical race politics, was cast under a shadow of suspicion. The motivations for supporting the Left were imagined as having a queer subtext. Both inside the homophile movement, then, and within a cultural context that was deeply suspicious of deviant politics, the relationship between homosexuality and the Left is central to making sense of the Cold War era.

THE HOMOPHILE MOVEMENT AND THE LEFT

In 1948, Harry Hay attended a political event supporting Henry Wallace's campaign for US president. Wallace was propped up by leftists as electoral heir to the Popular Front, campaigning on a progressive platform to the left of the Democratic incumbent, Harry S. Truman. Noting the preponderance of gay men in attendance at the party, Hay began to cook up a progressive organization that would connect the leftist politics of Wallace's supporters with their sexual dissidence. Hay invoked a rights framework to advocate for "the full first-class citizenship participation of Minorities everywhere, including ourselves." Hay's proposed group, Bachelors for Wallace, espoused the promise of American democracy sweeping through US culture at the time and ordered that membership "shall be limited only to those actively affirming the principles of majority democracy."

Bachelors for Wallace did not advance beyond the proposal stage, but Hay's outline established a blueprint for building the homophile movement, which kicked into high gear with the formation of groups such as Mattachine; ONE, Inc; and the Knights of the Clock—all founded over a span of three years.[15] Mattachine began as a discussion group in 1950, attended by a group of gay men with personal histories in the Communist Party. Their first gathering evolved into a series of meetings that included a small number of women, though the organization's male leadership and focus on entrapment presented an obstacle to full participation by the women who joined the discussions. Hay was insistent that his history on the Left prepared him for the work of organizing homosexuals into a political group. "I was pitching and stacking alfalfa during summers from 1925–31 side by side with old-time Wobblies," Hay recalled; "at Stanford I was introduced to the *New Masses* which I read every week; in the Spring of 1933 I threw my first brick at a mounted (horse) Cop in the LA Milk Riots; in April of 1934, on Black Thursday, I was beaten up by the Marines on a Longshoremen's Picket-line in San Francisco: in a way the CIO was born there at that time."[16] The founding of the Congress of Industrial Organizations in 1935 was a signature moment in the democratization of the radical labor movement, far closer to the Industrial Workers of the World than the American Federation of Labor. "The children of . . . proletarian migrants, the second-generation ethnic workers, were the rank and file of the CIO unions," Michael Denning writes. "And they were also the creators of a new militant working-class culture that was no longer marginalized in the 'foreign' ghettoes."[17] By concluding his leftist time line within that moment, Hay gestured toward the pluralistic populism of the Popular Front and its realignment of the Left.

While Harry Hay was the most prominent rallying figure in the organization of Mattachine, he might not have been the most militant of the leftist Mattachine founders. Others seemed to bring an even bolder revolutionary spirit to the proceedings. Jeff Winters, who wrote about the Mattachine's founding for *ONE Magazine* as early as 1954, had little space for the hagiography of Harry Hay, remembering the ways Hay's theoretical inclinations hampered his Mattachine comrades' efforts to take their message to the streets. "Scorning the warmth and passion of true leaders," Winters recalled decades later,

> Harry was less in the vanguard of his little herd of four than bringing up the rear with whip and goad to keep them in line. He literally wore these earnest but horny little heifers down to submission with a ceaseless flow of gray logic that ate up a major portion of their lives. Too holy earnest (sic), Harry never seemed to realize that these would-be psychos of his were young communists with a rage to get out and do something active like picketing and get themselves clobbered and perhaps laid. Instead he expatiated endlessly until the murmur went around, "For God's sake, vote yes so we can get on with the agenda!"[18]

Though picketing, if not clobbering, came years after Hay and the horny little heifers had been expelled, it took a form unrecognizable to what many of the Communist founders likely envisioned, and by then the strictly professional, gender-conforming dress code enforced at Mattachine protests—"conservative and conventional," regulations demanded—was not especially conducive to getting laid.

The vocabulary of the Popular Front offered language for connecting Hay's radical rejection of social prejudice with the promise of the

American "common man."[19] The recent history of global fascism remained a central rallying point for confronting the oppression of minorities in the United States. Whereas Third Period Communists had viewed the liberation of African Americans disenfranchised in the nation's Black Belt through the lens of anticolonialism, the antifascist Popular Front offered a softer narrative that emphasized strength in pluralism (the people, yes!). In the wake of that shift, fascism served as an especially effective point of reference for addressing the targeting of gay men and women in the United States during the Cold War. "Adlai Stevenson recently commented in Paris that McCarthyism in the US of 1953 might be compared to Hitlerism in the Germany of 1933," an author in ONE Magazine suggested. "This was a profound statement the implications of which touch our minority very directly. Have we so soon forgotten that Hitler, in making the world safe for fascism by pledging to destroy communism, found it expedient to destroy several million Jews, trade unionists, Catholics—and homosexuals?"[20]

Mattachine positioned homosexuals alongside other minority groups confronting discrimination. Its founding documents specifically refer-enced parallels between homosexuals and "the Negro, Mexican, and Jewish Peoples."[21] The analogous forms of discrimination confronted by racially and ethnically minoritized Americans offered a template for articulating the organization's conceptualization of homosexuals as a distinct and oppressed minority group, but it also imagined them as white.[22] The comparative logic connecting sexuality and race within Mattachine stood in contrast to the Knights of the Clock's central con-cern with contesting various legal restrictions on interracial same-sex couples.[23] Cofounded by Merton L. Bird and Dorr Legg around 1950, the Knights of the Clock made racist laws and housing restrictions their central target. The organization, Legg recalled, was "addressed prima-rily to interracial homosexual couples, both male and female. The organization would hope to be of assistance in finding housing for such couples, not at that time an easy thing to do; finding employment and other more generalized kinds of assistance."[24] Though the Knights of the Clock held meetings and, as Legg recounts, claimed a membership roster in the hundreds, they never had the national presence that Mat-tachine and ONE managed to achieve.

While Mattachine's founding documents were peppered with language familiar to Marxist organizations—"socially organic," "objective," and "discussion group" each made appearances—its particular emphasis on foregrounding homosexuality as an identity category that deserved to be woven into the American cultural fabric echoed the 100 percent Americanism of the antifascist Communist Party.[25] The Popular Front period had represented the peak years of Mattachine's founders' involvement in the Left. It can hardly be accidental that the principles advanced in the Mattachine's founding documents specifically referred to homosexuals as "our people." It was the Leftist critic Kenneth Burke, as we have seen, who advocated, at the 1935 American Writers' Congress, adopting the word "people" rather than "workers": "The symbol I should plead for, as more basic, more of an ideal incentive, than that of the worker, is that of 'the people.'"[26] In the wake of that moment, Michael Denning writes, "'The people' became the central trope of left culture in this period, the imagined ground of political and cultural activity, the rhetorical stake in ideological battle."[27] Harry Hay had himself participated in the leftist organization People's Songs in the late 1940s. The innocuous word brought with it deep associations drawn from leftist history and indexed the Mattachine as an heir to the Popular Front legacy.

In 1952 Mattachine launched one of its first actions: supporting the Edendale Civil Rights Congress after five Mexican American boys were arrested, shot, and beaten in the Echo Park neighborhood of Los Angeles, long a hotbed of Communist and homosexual activity.[28] The incident involved Horace Martinez, a seventeen-year-old boy who was entrapped by an undercover police officer in a restroom, and several of his friends.[29] While the arrested boys sought assistance from the local Civil Rights Congress, a leftist organization with chapters across the United States that had responded to incidents of racism since 1946, the homosexual dimensions of the case offered an opportunity for Mattachine to put its theories, developed over years of discussion, into practice. In response, Mattachine created the Citizen's Committee to Outlaw Entrapment (CCOE), offering support for the victims under the cover of resisting entrapment of "all minorities," specifically questioning "whether the Police Department is justified in using such methods."[30] "SO LONG AS ONE MINORITY GROUP (regardless of the justice or the injustice of the prejudice against them)—IS THUS HARRIED AND HOUNDED," one Mattachine leaflet read, "NO MINORITY GROUP OR COMMUNITY IS SAFE." Mattachine demanded "equal citizenship guarantees, privileges, and dignities under the law.[31] The Popular Front emphasis upon Americanism resonated in Mattachine's sweeping support for "minority groups," while also injecting an extra dash of Americanism to the affair by appealing to "citizenship guarantees."[32] Marxism yes, but revolutionary Marxism, perhaps not.

Within weeks of the Echo Park arrests, a white founding member of Mattachine, Dale Jennings, was arrested in another case of entrapment. In response, the CCOE shifted its focus to foreground Jennings's case, which lacked the overtly racist dynamics that had instantiated Mattachine's connecting with the Civil Rights Congress. This shift in focus effectively detached the homophile movement's efforts to "outlaw entrapment" from the broader leftist mission to protect civil rights for people of color. The homophile movement self-adjusted to prioritize ONE MINORITY GROUP. As historian Emily Hobson notes in her discussion of the case, "Mattachine stopped mentioning the Echo Park case and more generally ceased to note links between practices of entrapment and brutality, the policing of gay life and the policing of communities of color," even in the wake of further incidents in which Latino men, most notably Ramón Castellanos in the same year, were entrapped, beaten, and arrested.[33]

The relationship between the homophile movement and law enforcement also was far cozier than was typically found within leftist organizations. A 1953 article in *ONE Magazine* that encouraged readers to refuse volunteering self-incriminating information to police framed this strategy as an assertion of citizenship rights rather than a revolt against the state. "The person who is aware that he need not answer any of the questions of an arresting officer—or an agent of the FBI, for that matter—is far from overthrowing the government," the author reassured anxious readers. "He is strengthening it."[34]

On April 17, 1965, members of the Mattachine chapter in Washington, D.C., picketed outside the White House.[35] The protest's ostensible target was Cuba—specifically, opposing its persecution of homosexuals. The botched Bay of Pigs invasion in 1961 and the Cuban Missile Crisis in 1962 had made postrevolutionary Cuba a critical site in the mounting hostility between the United States and the Soviet Union and a key player in John F. Kennedy's Cold War strategy. As word spread about the Communist government's forcing homosexuals into labor camps, which had been reported in the *New York Times* the day before the protests, Mattachine members capitalized upon the public's distaste for Castro's six-year-old revolution to draw attention to homosexuals in the United States. Signs at the Mattachine protest implied that by discriminating against homosexuals in its own country, the US government was behaving like its Cold War nemesis. "15 MILLION U.S. HOMOSEXUALS PROTEST FEDERAL TREATMENT," one sign read, intentionally ambiguating about whose government was being protested. Another reading "FIRST CLASS CITIZENSHIP FOR HOMOSEXUALS" put a finer point on the affair. "Cuba's Government Persecutes Homosexuals. U.S. Government Beat Them to It," read a third, making no mistake about the strategic deployment of Cuban domestic policy to advance US goals.[36] The logic animating this protest was clear: Communists persecuted homosexuals; the United States persecuted homosexuals; thus the United States was behaving like Communists. Cold War anti-Communism was instrumentalized to exonerate homosexuals, who were, by virtue of their persecution at the hands of Communists, on the right side of history. Communists rejected homosexuals; therefore, homosexuals were good citizens.

The question of citizenship was hardly incidental to the relationship between homosexuality and Communism even in Mattachine's early years. Citizenship was never neutral ground, especially following the passage of the Immigration and Nationality Act, more commonly known as the McCarran-Walter Act, in 1952. Through that legislation, Siobhan B. Somerville writes, "Congress ensured that a finding of homosexuality could be used to exclude immigrants from eligibility for immigration and naturalization," codifying the inaccessibility of full citizenship for homosexuals.[37] While the final version of the act replaced the earlier text's usage of "homosexual" and "sex pervert" with the more coded "psychopathic personality," the Senate report registered that "this change in nomenclature is not to be construed in any way as modifying the intent to exclude all aliens who are sexual deviates."[38] The act further prevented immigration—and permitted deportation—of those who espoused Communism, defined in the act as "a revolutionary movement, the purpose of which is to establish eventually a Communist totalitarian dictatorship in any or all the countries of the world through the medium of an internationally coordinated Communist political movement."[39] The new restrictions on Communists and homosexuals within the already confining immigration law further entwined their fates as both domestic security risks and vehicles of contamination who deserved to be excluded from American life.

The Smith Act, which had been passed in 1940, made the un-Americanness of Communism crystal clear by retroactively rendering Party membership illegal, and the familiar practice of pleading the Fifth Amendment when questioned about membership in the Communist Party informed homophile strategies for resisting entrapment by refusing to speak to police. "This strange bedfellowship is brought about by the Fifth Amendment's rigid stipulations on self-incrimination," an author wrote in *ONE Magazine,* "which seems to put the homosexuals in the uncomfortable position of defending the rights of reds in order to defend their own."[40] The state-sponsored drift from cracking down on Communism to policing homosexuality was made even more explicit when the Florida Legislative Investigation Committee—formed in 1956, in the wake of the *Brown v. Board of Education* decision, to root out Communists in the civil rights movement—expanded its charge in 1961 to further investigate homosexuals.[41]

The strategic distancing of homosexuals from Communism represented a signature feature of homophile groups during the early years of their development. "The fledgling Mattachine Movement has not been without opposition and attack," James Whitman wrote in a 1953 article for *ONE Magazine.* "Because of its socially constructive ends it has been accused of Communist affiliation."[42] The expulsion of Mattachine's founding members from the organization in 1953 represented an especially critical moment when anti-Communism was baked into the homophile movement. The rationale behind purging Communists from the organization hinged on anxiety about the threat that harboring "un-American" Communists could bring down the entire homophile movement. "No one engaged in any position on the magazine should have any association whatsoever—on any basis—with any one who has played a part in the Communist party," wrote a *ONE Magazine* editor. "One such association could be used in Washington to wreck the entire magazine if the hands of some clever operator seized on it for that purpose."[43]

Occasionally homophile activists acknowledged, quixotic though it appeared to be, that gay Communists did exist. "It would be ridiculous to argue that there are no homosexuals who are communists," wrote Harry Johnson in *ONE Magazine.* "We know that in the past there have been some who were, and it is likely that there are still undetected homosexuals within the organization. It is hard to imagine the mental convulsions such people must experience in attempting to reconcile the irreconcilable contradictions in their thinking."[44] That "irreconcilable contradiction" was not mere fantasy, as the anti-Communism within the homophile movement corresponded with an uptick in the Communist Party's own disciplinary procedures, which had banned "degenerates" as early as 1938, and later specifically named "homosexuality" as grounds for disciplinary action.[45] Yet the targeting of homosexuals and Communists created, as Elizabeth Lalo despaired in a 1953 issue of *ONE Magazine,* "strange bedfellows." "Deviants who pride themselves in having no interest whatever in dull-old-politics, are shocked to find themselves classed with communists and criminals as far as Senator McCarthy and the present and previous administrations are concerned," Lalo complained.[46] The prevailing logic, according to Harry Johnson, followed a specious algorithm: "[C]ommunists are bad. Homosexuals are bad. Therefore communists are homosexuals. Illogical? Of course, but who gives a thought to logic when writing against homosexuals or communists? We live in the age of McCarthyism, and to question even the *logic* of anti-communist or anti-homosexual arguments is to commit treason."[47]

Mattachine's founders wound up in the crosshairs of anti-Communist forces within their own ranks. In 1953, the organization engaged in a vigorous discussion about whether members with histories on the Left should be expunged. This was a slippery slope for an organization ostensibly committed to social justice. If Mattachine sought to purge its communist members, a report on the discussion noted,

[w]e would find that if a person were a believer in low-cost public housing,— if a person ever signed a petition to end lynching in the South or to end restrictive covenants in California,—if a person had attended Wallace-for President rallies in 1948,—if a person objected to anti-Semitic outbreaks or if he had written a letter to congress urging the free State of Israel in 1948— if a person were one of the 80,000,000 warm supporters of Mr. Roosevelt's war-time international agreements,—if a person had been anti-Nazi or anti-Franco in 1939,—we would be informed by this or that feature writer of the press that all such persons previously described were either Communist-led or Communist-dominated by association. In the absence of a clear analytical definition of a Communist,—in the absence of any clear definition between acts and attitudes of Progressives, Liberals, and Humanitarians, as distinguished from Communists,—we would be forced to conclude that, in brief, anyone not 100% anti-humanitarian, and 100% pro the present political status-quo (whatever it might happen to be), is Communist by inspiration or by application. To be 100% pro-American then, one is required to be not only 100% New Deal *but also 100% anti-homosexual.*[48]

Nonetheless, Mattachine moved ahead with its expulsion of the Communist founders of the movement.[49] New leadership favored a less militant organization, advancing "evolutionary methods, not revolutionary methods," according to Hal Call, an architect of the society's post-Communist incarnation.[50] Call was a World War II veteran who was fanatical about replacing Mattachine's underground "cell structure" with a public-facing organization. Call was concerned that his open organization would reveal the Communist histories of Mattachine's original leaders, which, in the McCarthy era, spelled doom for the organization. The founders, Call determined, "had to go."[51] Though Call conceived this as a necessary measure to achieve his practical goals of eliminating police entrapment and other legal challenges, his distaste for the original Mattachine founders, whom he characterized as "pie in the sky, erudite, and artistically inclined," suggests a broader animus towards the Left.[52] After little debate, the former Communists were removed.

The trauma of being excised from Mattachine exacted a devastating toll on the former Communists, who found themselves ejected from an organization they had built from the ground up. Though the early leaders maintained a respectful, if chilly, relationship with the Communist Party, they harbored no lingering fondness for the gay leaders who unceremoniously pushed them out of Mattachine. "[T]he trauma of it is everlastingly etched in my brain," Harry Hay wrote in a letter more than twenty years later.[53] Nearly forty years after the split, Chuck Rowland's memory of the moment retained a palpable sense of hurt. "I became absolutely suicidal," he recalled. "I was prepared to quite literally devote my life to the Mattachine, and here this bright glory was all gone. It all turned to shit.[54] Founding member Bob Hull actually did commit suicide in 1962, which Chuck Rowland attributed to the split in Mattachine. Though Harry Hay wrote a small memorial in *ONE Magazine*, scant attention was paid to Hull's death.[55]

As the pressures of the Cold War intensified, homophile organizations differentiated their movement from the Left, even in its Popular Front iteration, with bolder insistence. The commitment within the movement to casting homosexuals as deserving of full citizenship impelled them to loosen the ties that had connected sexual dissidents to the Left. Homophile organizations rallied around the idea that joining in the fight against Communism was essential to advancing the rights of homosexuals. Homosexuals and leftists forged separate paths, by turns electively and coercively, at precisely the same time as narratives that imagined both as clear and present threats to American culture took hold.

SEXUAL DISSIDENTS AND THE COLD WAR LEFT

For sexual dissidents on the Left, the Cold War represented an extension of the surveillance and discipline that had long plagued American radicals. While McCarthyism represented a more aggressive chapter in a long history of red scares, it also animated the deviant politics that had attracted sexual dissidents to the Left for decades. Some gay Communists, such as Willard Motley and Dorsey Gassaway Fisher, joined communities of leftist exiles in Mexico. Fisher, who worked for the US State Department, was questioned about his radical activities in Mexico, including tipping off a veteran of the Spanish Civil War about the notes in his file.[56] For sexual dissidents who remained in the United States, the dragnet of the red and lavender scares deeply affected their lives and work, but the growing anxiety about homosexuality within the Communist Party made their lives equally precarious.

"The party leadership made a decision to drop all homosexuals from the party because of their presumed openness to blackmail as state repression increased," one Communist Party organizer recalled. "A local organizer was asked to speak to several known lesbians to request their resignations. These lesbians were friends of the organizer, although she never discussed their sexual preference with them. When she met them, they all cried, but the lesbians 'obeyed' and resigned."[57] Junius Scales, a well-known southern organizer for the Communist Party, remembered how in the late 1940s he was directed to inquire about homosexuality of Communists under his command. "The number of affirmative replies was startling: they came from young and old, men and women, Negro and white, married and single, workers and students," Scales writes. "Two prominent Negro unionists, two outstanding student leaders, and others exceptional in their ability and activity included themselves among the homosexuals."[58] Scales further recounted his unwillingness to participate in their expulsion.

For some gay Communists, electively leaving the Party was unrelated to such policies. Chuck Rowland asserted that he "left the Communist party in 1948, not because I was kicked out, not because I disagreed with anything, but because I wanted out. Joining the Communist party is very much like joining a monastery or becoming a priest. It is total dedication, 24-hours-a-day, 365-days-a-year. I thought I wanted that, and I did for awhile, but I realized that I was getting very little sex, and I didn't want a lover."[59] It was not the Party's homophobic policy that led to Rowland's leaving the Communist Party, then, but rather the intense time commitment—a factor that often led members to renounce their Party membership without abandoning their Communist sympathies.

Yet the Left continued to attract homosexual members, some of whom incorporated sexual dissidence into their critique of capitalism. In some cases, the Communist Party made exceptions to its antigay policy, "especially," Alan M. Wald notes, "if the individuals could 'pass' as heterosexuals or did not draw attention to themselves (for example, by being arrested) or if they were famous and of unquestionable political zeal."[60] The latter seemed to be the case for Marc Blitzstein, who was remarkably open about his homosexuality and his connections to the Left. More commonly, Communists kept their homosexuality and Party activities separate from one another, even if some of these individuals, such as the poet T.C. Wilson, confessed their homosexuality to heterosexual Communists whom they trusted to keep their revelations in confidence.[61] Dorothy Brewster and Lillian Barnard Gilkes were both professors in New York, and they each produced work on women writers while maintaining an intimate relationship. They were sympathetic toward the Soviet Union and friendly with Martha Dodd, who was accused of spying for the Soviets.[62] The pair was circumspect about their leftist sympathies and sexual dissidence. Still others, such as the radical writer Lee Hays, never joined the Party in spite of his leftist sympathies. "He may have stayed out—or been kept out—because of his homosexuality," leftist Irwin Silber suggested.[63] Aaron Copland, the prominent gay leftist composer, similarly stopped short of joining the Party even as his political orientation was decidedly consistent with the Party's goals.

Outside the Communist Party, gay leftists were occasionally more outspoken about politicizing their sexual dissidence. "Indeed," the perpetually cranky critic Leslie Fiedler wrote in 1958, "one feels sometimes that homosexuality is the purest and truest protest of the latest generation, not a burden merely, an affliction to be borne, but a politics to be flaunted."[64] In 1952, the *Young Socialist,* a bulletin for youth in the Socialist Party, published an essay titled "On Socialism and Sex," by the pseudonymous H.L. Small.[65] The short manifesto offered a three-pronged attack. First, the author suggested that American Socialists should look to other nations for sexual liberation. "The freedom of the legally of-age adult of both sexes to have sexual relations with whomever he or she wishes of the same or opposite sex, without fear of sanction," Small wrote, "is an important libertarian principle that is part of the law in many socialist and semi-socialist countries today." Second, decriminalizing and destigmatizing homosexuality would mean "to the individual 'deviant' that the fear of legal sanction, as well as illegal repression, blackmail, etc., are forever banished from his mind." That is to say, decriminalization would obviate charges of homosexuals as security risks. Finally, Small argued that prohibitions on homosexuality harmed individuals, in turn excluding them from joining radical movements. Dominant narratives suggested "that sexual deviancy is a mark of ill health," but the Socialist future required a wholesale rejection of unhealthy thought patterns. "Whether we individually consider it right or wrong, healthy or unhealthy, to have a large or small vocabulary of libidinal expression," Small concluded, "repression of such expression, or practice under fear, does not make for a whole, productive individual."[66]

Small's essay did not result in the adoption of a new Socialist Party platform embracing sexual dissidents, but, as Christopher Phelps notes, neither did the party discipline members for homosexuality, even during the repressive 1950s.[67] Vern Davidson, a Socialist beginning in 1948, recalled to Phelps that "[b]efore the 1952 party convention, when I was still in New York, I was instructed by the YPSLs [Young People's Socialist League] to attempt to put a homosexual rights plank before the platform committee."[68] Davidson did exactly that, and he was encouraged by the committee to draft a platform, which he failed to deliver. Other Socialists, such as David McReynolds and Ralph Shaffer, discovered numerous gay men working within the Socialist Party during the 1950s.

The US Socialist Workers Party (SWP) represented another such radical network, making up what Alan M. Wald refers to as a "cultural minority within a political minority," whereby a "longtime presence" was established within "the Trotskyist movement of sexual nonconformists." The SWP extended the anti-Stalinist Left that had included among its earlier ranks writers as diverse as Claude McKay, Parker Tyler, and Robert Duncan into the 1950s. During the Cold War, the SWP counted among its ranks Peter Bloch, a gay journalist who wrote about US imperialism for the leftist press, and Laura Slobe, a bisexual cartoonist and artist.[69]

While the Left continued to advance its anticapitalist agenda throughout the Cold War, radicals increasingly saw their work as connected with the blossoming civil rights movement. While this alliance represented an extension of the Left's long-standing interest in Black liberation—"The CP," Martha Biondi writes, "was the only major political party that formally opposed racial discrimination; it devoted considerable resources to an array of anti-discrimination campaigns; and it created a rare space for Black leadership in a multiracial institution"—the emergence of the Southern Christian Leadership Conference in 1957 and the Student Nonviolent Coordinating Committee in 1960 broadened the points of entry for addressing racism. For many Black sexual dissidents, the civil rights movement offered a more compelling launching point for leveling broad challenges to American structures of power than the overly narrow homophile movement.[70] Especially following the Montgomery bus boycott in 1955, which exposed the ferocity of white supremacy roiling throughout the United States, leftists perceived the brutality of segregation's defenders as an indictment of American liberalism. Sexual dissidents with long histories on the Left such as Bayard Rustin assumed leadership positions within the civil rights movement.[71] Meanwhile, American Cold Warriors worried about how the Communist propaganda that was successfully mobilizing anti-American sentiment in the Soviet Union, where images from Birmingham were splashed across the front page of *Pravda*, could frustrate their efforts to sell the American way of life to nations emerging from under the thumb of colonialism.[72]

Black challenges to Jim Crow segregation were central to Cold War leftist activism and writing. "From the 1930s to the 1960s," Mary Helen Washington writes, "African American literary criticism and practice was, in fact, significantly influenced by the formulas of the Marxist-Leninist nation thesis and its focus on black folk culture as the basis for a national, oppositional culture."[73] This was especially true of Black women, whose analysis, as Dayo F. Gore argues, "also carried with it a commitment to advancing women's equality and an internationalist vision of the black freedom struggle." These women spearheaded a reinvigorated Black feminist Left as "they demanded that left-leaning organizations embrace an intersecting analysis that centered race and gender, as well as economics. They enacted a vision of liberation and resistance anchored at these points of intersection."[74]

Some of the most prominent figures in what Martha Biondi terms the Cold War era's "Black Popular Front" incorporated sexuality in their critique of American racism. Two of the most significant Black writers of the period, James Baldwin and Lorraine Hansberry, were sexual dissidents with connections to the Left.[75] Baldwin, who had participated in a New York May Day parade in his youth ("carrying banners," he recalled, and "shouting, *East Side, West Side, all around the town, We want the landlords to tear the slums down!*"), published an early poem in a 1946 issue of *New Masses* and contributed to the *Partisan Review* and the *New Leader* in the 1940s.[76] "I didn't know anything about Communism," he claimed, "but I knew a lot about slums."[77] Later in his career, Baldwin disavowed his history with the Left, especially forcefully in his introduction to a collection of his nonfiction writing published in 1985. "My life on the Left is of absolutely no interest," Baldwin wrote in his introduction. "It did not last long. It was useful in that I learned that it may be impossible to indoctrinate me."[78]

Indoctrinated or not, Baldwin, by his own admission, had been involved in the Left, partly at the urging of his dear friend Eugene Worth, who "was a Socialist—a member of the Young People's Socialist League (YPSL) and urged me to join, and I did. I, then, outdistanced him by becoming a Trotskyite—so that I was in the interesting position (at the age of nineteen) of being an anti-Stalinist when America and Russia were allies."[79] Baldwin was especially disturbed by McCarthyist targeting of Communists. "The pretext for all this," he wrote in No Name in the Street, was "the necessity of 'containing' Communism, which, they unblushingly informed me, was a threat to the 'free' world. I did not say to what extent this free world menaced me, and millions like me."[80] Baldwin's sexual dissidence presented an obstacle to full participation in the Left. Stan Weir, a friend and coworker of Baldwin's in the 1940s, attempted to convince Baldwin to join the Workers Party. "I know that your group does not expel those who join and then are 'discovered' after the fact," he recalls Baldwin saying to him. "But like you they attempt to ignore this human difference. That it is a matter which cannot be discussed means that the discussion of every subject leads always to the closed door."[81] In response, Baldwin carved out a unique and significant place in American literature that resisted both a narrow understanding of sexuality as a singular centerpiece of political organizing and a leftist orientation that treated race, sexuality, and gender as secondary to class.[82]

Lorraine Hansberry is rightfully remembered most often as the author of the tremendously successful play A Raisin in the Sun, which debuted on Broadway in 1959. While that play launched her into a stratosphere of success unheard of for a Black woman playwright, it also bracketed off one text in Hansberry's career at the expense of many other writings. In a list cataloguing things she was "bored to death of," Hansberry began with "A Raisin in the Sun!"[83] While she also claimed to be bored with "'Lesbians' (the capital L variety)" and "SEX," she retained a hint of her radical history by also including "the Great American money obsession."[84] Her ambivalence around her homosexuality, which she otherwise seemed to embrace, if not publicly, could be observed in a list of things "I like" and "I hate" in a 1960 notebook: "my homosexuality" appears on both lists.[85]

Hansberry connected with the Communist Party as she drew closer to Paul Robeson. In 1952, she traveled in Robeson's stead to the Inter-American Peace Conference in Uruguay. She wrote letters for the Daily Worker under the name John Henry—a sly masquerade on the Black folk hero.[86] As Cheryl Higashida argues, Hansberry was deeply connected with Left internationalism, which was reflected in her journalism for Robeson's Freedom magazine. "The internationalism of the Black

Left, and the *Freedom* group in particular," Higashida writes, "crucially shaped Hansberry's gender and sexual politics."[87] Beginning in 1957, Hansberry also sent letters to *The Ladder*, a lesbian publication of the Daughters of Bilitis—a homophile organization formed in 1955—which she signed "L.H.N." or "L.N.," her initials while married to Robert Nemiroff.[88] In one letter from May 1957, Hansberry observed that "women, like other oppressed groups of one kind or another, have particularly had to pay a price for the intellectual impoverishment that the second class status imposed on us for centuries created and sustained." Popular Front echoes could be heard in Hansberry's declaration that "women, without wishing to foster any strict separatist notions, homo or hetero, indeed have a need for their own publications and organizations."[89] In another letter, she foregrounded the intersection of sexuality and gender she believed was essential to the liberation of homosexuals. "In this kind of work," she wrote in August 1957, "there may be women to emerge who will be able to formulate a new and possible concept that homosexual persecution and condemnation has at its roots not only social ignorance, but a philosophically active anti-feminist dogma."[90] Hansberry also wrote fiction under the name Emily Jones, including short stories titled "The Anticipation of Eve" and "Chanson du Konallis"—both published in *The Ladder* in 1958—as well as work that never found its way into print.

While repression was often cast as a deleterious force serving to suppress leftists, the painful dispossession of marginalized Americans during the Cold War was occasionally reframed as a site of solidarity working toward revolution. Among those who continued to participate in the Communist Party during the 1950s was the Black writer Lloyd L. Brown, whose 1951 novel *Iron City* drew heavily from his experiences in Allegheny County Jail a decade earlier. Brown was a managing editor for *New Masses*, later editing *Masses and Mainstream* (which replaced *New Masses*), and he worked on *Freedom* through the 1950s. Brown had joined the Young Communist League after visiting the Soviet Union in the 1930s, and he remained in the Party until 1952.[91] He was a defiant radical, as testified in his FBI file, which describes his encountering two agents on the streets of New York in 1962. After taunting the agents, he "continued by advising the Agents to go back and tell whoever they tell that he is the meanest, rottenest s—o—b——— they ever met and that is the way he is going to be until he gets his freedom."[92]

Iron City reflects the fiery imagination of its author, whose publishing the book during the Cold War was, according to blacklisted screenwriter Dalton Trumbo, "like setting a match to kerosene."[93] The novel imagines a radical politics that emerges in the homosocial space of a prison—a space that reframes Black targets of police repression and Communist organizers as defiant agents mutually engaged in challenging the state. As scholars such as Regina Kunzel have argued, prisons represented an important site for navigating modern sexuality.[94] Within his novel, Brown produced a transgressive list of social deviants and sexual dissidents, a catalogue of the lumpenproletariat who demanded inclusion in any radical program:

> A thousand men on fifty ranges were standing and waiting—the young and the old, the crippled and whole, the tried-and-found-guilty and the yet-to-be-tried: the F&B's, the A&B's, the drunk-and-disorderlies, rapists, riflers, tinhorns, triflers, swindlers, bindlers, peepers, punks, tipsters, hipsters, snatchers, pimps, unlawful disclosers, indecent exposers, delayed marriage, lascivious carriage, unlicensed selling, fortune telling, sex perversion, unlawful conversion, dips, dopes, dandlers, deceivers, buggers, huggers, writers, receivers, larceny, arsony, forgery, jobbery, felonious assault, trespassing, robbery, shooting, looting, gambling, shilling, drinking, winking, rambling, killing, wife-beating, breaking in, tax-cheating, making gin, Mann Act, woman-act, being-black-and-talking-back, and conspiring to overthrow the government of the Commonwealth by force and violence.[95]

For Brown, the possibility that a Black Communist who "talks back" and conspires against the state might find himself in a cell with sexual perverts represents a world of radical possibilities. Try though the state might to marginalize perverts and insurrectionists by separating them from the masses and mainstream of society, Brown acknowledges how mass incarceration also created a space within which one might envision state repression as a mobilizing tool for leftist organizing. Marked by rhyme, alliteration, and word play, Brown's list moves easily between official and vernacular language—at some points parroting the language of the state through legal language; at others invoking slang usages such as "peepers" and "punks." Brown asserts control over his narrative, as well as his irreverent refusal to reinscribe legal discourse, by riffing on the language games lawbreaking makes possible: Mann Act playfully becomes "woman act;" "buggers" are harmlessly juxtaposed alongside "huggers." His narrative accelerates as it reaches its crescendoing climax of force and violence.

For leftists in the Cold War era, homosexuality represented a site of conflict and resistance. The increased discipline required of homosexuals within the Communist Party threatened the ability of many sexual dissidents to participate fully in the movement. At the same time, leftists continued to work both within the Left and by repurposing radical discourse to push against the state, and the increasingly radical civil rights movement offered a plethora of new venues for sexually dissident leftists to confront American racism. Still, within a Cold War cultural context where normativity was aligned with Americanism, leftist activity cast further suspicion on radicals' deviant politics. Even when leftists remained silent on homosexuality, their rejection of normativity brought them deeper under a shadow of suspicion. The perceived deviance of homosexuals and Communists in a time of tremendous state repression ensured that their fates remained intertwined.

COMMUNISM AS DEVIANCE DURING THE COLD WAR

In 1954, Granville Hicks, a *New Masses* editor turned anti-Communist Cold Warrior, published an autobiographical study of the weird attraction to Communism that he perceived among his friends and acquaintances in the Depression-era United States. His hefty tell-all memoir, curiously titled *Where We Came Out,* speculated on the pull toward radical politics experienced by many outcasts in the 1930s. "The party had more than its share of lost souls," Hicks recalled. "There are always such people about and at that time the party was the fashionable haven for them." Yet in addition to offering a fabulous "haven" for those alienated from the American dream, Hicks detected a particularly deviant motivation behind radical attachment and membership in the party: "Some were cases from textbooks in psychopathology," he observed, whereas "others suffered from simpler kinds of frustration—the unsuccessful writers and artists, the sex-starved women, and so on."[96] The stirrings of radicalism, according to Hicks, were born of frustrations artistic and sexual. Communism represented just the perversion necessary to divert such un-American desires as artistic expression and female sexuality, and it was in light of such deviance that the famous leftist finally found his courage—or his weakness, as he later determined—and came out.

In diagnosing deviance as a cause for joining the Party, Hicks was not alone. Former Communist Benjamin Gitlow had suggested similarly suspect motivations leading young people into Communism in his 1949 memoir, *I Confess.* "Many came from homes where the parental influence was not very strong," Gitlow recalled. "The young Communists . . . fell easy prey to all the vices in the Party, which to them were not vices but expressions of rebellion against bourgeois society and the hypocrisy of bourgeois morals."[97] The lack of parental control in homes yielding incipient leftists impelled young people to throw off the shackles of American morality, and their rejection of bourgeois values was not only tolerated within the Communist Party, it was actively encouraged. As they attempted to overthrow the American government, Communists acted out against all irrational expectations of propriety. By opposing the standards of American morality, these militant radicals chipped away at the social order cementing capitalism in place. Following Gitlow's formulation, deviants were attracted to the Party, which in turn made its members into deviants.

Benjamin Gitlow took note of the randy young adults who had made up a sizable proportion of the rank and file in the 1930s, many of whom apparently took full advantage of the licentious leanings of their comrades. "The orgies and debaucheries among the youth were spoken about in whispers in the Party," Gitlow writes in his memoir, confirming both the limited visibility of sex in the Party and the gossipy networks that brought it to light. "We felt that the profligate sex relations among the youth was something we could not control and that as long as the youth could be depended upon to serve the interests of the movement it was best to leave the matter alone."[98] The Communist Party attempted to discipline its oversexed members, but its leaders were sometimes unwilling to become involved in sexual matters that were not impinging on members' work. Though he stopped short of theorizing sexual practices among members as ideological, Gitlow did recognize that sex was "profligate" in the Communist Party—a far cry from the myths of abstemiousness or unrelenting discipline that competed for space in the 1930s.

At the very least, Communism seemed to represent a hotbed of sexual license that left family members bemused and disturbed. Parents were perplexed by the sexual permissiveness they observed once their children joined the Party. "My daughter is only fifteen," one mother complained in an anecdote recounted in Gitlow's memoir.

> Before she joined the young Communists she was a very quiet and good girl. But now she is different. She smokes. When I tell her something, she laughs and tells me I am ignorant and think like a bourgeois. She has neglected her school and studies. She is seldom home. When she does come, it is around two or three o'clock in the morning.[99]

Communist membership is recalled here as a form of juvenile delinquency, with insinuations of defiance but also late-night rendezvous that can hardly be spoken aloud.[100] "Inevitably sex plays a great psychological role in any youth movement," Eugene Lyons warned in a 1941 book that was cited in the California Senate's 1951 investigation into Communist infiltration of the state's young people. "The unorthodox attitudes that go with radicalism helped to attract followers for the organization."[101]

The transgressive dimensions of Communism defied not only puritanical expectations of sexual propriety among women, but also gender normativity in the 1950s. In *I Led 3 Lives,* a 1952 memoir of his life as a spy within the Communist Party, Herbert Philbrick described Alice Gordon, the chairman of the Massachusetts Young Communist League, in terms that suggested the markings of a female masculinity that drifted into 1950s butch. "Alice was a squat, stocky, square-jawed functionary of the party, a paid professional of communism," Philbrick writes. "She was a plain proletarian, and like most party women she gave an impression of drab grayness, almost the uniform of Communist femininity. She was bossy and could tell me what to do as well as she could tell her own sex." As though her personal presentation were not bad enough, Gordon's housekeeping skills similarly repelled Philbrick when he visited her "unkempt, bug-infested, walk up apartment," where he "sat on an incredibly lumpy sofa covered with material grown slick and harsh through time and wear" as "two poorly shaded bridge lamps illuminated the room and threw a wretched glare into my eyes."[102] Perhaps most revealingly, Alice attempted to instruct Philbrick's wife, Eva, on the revolutionary gender upheaval Communists sought to spread throughout the world. "The function of women and girls is changing," Philbrick recalls Alice telling Eva. "A growing girl can look forward to motherhood, but should not be taught that this is her only function. . . . Boys who want to be modern have to include girls in their games when they play soldier. . . . If we prepare our children for their vanguard role we must not hem them in by the narrow restrictions of conventional middle-class sex patterns of behavior."[103]

Philbrick's memoir insisted upon Communist gender nonconformity. Fanny Hartman, "a vest-pocket edition of party stalwart Elizabeth Gurley Flynn," was "a mannish woman, at home in a man's world, and yet she commanded genuine affection and deep friendship from other women," while Comrade Frances was "one of the party's 'plain Janes,' a heavy-set, studious, and serious girl." Anne Burlak was "not averse to physical combat with the police, and had been known to tangle with as many as three at a time." In Philbrick's account, gender nonconformity extended at times to men as well as women. Harry, for example, was "an insufferable, overeducated bore" who "lived in comfortable good taste," and who, Philbrick was "convinced[,] . . . was too effete to be a Communist," while "Butch . . . was a young artist, also with rather Bohemian ways, who lived on Beacon Hill."[104] In cases where women were not masculine, Philbrick sometimes questioned their actual commitment to the Party. Norma, for example, who hosted a high-level Communist meeting, was "the homey type and obviously frightened by some of the things she heard in cell meetings." Philbrick characterizes her as "infatuated" with the Left, but "in truth she would have been better off reading love stories instead for her relaxation, with a box of chocolates on the arm of her chair."[105] Philbrick's characterizations of Communist deviance must be viewed in the context of his persistent efforts to justify his own curious ability to "pass" in the Party for so many years without being suspected of being a secret agent. By representing the women and men around him as gender transgressive, Philbrick performed his normativity and reminded readers that he was an outsider in this bizarre world.

Of course, one of the reasons why the Communist Party was looked upon with suspicion was that the International represented for American Communists an illicit love object that rendered its adherents deviant. At a time when the United States was envisioned as "one nation, under god," Communists replaced healthy allegiance to the United States with transgressive desire for an immoral (and international) utopia. They refused the emerging consumer culture and quest for suburban whiteness in favor of yearning for a collectivist future. In an age of home ownership and smug national belonging, Communists weirdly rejected material strivings in favor of materialist analysis.[106] In his 1958 ex-Communist memoir, *The Story of an American Communist*, John Gates recalled how "love can blind us to the evil in the object of our affection, as happened with American Communists in their attitude to the communist world," suggesting the abjection of desire for a bad political object.[107] During a period when the American family was conceived as foundational to the appropriate functioning of democracy, threats to the familial and national order took on a particularly grave tenor as Communists looked beyond the family and even outside the nation for hope and futurity—and also love. In this regard, Cold War–era anti-Communists confirmed an earlier Communist script that had defiantly refused to be woven into the American national fabric and resisted sitting at the hearth of domestic politics. The Communist poet H. H. Lewis, in his 1930 poem "Thinking of Russia," had articulated an obsessive relationship with the Soviet Union that drifted from compulsive desire into a bold proclamation of antifamilial deviance:

> I'm always thinking of Russia
> I can't keep her out of my head
> I don't give a damn for Old Uncle Sham
> I'm a left-wing radical Red.[108]

Though his was an ostensibly "straight" affair, Lewis's ode to Russia articulated the slipperiness between sexual radicalism and the leftist cultural vocabulary: Uncle Sam's assumed kinship—both traditional and chummy—was revealed to be a sham; fantasies of Russia were made to signify transgressive desire; and "left-wing radical Red"–ness became a site for camp appropriation of the unconflicted coupling of deviance with defiance. The jaunty affections of Uncle Sam were eschewed in favor of an unhealthy attraction to Mother Russia. An even more direct connection between susceptibility to Communism and illicit desire can be detected in Eugene Lyons's unsubtle title for his influential 1941 study of the Communist menace, *The Red Decade: The Stalinist Penetration of America*. Here American Communists not only gazed longingly toward the Soviet Union; they actually let themselves get fucked by Stalin.

During the Cold War, Communism seemed to promote domestic arrangements that threatened the sanctity of the family. In 1958, Leslie Fiedler argued that homosexuality, which he described as the "staunchest party of them all," was "the last possible protest against bourgeois security and the home in the suburbs in a world where adultery is old hat."[109] At times, the threats posed by Communism and homosexuality were represented as intersecting. In an early scene in Ann Petry's 1953 novel *The Narrows*, for example, Peter Bollock, a newspaper tycoon, lies in bed with his wife, Lola, complaining about both Communism and the interior decorator who has recently refurnished their home. "When he turned out the light in their bedroom," Petry writes,

> he thought, Well, at least that pansy who picked out the furniture knew what he was doing when he put a kingsize bed in here, or maybe it was Lola's idea. And [he] asked her, and she giggled, then whispered, "Stalin thought it up—part of the Communist plot to hasten the downfall of the capitalist class."[110]

Lola's teasing retort, reported from the cozy bed selected by a queer decorator, diminishes her husband's anxiety about reds and "pansies" by collapsing these categories in a grand ironic gesture—a move that signals the hysteria surrounding homosexuality and Communism during the Cold War. That this anecdote appeared in a novel that dissected with remarkable precision the anatomy of an interracial love affair is also not incidental. Petry's sensitivity to the chilling effects of American racism on sexual desire, and her commitment to exploring radical alternatives, offers a compelling explanation for the tongue-in-cheek specter of queer Communism that haunts her work. Neither should it be overlooked that Petry was a meticulous chronicler of the meanings of domesticity, race, and class in American culture, all filtered through her radical imagination.

Petry's conspiracy theory about Stalin's army of interior decorators might be filed under McCarthy-era camp, but the theory that homosexuality was being inflicted upon the United States by Communist agents represented a Cold War American trope. *Physical Culture* magazine postulated in 1953 that "[h]omosexuality is Stalin's atom bomb to destroy America."[111] Attorney General William Rogers feared that "the Soviets are exploiting sex situations" and "seem to have a list of homosexuals."[112] Even President Harry S. Truman joined the fun, complaining of "the parlor pinks and the soprano voiced men" who might represent "a sabotage front for Uncle Joe Stalin."[113] Meanwhile, in *U.S.A. Confidential*—a 1951 screed characterized by the Cornell University student newspaper as "a blunt and often obscene volume devoted to exposing communism, corruption, dope addiction, and sexual perversion throughout the United States and its territories"[114]—Jack Lait and Lee Mortimer connected sexual dissidence with Communism. "There is no place for love and emotion in proletarian society," they declared. "Sex is offered as an inducement to comrades for attending meetings." Lait and Mortimer further argued that "Communism actively promotes and supports sex deviation to sap the strength of the new generation and make the birth of another problematical." Communist parties, they claimed, were heady affairs that "mix Marx with cocaine, and sex."[115] Senator Kenneth Wherry complained to the *New York Post* in 1950 that "you can't hardly separate homosexuals from subversives."[116]

Arthur Schlesinger Jr. meditated upon the perversity of leftist attachment in *The Vital Center*, his best-selling 1949 treatise on "the politics of freedom."[117] Schlesinger described those who joined or followed along the Communist Party as "secret, sweaty, and furtive like nothing so much . . . as homosexuals in a boys' school." For Schlesinger, falling to the left of center was both queer metaphor and symptom; the attraction to the Communist Party was, for him, a sexual attraction, similar to that imagined by Granville Hicks. The Party rank and file comprised "lonely and frustrated people, craving social, intellectual and even sexual fulfillment they cannot obtain in existing society." The Party attracted members through "half-concealed exercises in penetration and manipulation." Cold Warriors were *very* anxious about penetration. "For these people," Schlesinger concluded, "party discipline is no obstacle; it is an attraction."[118]

"For weaklings floundering in a sea of trouble," Herbert Philbrick suggested, "Marxist-Leninist philosophy appears as a solid rock on which they can gain a footing—oblivious to the fact that the tide ultimately will come in and sweep them away."[119] Long-standing representations of Communist Party membership as demanding asexual devotion were replaced with images of fiendish sexual passion and mental instability during the Cold War. Under questioning during a 1950 State Department employee-loyalty investigation, Senator Millard E. Tydings quoted back to Joseph McCarthy a conversation the latter had recounted with "one of our top intelligence men," who stated that "you will find that practically every active Communist is twisted mentally or physically in some way." Senator McCarthy went to great pains to correct the record. "Let me interrupt you there, Mr. Chairman," McCarthy stated. "I do not agree with the 'or physically.'"[120]

Morris L. Ernst and David Loth confirmed the queer compulsion toward Communism in their *Report on the American Communist* in 1952. The authors had collaborated on earlier studies, including *American Sexual Behavior and the Kinsey Report* in 1948. Their credentials as experts on American sexuality established their expertise in offering their later report. In this book, Ernst and Loth aimed to "understand Communists," without which knowledge "the people of the United States cannot wisely and successfully combat communism." That understanding began by acknowledging a series of easily categorizable motivations that drew Communists into the Party, ranging from "youthful errors" to "damaged souls." The latter category was explained through convincing, if circumstantial, evidence: "Communists themselves sometimes explain the relatively large number of weak, physically unattractive, or emotionally unstable members by saying these people have been freed by their suffering for serious study and so turn to communism."[121] Perhaps most scandalous was "sex patterns," to which the authors dedicated nearly twenty pages. Based on a nonscientific collection of interviews conducted by Ernst and Loth, the authors sought to look unblinkingly into the bedrooms of American Communists.

"It was extensively reported and often believed," Ernst and Loth reported, "that life in the Communist party was one long sexual orgy. At one time there were probably more Americans who thought that all Communists practiced 'free love' and promiscuity than knew the name of Lenin." Ernst and Loth offered "informed guesses" into Communist sex practices, hoping that perhaps "a full research job" might be forthcoming.[122] Unsurprisingly, the authors found that the Communist's "sex life is casual, rather random, somewhat less monogamous . . . and also less sentimental or even intimate." In light of the curbing of sexual impulses in favor of a disciplined family order that governed Cold War structures of kinship, the idea that Communist men were "more inclined to take their sexual activity in the light of a form of calisthenics" suggested the depth of their depravity: it was not only the having of free-love relations that pointed to Communist deviance; the refusal to categorize sex differently from daily exercise indicated a turning away from the basic demands of reproductive citizenship. Communists were also hypersexual. The incidence of impotence among Communists was, Ernst and Loth found, lower than in the general population.[123]

The high number of gay Communists further confirmed both that sexual dissidents were drawn into the Party and that the particular ideological pressures of Communism resulted in homosexual behavior. The authors noted that "there is a slight analogy of a Communist and a that of a homosexual," noting that individuals in both categories "want their shame and enjoy the guilt of lying, cheating, and deceiving their friends."[124] The refusal of homosexuals and Communists to retreat in the face of social stigma was thus reframed as evidence for their enjoyment of stigmatization: theirs was a deviant pleasure based upon both desire for abjection and taking pleasure in the social demands of belonging to a community kept in the closet.

The structure of commitment, collectivity, secrecy, and intimacy demanded of Communists cast them under a cloud of suspicion. At the same time, these features of Communists bore a striking resemblance to the characterizations of an increasingly visible coterie of homosexuals who were similarly marked by their relentless pursuit of sexual partners in the face of moral and legal restrictions, propensity for leading double lives, and curious orientation toward homosociality. The Cold War targeting of both homosexuals and Communists was not, then, an entirely irrational coupling, but rather responded to the very real—and legitimately overlapping—threats each group posed to the dominant social order of the postwar United States. While the furtive fumblings of

Communists might have drawn many into the orbit of the Party, the narrative of leaving this embarrassing phase behind suggests how public confession could put such indiscretions in the past.

EX-COMMUNIST CONFESSION

In the opening pages of *Witness,* Whittaker Chambers's 1952 memoir of his transformation from a deviant Communist into a red-blooded American patriot, Chambers presented readers with a "foreword in the form of a letter to my children." "Beloved Children," Chambers writes to his offspring, "I am sitting in the kitchen of the little house at Medfield, our second farm which is cut off by the ridge and a quarter-mile across the fields from our home place, where you are."[125] This opening epistolary image, rich with bucolic fields and agricultural idyll transecting houses both present and distant, establishes Chambers's stirring desire for reconciliation on his private land, which, as readers in 1952 would surely have recalled from the sensationalistic 1948 Alger Hiss affair, was corrupted through a pumpkin's famously being violated with secret microfilmed documents shoved into its core.

"My children," Chambers suggestively pleads in this letter opening what he describes as his "terrible book,"

> [a]s long as you live, the shadow of the Hiss Case will brush you. In every pair of eyes that rests on you, you will see pass, like a cloud passing behind a woods in winter, the memory of your father—dissembled in friendly eyes, lurking in unfriendly eyes. . . . In time, therefore, when the sum of your experience of life gives you authority, you will ask yourselves the question: What was my father?[126]

As it turns out, that tawdry ontological question, steeped in the language of fractured paternalism, required close to one thousand pages to answer. Over the course of his book, and without even naming his homosexuality, about which there was much public speculation and a private confession to the FBI, Chambers reveals his children's father to have been a social and political deviant. Those shadows over his personal history, which he projects onto the eyes of strangers, speak to a knowledge of abjection so grave that it cast even those connected through kinship as unclean.[127] In spite of the chilling impact his revelations were sure to have upon his progeny, Chambers's confessional narrative ultimately serves to distance him from his deviance, in turn bringing him closer into a redemptive family structure. The public nature of his confession takes a toll on his children, but the necessity of restoring his patriarchal stature within his family impels him to accept those consequences.

Chambers stages the writing of *Witness*, then, as a performance of abjection for a readership representing, as his final chapter is titled, "tomorrow and tomorrow and tomorrow."[128] Bracketing off his narrative with bookended chapters detailing the setting, audience, and conditions precipitating his writing his memoirs, he reminds readers that it is precisely the act of *remembering* and *confessing* that distinguishes this Catholic, repentant Chambers from the deviant one whose scandalous past, marked by secrecy and subversion, he meticulously recounts. Completing his confession—which concludes with his wife older and his children grown, and resolving the division in the real estate that opens the book with a union, Sistine Chapel–like, of "two trees . . . whose branches met and touched when the wind blew"—allows Chambers to return to his family in the house across the field.[129] Readers of his memoir are likewise enjoined to enter into an intimate conversation with Chambers that will permit them entrance into this family reunion, and, by extension, to find redemption for the transgressions of a nation led astray by the seductions of the Left. The project of *confessing*, then, which consumed many former Communists during the Cold War, not only involved detailing and reflecting on a narrator's radical past, but also foregrounded the process of making visible aspects of one's identity that were hidden away. The confession performed individual penance for past transgressions, revealed the seduction of Communist belonging to which many troubled souls were susceptible, and ineluctably associated leftist commitment with a totalizing identity that could be excised only through ritualistic literary mortification.[130]

The religious and sexual implications of confession are not incidental here. It was, as Foucault has famously argued, the structure of confession, inaugurated through religious practice, that produced the modern sexual subject. In his *History of Sexuality*, Foucault foregrounds confession as the privileged form of self-narration in which the truth of oneself was uttered:

> We have passed from a pleasure to be recounted and heard, centering on the heroic or marvelous narration of "trials" of bravery or sainthood, to a literature ordered according to the infinite task of extracting from the depths of oneself, in between the words, a truth which the very form of the confession holds out like a shimmering mirage. . . . What secrecy it presupposes is not owing to the high price of what it has to say and the small number of those who are worthy of its benefits, but to its obscure familiarity and its

general baseness. Its veracity is not guaranteed by the lofty authority of the magistery, nor by the tradition it transmits, but by the bond, the basic intimacy in discourse, between one who speaks and what he is speaking about.[131]

For ex-Communists in Cold War American culture, the confession functioned similarly to perform abjection in the service of truth. It was not only, then, the shared features of homosexuality and Communism, or the organizations that attracted both groups, that linked them in Cold War history, but also the narrative form of confession that gave rise to the uncomfortable truth of modern subjectivity shared between these groups: the sexual self was produced through the confessional subject, and the Communist was conceivable only through a selfsame act of identification with the abject. In John Gates's words, from his 1958 *Story of an American Communist,* "[O]ne's life is wasted only if one fails to learn from the past in order to become a better human being in the future. I am today trying to learn from my experiences of yesterday."[132]

Whittaker Chambers was certainly aware of the significance of confession as a narrative form and religious practice. In fact, in response to dogged speculation about his homosexuality from Alger Hiss and his legal team, Chambers inaugurated the disclosure of his many same-sex affairs to the FBI in 1950 through a letter in which he announced, "I must testify to certain facts that should be told only to a priest."[133] Chambers thus not only acknowledged the relevance of his homosexual hook-ups to the narrative of his Communism, but also associated the very discussion of homosexuality with the need for a priest rather than an FBI agent. Privately, Chambers revealed his persistent struggles with homosexual urges, beginning with a man he met on the streets of Manhattan, and continuing through liaisons in several hotels in New York and Washington, D.C. Still, even if Chambers spared the public the details of his nights spent in "the typical 'flea bag' type of hotel one finds in certain parts of Manhattan," he confessed to the FBI that he "managed to break" free of homosexuality along with his Communism, thus explicitly linking his political and sexual deviance.[134]

It is noteworthy, in this light, how many books written by ex-Communists (or FBI informants who passed as Communists) include the first person in their titles, as though self-revelation were the required penance for having lost oneself in the Party. Julia Brown's *I Testify,* Herbert Philbrick's *I Led 3 Lives,* Bertram D. Wolfe's *Strange Communists I Have Known,* and, of course, Benjamin Gitlow's *I Confess* each foreground the author's relationship to both a Communist past and its Cold

War narration.[135] Praising Benjamin Gitlow's confessional mood in his introduction to the latter book, Max Eastman, himself an outspoken critic of the Left with a tangled history of his own, declared that "nothing less than a confession by one of those guilty of leadership in these crimes of insane zealotry could adequately reveal them."[136] The genre of the Cold War Communist confession shared a cosmology with the modern sexual subject, producing discursive overlap that inexorably linked Communists with homosexuals and cast both under a veil of suspicion.

Newly inaugurated Cold Warriors guiltily confessed the heady days of their radical youth, coyly offering a teasing catalogue of their past transgressions. Irving Howe recounted with disappointment how he was swayed toward the Communist Party by "the security of a set orientation."[137] Max Eastman confessed in his salacious memoir, *Love and Revolution,* that "I was passionately, not to say licentiously, addicted to revolutionary politics."[138] Alfred Kazin's memories of his Socialist mentor, John Chamberlain, fetishized Chamberlain's irresistible virility. "Chamberlain astounded me; in those days he astounded everyone. He looked young, ingenuous, carelessly one of the boys, with his tousled blond hair and his torn white shirt. . . . Chamberlain looked like Charles Augustus Lindbergh shyly starting out alone for Paris, like Gary Cooper at the end of a western modestly warding off a kiss. He was lean, handsome, kindly and awkward."[139] Kazin's attraction to radicalism was inextricable from his attraction to his astounding mentor, queer in both its ideological and homoerotic details.

The memories and confessions of ex-Communists represented a significant genre of Cold War autobiography that offered them penance for the unimaginable perversity that had overtaken them in the 1930s. The act of confessing one's Communist past confirmed that the self under Communism was fundamentally at odds with the healthy, fully realized subjectivity achieved through normative adherence to American values such as freedom, family, honesty, and forthrightness. Ex-Communists emphasized the integrity of their decision to abandon the Party and align themselves with anti-Communism, and their confessions distanced them from deviance and cemented the relationship between illicit desire and radical politics.

Nonetheless, not everyone piled into the Cold War confessional. Just a few years after *Witness* confirmed the genre of Cold War confession, the influential beat poet, committed homosexual, and emerging countercultural icon Allen Ginsberg published his influential poem "America."[140] In this work Ginsberg similarly invokes family, place, and kinship as he recounts his past subversion, flipping the switch on the Cold War confession to instead affirm his radical queerness. "I used to be a communist when I was a kid," Ginsberg perversely pronounces, "and I'm not sorry."[141] Refusing to seek redemption, Ginsberg defiantly catalogues the deviance in his past, turning out a dossier of disillusionment, by turns maudlin and cathartic, with a nation whose citizens seeks to exclude his Left history from its national narrative of belonging. Ginsberg balances an unapologetic nostalgia for growing up red with a celebration of his own queer present: the poem locates its radical futurity in a decisive conclusion where Ginsberg declares, "America I'm putting my queer shoulder to the wheel."[142]

Ginsberg's concluding call to action (indexed as a form of *work*) stands in contrast to the poem's helpless, depleted beginning ("I've given you all and now I'm nothing"). The body of the poem represents the locus of Ginsberg's transformation from apathetic nihilist into defiantly queer radical. And significantly, the body of the poem catalogues an increasingly transgressive set of memories about Ginsberg's radical attachment to un-American activities. "You should have seen me reading Marx. / My psychoanalyst thinks I'm perfectly right."[143] For Ginsberg, his refusal to either hide his leftist past or couch its narration in the form of a confession represents a queerly performative gesture. It is precisely his willingness to unapologetically announce his transgressive desire by gesturing toward touchstones in US leftist history that confirms Ginsberg's queer radicalism:

> America free Tom Mooney
> America save the Spanish Loyalists
> America Sacco and Vanzetti must not die
> America I am the Scottsboro Boys
> America when I was seven momma took me to Communist Cell
>   meetings they sold us garbanzos a handful per ticket a ticket costs a
>   nickel and the speeches were free everybody was angelic and senti-
>   mental about the workers it was all so sincere you have no idea what
>   a good thing the party was in 1835.[144]

As is so common with memories, especially those laced with nostalgia, Ginsberg gets some key details wrong. Backdating his Communist childhood by a full century—substituting 1835 for 1935—suggests the impossible distance between the United States of the 1950s and of the 1930s: Ginsberg's youth and the Left's optimism both felt a hundred years away. The error also points to Ginsberg's yearning for a longer leftist history in America. Yet it is his radical memories, framed in the context of the Cold War, that mobilize his determination to put his "queer shoulder to the wheel." The experiences of belonging, desire, and attachment within the Communist Party presented an alternative to the structure of feeling that demanded either dispassionate pragmatism in relation to political discourse or a normative love of country. Ginsberg's poem offered a counterpoint to Chambers's confession, replacing the latter's heteronormative redemption with the ongoing labor of sexual dissidence. Readers might have had no idea what a good thing the Party was, but Ginsberg and many other sexual dissidents on the Left knew. "Those bad things . . . were good things," one might hear Edward Melcarth echoing from the past, "when I did them with you."

CONTENDING WITH HISTORY: A CONCLUSION

At some point, likely during the Cold War, the lesbian Communist Betty Millard took a scalpel to her diaries, neatly excising passages from the 1930s that were either too racy or too radical (or maybe both) to bear scrutiny should a G-man show up at her door. Her intimate reflections on her daily life testified to activities that, if exposed to the light of day, might destroy her. Millard's carefully crafted memories now stop mid-sentence, the palimpsest of her queer radicalism sliced from her journal's pages, leaving behind a patchwork of lacunae where her personal history dematerializes. In 1959, Chuck Rowland set fire to a cache of documents relating to the early years of Mattachine, sending the only extant copies of these materials into the air in plumes of smoke. It was, Harry Hay recalled, a "dreadful loss."[145] If the erasure of one's history represents a form of trauma, living in fear of being remembered, especially for those who committed themselves to changing the world, must have been especially devastating. Records of lives and movements that were deeply meaningful to those who held them were transformed during the Cold War into dangerous contraband, and maintaining documents from the past introduced another form of vulnerability for people whose lives were already marked by risk.

Against the backdrop of a cultural imperative to frame radical politics as un-American activities, political commitments and intimate desires that fell outside the acceptable patriotic repertoire were viewed with tremendous suspicion and strategically suppressed. Americans dutifully adhering to the social norms that ostensibly kept the nation safe repudiated those driven by perverse passions, be they artists consumed by aesthetics or intellectuals overstuffed with ideas. Proper familial order, banal on its surface, was conceived as symptomatic of a proper national orientation, and any deviation from the homogeneity of American family life was taken as a rejection of the comforts offered in a capitalist society. The domestic sphere was conceived as a metonym for the republic, and Americans found themselves inundated with consumer options while restricted in acceptable political choices. Communists threatened each of these things. They looked outside the United States for a model society. They valued politics over family. They chose to defy American norms and disavowed consumer culture. And they engaged in forms of intimacy that were profoundly threatening to the existing social order. They were uncomfortably queer.

The Cold War also inaugurated a period in which submerged connections between homosexuality and the Left were brought to the surface and acknowledged in highly public, but deeply distrustful, ways. This increased surveillance was facilitated to a large extent by anti-Communists on the Right, who highlighted shared cultural practices among leftists and sexual dissidents such as gender transgression, non-normative familial relations, urban anonymity, secrecy, and sexual pathology. Former Communists perpetuated these characterizations by narrating their own leftist pasts through discursive nods to deviance. Though the connection between homosexuality and the Left was over-determined and sensationalized throughout the 1950s, it also confirmed dimensions of the Left that had made Communism attractive to sexual dissidents for decades. This historical imbrication was instrumentalized at the same moment that it was being repressed.

The Cold War abrogation of historical connections between homosexuality and the Left was precipitated by—and contributed to—a cultural climate that cast a pall over any acknowledgment of one's leftist past. Activists within the homophile movement determined there was more to be gained by working within a system that left the dispossessed behind than by building a movement that put them at the center. Former Communists confessed the sins of their past, offering carte blanche to those who sought to discredit their work. Looking to leftist history in search of radical sexual dissidents demanded contending with the cognitive dissonance of recovering a movement that fought for freedom but failed to fully embrace homosexuality. It required reconsidering a radical queer history that, in the context of McCarthyism, seemed terribly naive. And to what end? What could that history possibly teach anyone?

Connections between homosexuality and the Left had emerged out of a revolutionary foment that brought sexual and political dissidents together in a shared project of rejecting Americanism outright. The homophile movement that appeared in the 1950s, in opposition to its radical founders' connections to the Left, sought to distance itself from leftist organizations, legacies, and rhetoric. Anticapitalism was recast as less a solution than a problem. Citizenship was less something to be approached with skepticism and more something to be embraced as a desired outcome. As the state began to treat homosexuals as subversives, the homophile movement adopted a position that foregrounded the antagonistic relationship between homosexuality and the Left. Homosexuals needed to prove themselves to be good capitalists and model citizens in order to secure protection under law.

For leftists, acknowledging sexual diversity extended the Popular Front line that imagined the United States as a pluralist country while rejecting the dominant narrative that ascribed American greatness to the freedom afforded by capitalism. Steeped in the heady brew of antifascism that had correctly identified the cost of monolithic national identity, this Popular Front perspective also opened the door to a disaggregated politics of inclusion that exploited the space created by leftists to challenge American culture—its whiteness, its heterosexuality, its capitalism—and repurposed it to conceive homosexuals as rightful heirs to the American dream from which they had been excluded. Erasing the history of interconnections between homosexuality and the Left was an essential component of this work. Disavowing that relationship was not an unintended consequence of building a gay rights movement. It was a strategy born out of a commitment to rejecting a broader revolutionary struggle.

There were exceptions to this narrative, as figures such as Lorraine Hansberry and James Baldwin demonstrate. Especially as the civil rights movement introduced large-scale challenges to racism, Black Americans boldly rejected the foundations of US citizenship that had been built to exclude them. The stakes for signing onto Americanism were made all too clear as examples of the brutal force unleashed on those who challenged Jim Crow institutions were splashed across the front page. Antiracism was frequently attacked by its opponents as spearheaded by Communists rejecting American values. The civil rights movement of the 1950s incubated groups such as the Student Non-Violent Coordinating Committee and the Black Panther Party in the 1960s. These organizations, alongside the artists and writers associated with the Black Arts Movement, were less concerned with being smeared by the Communist label, and many of their goals coincided with—and expanded upon—the long history of leftist struggle.

While its organizations might have been inspired by the civil rights movement, the emerging homophile movement developed on a separate track. It remained a safe haven for white middle-class gay men and lesbians who adhered to principles upholding dominant American values while adjusting them in small ways to stitch gay women and men into the national fabric. The undesirables who had brought together homosexuality and the Left in earlier decades were hardly the same people Mattachine wished to splash across the front pages of newspapers covering their pickets or challenges to legal discrimination. Sex workers, militant labor activists, butch Communists, Black proletarian novelists, and many others were sidelined in favor of neatly pressed women and men, many of them government employees, who just wanted to make an honest day's living without being arrested or having their livelihoods threatened. Overthrowing the state was supplanted by using the tools of the system to access rights under law. The calcification within the homophile movement of a narrative that conceived the Left as a nagging inconvenience threatening to bring down gay people in a revolution that had nothing to offer them made it more difficult to learn from earlier intersections of homosexuality and the Left.

This was not a permanent condition. The 1960s brought thunderous waves of uprisings and protest, and the radical energy that swept across the globe during that decade created some space for developing alliances between American homophile organizations and the student-centered New Left. These tentative stirrings blossomed into a gay liberation movement that, in fits and starts, placed sexual dissidents into productive conversation with a broader revolutionary struggle. But by the time organizations such as Gay Liberation Front—a radical group that connected gay liberation with ongoing battles against racial, gender, and class inequality—formed in 1969, amid the foment of movement building that closed out the 1960s, the historical intersections of homosexuality and the Left had been largely dismissed as anti-Communist hysteria, if they were remembered at all.

The radicalism that guided leftists such as Willard Motley, Betty Millard, and H.T. Tsiang conceived liberation as spearheaded by those furthest on the margins of American society. This form of liberation did not fit comfortably into a narrative prioritizing gay citizenship. Neither did it fit into a history of the Left that was cast as anathematic to sexual dissidence. Theirs was a messier story of radicals who worked toward revolution, repurposed it to their own ends, resisted efforts at assimilation, produced art and literature bringing together sexual dissidence and the

Left, and participated in a political movement that failed to bring about the revolutionary society that had inspired their passion and required so many meetings. As he stubbornly held to his radical principles and continued to say what he thought about the "nation of Stool-pigeons" he felt American was becoming during the Cold War, Edward Melcarth had worried that "I may be almost unique." Almost. For even with gaps and redactions and fires and excisions and smears and hearings and expulsions and narrative displacements that coalesced during the Cold War to conceal the knotty history of homosexuality and the Left, the pieces that remain confirm that Melcarth was never truly alone.

POSTSCRIPT

Sitting in the Special Collections reading room at the University of Delaware Library in 2013, I open an envelope containing a letter sent from Kimon Friar to John Malcolm Brinnin in the 1930s. When I pull out the document, an overpowering smell permeates the room. I unfold the letter and a feather floats onto the table. A feather that had been exchanged between two men who shared a utopian belief that the revolution they were building would set them free; who believed that their idealism, given a chance to take flight, would carry them into a world where everyone would share ownership of the collective good; who believed that sexual desire and political liberation belonged in the same conversation. Eighty-plus years later, that same gesture, one of intimacy and hope, nearly clears out the reading room with its pungent stench. Bits of flesh from whatever bird carried this feather high above the earth, desiccated and raw, remain on the tip of the quill.

What impelled Brinnin to hold on to this feather for his entire life? What story did he hope would be told about him; about others like him; about the movement he participated in building; about how he negotiated homosexuality and the Left; about love's next meeting? That feather had arrived with the promise of a shared future. Shut away from the public eye, it continued its process of decomposition. Exposed to the air, its stark physicality, its fleshy reminder that it had once been attached to something that lived and breathed, reveals a complicated story of faith and loss; promise and betrayal; closeness and distance; fall and lift. It is, like the men who exchanged it, riddled with contradiction.

I send a text to my friend Mark. He is a naturalist; a cartographer and artist; a sexual dissident. He recently flew home from Greece, where he volunteered at a camp for Syrian refugees. He was forced to take flight out of Lesvos after the camp was attacked by neo-Nazis. He showed up at the opening for a show of his work at the Schoolhouse Gallery in Provincetown wearing a T-shirt that read, "Save Idlib."

Mark, what is the correct word for the part of a feather that attaches to a bird's flesh; the part that anchors it to the body; the part that, when plucked, tears at the skin, leaving behind an open wound?

He replies with one word:

Calamus.

Abbreviations

JKP   Jim Kepner Papers, ONE National Gay and Lesbian Archives

JMB   Collection of John Malcolm Brinnin-Kimon Friar Correspondence and Brinnin Literary Manuscripts, Special Collections Department, University of Delaware

JPP   John Pittman Papers, Tamiment Library, and Robert F. Wagner Labor Archives, New York University

JSC   Sinclair, [Ruth Seid] (1913–1995) Collection, Howard Gotlieb Archival Research Center, Boston University

KFP   Kimon Friar Papers, Department of Special Collections, Princeton University Library

REES   Ruth Erickson and Eleanor Stevenson Papers, 1910–1971, Special Collections and University Archives, University of Oregon

RKP   Rockwell Kent Papers (ca. 1840–1993), Archives of American Art, Smithsonian Institution

TLW   Tamiment Library & Robert F. Wagner Labor Archives, New York University

VFC   V. F. Calverton Papers, Manuscripts and Archives Division, New York Public Library

WMAC   Willard Maas Collection, Harry Ransom Center, University of Texas Austin

WMOP   Willard Motley Papers, Rare Books and Special Collections, Northern Illinois University

PERIODICALS

DW   *Daily Worker*

MQ   *Modern Quarterly*

NM   *New Masses*

Notes

INTRODUCTION

1. For an overview of sex and Melcarth's career, see Barry Reay and Erin Griffey, "Sexual Portraits: Edward Melcarth and Homoeroticism in Modern American Art," chap. 2 in Barry Reay, *Sex in the Archives: Writing American Sexual Histories* (Manchester, UK: Manchester University Press, 2019).

2. Edward Melcarth, "Guerilla Warfare," n.d., EMC, box 1, folder "Personal Correspondence Undated."

3. Federal Bureau of Investigation, file on Edward Melcarth, file no. 100-387350.

4. Edward Melcarth, letter to Sara, n.d., EMC, box 1, folder "Personal Correspondence Undated." Ellipsis in original.

5. Edward Melcarth, letter to *Life* magazine, Smithsonian Archives of American Art, box 1, folder "Personal Correspondence Undated."

6. Edward Melcarth, letter to Sara, n.d., EMC, box 1, folder "Personal Correspondence Undated."

7. EMC, box 4.

8. EMC, box 4.

9. EMC, box 1.

10. Edward Melcarth, untitled poem, EMC, box 2, folder "Untitled Poems."

11. Edward Melcarth, letter to Sara, n.d., EMC, box 1, folder "Personal Correspondence Undated." Ellipses in original.

12. Sociologist Stephen Valocchi wrote in a 2001 article that "the organizational centralization of the Old Left in the CPUSA prevented the early homophile activists from extending the collective identity of the Left to accommodate issues of same-sex oppression." Stephen Valocchi, "Individual Identities, Collective Identities, and Organizational Structure: The Relationship of the

Political Left and Gay Liberation in the United States" *Sociological Perspectives* 44, no. 4 (December 2001): 450. Martin Meeker echoed this claim in a 2001 essay in the *Journal of Homosexuality,* when he wrote that "the use of Communist Party tactics did not serve the foundation [for a gay political movement] well because its ideology ultimately undermined its politics." Martin Meeker, "Behind the Mask of Respectability: Reconsidering the Mattachine Society and Male Homophile Practice, 1950s and 1960s," *Journal of Homosexuality* 10, no. 1 (January 2001), 88. Terence Kissack, while attentive to the ways early-twentieth-century anarchists explored homosexuality and radicalism, wrote in 2008 that "the [Communist Party] took a dim view of homosexuality. When homosexuality did appear in the pages of CP publications it was most often as an occasion for satire." Terence Kissack, *Free Comrades: Anarchism and Homosexuality in the United States, 1895–1917* (Oakland, CA: AK Press, 2008), 170.

13. Owen Dodson, *Powerful Long Ladder* (New York: Farrar, Straus, and Giroux, 1946), 83; Harry Hay, letter to Jonathan Ned Katz, February 20, 1974, Jonathan Ned Katz Papers, Manuscripts and Archives Division, New York Public Library, Correspondence. On Dodson, see James V. Hatch, *Sorrow Is the Only Faithful One: The Life of Owen Dodson* (Urbana and Chicago: University of Illinois Press, 1995); James Edward Smethurst, *The New Red Negro: The Literary Left and African American Poetry, 1930–1946* (New York: Oxford University Press, 1999), 203–7.

14. Regina Kunzel, *Criminal Intimacy: Prison and the Uneven History of Modern American Sexuality* (Chicago: University of Chicago Press, 2008), 9.

15. Kevin Mumford, *Interzones: Black/White Sex Districts in Chicago and New York in the Early Twentieth Century* (New York: Columbia University Press, 1997), 20.

16. Ted Rolfs, quoted in Daniel Hurewitz, *Bohemian Los Angeles and the Making of Modern Politics* (Berkeley: University of California Press, 2008), 243.

17. David O. Cauldwell and E. Haldeman Julius, eds., *Private Letters from Homosexuals to a Doctor* (Girard, KS: Haldeman-Julius, 1949), 16.

18. Arthur Laurents, *Original Story By: A Memoir of Broadway and Hollywood* (New York: Knopf, 2000), 36.

19. Dick T., letter to William J. Fielding, April 24, 1938, William J. Fielding Collection (TAM 069), Tamiment Library and Robert F. Wagner Labor Archives, New York University, box 1, folder 44.

20. Glyn Salton-Cox, *Queer Communism and the Ministry of Love: Sexual Revolution in British Writing of the 1930s* (Edinburgh: Edinburgh University Press, 2018), 1. Salton-Cox writes specifically of the British context, but Florence Tamagne notes a broader European history of homosexuals "as leftist activists" between 1919 and 1939. "To be a homosexual is to be on the outside," she writes; "to choose an extreme political position is to push that exclusion to its logical end, to retaliate for society's charges that the homosexual is a potential danger." Florence Tamagne, *A History of Homosexuality in Europe: Berlin, London, Paris, 1919–1939* (New York: Algora, 2004; first published 2000 by Éditions du Seuil [Paris]), 86.

21. Stuart Hall, "Deviance, Politics, and the Media," in *The Lesbian and Gay Studies Reader,* ed. Henry Abelove, Michèle Aina Barale, and David M. Halperin (New York and London: Routledge, 1993), 63.

22. Hall, "Deviance, Politics, and the Media," 67.

23. George Jarrboe, "7 Months in a Y.M.C.A.," *NM,* August 1928, 11.

24. Michel Foucault, *The History of Sexuality,* vol. 1, *An Introduction,* trans. Robert Hurley (New York: Pantheon, 1978; first published 1976 by Gallimard [Paris]), 27.

25. Cedric J. Robinson, *Black Marxism: The Making of the Black Radical Tradition* (London: Zed Press, 1983).

26. Eithne Luibhéid, introduction to *Queer Migrations: Sexuality, U.S. Citizenship, and Border Crossings,* ed. Eithne Luibhéid and Lionel Cantú Jr. (Minneapolis: University of Minnesota Press, 2005), xii.

27. In part this intense engagement was possible because Communist artists promoted a diverse set of aesthetic practices. Debates about the form and content in proletarian fiction impacted the degree to which homosexuality could be made visible and the meanings it was assigned within radical literature. See, e.g., Barbara Foley, *Radical Representations: Politics and Form in U.S. Proletarian Fiction, 1929–1941* (Durham, NC: Duke University Press, 1993).

28. Walter Rideout, *The Radical Novel in the United States: Some Interrelations of Literature and Society, 1900–1954* (New York: Columbia University Press, 1992; first published 1956 by Harvard University Press [Cambridge, MA]), 174.

29. Daniel Aaron, *Writers on the Left: Episodes in American Literary Communism* (New York: Harcourt, Brace & World, 1961), 99.

30. Junius Scales, *Cause at Heart: A Former Communist Remembers* (Athens: University of Georgia Press, 1987), 224.

CHAPTER 1. "FLAUNTING THE TRANSATLANTIC BREEZE"

1. John Malcolm Brinnin, letter to Kimon Friar, July 22, 1936, JMB, box 1, folder 1..

2. John Malcolm Brinnin, unpublished memoir, n.d., JMB, box 54, folder 140; Lillian Hellman, letter to John Malcolm Brinnin, March 3, 1937, JMB, box 8, folder 186.

3. John Malcolm Brinnin, letter to Kimon Friar, July 22, 1936, JMB, box 1, folder 1.

4. Brinnin, letter to Friar, n.d., JMB, box 1, folder 1.

5. Kevin P. Murphy, *Political Manhood: Red Bloods, Mollycoddles, and the Politics of Progressive Era Reform* (New York: Columbia University Press, 2008), 150.

6. Ben L. Reitman, *Sister of the Road: The Autobiography of Box-Car Bertha, as told to Dr Ben L. Reitman* (New York: Sheridan House, 1937; repr., New York: Amok Press, 1988), 62. Citations refer to the 1988 edition. On the contested authorship of Box-Car Bertha's autobiography, see Joanne Hall, "Sisters of the Road? The Construction of Female Hobo Identity in the

Autobiographies of Ethel Lynn, Barbara Starke, and 'Box-Car' Bertha Thompson," *Women's Studies* 39, no. 3 (April/May 2010): 223–33.

7. Reitman, *Sister of the Road,* 66.

8. Reitman, 228–29.

9. Ben L. Reitman, "The Joys and Hazards of Sex," unpublished manuscript, n.d., p. 21, BRP, box 3, folder 49.

10. Nels Anderson, *The Hobo: The Sociology of the Homeless Man* (Chicago: University of Chicago Press, 1923); Peter Boag, *Same-Sex Affairs: Constructing and Controlling Homosexuality in the Pacific Northwest* (Berkeley: University of California Press, 2003); Todd DePastino, *Citizen Hobo: How a Century of Homelessness Shaped America* (Amherst: University of Massachusetts Press, 2003).

11. Kevin Mumford, "Homosex Changes: Race, Cultural Geography, and the Emergence of the Gay," *American Quarterly* 48, no. 3 (September 1996): 402; Randi Storch, *Red Chicago: American Communism at Its Grassroots, 1928–1935* (Urbana: University of Illinois Press, 2007), 46.

12. Chad Heap, *Slumming: Sexual and Racial Encounters in American Nightlife, 1885–1940* (Chicago: University of Chicago Press, 2009), 184–85; Terence Kissack, *Free Comrades: Anarchism and Homosexuality in the United States, 1895–1917* (Oakland, CA: AK Press, 2008), 177–78; Frank Rosemont, *The Rise & Fall of the Dil Pickle: Jazz-Age Chicago's Wildest & Most Outrageously Creative Bohemian Nightspot* (Chicago: Charles H. Kerr, 2003).

13. Sherwood Anderson, "Jack Jones—'The Pickler,'" *Chicago Daily News,* June 18, 1919.

14. Rosemont, *Rise & Fall of the Dil Pickle.*

15. DPC, Newberry Library, box 1, folder 22.

16. Ben Reitman, "Highlights in Dill Pickle History, Prepared by Dr. Ben L. Reitman," n.d., DPC, box 3, folder 291.

17. Rosemont, *Rise & Fall of the Dil Pickle,* 146.

18. Flier, DPC, box 1, folder 46; flier, DPC, box 3, folder 219.

19. DPC, box 3, folder 290.

20. Reitman, "Highlights in Dill Pickle History."

21. Quoted in St. Sukie de la Croix, *Chicago Whispers: A History of LGBT Chicago before Stonewall* (Madison: University of Wisconsin Press, 2012), 68. See also Heap, *Slumming,* 236.

22. Leo Adams, letter to Merle Macbain, November 29, 1931, OutHistory. org, accessed January 28, 2012, http://outhistory.org/exhibits/show/leo-adams-a-gay-life-in-letter/language-and-self-representati.

23. David W. Dunlap, "Jim Kepner, in 70's, Is Dead; Historian of Gay Rights Effort," *New York Times,* November 20, 1997.

24. Jim Kepner, unpublished autobiography, n.d., 92, JKP, box 5, folder 6.

25. On the origins of factionalizing on the Left, see Theodore Draper, *The Roots of American Communism* (New York: Viking, 1957); and Bryan D. Palmer, *James P. Cannon and the Origins of the American Revolutionary Left, 1890–1928* (Urbana: University of Illinois Press, 2007).

26. Kepner, autobiography, 78.

27. Kepner, 78.

28. Kepner, 92.

29. Kepner, 113.

30. Kepner, 114.

31. Alan M. Wald, "Sexual Bohemians in Cold War America: A Minority within a Minority," in *Red Love across the Pacific: Political and Sexual Revolutions of the Twentieth Century,* ed. Paula Rabinowitz, Ruth Barraclough, and Heather Bowen-Struyk (New York: Palgrave, 2015), 101–21.

32. Donald Vining, *A Gay Diary,* 5 vols. (New York: Pepys Press, 1979–1981). See also Arthur D. Kahn, *The Education of a 20th Century Political Animal,* a five-volume self-published autobiography recounting his history as a gay leftist (AuthorHouse, 2005–2009).

33. Justin Spring, *Secret Historian: The Life and Times of Samuel Steward, Professor, Tattoo Artist, and Sexual Renegade* (New York: Farrar, Straus and Giroux, 2011); Scott Herring, *The Hoarders: Material Deviance in Modern American Culture* (Chicago: University of Chicago Press, 2014).

34. Brinnin, letter to Friar, July 30, 1936, JMB, box 1, folder 1.

35. Friar, letter to Brinnin, August 28, 1936, JMB, box 9, folder 51.

36. CMC, box 18. For extended discussion of McKay's travels to the Soviet Union and his sexuality, see Gary Edward Holcomb, *Claude McKay, Code Name Sasha: Queer Black Marxism and the Harlem Renaissance* (Gainesville: University of Florida Press, 2007), 22–53.

37. Photograph, HWLD, IX ("Collected Material"): D ("Photographs and Negatives").

38. Quoted in Lillian Symes, "Reverend Go-Getter," *NM,* July 1926, 23.

39. Hugo Gellert, "I Meet an Individualist," *NM,* September 1927, 25.

40. JMB, box 54, folder 140.

41. Lucy Bland and Laura Doan, *Sexology in Culture: Labelling Bodies and Desires* (Chicago: University of Chicago Press, 1999).

42. Friar, diary entry from June 1929, KFP, box 6, folder 3.

43. Friar, "Camouflage," 1929, KFP, box 6, folder 1.

44. Friar, diary, n.d., KFP, box 6, folder 1.

45. Justine Silverstein letter to "Mrs. Friar," March 5, 1930, KFP, box 6, folder 6.

46. Friar, letter to Ed, August 25, 1931, KFP, box 6, folder 7.

47. Friar, letter to Brinnin, July 7, 1938, JMB, box 9, folder 56.

48. Friar, letter to Jack Thompson, March 19, 1940. JMB, box 7, folder 141.

49. Phillips Garman, letter to Friar, July 30, 1934, KFP, box 7 folder 5.

50. Phillips Garman, letter to Friar, November 5, 1934, KFP, box 7 folder 5.

51. Friar, letter to Phillips Garman, n.d., KFP, box 7, folder 7

52. Friar, letter to Ed, December 20, 1934, KFP, box 7, folder 7; letter from Friar to Shigeto Tsuru, September 6, 1935, KFP, box 7, folder 8.

53. Friar, letter to Anna, November 6, 1935, KFP, box 7, folder 8.

54. Friar, letter to Evie, August 13, 1934, KFP, box 7, folder 7

55. Brinnin, unpublished memoir, n.d., JMB, box 54, folder 140.

56. Collette Colligan, *A Publisher's Paradise: Expatriate Literary Culture in Paris, 1890–1960* (Amherst: University of Massachusetts Press, 2014).

57. Phillips Garman, letter to Brinnin, November 15, 1936, JMB, box 11, folder 67.

58. Max Eastman, *Artists in Uniform; A Study of Literature and Bureaucratism* (New York: Alfred A. Knopf, 1934).

59. Brinnin, "The Poet as Political Man," unpublished essay, n.d., JMB, box 13, folder 87.

60. Alan M. Wald, *Exiles from a Future Time: The Forging of the Mid-Twentieth Century Literary Left* (Chapel Hill: University of North Carolina Press, 2002), 307.

61. Alan Filreis, *Counter-Revolution of the Word: The Conservative Attack on Modern Poetry, 1945–1960* (Chapel Hill: University of North Carolina Press, 2008), 83.

62. Brinnin, letter to Friar, October 1936, JMB, box 1, folder 3.

63. Quoted in Wald, *Exiles from a Future Time,* 307.

64. Brinnin, letter to Friar, October 1936, JMB, box 1, folder 3.

65. Brinnin to Friar, November 1936, JMB, box 1, folder 3.

66. Brinnin, letter to Friar, August 16, 1937, JMB, box 3, folder 6.

67. Brinnin, letter to Friar, December 11, 1939, JMB, box 3, folder 14.

68. Friar, letter to Brinnin, February 16, 1937, KFP, box 134, folder 18.

69. Barry Werth, *The Scarlet Professor: Newton Arvin: A Literary Life Shattered by Scandal* (New York: Nan A. Talese, 2001), 101-6.

70. "Publisher's Note" in André Gide, *Corydon,* trans. Hugh Gibb (New York: Farrar, Straus, 1950), *vii–ix*.

71. Edward Sagarin, "André Gide Goes Left," *NM,* April 1933, 20.

72. Truman Capote, letter to Brinnin, n.d., JMB, box 4, folder 64.

73. Macmillan Company (Jerome Putnam), letter to Brinnin, December 27, 1939, JMB, box 28, folder 530.

74. John Malcolm Brinnin, *No Arch, No Triumph* (New York: Alfred A. Knopf, 1944), 31.

75. On counterpublics and queer culture, see Michael Warner, *Publics and Counterpublics* (New York: Zone Books, 2005).

76. Richard Wright, letter to Willard Maas, n.d., WMAC, box 8, folder 8.

77. Willard Maas, unpublished manuscript, n.d., WMAC, box 1, folder 1.

78. Raymond Larsson, letter to Maas, 1938, WMAC, box 5, folder 3.

79. Anna Norma Porter, letter to Maas, July 6, 1937, WMAC, box 7, folder 6.

80. Harry Waldman, *Hollywood and the Foreign Touch: A Dictionary of Foreign Filmmakers and Their Films from America, 1910–1995* (Lanham, MD: Scarecrow Press, 1996), 174–75.

81. Norman McLaren, letter to Maas, n.d., WMAC, box 5, folder 1.

82. Norman McLaren, letter to Maas, n.d., WMAC, box 5, folder 2.

83. Norman McLaren, letter to Maas, n.d., WMAC, box 5, folder 2.

84. Guy Glover, letter to Maas, n.d., WMAC, box 5, folder 2.

85. Rupert Barneby, letter to Maas, n.d., WMAC, box 4, folder 1.

86. Willard Maas, "Park Avenue Analyst Blues," n.d., WMAC, box 2, folder 3.

87. Norman McLaren, "To Willard from Norman," n.d., WMAC, box 2, folder 1.

88. McLaren, letter to Maas, n.d., WMAC, box 6, folder 1.

89. McLaren, letter to Maas, n.d., WMAC, box 6, folder 1.

90. Willard Maas, "The Priest Insults the Sailor," n.d., WMAC, box 1, folder 10.

91. Willard Maas, untitled poem, n.d., WMAC, box 1, folder 1.

92. Maas's first book, *Fire Testament* (New York: Alcestis, 1935), had been published in a limited edition of 165 copies in 1935.

93. Willard Maas, *Concerning the Young* (New York: Farrar and Rinehart, 1938), 6.

94. Mass, 16.

95. Mass, 16.

96. Richard Bruce Nugent, *Gay Rebel of the Harlem Renaissance: Selections from the Work of Richard Bruce Nugent*, ed. Thomas H. Wirth (Durham, NC: Duke University Press, 2002); Christopher Reed, *Art and Homosexuality: A History of Ideas* (New York: Oxford University Press, 2011), 130; A. B. Christa Schwartz, *Gay Voices of the Harlem Renaissance* (Bloomington: Indiana University Press, 2003); Jonathan Weinberg, *Speaking for Vice: Homosexuality in the Art of Charles Demuth, Marsden Hartley, and the First American Avant-Garde* (New Haven, CT: Yale University Press, 2003).

97. Granville Hicks, Michael Gold, Isidor Schneider, Joseph North, Paul Peters, Alan Calmer, and Joseph Freeman, eds., *Proletarian Literature in the United States: An Anthology* (New York: International Publishers, 1935), 146.

98. Constance Coiner, *Better Red: The Writing and Resistance of Tillie Olsen and Meridel Le Sueur* (New York: Oxford University Press, 1995), 39–71.

99. James Kepner, unpublished autobiography, n.d., JKP, box 5, folder 6; Helen Camp, *Iron in Her Soul: Elizabeth Gurley Flynn and the American Left* (Detroit: Wayne State University Press, 1995).

100. Kate Weigand, *Red Feminism: American Communism and the Making of Women's Liberation* (Baltimore: Johns Hopkins University Press, 2001), 34, 35.

101. Rosalyn Baxandall, "The Question Seldom Asked: Women and the CPUSA," in *New Studies in the Politics and Culture of U.S. Communism*, ed. Michael Brown, Randy Martin, Frank Rosengarten, and George Snedeker (New York: Monthly Review Press, 1993), 145.

102. Ann Snitow, Christine Stansell, and Sharon Thompson, *Powers of Desire: The Politics of Sexuality* (New York: Monthly Review Press, 1983). The formative influence of socialist feminism for opening this discourse was also important. See Zillah R. Eisenstein, ed., *Capitalist Patriarchy and the Case for Socialist Feminism* (New York: Monthly Review Press, 1979), 19.

103. Ernest Freeberg, *Democracy's Prisoner: Eugene V. Debs, the Great War, and the Right to Dissent* (Cambridge, MA: Harvard University Press, 2008), 17.

104. Beatrice Lumpkin, *Joy in the Struggle: My Life and Love* (New York: International Publishers, 2013).

105. Julia M. Allen, *Passionate Commitments: The Lives of Anna Rochester and Grace Hutchins* (Albany: State University of New York Press, 2013), 161. On Hutchins and Rochester, see also Janet Lee, *Comrades and Partners: The Shared Lives of Grace Hutchins and Anna Rochester* (Lanham, MD: Rowman & Littlefield, 2000).

106. Allen, *Passionate Commitments,* 120–21.

107. Quoted in Allen, 124.

108. Quoted in Allen, 124.

109. Alix Holt, ed., *Alexandra Kollontai: Selected Writings,* trans. Alix Holt (New York: Norton, 1977), 289.

110. Allen, *Passionate Commitments,* 285.

111. Allen, 151.

112. Allen, 229.

113. Elinor Ferry, unpublished manuscript, n.d., EFP, box 16, folder 7.

114. "Memo on interview with A. B. Magil of October 7, 1952," EFP, box 17, folder 19.

115. Elinor Ferry, unpublished manuscript, n.d., EFP, box 16, folder 7.

116. Elinor Ferry, unpublished manuscript, n.d. EFP, box 16, folder 7.

117. Allen, *Passionate Commitments,* 128–29.

118. Sidney Streat, "Grace Hutchins—Revolutionary," *DW,* September 16, 1936, 7.

119. Grace Hutchins, *Women Who Work* (New York: International Publishers, 1934), 9.

120. Hutchins, 16.

121. Grace Lumpkin, "Emancipation and Exploitation," *NM,* May 15, 1934, 26–27.

122. Allen, *Passionate Commitments,* 133.

123. "Resolution on the Negro Question in the United States," *The Communist* 10, no. 2 (February 1931): 153–67.

124. Grace Hutchins, "Negro Women Workers Fight against Conditions of Slavery," *Working Woman,* February 1930, 6.

125. Quoted in Allen, *Passionate Commitments,* 221.

126. Allen, 242.

CHAPTER 2. "AFTER SEX, WHAT?"

1. Advertisement in *NM,* March 1927, 32.

2. Daniel Aaron, *Writers on the Left: Episodes in American Literary Communism* (New York: Harcourt, Brace & World, 1961), 102.

3. Advertisement, *NM,* May 1931, 2.

4. Cartoon by Art Young, *NM,* July 1926, 16–17.

5. Michael Gold, "Write for Us!," *NM,* July 1928, 2. Michael Denning tacitly acknowledges the mildly salacious tone of the magazine when he suggests that "*NM* can be seen as a radical mutation of *True Story,* an attempt to build a new culture out of the stories and confessions of ordinary workers." Michael Denning, *The Cultural Front: The Laboring of American Culture in the Twentieth Century* (New York: Verso, 1997), 204.

6. Quoted in Aaron, *Writers on the Left,* 97.

7. Cartoon by William Sanderson, *NM,* January 5, 1937, 13.

8. Interestingly, the *Modern Quarterly* published an article in 1928 that acknowledged that "the McFadden Publications and their like . . . are likely to do much good in combatting the imbecilities of the prudes." Harry Elmer

Barnes, "Some Tranquil Reflections on the Jazz Age," *MQ*, November 1928–February 1929, 234.

9. John Darmstadt, "The Sexual Revolution," *MQ*, June–September 1927, 137. On the concept of sexual revolution in the 1920s and 1930s, see John Levi Martin, "Structuring the Sexual Revolution," *Theory & Society* 25, no. 1 (February 1996): 105–51.

10. Samuel D. Schmalhausen, "Will the Family Pass?" *MQ*, June–September 1927, 106.

11. Charles W. Wood, "Don't Fight with Sex: The Scientific Attitude for Proletarian Revolutionists," *NM*, February 1927, 7.

12. H. M. Wicks, "An Apology for Sex Anarchism Disguised as Marxism," *DW*, June 19, 1927, 4.

13. On slumming, see Chad Heap, *Slumming: Sexual and Racial Encounters in American Nightlife, 1885–1940* (Chicago: University of Chicago Press, 2009); and Scott Herring, *Queering the Underworld: Slumming, Literature, and the Undoing of Lesbian and Gay History* (Chicago: University of Chicago Press, 2007). On Marxist representations of the lumpenproletariat, particularly among Black writers, see Nathaniel Mills, *Ragged Revolutionaries: The Lumpenproletariat and African American Marxism in Depression-Era Literature* (Amherst: University of Massachusetts Press, 2017).

14. Mrs. W. W. Wallace, "Still Up in the Air," *NM*, March 24, 1936, 20.

15. Quoted in Aaron, *Writers on the Left*, 97.

16. Walter S. Hankel, ed., *Whither, Whither, or After Sex, What?* (New York: Macaulay, 1930).

17. Malcolm Cowley, "OEDIPUS: or the Future of Love," in Hankel, 262.

18. Corey Ford, "LIBIDO, or the Future of Debauchery," in Hankel, 35, 36.

19. "Obscenity or Heterodoxy? A Case against the Censorship," *NM*, June 1926, 15.

20. Leonard Wilcox, "Sex Boys in a Balloon: V. F. Calverton and the Abortive Sexual Revolution," *Journal of American Studies* 23, no. 1 (1989): 8.

21. "Obscenity or Heterodoxy?," 15.

22. Samuel Ornitz, "Do the Churches Corrupt Youth?" *NM*, September 1926, 19.

23. On obscenity law, see Whitney Strub, *Obscenity Rules: Roth v. United States and the Long Struggle over Sexual Expression* (Lawrence: University of Kansas Press, 2013).

24. Editorial, *NM*, July 1926, 3.

25. "Liberator to Have Second Class Rates," *The Toiler*, June 4, 1921, 1; Aaron, *Writers on the Left*, 92.

26. "Hays Removes Ban on the *Liberator*," *New York Times*, May 26, 1921.

27. "Censored!," *NM*, July 1926, 3.

28. "Smut-Hounds Expel 3," *DW*, March 21, 1929, 1.

29. "3,000 Students Protest Dismissal of Teachers for Sex Questionnaire," *DW*, March 22, 1929, 3.

30. Harold Stearns, *America and the Young Intellectual* (New York: George H. Doran, 1921), 65.

31. "Citizen's Jury Says O'Neill's Play Is Clean," *DW*, March 18, 1925, 4.

32. George Baron, "Don't Be Smutty," *NM,* August 1929, 22.

33. Upton Sinclair, "Poor Me and Pure Boston," *The Nation,* June 29, 1927, 16.

34. Upton Sinclair, "Revolution—Not Sex," *NM,* March 1927, 11.

35. Upton Sinclair, *Mammonart: An Essay in Economic Interpretation* (self-pub., Pasadena, CA, 1925), 302, 304, 205, 306.

36. Edmund Wilson, *The American Earthquake: A Documentary of the Twenties and Thirties* (New York: Doubleday, 1958), 367–413.

37. Upton Sinclair, letter to Marie Seton, April 5, 1950, reproduced in *Sergei M. Eisenstein: A Biography,* rev. ed. (London: Dennis Dobson, 1978; first published 1952 by Bodley Head [London]), 516, 515.

38. Upton Sinclair, ed., *My Lifetime in Letters* (Columbia: University of Missouri Press, 1960), 125–26.

39. "Will the Family Pass? A Debate Entitled: Is Monogamy Desirable? Affirmative: Upton Sinclair, Negative: V. F. Calverton," *MQ,* January–April 1927, 34–41.

40. Haim Genizi, "The *Modern Quarterly*: 1923–1940: An Independent Radical Magazine," *Labor History* 15, no. 2 (1974): 199–214; Wilcox, "Sex Boys in a Balloon," 7–26.

41. Sidney Hook, "*Modern Quarterly,* a Chapter in American Radical History: V. F. Calverton and His Periodicals," *Labor History* 10, no. 2 (1969): 242, 241.

42. V. F. Calverton, "Sex and Economics," *NM,* March 1927, 12.

43. Calverton, 11.

44. Quoted in Anthony Arthur, *Radical Innocent: Upton Sinclair* (New York: Random House, 2006), 212; see also Upton Sinclair, *Money Writes!* (New York: Albert and Charles Boni, 1927), 181.

45. "Open Kissing Openly Arrived at Slogan of Baltimore Bill," *DW,* August 14, 1924, 4; *New Student,* April 7, 1926; Harry Elmer Barnes, "Some Tranquil Reflections on the Jazz Age," *MQ,* November 1927–February 1928, 231.

46. Upton Sinclair, *Oil!* (New York: Albert & Charles Boni, 1927; repr., New York: Penguin, 2007), 194, 195. Citations refer to the 2007 edition.

47. Sinclair, 205.

48. Leon Harris, *Upton Sinclair: American Rebel* (New York: Thomas Y. Crowell, 1975), 241.

49. J. Louis Engdahl, "Bathtub Orgy Not an Isolated Incident in the Life of Bourgeoisie," *DW,* June 5, 1926, 2.

50. John Vincent Healy, "Portrait of a Bachelor Broker," *NM,* February 18, 1936, 10.

51. "Investigation of Wild Orgy Is Under Way," *DW,* February 26, 1926, 1.

52. "Bath-Tub Girl Appears before Grand Jury," *DW,* March 3, 1926, 2.

53. "Sex License Charges of University Heads Come Home to Roost," *DW,* September 21, 1926, 6.

54. Benjamin Gitlow, *I Confess; The Truth about American Communism* (New York: E. P. Dutton, 1940), 313.

55. Upton Sinclair, letter to V. F. Calverton, June 2, 1927, VFC, box 14; Sinclair, *Money Writes!,* 178–84.

56. Sinclair, letter to Calverton, September 24, 1928, VFC, box 14.

57. Sinclair, letter to Calverton, June 2, 1927, VFC, box 14.

58. Floyd Dell, "Marriage and Freedom," *Liberator*, August 1921, 17.

59. Floyd Dell, "Some Gifts of the Machine Age," *NM*, March 1927, 22.

60. "Poverty, Mother of Prostitution, German Shows," *DW*, April 23, 1924, 1; "League Admits Poverty Makes Prostitution," *DW*, March 10, 1927, 3.

61. H. M. Wicks, "'Desire under the Elms' Pictures New England," *DW*, October 13, 1925, 6.

62. V. S. Calverton, "'Luckee Girl' at the Casino Is Quite Amusing," *DW*, September 21, 1928, 4.

63. A. B. Magil, "Straight from the Street," *DW*, February 15, 1927, 4.

64. Quoted in Marybeth Hamilton, *The Queen of Camp: Mae West, Sex, and Popular Culture* (New York: HarperCollins, 1995), 46. Hamilton describes *Sex*'s lead character Margy as "bitterly conscious of herself as a member of an oppressed class" and the setting as "a mean and distinctly unglamorous place, rife with class antagonisms" (54).

65. "Still Prosecuting 'Sex,'" *DW*, March 5, 1927, 3.

66. "Novel of College Life Barred from Mails as 'Indecent,'" *DW*, June 12, 1925, 3.

67. "Boston Catholic Jury Finds the 'American Tragedy' Is 'Obscene,'" *DW*, April 19, 1929, 5.

68. "Warned Women Seek Forbidden Floyd Dell Book," *DW*, May 3, 1924, 3.

69. "Fight These Bills," *NM*, February 18, 1936, 6.

70. "Moron Kansas City Censors Play Their Tricks on Fifth Year," *DW*, April 23, 1924, 4; William F. Kruse, "Censorship, Sense, and the Labor Movies," *DW*, April 14, 1924, 6.

71. "Free Speech," *NM*, August 1927, 3.

72. Bill Smith, "Cupid's Letterbox," *NM*, April 16, 1934, 30.

73. Erin A. Smith, *Hard Boiled: Working-Class Readers and Pulp Magazines* (Philadelphia: Temple University Press, 2000).

74. Chris Vials, *Realism for the Masses: Aesthetics, Popular Front Pluralism, and U.S. Culture, 1935–1947* (Jackson: University Press of Mississippi, 2010).

75. Advertisement, *NM*, February 5, 1935, back cover.

76. Jack Lindsay, "Freud's Error," *NM*, December 22, 1936, 17.

77. On pulp in American culture, see Paula Rabinowitz, *American Pulp: How Paperbacks Brought Modernism to Main Street* (Princeton, NJ: Princeton University Press, 2014).

78. Smith, "Cupid's Letter Box," 30.

79. Burn Starr, review of *The Natural History of Revolution*, by Lyford P. Edwards, *The Communist*, July 1928, 453.

80. Michael Gold, "A Bourgeois Hamlet for Our Time," *NM*, April 10, 1934, 29.

81. Pitirim A. Sorokin, *The Sociology of Revolution* (Philadelphia and London: J. B. Lippincott Company, 1925), 86.

82. Gitlow, *I Confess*, 316.

83. Tess Slesinger, *Time: The Present: A Book of Short Stories* (New York: Simon & Schuster, 1935), 23.

84. Slesinger, 29.

85. Quoted in V. F. Calverton, "Red Love in Soviet Russia," *MQ*, November 1927–February 1928, 180.

86. On actual sexual practices in the Soviet Union, see especially Daniel Healey, *Homosexual Desire in Revolutionary Russia: The Regulation of Sexual and Gender Dissent* (Chicago: University of Chicago Press, 2001).

87. Floyd Dell, "The Outline of Marriage," *Liberator*, June 1923, 27.

88. "Reduced to This," *DW*, August 28, 1928, 4.

89. Edward Newhouse, *This Is Your Day* (New York: Lee Furman, 1937), 9–10.

90. Vern Smith, "Beginnings of Revolutionary Political Action in the U.S.A., *The Communist*, October 1933, 1041.

91. Sherwood Anderson, *Beyond Desire* (New York: Liveright, 1932), 4.

92. Anderson, 6. Ellipsis in original.

93. This claim is repeated by many scholars. Christine Simmons, for example, writes in a section on sex radicals that "many communists and supporters turned against sexual freedom in the 1920s, defining it as bourgeois self-indulgence." Christine Simmons, *Making Marriage Modern: Women's Sexuality from the Progressive Era to World War II* (New York: Oxford University Press, 2009), 65.

94. John Darmstadt, "The Sexual Revolution," 142. The *Daily Worker* noted this *j'accuse* and offered its own rejoinder several months later. H. M. Wicks, "An Apology for Sex Anarchism Disguised as Marxism," *DW*, June 9, 1927, 4.

95. Darmstadt, "The Sexual Revolution," 144.

96. Samuel D. Schmalhausen, "The New Candor in Sex," *DW*, April 12, 1927, 6.

97. Calverton, "Sex and Economics," 12.

98. "Horthy Ban on Flirting and Bare Wax Shoulder," *DW*, March 28, 1927, 3.

99. "Communists Demand Change in Germany's Divorce Legislation," *DW*, November 23, 1928, 3.

100. "World Sexology Congress," *DW*, October 18, 1926, 4.

101. Louis P. Lochner, "Birth Control Clinic Opens in Germany," *DW*, March 4, 1924, 4.

102. Havelock Ellis, "The Physician and Sex," *American Spectator*, November 1932, 1.

103. Wilhelm Reich, "What Is Class Consciousness?," in *Sex-Pol: Essays 1929–1934*, ed. Lee Baxandall, trans. Anna Bostock, Tom DuBose, and Lee Baxandall (New York: Random House, 1972; originally published 1934 as a pamphlet), 297.

104. Calverton, "Red Love in Soviet Russia," 190.

105. "Russia Today," *DW*, August 13, 1925, 4. This report came from the official British trade- union delegation to Soviet Russia.

106. Ella Winter, "Love in Two Worlds," *NM*, July 16, 1935, 17

107. Winter, 19. Ellipsis in original.

108. Calverton, "Red Love in Soviet Russia,"183.

109. Calverton, 183.

110. V. F. Calverton, letter to Phyllis Blanchard, March 10, 1930, VFC, box 26, folder "Manuscripts Submitted to the *Modern Quarterly*, 'A' and 'B.'"

111. Phyllis Blanchard, letter to V. F. Calverton, April 6, 1933, VFC, box 26, folder "Manuscripts Submitted to the *Modern Quarterly* 'A' and 'B.'"

112. Calverton, "Sex and Economics," 11.

113. Mark Solomon, *The Cry Was Unity: Communists and African Americans, 1917–1936* (Jackson: University Press of Mississippi, 1998), 282–83; Mark Naison, *Communists in Harlem during the Depression* (New York: Grove Press, 1983), 136–37.

114. "Negroes with White Friends Law Violators; At Least That Is What Chicago Police Think," *DW*, October 22, 1924, 3.

115. B. B. Rubinstein, "Workers Party Opposes Intermarriage Bill," *DW*, July 25, 1927, 3.

116. Naison, *Communists in Harlem*, 137.

117. "Faces Jail for Marrying White; Negro Worker Victim of Capitalist Hate," *DW*, August 7, 1930, 3.

118. Gordon W. Owens, "Anti-Intermarriage Laws," *DW*, November 25, 1924, 6.

119. Robin D. G. Kelley, *Hammer and Hoe: Alabama Communists during the Great Depression* (Chapel Hill: University of North Carolina Press, 1990), 78–91.

120. Cheryl Higashida, "Aunt Sue's Children: Re-viewing the Gender(ed) Politics of Richard Wright's Radicalism," *American Literature* 75, no. 2 (June 2003): 411.

121. John Lennon, *Boxcar Politics: The Hobo in U.S. Culture and Literature, 1869–1956* (Amherst: University of Massachusetts Press, 2014), 132–45.

122. Edmund Wilson, "The Freight-Car Case," *New Republic*, August 26, 1931. The accuser's "men's clothing" figures into most accounts of the Scottsboro case, including Daniel T. Carter's *Scottsboro: A Tragedy of the American South* (Baton Rouge: Louisiana State University Press, 1969); see also Glenda Gilmore, *Defying Dixie: The Radical Roots of Civil Rights, 1919–1950* (New York: W. W. Norton, 2009), 120.

123. Walter White, "The Negro and the Communists," *Harper's Magazine*, December 1931, 63.

124. *Patterson v. Alabama*, 294 U.S 599, Tr., (1933), 356–57.

125. In *Powell et al. v. Alabama*, Price had testified that "three boys had to gang up on her to remove her overalls," further suggesting how gender-nonconforming clothing served a functional purpose for train-hopping women who wore overalls. James R. Acker, *Scottsboro and Its Legacy: The Case that Challenged American Legal and Social Justice* (Westport, CT: Praeger, 2008), 31.

126. Lin Shi Khan and Tony Perez, *Scottsboro Alabama: A Story in Linoleum Cuts,* ed. Andrew H. Lee (New York: New York University Press, 2002), 77.

127. Josephine Herbst, "Lynching in the Quiet Manner," *NM*, July 1931, 11.

128. Langston Hughes, "Southern Gentlemen, White Prostitutes, Mill-Owners, and Negroes," *Contempo*, December 1, 1931, 1. Ellipsis in original.

129. Quoted in James A. Miller, *Remembering Scottsboro: The Legacy of an Infamous Trial* (Princeton, NJ: Princeton University Press, 2009), 16.

130. Hughes, "Southern Gentlemen," 1. Ellipsis in original.

CHAPTER 3. "TO BE ONE WITH THE PEOPLE"

1. "Prejudice against Homosexuals," *San Francisco Spokesman*, November 3, 1932, 8.

2. Albert S. Broussard, *Black San Francisco: The Struggle for Racial Equality in the West, 1900–1954* (Lawrence: University of Kanas Press, 1993), 62, 98–99.

3. John Pittman, oral history interview, n.d., Tamiment Library at New York University, https://wp.nyu.edu/tamimentcpusa/john-pittman/.

4. Nan Alamilla Boyd, *Wide-Open Town: A History of Queer San Francisco to 1965* (Berkeley: University of California Press, 2005); Josh Sides, *Erotic City: Sexual Revolutions and the Making of Modern San Francisco* (Oxford: Oxford University Press, 2011).

5. Though Pittman had some connection with A. Philip Randolph that informed his movement to the Left, he attributed his move into the Communist Party to a visit from Angelo Herndon in the 1930s. Pittman, oral history interview.

6. H.H.C., "From a College Student," *NM*, January 1929, 30. Ellipses in original.

7. H.H.C., 30.

8. "For College Student H.H.C.," *NM*, March 1929, 29.

9. H.H.C., "From a College Student," 30.

10. On homosexuality and the Soviet Union, see Daniel Healey, *Homosexual Desire in Revolutionary Russia: The Regulation of Sexual and Gender Dissent* (Chicago: University of Chicago Press, 2001); and Daniel P. Schluter, *Gay Life in the Former USSR: Fraternity without Community* (New York: Routledge, 2002).

11. Healey, *Homosexual Desire in Revolutionary Russia*, 123.

12. Quoted in Healey, 113.

13. E.P. Frenkel', *Polovye prestupleniia* (Odessa: Svetoch, 1927), 12, translated by Dan Healey and quoted in Healey, *Homosexual Desire in Revolutionary Russia*, 129.

14. M. Sereinski, "Homosexuality [Gomoseksualizm]," entry in *Bol'shaia sovetskaia entsiklopediia* (1930), trans. Laura Engelstein, excerpted in *We Are Everywhere: A Historical Sourcebook of Gay and Lesbian Politics*, ed. Mark Blasius and Shane Phelan (New York: Routledge, 1997), 215.

15. Quoted in Healey, *Homosexual Desire in Revolutionary Russia*, 133.

16. Healey, 128.

17. Healey, 181–204.

18. On American travels to the Soviet Union, see Kate Baldwin, *Beyond the Color Line and the Iron Curtain: Reading Encounters between Black and Red, 1922–1963* (Durham, NC: Duke University Press, 2002); and Julia L. Mickenberg, *American Girls in Red Russia: Chasing the Soviet Dream* (Chicago: University of Chicago Press, 2017).

19. Harry Whyte, letter to Joseph Stalin, trans. Thomas Campbell, in *Moscow*, by Yevginiy Fiks (New York: Ugly Duckling Press, 2013), n.p.

20. Healey, *Homosexual Desire in Revolutionary Russia*, 189.

21. Cartoon by William Gropper, *Liberator*, April 1922, 25.

22. Cartoon by Sandy Calder, *NM*, November 1926, 21.

23. John Dos Passos, *The Big Money* (New York: Modern Library, 1937), 97, 98.

24. Pietro Di Donato, *Christ in Concrete* (New York: Bobbs-Merrill, 1939), 140, 240.

25. "Britons Clamp the Cover on Sexual Sewer," *DW*, June 20, 1925, 3; T. J. O'Flaherty, "As We See It," *DW*, August 18, 1925, 2

26. "Pastimes of the Bourgeoisie," *DW*, February 25, 1926, 6.

27. Kevin P. Murphy, *Political Manhood: Red Bloods, Mollycoddles, and the Politics of Progressive Era Reform* (New York: Columbia University Press, 2008).

28. Alan M. Wald suggests the murder in *The Big Clock* relates to an actual 1943 murder case: Wayne Onergan's murder of Patricia Burton with a candelabra. An excellent discussion of Fearing's political trajectory and the cultural politics of *The Big Clock* can be found in Alan M. Wald, *American Night: The Literary Left in the Era of the Cold War* (Chapel Hill: University of North Carolina Press, 2012), 22–48.

29. Kenneth Fearing, *The Big Clock* (New York: Harcourt, Brace, 1946), 64, 71, 122.

30. Fearing, 65, 66.

31. Regina Kunzel urges historians to recognize how sexuality in homosocial spaces, often conceived as "situational," reveals the tensions, contradictions, and motivations animating "modern sexuality" more broadly. See Regina Kunzel, *Criminal Intimacy: Prison and the Uneven History of Modern American Sexuality* (Chicago: University of Chicago Press, 2008). Terence Kissack offers an excellent discussion on anarchists and prison earlier in the twentieth century in his important book *Free Comrades: Anarchism and Homosexuality in the United States, 1895–1917* (Oakland, CA: AK Press, 2008), 97–125.

32. Harrison George, "Ten Acres of Hell," *Liberator*, August 1923, 23.

33. David Gordon, "Inside the Reformatory," *NM*, August 1928, 9.

34. Daniel Allen, "Rose Water for a Sewer," *NM*, February 6, 1934, 19.

35. Charles H. Martin, *The Angelo Herndon Case and Southern Justice* (Baton Rouge: Louisiana State University Press, 1976); John Hammond Moore, "The Angelo Herndon Case, 1932–1937," *Phylon* 32, no. 1 (1971): 60–71.

36. Editorial, *NM*, March 27, 1934, 4.

37. Peter W. Madison, "I Saw Angelo Herndon . . .," August 7, 1934, 19.

38. Angelo Herndon, *Let Me Live* (New York: Random House, 1937), 210.

39. Joseph F. Fishman, *Sex in Prison: Revealing Sex Conditions in American Prisons* (New York: National Library Press, 1934), 142.

40. Herndon, *Let Me Live*, 211

41. Angelo Herndon, draft of "Let Me Live," AHC, box 1, folder 8.

42. Herndon, draft.

43. Quoted in Frederick Vanderbilt Field, *From Right to Left: An Autobiography* (Westport, CT: Lawrence Hill, 1983), 240.

44. Field, 242.

45. Benjamin Gitlow, *I Confess: The Truth about American Communism* (New York: E. P. Dutton, 1940), 75, 8.

46. John Gates, *The Story of an American Communist* (New York: Thomas Nelson, 1958), 138.

47. See Kissack, *Free Comrades*.

48. Kathy E. Ferguson, *Emma Goldman: Political Thinking in the Streets* (Lanham, MD: Rowman and Littlefield, 2011), 213.

49. Otto E. Huiswoud, "World Aspects of the Negro Question," *The Communist* 9, no. 2 (February 1930): 132.

50. Dayo F. Gore, *Radicalism at the Crossroads: African American Women Activists in the Cold War* (New York: New York University Press, 2011); Cheryl Higashida, *Black Internationalist Feminism: Women Writers of the Black Left, 1955–1995* (Urbana: University of Illinois Press, 2011); Robin D. G. Kelley, *Hammer and Hoe: Alabama Communists during the Great Depression* (Chapel Hill: University of North Carolina Press, 1990; Erik S. McDuffie, *Sojourning for Freedom: Black Women, American Communism, and the Making of Black Left Feminism* (Durham, NC: Duke University Press, 2011); Mark Naison, *Communists in Harlem during the Depression* (New York: Grove Press, 1983); Mark Solomon, *The Cry Was Unity: Communists and African Americans, 1917–1936* (Jackson: University Press of Mississippi, 1998.

51. Cora Ball Moten, "Soiled Goods," *San Francisco Spokesman*, April 23, 1932, 10.

52. Quoted in Broussard, *Black San Francisco*, 97.

53. "Scottsboro Demonstrations," *San Francisco Spokesman*, September 29, 1932, 8.

54. Catherine, letter to John Pittman, n.d., JPP, box 1, folder "Correspondence (undated) c. 1930s."

55. Boyd, *Wide-Open Town*, 2, 5.

56. Broussard, *Black San Francisco*, 97–99.

57. All further citations from *The Spokesman* refer to "Prejudice against Homosexuals," November 3, 1932, 8.

58. Broussard, *Black San Francisco*, 102–5.

59. "Resolution on the Negro Question in the United States," *The Communist* 10, no. 2 (February 1931): 153–67.

60. Solomon, *The Cry Was Unity*, 185–206.

61. Gary Edward Holcomb, *Claude McKay, Code Name Sasha: Queer Black Marxism and the Harlem Renaissance* (Gainesville: University of Florida Press, 2007).

62. Holcomb, 19.

63. Charles Henri Ford, postcard to Claude McKay, n.d., CMC, box 3, folder 82.

64. Charles Henri Ford and Parker Tyler, *The Young and Evil* (Paris: Obelisk Press, 1933), 37, 28.

65. Charles Henri Ford, letter to Claude McKay, July 8, 1938, CMC, box 3, folder 82.

66. Claude McKay, letter to Charles Henri Ford, July 20, 1938, Yale University CMC, box 3, folder 82.

67. Charles Henri Ford, letter to Claude McKay, CMC, box 3, folder 82.

68. Claude McKay, letter to Charles Henri Ford, CMC, box 3, folder 82.

69. Randi Storch, *Red Chicago: American Communism at Its Grassroots, 1928–1935* (Urbana: University of Illinois Press, 2007), 2.

70. Bill V. Mullen, *Popular Fronts: Chicago and African-American Cultural Politics, 1935–1946* (Urbana and Chicago: University of Illinois Press, 1999).

71. Chad Heap, *Slumming: Sexual and Racial Encounters in American Nightlife, 1885–1940* (Chicago: University of Chicago Press, 2009), 231–76.

72. Kevin Mumford, *Interzones: Black/White Sex Districts in Chicago and New York in the Early Twentieth Century* (New York: Columbia University Press, 1997).

73. As many scholars have noted, the Harlem Renaissance was no less centered in Chicago than in New York. See, for example, Robert Bone and Richard A. Courage, *The Muse in Bronzeville: African American Creative Expression in Chicago, 1932–1950* (New Brunswick, NJ: Rutgers University Press, 2011).

74. William J. Maxwell, *New Negro, Old Left: African-American Writing and Communism Between the Wars* (New York: Columbia University Press, 1999).

75. Richard Wright, "Blueprint for Negro Writing," *New Challenge* 2, no. 1 (Fall 1937): 53–65.

76. Wallace Thurman, *Infants of Spring* (New York: Macauley Company, 1932), 218.

77. See Janice A. Radway, *A Feeling for Books: The Book-of-the-Month Club, Literary Taste, and Middle-Class Desire* (Chapel Hill: University of North Carolina Press, 1997).

78. Roderick Ferguson, *Aberrations in Black: Toward a Queer of Color Critique* (Minneapolis: University of Minnesota Press, 2004), 48.

79. Richard Wright, *Native Son* (New York: Harper, 1940; repr., Harper, 1993), 30. Citations refer to the 1993 edition.

80. Wright, 30. Ellipsis in original.

81. Wright, 306.

82. Quoted in "Required Reading," *Manhattan Mercury*, February 12, 1988, 6.

83. A. W. Richard Sipe, *The Serpent and the Dove: Celibacy in Literature and Life* (New York: Praeger, 2007), 114.

84. Alan M. Wald, *James T. Farrell: The Revolutionary Socialist Years* (New York: New York University Press, 1978).

85. James T. Farrell, *A Note on Literary Criticism* (New York: Vanguard Press, 1936; New York: Columbia University Press, 1992), 169. Citations are to Columbia University Press edition.

86. James T. Farrell, *Calico Shoes* (New York: Vanguard Press, 1934), 147.

87. Herman Michelson, review of *Calico Shoes, NM*, October 30, 1934, 21.

88. Scott Herring, *Queering the Underworld: Slumming, Literature, and the Undoing of Lesbian and Gay History* (Chicago: University of Chicago Press, 2007), 14.

89. Eric Gordon, *Mark the Music: The Life and Work of Marc Blitzstein* (New York: St. Martin's, 1989); Howard Pollack, *Marc Blitzstein: His Life, His Work, His World* (New York: Oxford University Press, 2012). For a related discussion of Blitzstein and "Popular Front camp," see Rachel Rubin and James Smethurst, "Camp Unity: Camp and Popular Front Aesthetics and Reception," *English Language Notes* 53, no. 1 (Spring/Summer 2015): 83–96.

90. Michael Denning, *The Cultural Front: The Laboring of American Culture in the Twentieth Century* (New York: Verso, 1997), 285–95.

91. "Leaflets & Art for Art's Sake" (from *The Cradle Will Rock*). Words and Music by Marc Blitzstein © 1938 Chappell & Co. Inc. (ASCAP). All Rights Reserved. Used by Permission of Alfred Music.

92. Edwin Seaver, ed., *Cross Section 1945: A Collection of New American Writing* (New York: Book Find Club, 1945), vii.

93. Donald Vining, "Show Me the Way to Go Home," in Seaver, *Cross Section 1945*, 272, 273.

94. Vining, 280, 281.

95. Vining, 275, 276.

96. Alan M. Wald discusses Rollins's sexuality in *American Night*, 139–43.

97. William Rollins Jr., "What Is a Proletarian Writer?," *NM*, January 29, 1935, 22.

98. Rollins Jr., 23.

99. Ivan Beede, "Bertie—A Story," *NM*, September 1926, 9–10, 30.

100. *Nebraska: A Guide to the Cornhusker State; Compiled by the Federal Writers' Program of the Works Progress Administration in the State of Nevada* (Lincoln: Nebraska State Historical Society, 1939), 141; Ivan Beede, *Prairie Woman: A Novel* (New York: Harper, 1930).

101. Quoted in Malcolm Cowley, "More about Neglected Books," *New Republic*, May 23, 1934.

102. Beede, "Bertie—A Story," 9.

CHAPTER 4. "IF I CAN DIE UNDER YOU"

1. Alan M. Wald, *The Forging of the Mid-Twentieth Century Literary Left* (Chapel Hill: University of North Carolina Press, 2002), 12–13.

2. George Granich, "In Jail with Idiots," *NM*, August 1928, 18.

3. Lee Alexander Stone, *Sex Searchlights and Sane Sexual Ethics: An Anthology of Sex Knowledge* (Chicago: Science Publishing Company, 1922), 752.

4. Granich, "In Jail with Idiots," 18.

5. On gay decorators, see John Potvin, "Designing the Gender Contest: (Re) Locating the Gay Decorator in the History of Interior Design," in *Shaping the American Interior: Structures, Contexts and Practices*, ed. Paula Lupkin and Penny Sparke (New York: Routledge, 2018), 59–68.

6. Merrit Brunies & His Friar's Inn Orchestra, "Masculine Women, Feminine Men," 1926, by Edgar Leslie and James V. Monaco (New York: Okeh).

7. Havelock Ellis, *Psychology of Sex; A Manual for Students* (New York: Emerson Books, 1946), 221.

8. Alfred C. Kinsey, Wardell B. Pomeroy, and Clyde E. Martin, *Sexual Behavior in the Human Male* (Bloomington and Indianapolis: Indiana University Press, 1948), 77, 331.

9. Kinsey, Pomeroy, and Martin, 433.

10. Kinsey, Pomeroy, and Martin, 436.

11. Steven C. McKay, "Racializing the High Seas: Filipino Migrants and Global Shipping," in *The Nation and Its Peoples: Citizens, Denizens, Migrants,* ed. John Park and Shannon Gleeson (New York: Routledge, 2014), 160.

12. McKay, 160; Bruce Nelson, *Workers on the Waterfront: Seamen, Longshoremen, and Unionism in the 1930s* (Urbana: University of Illinois Press, 1988), 48.

13. George Robertson, "Desegregating a Maritime Union: The Marine Cooks and Stewards," Waterfront Workers History Project, n.d., http://depts.washington.edu/dock/mcs_desegregation.shtml; Allan Bérubé, "My Desire for History," in *Essays in Gay, Community, and Labor History,* ed. John D'Emilio and Estelle B. Freedman (Chapel Hill: University of North Carolina Press, 2011), 300–301; Nelson, *Workers on the Waterfront,* 259.

14. Richard S. Hobbs, *The Cayton Legacy: An African American Family* (Pullman: Washington State University Press, 2002), 94.

15. On the general strike, see David F. Selvin, *A Terrible Anger: The 1934 Waterfront and General Strikes in San Francisco* (Detroit, MI: Wayne State University Press, 1996); and Mike Quin, *The Big Strike* (Olema, CA: Olema Publishing Company, 1949).

16. Nelson, *Workers on the Waterfront,* 259.

17. Hobbs, *The Cayton Legacy,* 152.

18. Allan Bérubé was doing invaluable research on the MCS up until his untimely death in 2007. I would like to acknowledge that much of this section draws upon the oral histories he conducted, housed now at the Gay, Lesbian, Bisexual, and Transgender Historical Society in San Francisco. While I did not have a chance to meet Allan, I owe a tremendous debt to him for the work he did collecting materials I was able to access for my research, and to John D'Emilio and Estelle Freedman for working to bring some of his unpublished work on the MCS to print.

19. Allan Bérubé, interview with Archie Green, ABP, box 41, folder 3.

20. Allan Bérubé, interview with Stephen Blair, ABP, box 45, folder 12.

21. Nan Alamilla Boyd, *Wide-Open Town: A History of Queer San Francisco to 1965* (Berkeley: University of California Press, 2005), 5, 57.

22. Al Richmond, *A Long View from the Left: Memoirs of an American Revolutionary* (Boston: Houghton Mifflin, 1972).

23. See Phil Tiemeyer, *Plane Queer: Labor, Sexuality, and AIDS in the History of Male Flight Attendants* (Berkeley: University of California Press, 2013), 7.

24. Nayan Shah, *Stranger Intimacy: Contesting Race, Sexuality and the Law in the North American West* (Berkeley: University of California Press, 2012).

25. Paul Baker and Jo Stanley, *Hello Sailor: The Hidden History of Gay Life at Sea* (New York: Routledge, 2014), 1.

26. Albert S. Broussard, *Black San Francisco: The Struggle for Racial Equality in the West, 1900–1954* (Lawrence: University of Kanas Press, 1993); Howard Kimeldorf, *Reds or Rackets?: The Making of Radical and Conservative Unions on the Waterfront* (Berkeley: University of California Press, 1988), 145–48.

27. Quoted in Allan Bérubé, "Queer Work," paper presented at San Francisco State University, February 1996, ABP, box 42, folder 20.

28. Paul Brownlee, interview by Allan Bérubé, n.d., ABP, box 46, folder 16.

29. Quoted in Allan Bérubé, unpublished paper, n.d., ABP, box 41, folder 3.

30. Ted Rolfs, interview by Allan Bérubé, February 8, 1984, ABP, box 46, folder 26.

31. Miriam Johnson, interview by Allan Bérubé, n.d., ABP, box 46, folder 17.

32. Stephen Blair, interview by Allan Bérubé, n.d., ABP, box 45, folder 13.

33. Rolfs, interview by Allan Bérubé.

34. Joseph O'Connor, letter to the editor, *MCS Voice*, January 25, 1943.

35. Quoted in Allan Bérubé, "'Dignity for All': The Role of Homosexuality in the Marine Cooks and Stewards Union (1930s-1950s)," n.d., ABP, box 42, folder 4.

36. Quoted in unpublished paper by Allan Bérubé, n.d., ABP, box 41, folder 3.

37. Johnson, interview with Allan Bérubé.

38. Frank McCormick, "McCormick Asks Comments on New 'VOICE,'" *MCS Voice*, February 10, 1943.

39. "Seattle's Port Hole Peeper," *MCS Voice*, March 17, 1949.

40. Judith Scherr, "Pele deLappe, Artist and Activist, Remembered—1916–2007," *Berkeley Daily Planet*, October 16, 2007, http://www.berkeley dailyplanet.com/issue/2007-10-16/article/28229.

41. Pele deLappe, *Pele: A Passionate Journey through Art & the Red Press* (self-pub., Petaluma, CA, 1999), 13, 24, 35.

42. Pele deLappe, "To Be Gay in Cuba," *People's Daily World*, March 29, 1980.

43. John Ott, "Graphic Consciousness: The Visual Cultures of Integrated Industrial Unions at Midcentury," *American Quarterly* 66, no. 4 (December 2014): 883–917.

44. Martin B. Duberman, *The Worlds of Lincoln Kirstein* (New York: Knopf, 2007), 118–20.

45. Richard Meyer, *Outlaw Representation: Censorship and Homosexuality in Twentieth-Century American Art* (New York: Oxford University Press, 2002), 37–56.

46. Erika Doss, *Benton, Pollock, and the Politics of Modernism: From Regionalism to Abstract Expressionism* (Chicago: University of Chicago Press, 1991), 192; Philip Eliasoph, *Paul Cadmus, Catalogue Raisonné: Paintings, 1931–1977* (New York: Philip Eliasoph, 1977), 45. On the ashcan artists, see Rebecca Zurier, *Metropolitan Lives: The Ashcan Artists and Their New York* (Washington, D.C.: National Museum of American Art, 1995).

47. Andrew Hemingway, *Artists on the Left: American Artists and the Communist Movement, 1926–1956* (New Haven, CT: Yale University Press, 2002);

Helen Langa, *Radical Art: Printmaking and the Left in 1930s New York* (Berkeley: University of California Press, 2004).

48. Paul M. Angle, *Bloody Williamson: A Chapter in American Lawlessness* (New York: Alfred A. Knopf, 1952); Philip Eliasoph, *Paul Cadmus: Catalogue Raisonné, Paintings, 1931–1977* (self-pub., 1977), 45.

49. Emily Genauer, *Art Digest*, December 12, 1940, 17.

50. David Leddick, *Intimate Companions: A Triography of George Platt Lynes, Paul Cadmus, Lincoln Kirstein, and Their Circle* (New York: St. Martin's Press, 2000), 41; Meyer, *Outlaw Representation*, 37; *Paul Cadmus: Enfant Terrible at 80*, directed by David Sutherland, (Chicago: Homevision, 1986), VHS recording; Alejandro Anreus, Diana L. Linden, and Jonathan Weinberg, introduction to *The Social and the Real: Political Art of the 1930s in the Western Hemisphere*, ed. Alejandro Anreus, Diana L. Linden, and Jonathan Weinberg (University Park: Pennsylvania State University Press, 2006), xvii; Matthew Baigell and Julia Williams, eds., *Artists against War and Fascism: Papers of the First American Artists' Congress* (New Brunswick, NJ: Rutgers University Press, 1986), 49.

51. Lincoln Kirstein, *Paul Cadmus* (New York: Imago, 1984), 45.

52. Jonathan Weinberg, "I Want Muscle: Male Desire and the Image of the Worker in American Art of the 1930s," in Anreus et al., *The Social and the Real*, 123.

53. Paul Cadmus, interview by Jared Tully, March 22, 1988, Archives of American Art, Smithsonian Institution.

54. Weinberg, "I Want Muscle," 119.

55. On homoeroticism in *Herrin Massacre*, see Bram Dijkstra, *American Expressionism: Art and Social Change, 1920-1950* (New York: Harry N. Abrams, 2003), 149-150; Kenneth E. Silver, "Homo Erectus and His Discontents," *The Young and Evil: Queer Modernism in New York, 1930-1955*, ed. Jarrett Earnest (New York: David Zwirner Books, 2019), 53-55.

56. Anreus et al., introduction to *The Social and the Real*, xvii.

57. Cadmus's negotiations with racial representations are discussed in Meyer, *Outlaw Representation*, 81–86.

58. Ellis, *Psychology of Sex*, 221.

59. Quoted in Barry Reay, *New York Hustlers: Masculinity and Sex in Modern America* (Manchester, UK: Manchester University Press, 2010), 13. For further discussion on Painter, see Henry L. Minton, *Departing from Deviance: A History of Homosexual Rights and Emancipatory Science in America* (Chicago: University of Chicago Press, 2002), 122–58.

60. George Chauncey, *Gay New York: The Making of the Gay Male World, 1890–1940* (New York: Basic Books, 1994), 82.

61. Reay's *New York Hustlers* brilliantly explores this topic in New York.

62. Ralph Werther, *Autobiography of an Androgyne*, ed. Scott Herring (New York: Medico-Legal Journal, 1918; repr., New Brunswick, NJ: Rutgers University Press, 2008), 125. Citations refer to the 2008 edition.

63. Werther, 109.

64. Polly Adler, *A House Is Not a Home*, ed. Rachel Rubin (New York: Rinehart, 1953; repr., Amherst, : University of Massachusetts Press, 2006), 230–31. Citations refer to the 2006 edition.

65. Chad Heap, *Slumming: Sexual and Racial Encounters in American Nightlife, 1885–1940* (Chicago: University of Chicago Press, 2009), 67; Shane Vogel, *The Scene of Harlem Cabaret: Race, Sexuality, Performance* (Chicago: University of Chicago Press, 2009).

66. Boyd, *Wide-Open Town,* 34.

67. Kevin Mumford, *Interzones: Black/White Sex Districts in Chicago and New York in the Early Twentieth Century* (New York: Columbia University Press, 1997), 35.

68. Reproduced in Elizabeth Faue, *Community of Suffering and Struggle: Women, Men, and the Labor Movement in Minneapolis, 1915–1945* (Chapel Hill: University of North Carolina Press, 1991), 74.

69. Michael Trask, *Cruising Modernism: Class and Sexuality in American Literature and Social Thought* (Ithaca, NY: Cornell University Press, 2003), 166–91.

70. Michael Gold, "Thoughts of a Great Thinker," *Liberator,* April 1922, 22.

71. Michael Gold, *Jews without Money* (New York: Horace Liveright, 1930), 18.

72. Albert Maltz, "Onward Christian Soldiers," *NM,* March 13, 1924, 23–24.

73. Barney Conal, letter, *NM,* April 24, 1934, 22.

74. Margot Canaday, *The Straight State: Sexuality and Citizenship in Twentieth-Century America* (Princeton, NJ: Princeton University Press, 2009), 117, 120. For an excellent discussion of queer camp in the CCC, see Colin Johnson, "Camp Life: The Queer History of 'Manhood' in the Civilian Conservation Corps, 1933–1937," *American Studies* 48, no. 2 (Summer 2007): 19–36.

75. Quoted in Arthur D. Casciato and James L.W. West III, "Afterword: In Search of Tom Kromer," in *Waiting for Nothing and Other Writings,* by Tom Kromer, ed. Arthur D. Casciato and James L.W. West III (Athens: University of Georgia Press, 1986), 272.

76. "Books and Authors," *New York Times Review of Books,* September 15, 1935, 12.

77. Quoted in Casciato and West, "Afterword," 274.

78. Tom Kromer, *Waiting for Nothing and Other Writings,* ed. Arthur D. Casciato and James L.W. West III (Athens: University of Georgia Press, 1986), 43

79. Sherwood Anderson, *Beyond Desire* (New York: Liveright, 1932), 124.

80. H.T. Tsiang, *The Hanging on Union Square* (self-pub., New York, 1935), 69.

81. Daniel Fuchs, *Summer in Williamsburg* (New York: Vanguard, 1934; repr., New York: Carroll & Graf, 1983), 274. Citations refer to the 1983 edition.

82. David Gordon, "Call Western Union," *NM,* August 1926, 7.

83. Walter Rideout, *The Radical Novel in the United States: Some Interrelations of Literature and Society, 1900–1954* (New York: Columbia University Press, 1992; first published 1956 by Harvard University Press [Cambridge, MA]), 174.

84. Barbara Foley, *Radical Representations: Politics and Form in U.S. Proletarian Fiction, 1929–1941* (Durham, NC: Duke University Press, 1993), 363.

85. William Rollins Jr., "What Is a Proletarian Writer?," *NM,* January 29, 1935, 22–23.

86. William Rollins Jr., *The Shadow Before* (New York: Robert M. McBride, 1934), 37.

87. Thomas Painter, quoted in Minton, *Departing from Deviance*, 142.

88. On futurity and queerness, see especially José Esteban Muñoz, *Cruising Utopia: The Then and There of Queer Futurity* (New York: New York University Press, 2009).

CHAPTER 5. "SOCIALISM & SEX IS WHAT I WANT"

1. Maxwell Bodenheim, "To a Revolutionary Girl," in *Proletarian Literature in the United States: An Anthology,* ed. Granville Hicks (New York: International Publishers, 1935), 147–49.

2. Betty Millard, personal notes, BMP, box 1, folder 11; Betty Millard, timeline, BMP, box 1, folder 12.

3. Betty Millard, diary, February 4, 1934, BMP, box 3, folder 3.

4. Elizabeth Gurley Flynn, letter to Joseph North, n.d., BMP, box 19, folder 12.

5. Jeanne Vermeersch, letter to Betty Millard, n.d., BMP, box 19, folder 12.

6. See Kathleen A. Brown and Elizabeth Faue, "Revolutionary Desire: Redefining the Politics of Sexuality of American Radicals, 1919–1945," in *Sexual Borderlands: Constructing an American Sexual Past,* ed. Kathleen Kennedy and Sharon Ullman (Columbus: Ohio State University Press, 2003), 273–302.

7. Mari Jo Buhle, *Women and American Socialism, 1870–1920* (Urbana: University of Illinois Press, 1981), xvii.

8. For further discussion of this movement, see Kevin P. Murphy's excellent chapter on the subject in *Political Manhood: Red Bloods, Mollycoddles, and the Politics of Progressive Era Reform* (New York: Columbia University Press, 2008), 104–24.

9. Daniel Aaron, *Writers on the Left: Episodes in Literary Communism* (New York: Harcourt, Brace, 1962), 13; Lois Palken Rudnick, ed., *The Suppressed Memoirs of Mabel Dodge Luhan: Sex, Syphilis, and Psychoanalysis in the Making of Modern American Culture* (Albuquerque: University of New Mexico Press, 2012); Lillian Faderman, *Odd Girls and Twilight Lovers: A History of Lesbian Life in Twentieth-Century America* (New York: Penguin, 1991), 82.

10. Mabel Dodge, "Speculations, or Post-Impressionism in Prose," *Arts and Decorations,* March 1913, 172.

11. Clement Wood, "The Greenwich Village Epic," *Bohemian Life in N.Y.'s Greenwich Village* (New York: Haldeman-Julius, 1926).

12. Granville Hicks, *John Reed: The Making of a Revolutionary* (New York: Macmillan, 1936), 92.

13. Rosalyn Baxandall, "The Question Seldom Asked: Women and the CPUSA," in *New Studies in the Politics and Culture of U.S. Communism,* ed. Michael Brown, Randy Martin, Frank Rosengarten, and George Snedeker (New York: Monthly Review Press, 1993), 142. For a general discussion of women in the Communist Party, see Constance Coiner, *Better Red: The Writing and Resistance of Tillie Olsen and Meridel Le Sueur* (New York: Oxford University Press, 1995), 3–71; and Kate Weigand, *Red Feminism: American Com-*

munism and the Making of Women's Liberation (Baltimore: Johns Hopkins University Press, 2001).

14. Quoted in Elaine Hedges, introduction to *Ripening*, by Meridel Le Sueur, ed. Elaine Hedges (Old Westbury, NY: Feminist Press, 1982), 14.

15. Quoted in Elinor Langer, *Josephine Herbst* (New York: Little, Brown, 1983), 120.

16. Ruth McKenney, "Women Are Human Beings," *NM*, December 17, 1940, 9–10.

17. Sheila Rowbotham, *Women, Resistance, and Revolution: A History of Women and Revolution in the Modern World* (New York: Vintage, 1974), 155.

18. Michael Denning, *The Cultural Front: The Laboring of American Culture in the Twentieth Century* (New York: Verso, 1997), 30.

19. "Changes to a Magazine," *Working Woman*, March 1933, 2.

20. Barbara Alexander, "Happiness for One Dime," *Working Woman*, November 1935, 13–14.

21. *Working Woman*, advertisement, January, 1935, 16.

22. "Bermuda Women Denied Vote," *Working Woman*, December 1929, 1; "Turkish Women Strike," *Working Woman*, February 1930, 4.

23. Erik S. McDuffie, *Sojourning for Freedom: Black Women, American Communism, and the Making of Black Left Feminism* (Durham, NC: Duke University Press, 2011), 4. See also Dayo F. Gore, *Radicalism at the Crossroads: African American Women Activists in the Cold War* (New York: New York University Press, 2011); and Cheryl Higashida, *Black Internationalist Feminism: Women Writers of the Black Left, 1945-1995* (Urbana and Chicago: University of Illinois Press, 2011).

24. "Women's Wage Lowest; Negroes Pay Is Poorest," *Working Woman*, February 1930, 1; "Bosses Speed Up Negro Women Workers," *Working Woman*, March 1930, 3.

25. Irma Watkins-Owens, *Blood Relations: Caribbean Immigrants and the Harlem Community, 1900–1930* (Bloomington: Indiana University Press, 1996), 92; McDuffie, *Sojourning for Freedom*, 35, 43.

26. "Told to 'Quit, Get Married or Die,'" *Working Woman*, February 1931, 2.

27. Dan Davis, "You're Telling Me!" *Working Woman*, March 1933, 7.

28. "Slave Market Up-to-Date," *Working Woman*, January 1935, 13.

29. M.S., "Conditions Forcing Women into Prostitution," *Working Woman*, September 1931, 6.

30. R.L.M., "Low Pay Leads to Girls' Degradation; Negro Girls Victims of Discrimination," *Working Woman*, December 1931, 5.

31. Irene Thirer, "Movies," *Working Woman*, April 1936, 3.

32. "Letters Received by the American Birth Control League," *Working Woman*, April 1933, 13.

33. Sasha Small, "Love—Bows to the Dollar," *Working Woman*, September 1934, 7.

34. Elizabeth McCausland, "The Blue Menace,'" Elizabeth McCausland Papers, Archives of American Art, Smithsonian Institution, Washington, D.C., box 5, folder 23.

35. Betty Millard, invitation, n.d., BMP, box 19, folder 12.

36. Daniel Hurewitz, *Bohemian Los Angeles: The Making of Modern Politics* (Berkeley: University of California Press, 2012).

37. Betty Millard, personal notes, BMP, box 1, folder 13.

38. Betty Millard, diary, October 7, 1933, BMP, box 3, folder 3.

39. Betty Millard, diary, May 20, 1934, BMP, box 3, folder 3.

40. Betty Millard, diary, July 8, 1934, BMP, box 3, folder 3.

41. Elizabeth Lapovsky Kennedy and Madeline D. Davis, *Boots of Leather, Slippers of Gold: The History of a Lesbian Community* (New York: Routledge, 1993). See also Faderman, *Odd Girls and Twilight Lovers.*

42. Michael Sherry, *Gay Artists in Modern America: An Imagined Conspiracy* (Chapel Hill: University of North Carolina Press, 2007).

43. Betty Millard, diary, July 31, 1934, BMP, box 3, folder 3.

44. Mrs. John Esser Dodson, letter to Betty Millard, December 31, 1940, BMP, box 9, folder 12.

45. Betty Millard, *Women against Myth* (New York: International Press, 1948), 21, 24.

46. Julia L. Mickenberg, *American Girls in Red Russia: Chasing the Soviet Dream* (Chicago: University of Chicago Press, 2017), 4.

47. Myra Page, *Moscow Yankee* (New York: G. P. Putnam's and Sons, 1935; repr., Urbana and Chicago: University of Illinois Press, 1995), 72. Citations refer to the 1995 edition.

48. Mickenberg, *American Girls in Red Russia,* 62.

49. Ruth Erickson and Eleanor Stevenson, letter to the *New Milford* [Connecticut] *Times,* 1947, REES, box 1, Outgoing Correspondence, 1940–1949.

50. Eleanor Stevenson, letter to Ted, May 8, 1925, REES, box 1, Outgoing Correspondence, 1920–1929.

51. Ruth Erickson, letter to Father Abraham, 1926, REES, box 1, Outgoing Correspondence, 1920–1929.

52. Eleanor Stevenson, letter, May 10, 1925, REES, box 1, Outgoing Correspondence, 1920–1929.

53. Eleanor Stevenson, letter, November 12, 1924, REES, box 1, Outgoing Correspondence, 1920–1929.

54. Eleanor Stevenson, letter, May 10, 1925, REES, box 1, Outgoing Correspondence, 1920–1929.

55. Eleanor Stevenson, letter, May 10, 1925, REES, box 1, Outgoing Correspondence, 1920–1929.

56. Eleanor Stevenson, letter, November 12, 1924, REES, box 1, Outgoing Correspondence, 1920–1929.

57. Eleanor Stevenson, letter to Ted, March 26, 1947, REES, box 1, Outgoing Correspondence, 1940–1949.

58. Eleanor Stevenson, draft of letter to the *New Milford* [Connecticut] *Times,* n.d., REES, box 1, Outgoing Correspondence, 1930–1939.

59. Eleanor Stevenson, letter to Woofie and Harry, February 5, 1947, REES, box 1, Outgoing Correspondence, 1940–1949.

60. Eleanor Stevenson, letter to the *New York Herald Tribune,* March 30, 1947, REES, box 1, Outgoing Correspondence, 1940–1949.

61. Eleanor Stevenson, letter to Representative Patterson, November 14, 1947, REES, box 1, Outgoing Correspondence, 1940–1949.

62. Eleanor Stevenson, letter to the *New Milford* [Connecticut]*Times,* 1947, REES, box 1, Outgoing Correspondence, 1940–1949.

63. Eleanor Stevenson, letter to Marion, February 18, 1947, REES, box 1, Outgoing Correspondence, 1940–1949.

64. Ruth Erickson, letter to Alma, February 19, 1947, REES, box 1, Outgoing Correspondence, 1940–1949.

65. Ruth Erickson and Eleanor Stevenson, letter to Chuck, Feb 26, 1945, REES, box 1, Outgoing Correspondence, 1940–1949

66. Ruth Erickson, "Birthday Poem," 1961, REES, box 2, Ruth Erickson: Manuscripts and Notes.

67. Ruth Erickson and Eleanor Stevenson, letter to "friends," January 27, 1954, REES, box 1, Outgoing Correspondence, 1950–1959.

68. Ruth Erickson and Eleanor Stevenson, letter to "Dear girls," March 10, 1926, REES, box 1, Outgoing Correspondence, 1920–1929.

69. Ruth Erickson and Eleanor Stevenson, letter to Rep. Chase Going Woodhouse, June 5, 1946, REES, box 1, Outgoing Correspondence, 1940–1949.

70. Eleanor Stevenson, letter to Woofie and Harry, February 5, 1947, REES, box 1, Outgoing Correspondence, 1940–1949. Ellipsis in original.

71. Eleanor Stevenson, letter to Mr. Bonosky, January 19, 1955, REES, box 1, Outgoing Correspondence, 1950–1959.

72. Michael Helquist, *Marie Equi: Radical Politics and Outlaw Passions* (Corvallis: Oregon State University Press, 2015), 121.

73. Elizabeth Gurley Flynn, *The Rebel Girl, an Autobiography: My First Life (1906–1926)* (New York: Masses & Mainstream, 1955; rev. ed., New York: International Publishers, 1973), 21. Citations refer to the 1973 edition.

74. Helquist, *Marie Equi,* 222–23.

75. Helquist, 176.

76. Helquist, 225, 230.

77. Julia Van Haaften, *Berenice Abbott: A Life in Photography* (New York: Norton, 2018), 17.

78. Claude McKay, *A Long Way from Home* (New York: L. Furman, 1937), 104.

79. Angela Calomiris, *Red Masquerade* (New York: Lippincott, 1950); Lisa E. Davis, *Undercover Girl: The Lesbian Informant Who Helped the FBI Bring Down the Communist Party* (Watertown, MA: Charlesbridge, 2017); Van Haaften, *Berenice Abbott,* 315.

80. Van Haaften, 194.

81. Van Haaften, 320.

82. Van Haaften, 306–7, 310, 312, 315, 316.

83. Elizabeth McCausland, "There Shall Be Day," 1940, EMP, box 5, folder 23.

84. Agnes Smedley, *Daughter of Earth* (New York: Coward-McCann, 1929; repr., New York: Feminist Press, 1973). Citations refer to the 1973 edition.

85. Ruth Price, *The Lives of Agnes Smedley* (New York: Oxford University Press, 1995), 83, 141.

86. Price, 158.

87. Agnes Smedley, "One Is Not Made of Wood: The True Story of a Life," *NM*, August 1927, 5–7; Price, *The Lives of Agnes Smedley,* 159.

88. Quoted in Price, 164.

89. Quoted in Price, 170.

90. Paula Rabinowitz, *Labor & Desire: Women's Revolutionary Fiction in Depression America* (Chapel Hill: University of North Carolina Press, 1991), 16.

91. Elinor Langer, *Josephine Herbst: The Story She Could Never Tell* (Boston: Little, Brown, 1984), 179.

92. Barbara Foley, *Radical Representations: Politics and Form in U.S. Proletarian Fiction, 1929-1941* (Durham, NC: Duke University Press, 1993), 237.

93. Paul Lauter, afterword to *Daughter of Earth,* by Agnes Smedley (New York: Feminist Press, 1973), 407–430, 489.

94. Ellipsis in original.

95. Mary Ann Rasmussen, introduction to *Pity Is Not Enough,* by Josephine Herbst (Urbana and Chicago: University of Illinois Press, 1998), x.

96. Elinor Langer, *Josephine Herbst* (New York: Atlantic Monthly Press, 1983), 127.

97. Quoted in Langer, 136.

98. Virginia Spencer Carr, *The Lonely Hunter: A Biography of Carson McCullers* (New York: Doubleday, 1976), 38, 49, 57.

99. Carson McCullers, *Illumination and Night Glare: The Unfinished Autobiography of Carson McCullers,* ed. Carlos L. Dews (Madison: University of Wisconsin Press, 1999), 56.

100. Virginia Spencer Carr, *The Lonely Hunter: A Biography of Carson McCullers* (New York: Doubleday, 1975), 117–40.

101. Melissa Dabakis, *Visualizing Labor in American Sculpture: Monuments, Manliness, and the Work Ethic, 1880–1935* (Cambridge: Cambridge University Press, 1999).

102. Foley, *Radical Representations,* 221.

103. Coiner, *Better Red,* 39–71.

104. Jack Halberstam, *Female Masculinity* (Durham, NC: Duke University Press, 1998), 9.

105. Faderman, *Odd Girls and Twilight Lovers,* 60.

106. Jen Manion, *Female Husbands: A Trans History* (Cambridge: Cambridge University Press, 2020), 11. See also Clare Sears, *Arresting Dress: Cross-Dressing, Law, and Fascination in Nineteenth-Century San Francisco* (Durham, NC: Duke University Press, 2014), 9–10. Susan Stryker, Paisley Currah, and Lisa Jean Moore describe how transing can "function as an escape vector, line of flight, or pathway toward liberation." Susan Stryker, Paisley Currah, and Lisa Jean Moore, "Introduction: Trans-, Trans, or Transgender?," *WSQ: Women's Studies Quarterly* 36, nos. 3/4 (Fall/Winter 2008): 13.

107. Quoted in Christina Kaier, *Imagine No Possessions: The Socialist Objects of Russian Constructivism* (Cambridge, MA: MIT Press, 2005), 119.

108. H. H. Lewis, "The Man from Moscow," in *Thinking of Russia* (Holt, MN: B. C. Hagglund, 1932), 19.

109. Lola Bullard, "You Can't Eat Romance," *Woman Today,* May 1935, 6.

110. Helen Morgan, "Paris Women Fashion New Weapons," *Woman Today,* December 1936, 3.

111. Joseph Freeman, "The Red Commander: Outline for a True Story," *NM,* January 1928, 26.

112. Rosalind Rosenberg, *Jane Crow: The Life of Pauli Murray* (Oxford: Oxford University Press, 2017), 49–50.

113. Rosenberg, 53–55.

114. Jo Sinclair, *Wasteland* (New York: Harper, 1946). An earlier version of some portions of this section and of chapter 7 appeared in Aaron Lecklider, "Public Excursions in Fierce Truth-Telling: Literary Cultures and Homosexuality in the 1940s," in *American Literature in Transition, 1940–1950,* ed. Christopher Vials (Cambridge: Cambridge University Press, 2017), 193–211.

115. Alan M. Wald, *American Night: The Literary Left in the Era of the Cold War* (Chapel Hill: University of North Carolina Press, 2012), 244.

116. Sinclair, *Wasteland,* 29.

117. "Ruth Seid's Novel Wins a $10,000 Harper Award," *Cleveland News,* January 2, 1946.

118. Mary D. Tufts, letter to Miss Herdman, JSC, box 36, folder 13.

119. Albert Stevens, "A Wasteland of Distorted Humans," *DW,* April 28, 1946, 9.

120. Clinton H. Edwards, letter to Jo Sinclair, July 13, 1946, JSC, box 36, folder 14.

121. Sinclair, *Wasteland,* 146, 133.

122. Sinclair, *Wasteland,* 289.

123. Carson McCullers, *The Member of the Wedding* (New York: Houghton Mifflin, 1946), 23.

124. Susan E. Lederer, *Flesh and Blood: Organ Transplantation and Blood Transfusion in Twentieth-Century America* (New York: Oxford University Press, 2008), 107.

125. Wald, *American Night,* 128.

126. Myron Brinig, *Singermann* (New York: Farrar & Rinehart, 1929).

127. Sinclair, *Wasteland,* 25, 26, 266.

128. Sinclair, 26, 31, 32, 26, 137.

129. Sinclair, 219, 220.

130. For an extended treatment of this topic, see Monica Bachmann, "'Someone like Debby': (De)Constructing a Lesbian Community of Readers," *GLQ: A Journal of Lesbian and Gay Studies* 6, no. 3 (2000): 377–88.

131. Robert I. Larus, letter to Jo Sinclair, March 15, 1947, JSC, box 36 folder 14.

132. Jo Sinclair, "The Seasons: Death and Transfiguration," n.d., JSC, box 40.

133. J. Shelley Wilks, letter to Jo Sinclair, November 8, 1948, JSC, box 36, folder 15.

134. Betty E. Breaux, letter to Jo Sinclair, May 29, 1946, JSC, box 36, folder 14.

135. Joan Willis, letter to Jo Sinclair, June 4, 1946, JSC, box 36, folder 15.

136. Rabbi Leo A. Bergman, letter to Jo Sinclair, April 5, 1946, JSC, box 36, folder 14.

137. Chester Himes, letter to Jo Sinclair, December 21, 1945, JSC, box 36, folder 14.

138. Quoted in Margaret Walker, *Richard Wright, Daemonic Genius: A Portrait of the Man; A Critical Look at His Work* (New York: Warner Books, 1988), 131.

139. Walker, 88.

140. Chester Himes, *Cast the First Stone* (New York: Howard McCann, 1952).

141. Alice Candow, letter to Jo Sinclair, n.d., JSC, box 36, folder 15.

CHAPTER 6. "PLAYING THE QUEERS"

1. Federal Bureau of Investigation, file on Willard Motley, file no. 100–382070. All FBI comments about Motley in this chapter are from this file.

2. Federal Bureau of Investigation, file on H. T. Tsiang, file no. 100–32590.

3. Walter Rideout, *The Radical Novel in the United States: Some Interrelations of Literature and Society, 1900–1954* (New York: Columbia University Press, 1992; first published 1956 by Harvard University Press [Cambridge, MA]), 23.

4. Michael Gold, "Notes of the Month," *NM*, September 1930, 5.

5. "Author Motley's Cops Come to Life," *DW*, October 9, 1949.

6. Michael Gold, "Notes of the Month," *NM*, September 1930, 5.

7. Gayle Rubin, "Thinking Sex: Notes for a Radical Theory of the Politics of Sexuality," in *Culture, Society, and Sexuality*, ed. Peter Aggleton and Richard Parker (New York: Routledge, 2006), 143–78.

8. Max Eastman, *Artists in Uniform; A Study of Literature and Bureaucratism* (New York: Alfred A. Knopf, 1934), 24.

9. Walter Kalaidjian, *American Culture between the Wars: Revisionary Modernism and Postmodern Critique* (New York: Columbia University Press, 1993), 3.

10. Barbara Foley, *Radical Representations: Politics and Form in U.S. Proletarian Fiction, 1929–1941* (Durham, NC: Duke University Press, 1993), 396.

11. Willard Motley, "Desire Is Sad," WMOP, box 22, folder 31.

12. Judy Baston, "Good & Welfare," *Publisher's Weekly*, March 12, 1966.

13. Willard Motley, notes for unpublished story, n.d., WMOP, box 54, folder 24.

14. Alan M. Wald, *American Night: The Literary Left in the Era of the Cold War* (Chapel Hill: University of North Carolina Press, 2012), 210–12.

15. Rebecca M. Schreiber, *Cold War Exiles in Mexico: U.S. Dissidents and the Culture of Critical Resistance* (Minneapolis: University of Minnesota Press, 2008), 13.

16. Schreiber, 67.

17. Willard Motley, "I Discover I'm a Negro," 1940, WMOP, box 54, folder 18.

18. Willard Motley, unpublished notes, WMOP, box 27.

19. Willard Motley, diary, Thursday, September 11, WMOP, box 6, folder 9.

20. Willard Motley, unpublished notes, WMOP, box 55, folder 27.

21. Donald MacCampbell, letter to Willard Motley, June 19, 1944, WMOP, box 8, folder 3.

22. Willard Motley, "The Juvenile Delinquency Problem," n.d., WMOP, box 53, folder 1.

23. Willard Motley, "The Slums Have a Mission; A New Slant on the Slums," [1946?], WMOP, box 55, folder 29.

24. Willard Motley, unpublished notes, WMOP, box 53, folder 37.

25. Bill V. Mullen, *Popular Fronts: Chicago and African-American Cultural Politics, 1935–46* (Urbana: University of Illinois Press, 1999).

26. Willard Motley, "Leo Clayton, Waterboy Substitutes," n.d., WMOP, box 53, folder 27

27. Stacy I. Morgan, *Rethinking Social Realism: African American Art and Literature, 1930–1953* (Athens: University of Georgia Press, 2004), 256; Schreiber, *Cold War Exiles,* 141.

28. Willard Motley, "Boy Meets Boy," n.d., WMOP, box 53, folder 21.

29. Keith Huntress, letter to Willard Motley, 1940, WMOP, box 7, folder 11.

30. Letter to Willard Motley, n.d., WMOP, box 7, folder 11.

31. Willard Motley, "The Beautiful Boy," n.d., WMOP, box 22, folder 8.

32. Motley, "The Beautiful Boy." .

33. Willard Motley, "Biography of a Character," n.d., WMOP, box 53, folder 17.

34. Willard Motley, letter to Ted Purdy, December 11, 1946, WMOP, box 8, folder 12.

35. Ted Purdy, letter to Willard Motley, November 11, 1945, WMOP, box 8, folder 3.

36. Willard Motley, list of obscenities, n.d., WMOP, box 16, folder 40.

37. George P. Barrett, letter to Willard Motley, June 11, 1946, WMOP, box 8, folder 12.

38. Robert E. Fleming, *Willard Motley* (Boston: Twayne, 1978), 61.

39. Willard Motley, unpublished notes, WMOP, box 15, folder 20.

40. Christopher Isherwood, letter to Willard Motley, May 12, 1947, WMOP, box 9, folder 5. On Isherwood's relation to the Left, see Glyn Salton-Cox, *Queer Communism and the Ministry of Love: Sexual Revolution in British Writing of the 1930s* (Edinburgh: Edinburgh University Press, 2018), 44–76.

41. Willard Motley, *Knock on Any Door* (New York: Appleton-Century, 1947), 87.

42. On policing homosexuality in Chicago in the postwar period, see Timothy Stewart-Winter, *Queer Clout: Chicago and the Rise of Gay Politics* (Philadelphia: University of Pennsylvania Press, 2016), 14–40.

43. On liking as a queer affect, see Jonathan Flatley, *Like Andy Warhol* (Chicago: University of Chicago Press, 2017), 34–51.

44. Willard Motley, unpublished draft of "Knock on Any Door" ("Leave No Illusions"), 558, WMOP, box 15.

45. Willard Motley, homosexual dictionary, n.d., WMOP, box 67, folder 17.

46. Willard Motley, notes, WMOP, box 23, folder 47.

47. Willard Motley, notes, WMOP, box 23, folder 4.

48. Willard Motley, notes, WMOP, box 67, folder 20.

49. John C. Charles, *Abandoning the Black Hero: Sympathy and Privacy in the Postwar African American White-Life Novel* (New Brunswick, NJ: Rutgers University Press, 2013), 114.

50. H. T. Tsiang, letter to Rockwell Kent, January 1941, RKP. On Tsiang's detention, see Hua Hsu, *A Floating Chinaman: Fantasy and Failure across the Pacific* (Cambridge, MA: Harvard University Press, 2016), 159–62.

An earlier version of some material in this section appeared in Aaron S. Lecklider, "H. T. Tsiang's Proletarian Burlesque: Performance and Perversion in *The Hanging on Union Square*," *MELUS: Multi-Ethnic Literature of the U.S* 36, no. 4 (Winter 2011): 87–113.

51. For an excellent reading of the novel, see Hsu, 105–33.

52. Robert C. Allen, *Horrible Prettiness: Burlesque and American Culture* (Chapel Hill: University of North Carolina Press, 1991), 26. The term "low other" comes from Peter Stallybrass and Allon White, *The Politics and Poetics of Transgression* (Ithaca, NY: Cornell University Press, 1986), 5.

53. Lucinda Jarrett, *Stripping in Time: A History of Erotic Dancing* (New York: HarperCollins, 1997), 137.

54. Samuel Ornitz, *Haunch, Paunch, and Jowl* (London: Wishardt, 1929), 132–33.

55. For a representative sample of scholars' varying definitions of proletarian literature, see Michael Denning, *The Cultural Front: The Laboring of American Culture in the Twentieth Century* (New York: Verso, 1997); Foley, *Radical Representations;* and Alan M. Wald, *Exiles from a Future Time: The Forging of the Mid-Twentieth Century Literary Left* (Chapel Hill: University of North Carolina Press).

56. Michael Gold, *The Hollow Men* (New York: International Publishers, 1941), 26.

57. Jill Dolan, *Utopia in Performance: Finding Hope at the Theater* (Ann Arbor: University of Michigan Press, 2005), 2.

58. Ann Petry, *The Street* (Boston: Houghton Mifflin, 1946), 8. Heather J. Hicks discusses Petry's rejection of realism through her use of performance and refusal of surveillance in "Rethinking Realism in Ann Petry's 'The Street,'" *MELUS* 27, no. 4 (Winter 2002): 89–105.

59. Claude McKay, *Complete Poems,* edited with an introduction by William J. Maxwell (Urbana and Chicago: University of Illinois Press, 2004), 238–39.

60. Tsiang's work is discussed most comprehensively in Hsu, *A Floating Chinaman.* Floyd Cheung offers a brilliant reading of the novel in his afterword to the Penguin Modern Classics reprint of *The Hanging on Union Square* (New York: Penguin Press, 2019). See also Alan M. Wald, "Introduction to H. T. Tsiang's *The Hanging on Union Square,*" in *Into the Fire: Asian American Prose,* ed. Sylvia Watanabe and Carol Bruchac (New York: Greenfield Review Press, 1996), 341–58.

61. H. T. Tsiang to Rockwell Kent, January 7, 1941, RKP.

62. *New Yorker,* July 6, 1935, 10–11; Floyd Cheung, introduction to *And China Has Hands,* by H. T. Tsiang (New York: Robert Speller, 1937; repr., New

York: Ironweed Press, 2003), 7–15 (citation refers to the 2003 edition); H. T. Tsiang, *The Hanging on Union Square* (self-pub., New York, 1935), 223.

63. Hsu, *A Floating Chinaman*, 205.

64. Stein's particular interest in framing her modernism as deviant sexual practice is discussed in Michael Trask, *Cruising Modernism: Class and Sexuality in American Literature and Social Thought* (Ithaca, NY: Cornell University Press, 2003), 74–107.

65. Tsiang, *And China Has Hands*, 35.

66. See Michael Denning, *Mechanic Accents: Dime Novels and Working-Class Culture in America* (New York: Verso, 1987).

67. Richard J. Walsh, letter to Rockwell Kent, October 20, 1941, RKP.

68. *The Hanging on Union Square* was made into a performance starring Tsiang, and he followed this with his one-man performance of Shakespeare, *Hamlet-ly Yours*. Katherine von Blon, "'Hanging on Union Square' Presented by H. T. Tsiang," *Los Angeles Times,* September 6, 1948. He continued to perform *The Hanging on Union Square* at least through 1950. Louis Calta, "Play by Manoff Closing Tonight," *New York Times,* February 11, 1950.

69. Tsiang, *The Hanging on Union Square*, 7.

70. Tsiang, 157.

71. I am following José Esteban Muñoz's definition of disidentification as a process that "scrambles and reconstructs the encoded messages of a cultural text in a fashion that both exposes the encoded message's universalizing and exclusionary machinations and recircuits its working to account for, include, and empower minority identities and identifications." José Esteban Muñoz, *Disidentifications: Queers of Color and the Performance of Politics* (Minneapolis: University of Minnesota Press, 1999), 31.

72. Waldo Frank, foreword to *The Hanging on Union Square*, 9.

73. Tsiang, *The Hanging on Union Square*, 7.

74. Nut both is and is not a Communist until he performs a public act of radicalism. In this respect, Nut's identity as a Communist parallel's the act of coming out described in Eve Kosofsky Sedgwick, *Epistemology of the Closet* (Berkeley: University of California Press, 1990).

75. This usage that was associated with working-class camaraderie and low culture on Union Square in texts ranging from Horatio Alger's bowery bums in *Raggedy Dick* to the 1931 reform publication *Commercialized Prostitution in New York City* ("she was 'lined up' about a year ago by a gang that 'hangs out' in a cigar store on East 14th Street"). George Jackson Kneeland, *Commercialized Prostitution in New York* (New York: Century Co., 1913), 65.

76. The Jewish gangster was also a convenient stand-in for radical modernist writers during the Depression. Rachel Rubin, *Jewish Gangsters of Modern Literature* (Urbana and Chicago: University of Illinois Press, 2000).

77. George Chauncey, *Gay New York: The Making of the Gay Male World, 1890–1940* (New York: Basic Books, 1994), 141–42, 185, 189, 190.

78. See Michael Sherry, *Gay Artists in Modern America: An Imagined Conspiracy* (Chapel Hill: University of North Carolina Press, 2007).

79. Kate Baldwin, *Beyond the Color Line and the Iron Curtain: Reading Encounters between Black and Red, 1922–1963* (Durham, NC: Duke University Press, 2002).

80. Tsiang's allusion is to Max Eastman, *Artists in Uniform.*

81. The audience for this performance comprises several pets: a bird, who "was inspired by the rhythm"; a bulldog, who "watched jealously"; and a cat, who "was suspicious" (145–46).

82. See Robert G. Lee, *Orientals: Asian Americans in Popular Culture* (Philadelphia: Temple University Press, 1999); and Krystyn R. Moon, *Yellowface: Creating the Chinese in American Popular Music and Performance, 1850s–1920s* (New Brunswick, NJ: Rutgers University Press, 2005).

CHAPTER 7. "WE WHO ARE NOT ILL"

1. George Orwell, *Homage to Catalonia* (London: Secker and Warburg, 1938), 1.

2. Orwell, 2.

3. Granville Hicks, *Where We Came Out* (New York: Viking, 1954), 43.

4. Orwell, *Homage to Catalonia*, 5.

5. Orwell, 21.

6. Stanley Burnshaw, review of *Those Who Perish*, *NM*, September 11, 1934, 26.

7. Edward Dahlberg, "Ajax's Sheep," *New York Review of Books*, October 12, 1967.

8. John Chamberlain, blurb on the back cover of *Those Who Perish*, by Edward Dahlberg, (New York: John Day, 1934). Dahlberg was probably more conflicted about homosexuality than *Those Who Perish* suggests: Andrew Delblanco has noted that he "accused Melville in 1960" of "'sodomy of the heart' and dismissed *Moby-Dick* as a book for 'hermaphrodites and spados.'" Andrew Delblanco, *Melville: His World and Work* (New York: Knopf, 2005), 363.

9. Charles DeFanti, *The Wages of Expectation: A Biography of Edward Dahlberg* (New York: New York University Press, 1978), 111.

10. Matthew Baigell and Julia Williams, eds., *Artists against War and Fascism: Papers of the First American Artists' Congress* (New Brunswick, NJ: Rutgers University Press, 1986), 9.

11. "The War Mongers," *Chicago Daily Tribune*, September 21, 1938.

12. Michael Denning, *The Cultural Front: The Laboring of American Culture in the Twentieth Century* (New York: Verso, 1997), 9.

13. "Hitler Commands Nazi Abstinences," *New York Times*, July 1, 1934, 1.

14. Paragraph 175 translated in Florence Tamagne, *A History of Homosexuality in Europe, Berlin, London, Paris 1919–1939*, 2 vols. (New York: Algora Publishing, 2004), 2: 285.

15. Robert Beachy, *Gay Berlin: Birthplace of a Modern Identity* (New York: Knopf, 2014), 98; Chris Vials, *Haunted by Hitler: Liberals, the Left, and the Fight against Fascism in the United States* (Amherst: University of Massachusetts Press, 2015), 204.

16. Beachy, *Gay Berlin,* 157.

17. Kurt Hiller, "Appeal to the Second International Congress for Sexual Reform on Behalf of an Oppressed Human Variety," trans. John Lauritsen, reprinted in John Lauritsen and David Thorstad, *The Early Homosexual Rights Movement (1864–1935),* rev. ed. (Ojai, CA: Times Change Press, 1995), 107.

18. Ruth McKenney, "Big Themes in the Theater," *NM,* November 15, 1938, 28.

19. Edward Dahlberg, "Hitler's Power over Germany: The Nazi Strength Analyzed," *New York Times,* April 9, 1933.

20. Edward Dahlberg, *Those Who Perish* (New York: John Day, 1934), 11, 208.

21. Dahlberg, 22, 86, 105, 23.

22. Dahlberg, 187. Ellipsis in original.

23. Harry Hay, "Little Jew Boy," Harry Hay Papers, James C. Hormel LGBTQIA Center, San Francisco Public Library, box 5, folder 14.

24. Judith E. Smith, *Visions of Belonging: Family Stories, Popular Culture, and Postwar Democracy, 1940–1960* (New York: Columbia University Press, 2004), 145.

25. Richard Brooks, *The Brick Foxhole* (New York: Harper, 1945).

26. Daniel K. Douglass, *Tough as Nails: The Life and Films of Richard Brooks* (Madison: University of Wisconsin Press, 2011), 32.

27. Brooks, *The Brick Foxhole,* 89.

28. Brooks, 93.

29. Vials, *Haunted by Hitler,* 210–14. For more information about this topic, see Richard Plant, *The Pink Triangle: The Nazi War Against Homosexuals* (New York: Henry Holt, 1986).

30. Quoted in Smith, *Visions of Belonging,* 149.

31. Richard Wright, "A Noncombat Soldier Strips Words for Action," *PM,* June 24, 1945.

32. Heather Love offers an important reading of Townsend Warner's queer and Left politics in *Feeling Backward: Loss and the Politics of Queer History* (Cambridge, MA: Harvard University Press, 2009), 129–45; as does Glyn Salton-Cox, *Queer Communism and the Ministry of Love: Sexual Revolution in British Writing of the 1930s* (Edinburgh: Edinburgh University Press, 2018), 77–112. For biographical coverage, see Peter Haring Judd, *The Akeing Heart: Letters between Sylvia Townsend Warner, Valentine Ackland and Elizabeth Wade White* (Bath, UK: Handheld Press, 2018); and Wendy Mulford, *This Narrow Place: Sylvia Townsend Warner and Valentine Ackland; Life, Letter and Politics, 1930–1951* (London: Pandora Press, 1998).

33. Quoted in Salton-Cox, *Queer Communism,* 94.

34. Valentine Ackland, "Teaching to Shoot," *New Yorker,* February 27, 1943, 24.

35. John Malcom Brinnin, *The Garden Is Political* (New York: Macmillan, 1942), 41.

36. Albert Fried, ed., *Communism in America: A History in Documents* (New York: Columbia University Press, 1997), 247, 248, 249.

37. Fried, 110.

38. Alan M. Wald offers biographical information on Dana in *American Night: The Literary Left in the Era of the Cold War* (Chapel Hill: University of North Carolina Press, 2012), 134–39.

39. Fried, *Communism in America,* 288, 276, 277, 279, 280, 281.

40. Fried, 253, 251, 253.

41. Quoted in Arthur J. Sabin, *Red Scare in the Court: New York versus the International Workers Order* (Philadelphia: University of Pennsylvania Press, 1993), 152. Michael Denning disputes the emphasis upon patriotism in many scholarly accounts of the Popular Front, arguing that "it is a mistake to see it simply as a 'politics of patriotism'" and suggesting instead that the "figure of 'America' became a locus for ideological battles over the trajectory of US history, the meaning of race, ethnicity, and region in the United States, and the relation between ethnic nationalism, Americanism, and internationalism." Denning, *The Cultural Front,* 129.

42. Andrew Hemingway, *Artists on the Left: American Artists and the Communist Movement, 1926–1956* (New Haven, CT: Yale University Press, 2002), 103.

43. James T. Farrell, letter to Rt. Hon. W. L. Mackenzie King, May 29, 1944, James T. Farrell Papers 1930–1948, Special Collections Research Center, University of Chicago Library, box 1, folder 3.

44. Denning, *The Cultural Front,* 116; Robert Warshow, "The Legacy of the 1930s: Middle-Class Mass Culture and the Intellectuals' Problem," *Commentary* (December 1947), 538.

45. Willard Motley, notes for speech, WMOP, box 23, folder 16.

46. Robert K. Martin, "Newton Arvin: Literary Critic and Lewd Person," *American Literary History* 16, no. 4 (Summer 2004): 296.

47. Quoted in Denning, *The Cultural Front,* 204.

48. Quoted in Barry Werth, *The Scarlet Professor: Newton Arvin, a Literary Life Shattered by Scandal* (New York: Nan A. Talese, 2001), 55–56.

49. Quoted in Fried, *Communism in America,* 284.

50. Quoted in Denning, *The Cultural Front,* 187.

51. Michael Gold, "Towards Proletarian Art," *The Liberator,* February 1921, 67.

52. Christopher Irmscher, *Max Eastman: A Life* (New Haven, CT: Yale University Press, 2017); Max Eastman, *Artists in Uniform; A Study of Literature and Bureaucratism* (New York: Alfred A. Knopf, 1934).

53. Max Eastman, "Menshevizing Walt Whitman," *NM,* December 1926, 12.

54. Newton Arvin, *Whitman* (New York: Macmillan, 1938), 2, 290, 289–90.

55. Floyd Dell, "Walt Whitman as an Anti-Socialist," *New Review,* June 15, 1915; V. F. Calverton, *The Liberation of American Literature* (New York: Scribner's, 1932), 296.

56. Arvin, *Whitman,* 71.

57. Arvin, 71, 35.

58. Frank O'Hara, *Standing Still and Walking in New York* (Bolinas, CA: Grey Stone Press, 1975), 31. On Frank O'Hara's relationship to the Spanish Civil War, see Jonathan Mayhew, *Apocryphal Lorca: Translation, Parody, Kitsch* (Chicago: University of Chicago Press, 2009), 124.

59. Aldon Lynn Nielsen, *Black Chant: Languages of African American Post-modernism* (New York: Cambridge University Press, 1997), 52.

60. Langston Hughes, ed. *New Negro Poets, U.S.A.* (Bloomington: Indiana University Press, 1964).

61. Frank O'Hara, "Failure of Spring," *Collected Poems,* ed. Donald Allen (New York: Knopf, 1971), 274.

62. On gay male appropriation of Federico García Lorca generally, see Mayhew, *Apocryphal Lorca,* 41–46.

63. Robert Duncan, "The Homosexual in Society," *Politics,* August 1944, 209–11; Robert Duncan, *Caesar's Gate: Poems 1949–1950* (Berkeley: Sand Dollar, 1972), xix.

64. Alan Ginsberg *Howl and Other Poems* (San Francisco: City Lights, 1957); Allen Ginsberg, "Death to Van Gogh's Ear!," *Collected Poems: 1947–1997* (New York: HarperCollins, 2006), 175.

65. Oscar Hunter, "700 Calendar Days," in *The Heart of Spain,* ed. Alvah Bessie (New York: Veterans of the Abraham Lincoln Brigade, 1952). See also Robin D. G. Kelley, "This Ain't Ethiopia, but It'll Do," in *African Americans in the Spanish Civil War,* ed. Danny Duncan Collum (New York: G.K. Hall, 1992), 5–57.

66. See Lisa A. Kirschenbaum, *International Communism and the Spanish Civil War: Solidarity and Suspicion* (Cambridge: Cambridge University Press, 2015), 151–79.

67. William Aalto, questionnaire [1942?], John Dollard Research Files for Fear and Courage under Battle Conditions, TLW, box 1, folder 16.

68. Quoted in George Henry, *Sex Variants: A Study of Homosexual Patterns* (New York: Paul B. Hoeber, 1941; repr., 1948), 27 (citation refers to the 1948 edition). For a discussion of this study, see Henry L. Minton, *Departing from Deviance: A History of Homosexual Rights and Emancipatory Science in America* (Chicago: University of Chicago Press, 2001), 58–93.

69. Quoted in Henry, *Sex Variants,* 28.

70. Cary Nelson and Jefferson Hendricks, eds., *Madrid 1937: Letters of the Abraham Lincoln Brigade from the Spanish Civil War* (New York: Routledge, 1996), 146.

71. Vincent Lossowski, interview transcript, John Gerassi Oral History Papers, TLW, box 4, folder 7.

72. Federal Bureau of Investigation, file on David McKelvy White, file no. 100–19129. All FBI comments about White in this chapter are from this file.

73. Hugh Ryan, *When Brooklyn Was Queer: A History* (New York: St. Martin's Press, 2019), 174–75.

74. Milt Felsen, *The Anti-Warrior: A Memoir* (Iowa City: University of Iowa Press, 1989), 55.

75. Felsen, 61.

76. David Gillis Kelly file, ALBVF, box 4, folder 100; Jack Mail file, ALBVF, box 5, folder 92.

77. James Foss, "A Hero on the Left," 17, unpublished manuscript, n.d., ALBVF, box 1, folder 2.

78. William Aalto files, ALBVF, box 1, folder 1.

79. Foss, "A Hero on the Left," 16.

80. Foss, 17.

81. William Aalto, questionnaire, n.d., John Dollard Research Files for Fear and Courage under Battle Conditions, TLW, box, 1 folder 16.

82. James Schuyler, *The Morning of the Poem* (New York: Farrar, Straus and Giroux, 1980), 36.

83. *DW*, January 12, 1937; Richard Davenport-Hines, *Auden* (New York: Pantheon, 1995), 164, 166, 167.

84. W. H. Auden, "Spain," *Spain* (London: Faber & Faber, 1937), 7.

85. William Aalto, letter to Irving Goff, March 8, 1942, Veterans of the Abraham Lincoln Brigade: Complaints of Discrimination during World War II, TLW, box 1, folder 4.

86. Peter N. Carroll, *The Odyssey of the Abraham Lincoln Brigade: Americans in the Spanish Civil War* (Stanford, CA: Stanford University Press, 1994), 256. Carroll also writes that Aalto was expelled from the Communist Party for his homosexuality (257).

87. Milton Felsen, interview transcript, John Gerassi Oral History Papers, TLW, box 2, folder 6.

88. Vincent Lossowski, letter to the editor, *Shmate: A Journal of Progressive Jewish Thought* 2, no. 7 (1983): 5.

89. Foss, "A Hero on the Left," 21.

90. Foss, "A Hero on the Left," 22.

91. Schuyler, *The Morning of the Poem*, 36–38.

92. William Aalto, letter to James Foss, January 1, 1958, TLW, box 1, folder 1.

93. Vincent Lossowski, interview transcript, John Gerassi Oral History Papers, TLW, box 4, folder 7.

CHAPTER 8. "THE SECRET ELEMENT OF THEIR VICE"

The three quotations that make up the epigraph are from, respectively, Morris L. Ernst and David Loth, *Report on the American Communist* (New York: Holt, 1952), 180; "More Confusion over McCarthy Case," *New York Times,* April 30, 1950; and Herbert Philbrick, *I Led 3 Lives: Citizen, "Communist," Counterspy* (New York: McGraw-Hill, 1952).

1. R. G. Waldeck, "Homosexual International," *Human Events,* September 29, 1960, 453.

2. Waldeck, 454, 454–55, 455.

3. Waldeck, 455.

4. Waldeck, 455. Waldeck's reference to a "Homosexual International" gestures toward the ironic neologism "homintern" that had appeared the early 1940s—a play on the Comintern (the term itself a shortening of "Communist International"). Though the homintern indexed a coterie of powerful artists and cultural influencers irrespective of their ideological orientation, the term's pithy reference to leftist history further suggests the melding of queer and the Left during the Cold War. See Gregory Woods, *Homintern: How Gay Culture Liberated the Modern World* (New Haven, CT: Yale University Press, 2016), 6.

5. "Another Sort of Wind," *ONE Confidential,* October 1960, 4.

6. Jim Kepner, letter to Wally Jordan, May 3, 1943, JNK, Research Notes and Papers—Kepner, James.

7. Daniel Hurewitz, *Bohemian Los Angeles: The Making of Modern Politics* (Berkeley: University of California Press, 2012).

8. "To the Friends of ONE," *ONE Confidential,* July 1959, 1.

9. K. A. Cuordileone, *Manhood and American Political Culture in the Cold War* (New York: Routledge, 2005), 64; Robert Dean, *Imperial Brotherhood: Gender and the Making of Cold War Foreign Policy* (Amherst: University of Massachusetts Press, 2001), 63–145.

10. David K. Johnson, *The Lavender Scare: The Cold War Persecution of Gays and Lesbians in the Federal Government* (Chicago: University of Chicago Press, 2004), 31.

11. For a discussion of this case, see Johnson, 144–46.

12. Quoted in Johnson, 145.

13. Editorial, *ONE Magazine,* October 1960, 4–5.

14. Dr. G. in North Hollywood, CA, letter to the editor, *ONE Magazine,* February 1961, p. 31.

15. While I primarily focus on the US homophile movement here, important work looking at transnational dimensions of the homophile movement is found in David S. Churchill, "Transnationalism and Homophile Political Culture in the Postwar Decades," *GLQ: A Journal of Lesbian and Gay Studies* 15 (2009): 31–66; Víctor M. Macías-González, "The Transnational Homophile Movement and the Development of Domesticity in Mexico City's Homosexual Community, 1930–1970," *Gender & History* 26, no. 3 (November 2014): 519–44; and Leila J. Rupp, "The Persistence of Transnational Organizing: The Case of the Homophile Movement," *American Historical Review* 116 (2011): 1014–39.

16. Harry Hay Papers, Special Collections, San Francisco Public Library, box 7, folder 50.

17. Michael Denning, *The Cultural Front: The Laboring of American Culture in the Twentieth Century* (New York: Verso, 1997), 7; Chris Vials, *Haunted by Hitler: Liberals, the Left, and the Fight against Fascism in the United States* (Amherst: University of Massachusetts Press, 2015), 203–15.

18. Jeff Winters, review of *Sexual Politics, Sexual Communities: The Making of a Homosexual Minority in the United States, 1940–1970,* by John D'Emilio, *ONE Letter,* March 1985, 2–3.

19. Other scholars have explored Hay's writings and concluded that he aligned more with Third Period Communism. For that perspective, see Stuart Timmons, *The Trouble with Harry Hay: Founder of the Modern Gay Movement* (Boston: Alyson, 1990); and Bettina Aptheker, "Queer Dialectics/Feminist Interventions: Harry Hay & the Quest for a Revolutionary Politics," *English Language Notes* 53, no. 1 (Spring/Summer 2015): 11–22.

20. Harry Johnson, "And a Red Too . . . ," *ONE Magazine,* September 1953, 3.

21. "Mattachine Society Missions and Purposes," adopted July 1951, Harry Hay Papers, San Francisco History Center, San Francisco Public Library, box 2, folder 8.

22. Christine B. Hanhardt discusses this idea extensively in *Safe Space: Gay Neighborhood History and the Politics of Violence* (Durham, NC: Duke University Press, 2013).

23. John D'Emilio, *Sexual Politics, Sexual Communities: The Making of a Homosexual Minority in the United States, 1940–1970* (Chicago: University of Chicago Press, 1983), 88; Martha E. Stone, "Unearthing the 'Knights of the Clock,'" *Gay & Lesbian Review Worldwide,* May/June 2010, 18–19.

24. W. Dorr Legg, "The Movement: How It Began," *ONE Letter,* September 1974, 2.

25. "Mattachine Society Missions and Purposes."

26. Kenneth Burke, "Revolutionary Symbolism in America," in *American Writers' Congress,* ed. Henry Hart (New York: International Publishers, 1935), 89.

27. Denning, *The Cultural Front,* 124.

28. On the history of the Civil Rights Congress, see Gerald Horne, *Communist Front? The Civil Rights Congress, 1946–1956* (Madison, NJ: Farleigh Dickinson University Press, 1988); Josh Sides, "'You Understand My Condition': The Civil Rights Congress in the Los Angeles African American Community, 1946–1952," *Pacific Historical Review* 67, no. 2 (May 1998): 233–57.

29. Emily Hobson, "Policing Gay LA: Mapping Racial Divides in the Homophile Era, 1950–1967," in *The Rising Tide of Color: Race, State Violence, and Radical Movements across the Pacific,* ed. Moon-Ho Jung (Seattle: University of Washington Press, 2014), 188.

30. Hurewitz, *Bohemian Los Angeles,* 232–33; Hobson, "Policing Gay LA," 189.

31. Quoted in Hurewitz, *Bohemian Los Angeles,* 260.

32. Earl Browder, "Who Are the Americans?," in *Communism in America: A History in Documents,* ed. Albert Fried (New York: Columbia University Press, 1997), 251.

33. Hobson, "Policing Gay LA," 190.

34. Elizabeth Lalo, "Must I Answer That Cop?" *ONE Magazine,* October 1953, 3.

35. Mattachine's New York chapter organized a smaller picket outside the United Nations building on Dag Hammarskjold Plaza the following day. The tenor of this protest was consistent with that of the picket in Washington.

36. For details on this protest, see Johnson, *The Lavender Scare,* 199–202.

37. Siobhan B. Somerville, "Sexual Aliens and the Racialized State: A Queer Reading of the 1952 U.S. Immigration and Nationality Act," in *Queer Migrations: Sexuality, U.S. Citizenship, and Border Crossings,* ed. Eithne Luibhéide and Lionel Cantú Jr (Minneapolis: University of Minnesota Press, 2002), 76.

38. Quoted in Margot Canaday, *The Straight State: Sexuality and Citizenship in Twentieth-Century America* (Princeton, NJ: Princeton University Press, 2009), 220.

39. *United States Statutes at Large,* 1952, vol. 66, 82nd Cong., 163–282.

40. Elizabeth Lalo, "Must I Answer That Cop?," *ONE Magazine,* October 1953, 3–6, 3.

41. Stacy Braukman, *Communists and Perverts under the Palms: The Johns Committee in Florida, 1956–1965* (Gainesville: University Press of Florida, 2012).

42. James Whitman, "The Answer to Homosexuality," *ONE Magazine,* July 1953, 14–17, 17.

43. Edwin F. Dakin, letters (1954/1962), ONE National Gay and Lesbian Archives, box 22, folder 127, item 1.

44. Johnson, "And a Red Too . . . ," 2.

45. Aptheker, "Queer Dialectics/Feminist Interventions," 20–21.

46. Elizabeth Lalo, "Must I Answer That Cop?," *ONE Magazine,* October 1953, 3.

47. Johnson, "And a Red Too . . . ," 2–3.

48. "Are You Now or Have You Ever Been a Homosexual," *ONE Magazine,* April 1953, 6.

49. D'Emilio, *Sexual Politics,* 75–91.

50. Quoted in Eric Marcus, *Making History: The Struggle for Gay and Lesbian Equal Rights, 1945–1990; An Oral History* (New York: HarperCollins, 1993), 63

51. Quoted in Marcus, 62.

52. Quoted in Marcus, 62.

53. Harry Hay, letter to Jonathan Ned Katz, March 22, 1974, Jonathan Ned Katz Papers, Correspondence, Manuscripts and Archives Division, New York Public Library.

54. Quoted in Marcus, *Making History,* 36.

55. Harry Hay, "To the Memory of Robert Hull," *ONE,* December 1962, 24.

56. Rebecca M. Schreiber, *Cold War Exiles in Mexico: U.S. Dissidents and the Culture of Critical Resistance* (Minneapolis: University of Minnesota Press, 2008); John Virtue, *Leonard and Reva Brooks: Artists in Exile in San Miguel de Allende* (Montreal and Kingston: McGill-Queen's University Press, 2001), 158.

57. Ellen Kay Trimberger, "Women in the Old and New Left: The Evolution of a Politics of Personal Life," *Feminist Studies* 5, no. 3 (Autumn 1979): 438.

58. Junius Scales, *Cause at Heart: A Former Communist Remembers* (Athens: University of Georgia Press, 1987), 223.

59. Quoted in Marcus, *Making History,* 28.

60. Alan M. Wald, *American Night: The Literary Left in the Era of the Cold War* (Chapel Hill: University of North Carolina Press, 2012), 119. The shared performances of queerness and Communism are discussed in relation to passing in Tony Perucci, "The Red Mask of Sanity: Paul Robeson, HUAC, and the Sound of Cold War Performance," *TDR: The Drama Review* 53, no. 4 (Winter 2009): 18–48.

61. Wald, *American Night,* 120.

62. Wald, 121.

63. Quoted in Wald, 119.

64. Leslie Fiedler, "The Un-Angry Young Men," in *The Collected Essays of Leslie Fiedler,* 2 vols. (New York: Stein and Day, 1971), 1:405.

65. H. L. Small [Christopher Phelps], "On Socialism and Sex: An Introduction," *New Politics* 12, no. 1 (Summer 2008): 12–17, 19–21.

66. Small, 21.

67. Christopher Phelps, "A Neglected Document on Socialism and Sex," *Journal of the History of Sexuality* 16, no. 1 (January 2007): 1–13.

68. Quoted in Phelps, 9.

69. Alan M. Wald, "Sexual Bohemians in Cold War America: A Minority within a Minority," in *Red Love across the Pacific: Political and Sexual Revolutions of the Twentieth Century,* ed. Paula Rabinowitz, Ruth Barraclough, and Heather Bowen-Struyk (New York: Palgrave, 2015), 102, 103.

70. Martha Biondi, *To Stand and Fight: The Struggle for Civil Rights in Postwar New York City* (Cambridge, MA: Harvard University Press, 2003), 6.

71. John D'Emilio, *Lost Prophet: The Life and Times of Bayard Rustin* (New York: Free Press, 2003).

72. Mary L. Dudziak, *Cold War Civil Rights: Race and the Image of American Democracy* (Princeton, NJ: Princeton University Press, 2002).

73. Mary Helen Washington, *The Other Blacklist: The African American Literary and Cultural Left of the 1950s* (New York: Columbia University Press, 2014), 15.

74. Dayo F. Gore, *Radicalism at the Crossroads: African American Women Activists in the Cold War* (New York: New York University Press, 2011), 3, 5. An important discussion on Black women and Communism is also to be found in Erik S. McDuffie, *Sojourning for Freedom: Black Women, American Communism, and the Making of Black Left Feminism* (Durham, NC: Duke University Press, 2011).

75. Biondi, *To Stand and Fight,* 6; Imani Perry, *Looking for Lorraine: The Radiant and Radical Life of Lorraine Hansberry* (Boston: Beacon Press, 2018), 78–96.

76. Douglas Field, "James Baldwin's Life on the Left: A Portrait of the Artist as a Young New York Intellectual," *ELH* 78, no. 4 (2011): 833–62; James Baldwin, *No Name in the Street* (New York: Laurel, 1972), 29; Wald, *American Night,* 131–33; Bill V. Mullen, *James Baldwin: Living in Fire* (London: Pluto Press, 2019).

77. Baldwin, *No Name in the Street,* 29.

78. James Baldwin, *The Price of the Ticket: Collected Nonfiction, 1948–1985* (New York: St. Martin's Press, 1985), xiii.

79. Baldwin, xii.

80. Baldwin, *No Name in the Street,* 29, 33.

81. Stan Weir, "Meetings with James Baldwin," *Against the Current,* no. 18 (January/February1989): 36.

82. On Baldwin and the "homosexualization of the left," see Robert J. Corber, *Homosexuality in Cold War America: Resistance and the Crisis of Masculinity* (Durham, NC: Duke University Press, 1997), 160–90.

83. "Lorraine Hansberry: Letters to 'The Ladder,'" June 4, 2018, *Illinois History and Lincoln Collections* (blog), https://publish.illinois.edu/ihlc-blog/2018/06/04/lorraine-hansberry-letters-to-the-ladder/.

84. "Lorraine Hansberry: Letters to "The Ladder."

85. Perry, *Looking for Lorraine,* 95.

86. Perry, 56–57, 83–84.

87. Cheryl Higashida, *Black Internationalist Feminism: Women Writers of the Black Left, 1945-1995* (Urbana and Chicago: University of Illinois Press, 2011), 58.

88. Hansberry's letters are discussed in Lisbeth Lipari, "The Rhetoric of Intersectionality: Lorraine Hansberry's 1957 Letters to the *Ladder*," in *Queering Public Address: Sexualities in American Historical Discourse*, ed. Charles E. Morris (Columbia: University of South Carolina Press, 2007), 220–48; and in Perry, *Looking for Lorraine*, 80–81.

89. L.H.N., *The Ladder*, May 1957, 26.

90. L.N., *The Ladder*, August 1957, 26.

91. Alan M. Wald, introduction to *Iron City*, by Lloyd L. Brown (Boston: Northeastern University Press,1994), viii, xvi–xvii. Extensive discussion of Lloyd L. Brown's career appears in Washington, *The Other Blacklist*, 33–68.

92. Federal Bureau of Investigation, file on Lloyd Brown, file no. 100–24615.

93. Quoted in Washington, *The Other Blacklist*, 35.

94. Regina Kunzel, *Criminal Intimacy: Prison and the Uneven History of Modern American Sexuality* (Chicago: University of Chicago Press, 2008).

95. Lloyd L. Brown, *Iron City* (New York: Masses and Mainstream, 1951), 31–32.

96. Granville Hicks, *Where We Came Out* (New York: Viking, 1954), 42, 42–43.

97. Benjamin Gitlow, *I Confess: The Truth about American Communism* (New York: E.P. Dutton, 1940), 315.

98. Gitlow, 317.

99. Gitlow, 316.

100. For a broader conversation on youth and sexuality during the Cold War, see Leerom Medovoi, *Rebels: Youth and the Cold War Origins of Identity* (Durham, NC: Duke University Press, 2005).

101. Eugene Lyons, *The Red Decade: The Stalinist Penetration of America* (Indianapolis, NY: Bobbs-Merrill, 1941), 215. These comments also appeared in the *Sixth Report, Un-American Activities in California, 1951: Report of the Senate Fact-Finding Committee on Un-American Activities to the Regular California Legislature* (Sacramento, 1951), 9.

102. Philbrick, *I Led 3 Lives*, 83, 192.

103. Philbrick, 165.

104. Philbrick, 122–23, 209, 124, 224.

105. Philbrick, 237.

106. On the relationship between normativity and anti-Communism, see Elaine Tyler May, *Homeward Bound: American Families in the Cold War Era* (New York: Basic Books, 1988).

107. John Gates, *The Story of an American Communist* (New York: Thomas Nelson, 1958), 126.

108. H.H. Lewis, "Thinking of Russia," in *Thinking of Russia* (Holt, MN: B.C. Hagglund, 1932), 1.

109. Fiedler, "The Un-Angry Young Men," 1:405, 406.

110. Ann Petry, *The Narrows* (Cambridge, MA: Riverside Press, 1953), 50.

111. Arthur Guy Mathews, "Homosexuality Is Stalin's Atom Bomb to Destroy America," *Physical Culture*, April 1953, 13.

112. Quoted in Johnson, *The Lavender Scare*, 145.

113. Quoted in Michael Sherry, *Gay Artists in Modern America: An Imagined Conspiracy* (Chapel Hill: University of North Carolina Press, 2007), 29.

114. E.L.K., "USA Confidential," *Cornell Daily Sun*, April 3, 1952, 4.

115. Jack Lait and Lee Mortimer, *USA Confidential* (New York: Crown, 1952), 52, 44, 51.

116. "The Senator and the Purge," *New York Post*, July 17, 1950.

117. An excellent discussion of *The Vital Center* in relation to masculinity is found in Cuordileone, *Manhood and American Political Culture*, 17–35. See also Robert J. Corber, *In the Name of National Security: Hitchcock, Homophobia, and the Political Construction of Gender in Postwar America* (Durham, NC: Duke University Press, 1993), 19–26.

118. Arthur M. Schlesinger Jr., *The Vital Center: The Politics of Freedom* (Boston: Houghton Mifflin, 1949), 151, 26, 104.

119. Philbrick, *I Led 3 Lives*, 111–12.

120. *Hearings before a Subcommittee of the Committee on Foreign Relations United States Senate Pursuant to S. Res. 231 A Resolution to Investigate whether the Employees in the State Department Disloyal to the United States*, 81st Cong., 2nd sess. (1950), 3.

121. Morris L. Ernst and David Loth, *Report on the American Communist* (New York: Holt, 1952), 1, 127.

122. Ernst and Loth, 162, 164, 165.

123. Ernst and Loth, 163, 164.

124. Ernst and Loth, 165.

125. Whittaker Chambers, *Witness* (New York: Random House, 1952), 3.

126. Chambers, 5.

127. On homosexuality in the Chambers case, see especially Cuordileone, *Manhood and American Political Culture*, 40–45.

128. Chambers, *Witness*, 797.

129. Chambers, 799.

130. Nikita Khrushchev's 1956 "Secret Speech," in which he revealed definitively the extent of Stalin's crimes against the Soviet people, precipitated a wave of disillusionment among committed leftists who, prior to the revelations, had been suspicious of such claims, often dismissing them as red-scare tactics. Grappling with this history pushed many members to leave the Communist Party, and it animated broad characterizations within mainstream American culture of Communists as either lost souls who were easily misled or adherents of murderous regimes.

131. Michel Foucault, *The History of Sexuality*, vol. 1, *An Introduction*, trans. Robert Hurley (New York: Pantheon, 1978; first published 1976 by Gallimard [Paris]), 59, 62.

132. Gates, *The Story of an American Communist*, 6.

133. Quoted in Sam Tanenhaus, *Whittaker Chambers: A Biography* (New York: Random House, 1997), 343.

134. Tanenhaus, 344–45.

135. Julia Brown, *I Testify: My Years as an Undercover Agent for the FBI* (Boston: Western Islands, 1966); Bertram D. Wolfe, *Strange Communists I Have Known* (New York: Stein and Day, 1965).

136. Max Eastman, introduction to *I Confess: The Truth about American Communism,* by Benjamin Gitlow (New York: E. P. Dutton, 1940), v.

137. Irving Howe, "New York in the Thirties: Some Fragments of Memory," *Dissent* 8, no. 3 (Summer 1961): 241–42.

138. Max Eastman, *Love and Revolution: My Journey through an Epoch* (New York: Random House, 1964), 12.

139. Alfred Kazin, *Starting Out in the Thirties* (Boston: Little, Brown, 1965), 7–8.

140. Allen Ginsberg, "America," in Allen Ginsberg, *Collected Poems 1947–1997* (New York: HarperCollins, 2006), 154–56.

141. Ginsberg, 154. From "America" in Collected Poems 1947–1997 by Allen Ginsberg. Copyright © 2006 by the Allen Ginsberg Trust. Used by permission of HarperCollins Publishers. "America" by Allen Ginsberg. Copyright © 2006 by Allen Ginsberg, used by permission of The Wylie Agency LLC.

142. Ginsberg, 156.

143. Ginsberg, 154.

144. Ginsberg, 155.

145. Harry Hay, letter to Jonathan Ned Katz, February 20, 1974, Jonathan Ned Katz Papers, Manuscripts and Archives Division, New York Public Library.

Index

Founded in 1893,
UNIVERSITY OF CALIFORNIA PRESS
publishes bold, progressive books and journals
on topics in the arts, humanities, social sciences,
and natural sciences—with a focus on social
justice issues—that inspire thought and action
among readers worldwide.

The UC PRESS FOUNDATION
raises funds to uphold the press's vital role
as an independent, nonprofit publisher, and
receives philanthropic support from a wide
range of individuals and institutions—and from
committed readers like you. To learn more, visit
ucpress.edu/supportus.